Multilateral Trade Negotiations

In this book Leslie Glick provides the information
and analysis necessary for understanding the impact
of the Tokyo Round of the Multilateral Trade Negotiations (MTN). Mr. Glick presents the background
leading up to the negotiations, analyzes the negotiations themselves, and discusses the implementation of their results. The GATT negotiations of
1982 are discussed, and there is an evaluation of
the current situation. Extensive appendices provide
a wealth of original source material, much of which
is not otherwise readily available. This book is a
valuable tool for businessmen, lawyers, consultants,
scholars and anyone who needs to understand the complex questions involved in contemporary international
trade.

Multilateral Trade Negotiations
World Trade After the Tokyo Round

LESLIE ALAN GLICK

Rowman & Allanheld
PUBLISHERS

ROWMAN & ALLANHELD

Published in the United States of America in 1984
by Rowman & Allanheld, Publishers
(A division of Littlefield, Adams & Company)
81 Adams Drive, Totowa, New Jersey 07512

Library of Congress Cataloging in Publication Data

Glick, Leslie Alan.
    Multilateral trade negotiations.

    1. Tokyo Round (1973-1979) 2. Tariff—Law and legis-
lation. 3. Foreign trade regulation. 4. Tariff—Law
and legislation—United States. 5. Foreign trade regulation—United States. I. Title.
K4603 1973.G55   1984   341.7'54'0265   80-70919
ISBN 0-86598-036-5

84 85 86 / 10 9 8 7 6 5 4 3 2 1

Printed in the United States of America

SUMMARY OF CONTENTS

TABLE OF CONTENTS

FOREWORD

Any publication of this length involves the investment of many hours and the help of many people. When this project was begun, it was intended to be a quick and brief overview of the Multilateral Trade Negotiations in Geneva. However, as new issues developed that grew out of the MTN, the book expanded to cover the implementation of the MTN. As the GATT Ministerial loomed on the horizon, this appeared to be too important an event not to discuss in a book on the MTN. Thus, this book is many pages longer and several years later than originally intended.

Numerous people have contributed to this effort in many ways. My wife, Melissa, provided both encouragement and angelic tolerance in enduring several years of my weekends lost in piles of documents, surrounded by yellow legal pads, felt tip pens, and clouds of pipe tobacco, turning our home into a miniature GATT library. Her help goes beyond spiritual support, for it was she who tackled the almost insurmountable task of organizing and indexing the thousands of documents and clippings that were necessary to the preparation of this book, and which still fill numerous banker's boxes in my home. Certainly, she deserves an M.L.S. and LL.M. degree for her efforts.

My secretary, Jan Crawford, had the unenviable task of translating the hieroglyphics that I pass off as handwriting into meaningful text. For this alone, she deserves a degree in advanced cryptanalysis. Yet adapting the work to the format of the publisher with the limitations of our word processing machine was also a feat worthy of Star Wars. In the end, human ingenuity and persistence won out over the machine that wanted to put my footnotes in the wrong places and refused to number them past 250, to name just a few mechanical aberrations. For her repeated typing of this manuscript I also owe her a lifetime of optical care, although I hope she will not need the seeing eye dog to which she claims this book will lead. Her efforts were crucial to the completion of this book and are truly appreciated.

One of the dullest tasks in a work of this size is proofreading and editing. This thankless task fell to the able talents of Karen Vogel, a third year law student at George Washington University and a staff member of the George Washington Journal of International Law & Economics. "Blue-book" in hand, Karen made sure that the citations were in proper form and spent countless hours proofreading and checking references, which undoubtedly aged her prematurely. Her hard work and dedication were invaluable to the completion of this work.

One limitation in my writing this book was my lack of hands-on, first person experience at the Multilateral Trade Negotiations. Fortunately, my law partner and friend, Jim Adduci, was in Geneva as part of the U.S. delegation and contributed the extra edge of authenticity that only experience can provide. Jim not only read the entire manuscript and provided incisive and thoughtful comments, but he contributed background and substantive information on a variety of topics relating to the MTN. This ranged from specific detail to sublime reflection on the state of mind and the feelings that existed at various stages of the MTN, all of which helped make the book more three-dimensional, rather than just a compilation of statistics. Certainly, this book would have been much less interesting and authentic without Jim's involvement.

Numerous other people contributed in large or small part. Some typing was done by Jackie Wilson and Linda Henderson. Able assistance in proofreading was provided by Dan Bosco, an LL.M candidate at American University, Rebecca Hardy, Maria Roble, Mary Pat Michel and Barbara Murphy.

I am grateful also to the staff of the United Nations Library in New York, who provided access to much original GATT source material on the MTN that otherwise would have been difficult to obtain.

INTRODUCTION

The problems facing the world's trading nations in the 1980's are undoubtedly as complex and potentially disruptive as those that existed in prior decades. Much progress has been made in strengthening international mechanisms for both establishing rules of conduct and resolving disputes. Nevertheless, the economic fragility of the economies of the western industrialized nations, the growing demands of the less developed countries, and the increased confrontations between western trading nations and the successful export oriented economies of Japan, Taiwan, and Hong Kong work together to create a serious threat to the continued liberalization of trade. Events occurring early in the Reagan Administration in the United States indicated that there were some areas for optimism for those that sought trade liberalization. The emphasis on less government spending and regulation appeared to some to be a harbinger of a new approach to American trade policy; one which would be based on competitiveness rather than protection; one where the fit would survive and the unfit might not, despite what generally in the past have been considered unacceptable political costs.

The cause for optimism appears to have been premature. The ideals of the Reagan Administration have apparently given way to political and economic realities of the marketplace. U.S. products were losing ground in world markets, while imports continued to increase and the U.S. economy has, as a whole, suffered a prolonged malaise that has become politically unacceptable. The Reagan Administration in early 1982 revealed a new policy which was to become the buzz word for 1982 -- "reciprocity". Reciprocity unfortunately had as many definitions as definers. Some advocates were quick to proclaim that "reciprocity" was not designed to take retaliatory actions against foreign products but only to provide an impetus for removal of trade barriers applied to U.S. goods in certain countries, notably, but not exclusively, Japan. Critics of reciprocity pointed out that such a policy is little incentive unless foreign countries believe actions will be taken against their U.S. imports, and the carrying out of this counter-threat is what could trigger the trade war of the 1980's.

At the time of this writing, reciprocity is still a theory rather than a cohesive program and it is too early to fully analyze its impact on world trade. However, several bills have been introduced to effectuate this policy and hearings have been held. Although a reciprocity bill (S.144) passed the Senate in April, 1983, the bill died in conference committee. The Administration's position is somewhat guarded. Although often espoused in speeches and briefings, the U.S. Administration appeared somewhat reluctant to put its full weight behind these proposals, hoping, as some have speculated, that the threat of legislation would provide bargaining leverage at the November, 1982, GATT Ministerial Meeting in Geneva, and thus be more valuable than legislation itself. However, the lackluster results of the GATT Ministerial belie this.

Many other difficult trade issues must be faced by the U.S. and its trading partners in the 1980's. Among these are restrictions on trade in services, subsidization of agricultural exports, increased use of "voluntary restraint agreements" as an alternative to actions under the GATT, and local content legislation. The U.S. has been engaged in an introspective re-evaluation of many basic concepts. Included in this is the concern of many U.S. businessmen and government officials over the need for the U.S. to develop an "industrial policy", comparable to that of Japan. Another major issue is the need for a reorganization of U.S. trade functions into a cabinet level Department of International Trade, similar to Japan's Ministry of International Trade and Industry.

The purpose, or focus of this book is to take a look both backwards and forwards to assess the state of world trade in the final decades of the Twentieth Century. The focal point of this analysis is the Tokyo Round of Trade Negotiations which began in Tokyo in 1973, and completed its major thrust in Geneva in 1979. We will begin by looking at the predecessor of the Tokyo Round, the Kennedy Round, to assess its achievement and shortcomings which set the stage for the negotiations of the 1970's. The events leading up to, and the actual negotiations of the Tokyo Round will be reviewed and analyzed. Hopefully, both the spirit and the substance of the negotiations will be captured to portray the thoughts and accomplishments that took place in Geneva. However, the most important focal point of this book will be to cast the results of the Tokyo Round against the background of current world trading problems. The codes of conduct and tariff concessions will be discussed in detail, along with the responses they received in various nations. The failures of the Tokyo Round, as well as the successes, are the key to understanding the prognosis for world trade in the 1980's and beyond. The reponse of the United States and other major trading nations to current trade issues will be analyzed in the search for clues that may lead to the discovery of the pattern in trade relations that is emerging. Attention will be devoted to the current issues and differing approaches to world trade that exist in the U.S., Japan, Europe, the less developed countries ("LDCs") and the "communist bloc", state-controlled economies. One of the key questions that will undoubtedly affect world trade in the 1980's is whether nations like the U.S. and Great Britain have learned anything from the Japanese super-economy that has come to dominate world exports in the past decade through a devotion to quality, worker motivation, and export sophistication. On the other hand, and of similar importance, is whether the traditionally restricted Japanese home market will respond to the needs of both its western trading partners and the less developed nations and help take over the role as "marketplace for the world" that the U.S. has for so long held on an almost unilateral basis.

Juxtaposed against this East/West scenario is the per-plexing and often inscrutable role of the communist/ socia-list economies in the traditional world trade framework. Such issues as politically motivated trade embargoes are a distor-tion to trade that have become more frequent and have in-creased the political input in trade decisions that might ordinarily remain largely economic. One cannot even conceive of the potential impact on world trade if such huge and product starved markets such as that of the U.S.S.R. and China were to be opened markedly to increased import penetration from both East and West. While recent political events have not been encouraging as to progress in further trade with the U.S.S.R., there has been a small but, nevertheless, signifi-cant aperture in the long dormant soviet marketplace. More-over, the participation of communist nations in the Tokyo Round was itself significant. In addition to the participation of GATT members, such as Czechoslovakia, Poland, Romania, Cuba and Yugoslavia, non-GATT countries such as Bulgaria and Vietnam participated, making the results of the Tokyo Round more than just a monolithic experience. East-West politico-economic problems have led to some of the greatest ironies in current world trading. For example, the U.S. concern over increasing exports would normally encourage the export of our top, high technology equipment such as computers, aircraft and scientific instruments in which the U.S. has a clear competi-tive advantage. However, concern over transfer of technology to the communist bloc has become more pronounced and is likely to result in less of these U.S. high technology exports.

Undoubtedly, this book will pose as many questions as it will answer. Hopefully, the questions themselves may provoke further thought and perhaps some answers. However, it is hoped that this book will provide a convenient source of

information about achievements and activities in world trade
during the past decade to enable practitioners, students,
scholars, and governments to have access to many of the
original source materials that are so often quickly dispersed.
Thus, the appendices to this book, with the original source
materials included therein, should be a useful tool for both
the practitioner in the trade area and the scholar alike. At
the same time, in view of the uncertain results of the GATT
Ministerial Meeting in November, 1982, and the many unresolved
issues in the world trade regime, it is hoped that this book
will provide assistance in analyzing current world trading
problems. This book is oriented primarily towards those
already basically familiar with world trading mechanisms and
does not attempt to explain or define such institutions as the
General Agreement on Tariffs and Trade (GATT), the Organization for Economic Cooperation and Development (OECD) and
similar bodies.

Finally, although this book will include much original
documentation and factual accounts of important trade events,
it is not without its share of opinion and, undoubtedly, bias.
As a U.S. attorney specializing in international trade law who
has represented both domestic and foreign interests since
1971, I have naturally formed certain opinions on a number of
trade issues. It is hoped that such opinions and biases will
be sufficiently transparent so as not to preclude effective
use of the factual and analytical portions of the book by
those who see it solely as a research tool rather than as a
foil for future thought and discussion.

KENNEDY ROUND

Prior to the Tokyo Round of trade negotiations, the most recent and comprehensive series of multilateral negotiations which resulted in worldwide trade concessions was the Kennedy Round in the early 1960s. The Kennedy Round was authorized by the Trade Expansion Act of 1962, and provided a broad delegation of negotiating power to President Kennedy. It is beyond the scope of this book to discuss in detail all the circumstances that led to the Kennedy Round,[1] or the background or details concerning the intimate aspects of the negotiating process. Our main purpose is to discuss the results of the Kennedy Round, insofar as these results planted the seeds for further negotiations in Geneva, which are the focus of this book.

It is difficult to measure results of trade negotiations strictly in quantitative terms since there are always political aspects to the negotiations, some of which are directly contrary to the objective achievements, in the form of quantitative or monetary value of concessions. Nevertheless, it is significant that the volume of trade affected by the Kennedy Round negotiations was in the area of forty billion dollars. On the part of the United States, this involved reductions in over 64% of the dutiable imports into the United States. During the Kennedy Round, in contrast to the Tokyo Round, the emphasis was placed on tariff cutting and therefore perhaps the appropriate measure of its achievements is from the viewpoint of the extent and percentage of tariff cuts. In this context an estimate of the average reductions on all dutiable non-agricultural items for products subject to negotiation in the Kennedy Round is approximately 35% of prior rates.[2] Although these tariff concessions were quite high compared to previous ones, they did not reach the goals set by the GATT in calling for the Kennedy Round.

Many of the participating countries in the Kennedy Round had limited their tariff cutting participation to certain products. They had excepted or excluded certain categories. A majority of the U.S. exceptions were in the area of textiles and metals. The tariff reductions in the Kennedy Round, although substantial and significant, were intended to take effect in stages over a five year period beginning January, 1968. At the request of certain Less Developed Countries (LDCs), certain tariff concessions on products of particular

---

1   For a more complete discussion see J. Evans, The Kennedy Round in American Trade Policy - The Twilight of the GATT 19-383 (1971). For those who do not wish to read this entire book, a review can be found by this author; see Glick, Book Review, Fordham Law Review 217-21 (Oct. 1972).
2   See Report on United States Negotiations, vol. I, pt. I, at v.

staging. As we will note later, this concept of more immediate tariff relief for less developed countries was carried forward and institutionalized in the Tokyo Round, which established two different standards of tariff reductions; one which took effect immediately, for the most underdeveloped nations, and another for all other eligible nations.

The role of the less developed countries in the Kennedy Round was significant insofar as it formed the basis for future action by the LDCs. It was clear that these countries had a greater desire for participation in trade negotiations that was not to be denied in the future. At the end of the Kennedy Round the less developed nations which participated issued a statement indicating their disappointment over the paucity of benefits that they had received. Major concerns were their failure to achieve a reduction or elimination of duties on particular products of special interest to these developing countries, particularly tropical products, and the continuation of non-tariff barriers in the developed countries, to name just two.[3] Whether or not the disappointment of the less developed countries was objectively valid is a matter of some disagreement. Reacting to this criticism, the GATT Secretariat prepared an analysis of the value of concessions to less developed countries granted by the major developed countries. The study showed that the Kennedy Round actually reduced duties on almost 60% of imports from the developing countries into the markets of the major developed countries, that almost 90% of these reductions were greater than 20%, and that almost half of the reductions were greater than 50%.[4] Major shortcomings, from the viewpoint of the less developed nations, were the lack of reductions in duties on various tropical products for which they had hoped for greater gains. On the other hand, major achievements were obtained in the area of textiles where duties were eliminated entirely on over 50% of the items negotiated. However, the United Nations Commission on Trade and Development (UNCTAD) did their own analysis, finding that the average tariff reductions on products of interest to the less developed countries were smaller than those of interest to the developing countries.[5]

One of the major contrasts between the Kennedy Round and the Tokyo Round was in the area of negotiations relating to non-tariff barriers ("NTBs"). While the inability of the Kennedy Round to produce results in the elimination of non-tariff barriers cannot be viewed as a failure because the primary emphasis and orientation of the Kennedy Round was linear tariff cutting, the absence of any progress in areas

3 Joint Statement by the Developing Participating Countries in the Kennedy Round Negotiations, GATT, Press Release, GATT/994 (June 30, 1967).
4 See GATT Doc. COM. TD/48/Rev. 1 (Nov. 21, 1967).
5 UNCTAD, Supp. 2 (Sept, 1967).

outside of the tariff cutting area in the Kennedy Round is in marked contrast to what we shall see as the major accomplishments in the Tokyo Round negotiations. The GATT contracting parties had hoped that the Kennedy Round would deal with the questions of non-tariff barriers. Multilateral negotiations on these issues had never been conducted in the past, and the problems relating to these non-tariff issues were much more complex and potentially disruptive than those dealing with straight tariff cutting issues. One of the major problems was the absence of a clear cut definition of non-tariff barriers, or a generally accepted list of the non-tariff barriers that each country considered to be in existence. Nevertheless, the GATT ministers directed the Trade Negotiations Committee to draft rules to be utilized in the negotiation of non-tariff barriers. The Committee attempted to first identify the various types of non-tariff barriers that were considered significant obstacles to international trade. In 1963, the Executive Secretary of the GATT requested participating nations to submit lists of non-tariff barriers to be subject to negotiations; however, only a small number of nations made such submissions.

Unlike negotiating tariff cuts, non-tariff barriers offered almost open ended areas for discussion.[6] The problem with eliminating non-tariff barriers is that they include many intangible, and sometimes undefinable, elements that make elimination and negotiation a difficult process. For example, the policies and practices applied by customs officials in any given nation can be a sizeable non-tariff barrier to trade. Such policies, however, may relate to the exercise of discretion in thoroughly inspecting certain types of shipments or in adhering to the letter of customs regulations which may be applied non-uniformly. To eliminate such forms of non-tariff barriers requires more than just rules and regulations. It also requires enforcement and policing of a nature that may be impractical in many instances. In general, negotiations on non-tariff barriers hope to deal with at least the elimination of formal policies and restrictive practices, which may or may not be intended to limit trade. Emphasis is also placed on "transparency", a term used to indicate a system of open and clearly discernible policies that can be understood and monitored by other nations as compared to the secret, unpublished, and discretionary practices that often exist in many countries.

Many NTBs are legitimate exercises of the police power of the state in protecting its citizens. Some examples are internal laws and regulations dealing with safety, purity of

---

6 For those not conversant with the term, a non-tariff barrier can include any impediment to the free flow of goods or services in international trade other than one caused by a high tariff.

foods and drugs, and sanitary regulations. However, they can, and in fact have in many instances, been used to create more onerous burdens on imports than on domestic products, either through formal regulations (such as requiring on-site inspection of plants, which of course is more difficult and expensive for foreign producers), or merely through selective enforcement procedures. The importance of non-tariff barriers to trade will be discussed further, and, as we shall see, they were in fact the most important focus of the trade negotiations which were completed in the Tokyo Round.   A detailed discussion of the particular types of non-tariff barriers will be provided in later chapters. However, for purposes of discussing the Kennedy Round, the principal areas of non-tariff barriers which were discussed included government procurement practices, methods of valuation of imports, use of quantitative restrictions, internal taxes, and administrative regulations, as well as policies and practices relating to antidumping and state trading.[7]

Although many important topics were identified for purposes of negotiation of non-tariff barriers during the Kennedy Round, in fact, little progress was made in actual negotiations. There are many reasons for this, including the genuine reluctance of many parties to make concessions in these areas no matter how well disguised.

Another, and perhaps more significant reason, was the limitation on the power of many nations to negotiate changes in non-tariff barriers. Any federal system, such as exists in the United States, lacks complete control over all forms of non-tariff barriers, chiefly those created by the states, and the authority to eliminate those barriers by the federal authorities is not always clear. Moreover, as we shall see from the negotiations in the Tokyo Round, the complexity of removing non-tariff barriers in itself was a significant obstacle to any quick results. Many nations undoubtedly found it easier to devote the greater part of their resources to tariff cutting, an area that was less complex and more likely to yield concrete results to take back home.

It would be unfair to consider the Kennedy Round a complete failure in the area of negotiations on non-tariff barriers. It might be argued that were it not for at least the initial attempts to negotiate in these areas, NTBs might never have been included as a major focus of the Tokyo Round. The Kennedy Round, in a sense, was a successful dry run at an attempt to negotiate non-tariff barriers; at least allowing the parties to form negotiating committees and to identify the issues, albeit not to successfully resolve the most important issues. However, the mistakes and, to a limited extent, the successes of negotiating and attempting to negotiate non-tariff barriers in the Kennedy Round provided guideposts to

---

7 See Evans, _supra_ note 1, at ch. 5.

the neogtiators in Geneva, and may have eliminated the
repetition of certain mistakes and undoubtedly eliminated some
unnecessary time-consuming activities. Moreover, the Kennedy
Round did result in the establishment of the Antidumping
Code.

THE TOKYO ROUND - THE STAGE IS SET

The Tokyo Round of trade negotiations received its name
form the largely coincidental event that its origins occurred
at the GATT meeting of Ministers held in Tokyo in September,
1973.   However, the ground work for the Tokyo Round commenced
long before 1973. As early as November, 1967, merely five
months after the conclusion of the Kennedy Round, the GATT
annual session decided to initiate the preparatory work for a
new round of trade negotiations. The preparatory program had
essentially three stages. These were the collection of the
basic documentation and information needed to negotiate, which
took place in 1968; the identification of issues to be discussed, which was completed by 1970; and the final step, the
search for solutions.

Many obstacles and problems existing during this preparatory period impeded progress and raised uncertainties about
the ability to actually commence negotiations. Many of these
problems were economic. The year 1967 included a worldwide
recession that resulted in the usual protectionist pressures.
Balance of payments problems were also a factor, leading to
the imposition of a 10% import surcharge on all U.S. imports
except those under quantitative restrictions in 1971.[8] This
comprehensive action, while not totally without precedent, did
little to enhance international cooperation in resolving trade
disputes. The situation was not helped by the fact that the
U.S. President, in imposing the 10% surcharge without legislative mandate, relied on the archaic Trading With The Enemy
Act, a fact which did not go unnoticed by our trading partners. Although the surcharge was temporary in nature, its
impact outlasted its lifespan. The question of how to deal
with payment imbalances without dictorting the entire world
trading system led to serious questioning and re-evaluation of
the international monetary system, which eventually led to
changes in the Bretton Woods Agreement.

Other politico-economic factors loomed large in the
United States, whose participation was crucial to any new
round of trade negotiations. Protectionist sentiment in the
United States in the early 70's led to a lengthy process in

---

8 For a discussion of the import surcharge, see Attacks on the
   United States Import Surcharge Under Domestic and Inter-
   national Law: A Pragmatic Approach, 6 J. Int'l L. & Econ. 269
   (Jan. 1972).

obtaining the necessary authorization for the U.S. President
to conduct further trade negotiations. This authority, in
fact, did not materialize until the Trade Act of 1974, which
did not become effective until January, 1975.

During the same period, there was considerable economic
uncertainty in Europe. Members of the European Free Trade
Association, such as Great Britain and Denmark, sought and
eventually became members of the European Economic Community
(EEC). Eventually, at the time of the Tokyo Round, the EEC
would be a major force to reckon with, significantly changing
the role of the European states that existed during the
Kennedy Round. One encouraging point was the declaration of
the U.S., Japan and the EEC in 1972 calling for the initiation
of multilateral negotiations in the framework of the GATT.
These declarations lent sufficient support and prestige to the
efforts to launch formal negotiations. An agreement in
principle on a new round of trade negotiations was reached at
the March, 1972 GATT annual meeting and endorsed at the 1972
GATT Plenary Session. A preparatory committee was established
under the chairmanship of Oliver Long, GATT Director-General,
and held three meetings during 1973 resulting in a draft
declaration being submitted to the Ministers in Tokyo.

The Tokyo Round was officially initiated at the conclusion of the September, 1973 GATT Ministerial Meeting in Tokyo.
The countries attending adopted unanimously what was called
the Tokyo Declaration, and the Multilateral Trade Negotiations
were officially launched. The text of the Declaration appears
in Appendix I. The Tokyo Declaration itself was an important
achievement in view of the fact that it was unanimously
adopted with its broad aims to "achieve the expansion and
greater liberalization of world trade ... through the progressive dismantling of obstacles to trade and the improvement of
the international framework for the conduct of world trade."[9]
Recognition was also given to the special needs of developing
countries "so as to achieve a substantial increase in their
foreign exchange earnings, the diversification of their
exports (and) the acceleration of the rate of growth of their
trade..."[10] This Declaration specifically recognized some of
the concerns expressed by the LCDs after the Kennedy Round,
particularly a recognition of the need for "a substantial
improvement in the conditions of access for the products of
interest to the developing countries ..."[11] Thus, the list of
aims of the negotiations specifically included a reference to
"tropical products as a special priority sector",[12] an area
considered by the LDCs to be a major shortcoming of the
Kennedy Round.

---

9 See Appendix I, Tokyo Declaration, para. 2.
10 Id.
11 Id.
12 Id.

The Declaration indicated that "the negotiations shall be conducted on the basis of the principles of mutual advantage, mutual commitment and overall reciprocity, while observing the most favored nation clause..."[13] The reference to the term "reciprocity" is quite significant, since the concept of reciprocity has become a source of controversy in current trade relations as a result of certain actions taken by the U.S. to encourage other nations to open their markets. While some claim the concept of reciprocity is completely alien to existing trade relations, it is, in fact, a term frequently used by the GATT and which appeared in the Tokyo Declaration. For example, the Declaration noted that, "... the developed countries do not expect reciprocity for commitments made by them in the negotiations to reduce or remove tariff and other barriers to trade of developing countries..."[14] This language could cast considerable doubt upon the legitimacy of any U.S. legislation seeking retaliation against LDCs that have less than open markets.   For example, while U.S. reciprocity legislation appears to be aimed primarily at Japan, a developed country, many also see it as an effective tool against certain LDCs that have had relatively free access to the U.S. market but have import license requirements and high tariffs that impact U.S. imports. However, in view of the clear objectives of the Tokyo Declaration, it would appear inappropriate to expect the same degree of reciprocity from the LDCs. Another important and somewhat controversial aspect of the Declaration was the reference in Paragraph 7 to the need for international monetary reform. This language was actually a compromise adopted after considerable differences of opinion between the European Economic Community and the U.S.

The Declaration ended with the establishment of a Trade Negotiations Committee whose membership was open to all governments, with the first meeting to be held not later than November, 1974. The Ministers concluded with a reference to their intent to conclude negotiations by 1975, a desire that was in retrospect, highly unrealistic.

It is important to emphasize that participation in the MTN negotiating process was not limited to GATT members. In fact, twenty-six of the ninety-nine participating countries were not GATT members and another three had only acceded provisionally. A complete list of the MTN participations, indicating non-GATT members, is contained in Appendix II. Since non-GATT members included such nations as Algeria, Bolivia, Iran, Mexico and Venezuela, it was a significant step to include these non-members in the negotiating process.

---

13 Id. at 5.
14 Id. at 5.

THE TRADE NEGOTIATING COMMITTEE AND WORKING GROUPS

After the preparatory meetings which culminated in the Tokyo Declaration, the most important development was the establishment of the Trade Negotiations Committee (TNC). Its goals were to effectuate detailed trade negotiating plans and to establish appropriate negotiating procedures. The Committee would also have a supervisory function over negotiations but little role in substantive negotiations, which were to be carried out by specific working groups. The Trade Negotiations Committee had set up six groups by 1975 to conduct the substantive negotiations, some of which contained sub-groups. These groups were as follows:

1. Tropical products.
2. Tariffs.
3. Non-tariff measures.
    a. Quantitative restrictions sub-group.
    b. Technical barriers to trade sub-group.
    c. Customs sub-group.
    d. Subsidies and countervailing sub-group.
    e. Government procurement sub-group.
4. Agriculture.
    a. Grains sub-group.
    b. Meat sub-group.
    c. Dairy products sub-group.
5. Sector Approach.
6. Safeguards.

A seventh group, known as the "Framework Group" was established in 1976 to work on improving the international framework for the conduct of world trade.

A discussion of the activities of each of these groups and the progress in the conduct of negotiations will be discussed infra. While the results of the Tokyo Round are perhaps of greater interest than how those results were achieved, it is important from both an historical viewpoint and as an aid to future negotiations to review some of the problems and sources of conflict in the negotiating process. The entire negotiation process, which spanned a period of four years (not including the preparatory stages and the uncompleted areas still being negotiated) was obviously not conducted in a vacuum. During this period there were numerous economic and political developments among the negotiating states that had an impact on the course and progress of negotiations. For example, unlike the period during which the Kennedy Round was negotiated which was characterized by a general world economic upturn, the Tokyo Round was conducted during a period of less than optimal world economic conditions. For example, the change in the price and availability of oil and gas in this period led to tremendous distortion in

the balance of payments that could not but help affect
countries' attitudes toward trade liberalization. This was
also a period of rampant inflation and increasing unemployment
in many countries which created additional uncertainties that
were counterproductive to trade liberalization.

On the political side were many unknown factors, such as
the outcome of the 1976 U. S. Presidential elections, which
left in limbo for some time a clear formulation of U.S.
policies on trade negotiation matters.

It was not until early 1977 when President Carter took
office that the U.S. began to firm up its policies and
approaches toward negotiations. The U.S. had been deadlocked
with the EEC as to certain basic policy questions, particularly with regard to agricultural negotiations. However, in
July, 1977, a meeting took place in Brussels between U.S.
Special Trade Representative Robert Strauss, and Wilhelm
Haferkamp, Commissioner for External Relations of the EEC,
which helped resolve a number of these problems. Of greatest
significance was an agreement to accelerate the Tokyo Round
negotiating process. Four phases were proposed. The first was
a general tariff plan to include a tariff-cutting formula,
methods for treating LDCs, methods for dealing with countries
not participating in the tariff-cutting formula and methods
for dealing with agricultural questions. The second phase
consisted of requests for tariff reductions by countries not
agreeing to the tariff-cutting formula, tariff cuts on
agricultural goods and non-tariff measures covered by specific
codes of conduct. The third phase consisted of proposals for
the various non-tariff codes and the fourth phase involved
specific offers in response to the requests already received.
The timetable for this procedure involved the submission of
requests by November, 1977, all four phases were to be
completed by January, 1978, when the substantive negotiations
would continue. After this timetable and "four-phase agreement" were worked out, intense negotiations took place during
1978 of both a bilateral and multilateral nature. One multilateral meeting was held by the Trade Negotiations Committee
in July, 1978, and the other was an informal meeting of all
participating countries later that month.

As a result of these meetings, on July 13, 1978, a major
pronouncement was issued entitled "Framework For Understanding", covering all the main issues of the Tokyo Round.
The "Framework For Understanding" was, in effect, an agreement
reached by a number of principal negotiating parties including
the EEC, the United States, Canada, Japan, New Zealand,
Australia, Norway, Sweden and Denmark. This pronouncement set
forth the basic elements that these nations considered should
be part of the final Tokyo Round results. While the countries
participating in the proclamation considered it a major step
forward, their enthusiasm was not shared by the LDCs who were
generally critical of the "Framework For Understanding",

largely because they had not been included in its formation. On July 14, 1978, they issued a critical statement indicating their displeasure at not having participated in the process for formulation of the "Framework".

Chapter 1

PREPARATORY STEPS IN MAJOR SUBSTANTIVE AREAS

While we have discussed in a general manner the overall
events leading up to the Tokyo Round negotiations, and some of
the specific preparatory problems, a more specific discussion
of certain preliminary steps which relate to the various
substantive areas of negotiation is desirable.[1]

TARIFF CUTTING

In order to provide a basis for tariff cutting negotiations, prior to the announcement of the Tokyo Round a tariff
study had been undertaken which provided a picture of the
tariff structure of each of the major participating countries
and provided accurate trade statistics. A file was established on each of the larger trading states that included
details on duty rates and imports. This tariff study was
updated as the negotiations took place. Also, prior to the
announcement of the Tokyo Round, procedures were undertaken to
develop various techniques to accomplish a tariff reduction.
Three possible approaches to tariff cutting were studied.

1.   Tariff Elimination. This involves the complete
     elimination of a tariff on an item. While this
     approach has certain benefits in ease of administra-
     tion, it was not one which had great appeal to most
     of the parties.

---

[1] Much of the background information that follows is based on
the Report of the GATT Director General, Oliver Long,
contained in GATT,The Tokyo Round of Multilateral Trade
Negotiations, GATT/1979-3, (Ap. 1979) as well as discussions
with individuals who attended the Tokyo Round and were
involved in the negotiations.

2. <u>Linear Reductions</u>. Linear reductions involve equal
    percentage cuts on all tariffs. This approach was
    used successfully in the Kennedy Round. The problem
    with linear cutting is that it preserves disparities
    that already exist and accomplishes little to reform
    tariff statutes.

3. <u>Harmonized Reductions</u>. Harmonized reductions
    involved larger percentage cuts in the higher tariff
    rates. This tends to equalize tariffs but also
    tends to have the greatest impact on the most
    sensitive items which are the ones generally subject
    to higher duties.

4. <u>Item-by-Item Reductions</u>. This approach received
    little support since it could only result in selec-
    tive tariff cutting on items of lesser significance.
    Although this approach was used prior to the Kennedy
    Round, it was abandoned at that time and it was not
    considered an appropriate vehicle for the Tokyo
    Round.

NON-TARIFF BARRIERS

As pointed out earlier, the inclusion of extensive
negotiations on non-tariff barriers was one aspect of the
Tokyo Round that was a major departure from previous rounds of
tariff negotiations. In contrast to tariff cutting where
there was a wealth of prior experience, it was obviously more
difficult to prepare for negotiations on non-tariff barriers
since there was little precedent for these types of negotiations. There was some precedent, such as the Antidumping
Code, but of much narrower scope than the ambitious plans
called for in the Tokyo Round. Among the issues that had to
be considered in preparation for negotiations on NTBs were
whether changes negotiated would apply only to the contracting
states or also to other GATT member countries on a most
favored nation basis.

As a basis for approaching negotiations, a comprehensive
list of NTBs was drawn up in 1968 and updated annually. This
list contained approximately 800 different trade distorting
barriers. These consisted of five general categories:

(1) price related controls on imports and exports;
(2) product standards applied to imports;
(3) government customs and administrative practices;
(4) special limitations on imports and exports (e.g.,
     license requirements);
(5) state trading practices and government subsidization
     and control of trade activities.

To facilitate negotiations, it was decided that various agreements would be submitted on an ad referendum basis, i.e., various codes or proposals would be submitted but not made binding on the government proposing them until formally approved.

Many of these topics had already been the subject of ad referendum proposals as early as the September, 1973 GATT Ministerial Meeting in Tokyo. These included customs valuation, standards and licensing. At the 1973 Preparatory Committee Meeting, a list of NTBs considered to be the principal focus of negotiations was drawn up. This list contained the following subject areas:

(1) Government procurement;
(2) Subsidies;
(3) Standards;
(4) Dumping and countervailing duties;
(5) Import documentation;
(6) Quantitative restrictions;
(7) Customs valuations.

Five subgroups were set up to begin negotiations in these areas. A brief discussion of the background preparatory activities in each area is useful.

A.   Subsidies and Countervailing Duties

In 1960, a list of prohibited export subsidies was drawn up. However, a general agreement on the definition of subsidies was more difficult to reach. As far back as the Kennedy Round there was discussion of the desireability of negotiating a code governing countervailing duties similar to the Antidumping Code. In 1967 the GATT set up a working party to begin studying this area. However, a dispute as to the scope of investigation resulted in the failure of the working party to ever meet. The dispute was largely between the U.S. and the EEC. The U.S. wanted negotiations to include state subsidy practices and not simply procedures for imposition of countervailing duties. The EEC, however, which was the source of many subsidies that concerned the U.S., wanted to limit the group to a discussion only of a code on countervailing duties.

B.   Technical Barriers to Trade

Technical barriers to trade generally concern product standards that inhibit the free flow of goods; they may be federally, state or locally imposed and consist of testing, certification and other requirements. Often such requirements are imposed without an overt intention to discriminate against foreign suppliers. However, often this is the result whether intended or not. In the standards area, an <u>ad referendum</u> code in draft form was prepared prior to the September, 1973 Tokyo Ministerial Meeting. This was the basis for the work of the subgroup.

C.   Customs Valuation

Customs valuation deals with the method used for determining the value of imported goods for purposes of calculating duties.   In 1950, the Customs Cooperation Council, an international group, drafted the Brussels Convention on Valuation, and currently, over 100 countries base their systems of customs valuation on the Brussels Convention.   However, despite this existing standard, there was a considerable lack of conformity between states, and often customs valuation constituted an impediment to imports, e.g., in systems where official prices are uniformly used for valuation pruposes, even when they are higher than the transaction price.

D.   Government Procurement

A sizeable market for imported goods consists of governmental entities.   Often governments impose restrictive conditions that inhibit import competition. This may be in the form of preferences for local goods within certain price perimeters (e.g., preference for local goods unless the imported goods are more than 15% cheaper).   Often policies, particularly of state and local governments, became restrictive as a result of informal practices rather than written legislation.   Article 111:8(a) of the GATT permitted discrimination by governments in procurement. This section provides:

> The provisions of this article shall not apply to laws, regulations or requirements governing the procurement by governmental agencies of products purchased for governmental purposes and not with a view to commercial resale or with a view to use in the production of goods for commercial sale.

Prior to the Tokyo Round negotiations, the Organization for Economic Cooperation and Development (OECD) undertook a study of this area which resulted in a document entitled "Draft Instrument on Government Purchasing Policies, Procedures and Practices".   This provided a starting point for the GATT subgroup.

E.   Quantitative Restrictions

Quantitative restrictions had presented a problem for
many years and the subgroup established to deal with them had
many issues to confront.   Among the issues was how to deal
with voluntary restraint programs such as the U.S. restraints
on European steel imports imposed during the late 1960's and
early 1970's.   Another area of concern was whether a country
that had quantitative restrictions was entitled to compensation for elimination of the program.   Also, many countries in
their protocols of accession to the GATT had grandfathered in
certain quantitative restrictions and these posed special
problems.

F.   Import Licensing

Prior to the 1973 Tokyo Ministerial Meeting, two ad
referendum texts had been submitted dealing with import
licensing.   One dealt with the area of administration of
quantitative restrictions and the other dealt with "automatic"
licenses which are generally given rather routinely.

AGRICULTURE

Traditionally, the GATT framework has not been utilized
to regulate trade in the agricultural sector.   Although
certain agricultural areas were addressed during the Kennedy
Round, the results of this were minimal.   The previous lack of
penetration into the agricultural area and the complexity of
the problems made this one of the most difficult fronts for
negotiation. Some groups wanted agricultural negotiations kept
separate from negotiations on industrial products; a continuing source of tension was the differing goals of the U.S.
and the EEC. While somewhat of an oversimplification, the aim
of the U.S. was to obtain greater penetration into the large
and relatively closed EEC market while reducing EEC subsidies
of its exports. The EEC sought more in terms of protection and
stabilization through various commodity agreements.   The U.S.
was willing to negotiate agricultural issues in the same
manner as industrial products but this was resisted by the EEC
which insisted that agriculture was a unique area that should
receive separate treatment.

TROPICAL PRODUCTS

As mentioned previously, tropical products were an
important issue to the LDCs and one which the Tokyo Declaration recognized as worthy of special priority.   The GATT Trade

and Development Committee had laid a foundation for negotiations in this area in its work prior to the Tokyo Round.

SAFEGUARDS

Safeguards refer to measures to protect countries granting tariff concessions from disruption to their markets by sudden flows of increased imports. Article XIX of the GATT permits the increase in duties on an item if imports have increased so as to cause or threaten to cause serious injury to domestic producers of like or directly competitive products. The U.S. has incorporated these standards into § 201 of the Trade Act of 1974, commonly known as the "escape clause". Generally, safeguard measures are imposed on a multilateral, non-discriminatory basis. Thus, for example, under U.S. law, a complaint under § 201 leads to an investigation by the U.S. International Trade Commission of imports from all countries producing the product and if relief is granted, it is imposed on all countries. This non-discrimination has frequently caused problems since a country was often forced to take actions against other countries that individually were not the main, or even an important, source of the problem. For example, if imports were increasing, 90% of which came from Japan and the other 10% from Belize, Jamaica and Haiti, under U.S. law, the duty would have to be raised for all countries. Also, the mere threat of injury has been considered by some countries to be too tenuous a basis to impose import restrictions. These and other issues led to the desire to negotiate a safeguards code. As we shall see, this has yet to take place and has been one of the major shortcomings of the Tokyo Round.

Chapter 2

THE NEGOTIATIONS

The MTN Negotiations were long and arduous. The results were seen as successes or failures from various perspectives. While the results are, of course, of greater interest to most observers, the study of the negotiating process is most illuminating both as a guide to understanding future GATT negotiations and to lend interpretation and perspective to the substantive results. In reviewing the negotiations, we shall look both at what occurred in Geneva and what took place in certain of the principal negotiating countries while the process was going on.

TARIFFS

The tariff negotiating group made little progress during 1975 and 1976 on actual tariff cutting although some agreement was reached on tariff cutting formulas, base rates and staging of tariff reductions. As discussed previously, two main approaches were considered. One was the linear approach, largely sponsored by the United States, which would have had the effect of across-the-board tariff cuts as implemented during the Kennedy Round. The other approach was the "harmonized" approach which varied tariff cuts with the level of duty, favored principally by the EEC and Japan. In 1977, negotiations began to result in concrete progress. Some of the key negotiators were U.S. Trade Representative Robert Strauss, EEC Commissioner William Haferkamp and Japanese Minister of State for External Economic Affairs Nopshiko Ushiba. Largely as a result of the meetings between Strauss and Haferkamp, there resulted a tentative proposal for a tariff cutting formula based on a methodology which was originally suggested by the Swiss delegation. This formula, or "working hypothesis", was a compromise between linear and harmonized tariff cuts but was more of a concession to those in favor of the harmonized cuts since it reduced higher

tariffs by a greater proportion than lower tariffs.   The
formula was based on an algebraic equation with the duty rate
equalling the present duty multiplied by a factor or coefficient divided by the present duty added to that factor.   Thus,
for example, if the factor was ten and the present duty was
20% the rate would be 200 divided by 30 or 6.66%.   On a higher
duty (for example 50%) applying the same formula, the rate
would be 8.3%.   Thus it can be seen that the percentage
reduction in duty was greater for the higher tariffs. Most
countries supported the Swiss formula but with some variations.

One area of disagreement concerned the appropriate factor
to be used.   The EEC supported the use of the number 16 as a
coefficient while the U.S. and Japan supported the use of the
number 14.[1] Another problem was what duty would be accepted
as the official rate of duty in a particular country. Some
countries had actual rates that were below official tariff
rates.   Due to the difficulty of determining variations from
official duties, each country was permitted to set forth its
rate of duty based on the rate it considered appropriate. This
no doubt resulted in benefits to certain countries which were
able to base tariff reductions on rates that were higher than
those practically enforced.

Certain countries emphasized particular products in their
tariff cutting.   For example, the U.S. placed its highest
priority on tariff concessions on film, paper, computers,
semiconductors, certain chemicals and other machinery.[2] Tariff
concessions were staged over an eight year period.   The term
"staging" of tariff cuts refers to the process of granting
concessions in small parts over a number of years. This
enables the affected domestic industries to better adjust to
the impact of the lower priced imports.   The Kennedy Round
provided a staging over a four year period in annual install-
ments.   However, certain countries that could not put their
reductions into effect fast enough were permitted to reduce
duties in two stages. Developing countries requested that
certain concessions affecting them be put into effect immediately and the developed countries agreed to do this when
possible.   In the Tokyo Round there was a consensus that an
eight year staging period seemed appropriate. Less developed
countries again favored immediate granting of reductions on
products of special interest to them.

---

[1] See U.S. International Trade Commission, Operation of the
Trade Agreements Program, 30th Report, 1978, U.S.I.T.C. Pub.
No. 1021, at 45-46 (1979).
[2] Id. at 46.

NON-TARIFF MEASURES

The negotiations in the area of non-tariff barriers were perhaps the most crucial to the success or failure of the Tokyo Round since non-tariff barriers were the principal focus of the negotiations. It was in this area which the success of the MTN would be measured. As mentioned previously, a number of sub-groups were set up to conduct specific negotiations in each area. The various groups progressed at different levels, and negotiations continued until the very last days of the Tokyo Round.

A.   Subsidies and Countervailing Duties

The issue of subsidies and countervailing duties was not entirely new to the GATT negotiators. In 1960, the GATT issued a "Declaration Giving Effect To The Provisions of Article XVI of the GATT" which stated that export subsidies on industrial products were prohibited. However, this declaration was not binding on non-signatories, a group which included many of the developing countries. Moreover, the GATT contained no restrictions on the use of domestic subsidies. These are subsidies which are not strictly designed to stimulate exports but rather to enhance development, production, employment and other socially related goals within the country. However, domestic subsidies may still have an impact on exports. Article XVI of the GATT did require notification of the existence of subsidies which either directly or indirectly increase exports, and requires GATT members to agree to consultations when so requested. However, the effects of this provision were limited. Moreover, the entire pre-MTN GATT framework on subsidies was largely confined to the industrialized countries, whereas the problems that arose due to subsidization in the 1970's was to a large degree the result of programs in the developing countries. This was particularly true of the advanced developing countries that were in the economic take-off stage and were devoting considerable government resources to developing exports as a source of foreign exchange.

The actual negotiations on subsidies and countervailing duties were heated. The principal adversaries were the United States and the European community. Differences on the subsidies issue were perhaps greater than on any other issue in the MTN.[3] The goal of the United States was to obtain tighter restrictions on export subsidies for industrial products, clarification of the rules on agricultural export subsidies, and restrictions on the use of domestic subsidies. The European Community, however, resisted these demands,

---

3 Id. at 50.

particularly those relating to agricultural products. It
concentrated its efforts on trying to establish an injury test
as a requirement for the imposition of countervailing duties.[4]
The EEC saw the primary goal in subsidies negotiations as the
imposition of an injury test by the U.S. which they considered
a requirement under the Article VI of the GATT and they did
not feel that there was a need for changing the basic rules on
subsidies since the U.S. was out of line with the existing
GATT rule.[5] As a result of this fundamental divergence in
viewpoints, negotiations went nowhere for the first three
years, and at one point the disagreement between the U.S. and
the EEC was so substantial that there was talk of dropping
subsidies and countervailing duties from the negotiating
effort.[6] One of the principle reasons for the difficulty in
negotiating on this issue was the importance of subsidies to
the EEC, particularly to its agricultural policy known as the
"Common Agricultural Policy" (CAP).[7] The American negotiators, on the other hand, were under pressure from U.S.
agricultural producers, who felt that the European Community
subsidies, particularly on agricultural products, were one of
the major distortions in international trade. The United
States, however, did not feel that its policy on countervailing duties should be the sole focus of negotiations since
the U.S. countervailing duty law preceded the GATT requirements for the injury test.[8] Nevertheless, the United States
had from the beginning been willing to negotiate the issue of
an injury test -- expecting that there would be reciprocal
concessions on subsidy policy, particularly from the Europeans.[9]

Thus the negotiations on the countervailing duty subsidies code began under less than optimum conditions. Rather
than having certain common agreements on objectives to provide
a framework from which to reach further agreements, the
parties in the negotiations of the subsidies code basically
started out in total disagreement on most of the important

---

[4] Id.
[5] Rivers & Greenwald, The Negotiations of a Code on Subsidies
     and Countervailing Measures: Bridging Fundamental Policy
     Differences, 2 Law & Pol'y Int'l Bus. 1447, 1449 (1979).
[6] Id.
[7] See MIN Studies: Tokyo-Geneva Round - Its Relation to Agri-
     culture Before the Subcomm. on International Trade of the
     Senate Comm. on Finance, 96th Cong., 1st Sess. (1979)
     [hereinafter cited as MIN Studies].
[8] Under the provisions by which the U.S. acceded to the GATT,
     legislation that was existing at the time of signature
     superseded provisions in the GATT. See Protocol of Pro-
     visional Application of the General Agreements on Tariffs and
     Trade, art. 2(b), 55 U.N.T.S. 308.
[9] See Rivers & Greenwald, supra note 5, at 1454.

issues.   The United States' approach had been to submit
various proposed agreements incorporating the various United
States' positions.   They met with little or no response or
success from the other negotiating parties.   Eventually, by the
second half of 1977, the United States agreed to work towards
the establishment of a framework for negotiations.   The United
States made several concessions including a commitment to use
the existing GATT rules as a basis for further negotiations
and to abandon its efforts to have subsidies classified solely
in terms of those that were acceptable and unacceptable.[10]   As
a result of these concessions, eventually the U.S. and the EEC
were able to circulate a paper that was to become the basis
for the framework of negotiations entitled "Subsidies/Counter-
vailing Duties -- Outline of an Approach".[11]   This paper deline-
ates the major issues that were the focus of the negotiations
on subsidies.   The basic features of the outline (not necessarily in the order or format of the original text) are set out
below.   The general premise of the outline was that subsidies
should be avoided if they would cause or threaten to cause
serious prejudice to other parties.

1.   Export subsidies

    a.   a recognition of the harmful effect of export
         subsidies;
    b.   an agreement not to use export subsidies on
         non-primary products;
    c.   a definition of export subsidies should be
         formulated;
    d.   an illustrative list of prohibited export
         subsidies;
    e.   export subsidies for agricultural products
         should be limited so a country does not obtain
         more than "an equitable share of the world
         market" (EEC position).   Agreements might be
         developed to restrict or limit export subsidies
         on specific agricultural products (U.S.
         position).

2.   Countervailing Duties

    a.   an injury test should be required with a
         definition of injury and improved consultation

---

[10] Id. at 1466.
[11] GATT Doc. MTN/INF 13 (Dec. 23, 1977).   This paper did not
      represent a complete agreement on all fundamental principles
      since both the U.S. and the EEC noted reservations as to
      certain portions of the text.

mechanisms should be implemented to improve the likelihood of resolving disputes.

3.   LDCs

a.   a recognition of the special problems of developing countries.

Although the outline does not specifically mention domestic subsidies, it contained general language applicable to both domestic and export subsidies and contained language (subject to an EEC reservation) that called for detailed guidelines with respect to use of certain subsidies.

The issue of domestic subsidies was in fact one of the most troublesome. Practically all countries, including the U.S., maintain such programs ranging from incentives to locate plants in depressed areas, to grants and tax credits for employing new workers, particularly the disadvantaged or handicapped. Such programs often seem innocuous; however, their impact on trade can sometimes be substantial. For example, grants to build a new plant and employ workers in an economically depressed area, while domestic in nature, can have a significant impact on trade if the plant receiving the aid manufactures products for which a small home market exists and will thus be primarily exported.

The more socialistic economies in certain European states exhibited a high degree of government ownership and assistance to major industries that made negotiations on these issues particularly sensitive. The U.S. proposed a special "supplementary understanding" to delineate the role of internal subsidies. A list of domestic subsidies that might cause "serious prejudice" to other signatories was enumerated which the U.S. hoped and the Europeans feared might create a standard for defining prohibited domestic subsidies.[12] Many of these principles did, in fact, become incorporated in Article II of the Subsidies/Countervailing Measures Code, and constituted a major accomplishment for the United States, the primary advocate of such standards.

Next to domestic subsidies, subsidies on agricultural products were a major stumbling block. The European Common Market Agricultural Policy was fraught with subsidies that the EEC did not wish to relinquish. The U.S. delegation was under pressure from the U.S. Congress to obtain concessions on agricultural products, while the EEC's goal was to keep agriculture separate from concessions made in other areas. Problems were sufficiently serious to cause Finn Gundelach, the EEC Commissioner of Agriculture to fly to Washington in March, 1977 to try to work out a compromise on some of these issues.[13]

---

[12] Id. at 1173.
[13] Bus. Wk. 23 (Mar. 7, 1977).

To many in the U.S., there was no reason to differentiate between agricultural and industrial products. However, to the EEC, subsidies comprise a major part of its Common Agricultural Policy (CAP) and it could not afford to risk a complete or sudden termination of these programs. In fact, the EEC itself noted that the Common Agricultural Policy was "the only really joint community program".[14] Under the CAP when surplus production occurs, it is either stored for future disposition or exported with whatever financial subsidy is needed to sell it abroad.[15] Thus, the EEC had a great deal at stake in negotiating on the issue of agricultural subsidies.

GATT Article XVI, Paragraph 3 permitted agricultural export subsidies so long as they did not give the subsidizing country more than an equitable share of the world market. Unfortunately, the concept of "equitable share" was not defined. This problem was resolved in the MTN by interpreting Article XVI, Paragraph 3 of the GATT as follows:

> "More than an equitable share of world export trade" shall include any case in which the effect of an export subsidy granted by a signatory is to displace the exports of another signatory bearing in mind the developments on world markets[.]...[16]

The Code further provided that the signatories agreed not to grant export subsidies on exports of certain agricultural products to a particular market in a manner which results in prices materially below those of other suppliers to the same market.[17]

A final important negotiating issue concerned the implementation of an injury test in U.S. law. Since the U.S. law antedated the GATT, the U.S. was not required under the Protocol of Provisional Application[18] to extend an injury test to other GATT members. This was the principal concession sought from the U.S. during the negotiations, and one which the U.S., in principle, was prepared to accept subject to the outcome of other negotiations. The U.S. did not want an injury test that required that subsidized exports be the principal cause of injury, following the injury test set out for dumped imports in the 1967 Antidumping Code.[19] Such a requirement would have made it more difficult for U.S.

---

14 European Communities, The Agricultural Policy of the European Communities (1976).

15 MTN Studies, supra note 7.

16 Agreement on Interpretation and Application of Articles VI, XVI and XXIII of the General Agreement on Tariffs and Trade, GATT Doc. MTN/NTM/W/236, pt. II, art. 10, para.2.

17 Id. at para. 3.

18 See 55 U.N.T.S. 308.

19 19 U.S.T. 4348, art. 31a.

domestic industries to prove injury. However, EEC negotiators supported the U.S. on this point and compromise language suggested by Canada was finally adopted. This language kept the causation requirement but did not require that subsidized imports be the principal cause of injury, but only that subsidized imports, through the effects of the subsidy are causing injury.[20]

A second issue was whether simply injury alone would suffice or some higher standard such as "substantial" or "material" injury was needed. The U.S. negotiators favored a straight "injury" criteria since this would provide the most protection to domestic industries. However, the U.S. eventually acceded to a "material injury" test after a list of criteria for interpreting "material injury" was set forth.[21]

B.   Technical Barriers To Trade

Although one of the less glamorous areas of negotiation, technical barriers such as product standards, were an important issue in the overall process of negotiating removal of non-tariff barriers. The Draft Code, prepared far in advance of the Tokyo Round, was used as a starting point for negotiations, despite the fact that many members of the technical barriers subgroup were not involved in preparing the draft. The technical barriers subgroup met a number of times and made considerable progress, perhaps due to the less political nature of their task as compared to sensitive areas as subsidies and government procurement. Negotiations covered such areas as testing and certification by governmental bodies and included the areas of packaging, labeling and marking of origin. The negotiators worked with representatives of various international standards groups such as the International Organization for Standardization.

C.   Customs Valuation

The Customs Valuation subgroup had its first meeting in May, 1975. Among the topics discussed were provisions for uniformity in publication of customs valuation laws and regulations and for administrative review procedures. Another important topic was the need for standard definitions. Some countries already subscribed to standard definitions contained in the Brussels Definition, while others did not. Efforts were focused upon harmonizing the views of these two groups

---

[20] Rivers & Greenwald, supra note 5, at 1484.
[21] Id. at 1485. These criteria included such factors as lost sales, lost market, market share, price supression, and the ability to raise capital.

and a compromise combining several systems was first presented
in 1977 and became the basis for negotiations subject to
reservations by some participants.   However, sources of
continued disagreement were in such areas as the need for
separate rules for developing countries and methods for
dispute settlement.   By late 1978 a new draft was completed;
but a consensus was still quite far away.   A particular
stumbling block was found in the area of transactions between
related parties.   This and certain other issues were sources
of disagreement between the LDCs and the developed countries
who preferred their own position paper.   Due to the failure of
these two groups to reach an agreement, both groups were
permitted to put forth texts that were opened for signature to
the participants.

D.   Government Procurement

The Government Procurement subgroup circulated a draft in
December, 1977 entitled "Draft Integrated Text for Negotiations on Government Procurement".   A second draft was submitted in July, 1978.   Among the various issues discussed were
non-discrimination in procurement, dispute settlement procedures, and the issue of "transparency" of procurement procedures.   The issue of transparency, or the openness and
visibility of the procurement process was an important one and
constituted one of the major areas of negotiations.[22] Another
issue was the value threshold that would trigger applicability
of the Code provisions.   It was realized that it would be
impractical to apply any complex Code procedures to various
small government procurements; and some governments claimed by
eliminating small contracts, the costs of administration would
be reduced.   The U.S., on the other hand, as discussed in
detail below, favored a lower threshold.[23] Much of the
negotiations on government procurement had as its antecedent
negotiations conducted by many of the same parties within of
the Organization for Economic Cooperation and Development
(OECD).[24] Perhaps as a result of this, there was considerable
focus on and consideration of the needs of the LDCs resulting
in special provisions in the final agreement.

A document produced by the OECD entitled "Draft Instrument on Government Purchasing Policies, Procedures, and
Practices" was made available to the GATT subgroup working on
the Government Procurement Code, and understandably formed a

---

22 Pomeranz, Toward a New International Order in Government
    Procurement, 11 Law & Pol'y Int'l Bus. 1263, 1278 (1979). The
    author served as Senior Industrial Advisor to the U.S.
    Special Trade Representative during the MTN.

23 Id.

24 Id. at 1275.

basis for the "Draft Integrated Text for Negotiations on Government Procurement".

There were a number of primary issues discussed by the Government Procurement subgroup of which some will be discussed breifly below:

1.   Applicability Threshold

The minimum value that would trigger applicability of the Code provisions was a crucial issue. Efforts were made to reach a threshold low enough to accomplish the goals of opening up new markets, but high enough so not to cause an administrative nightmare for the authorities in the signatory countries. Most of the developing countries generally favored a low value threshold in developed countries since they believed they had the greatest opportunity to obtain smaller contracts involving smaller and lesser technology equipment. Interestingly enough, the United States also supported a lower value threshold apparently since it felt that the value of procurement contracts in countries that U.S. companies might benefit from would be lower than those in the U.S.[25]

2.   Governmental Bodies Subject to the Code

Because of the differing degrees of governmental ownership of various sectors in individual negotiating countries, it was important but difficult to delineate the entities subject to the Code.

The systems varied considerably, particularly between the more socialistic economies where government ownership of utilities and transportation was common and to the U.S. system in which government purchasing was largely for governmental type activities rather than for proprietary activities. This also led to some negotiating inequities since if each country agreed to open up all its government procurement to foreign purchasers, some countries would obviously be opening up more than others. The problem was eventually solved in the Code by providing for a mix of entities from each country in relationship to the size of the countries' procurement market. The exact mix was never reduced to a formula. In 1978, a procedure was adopted for negotiations on the questions of entities through the system of offers and requests, whereby each country would notify the others of those entities in its own country that would be subject to the Code and those entities in other countries which they would like to see covered.

Developing countries were permitted to limit their offers to a degree consistent with their level of development.

---

[25] Id. at 1278.

3.   Non-Central Governments

Negotiations, offers and requests were generally concerned with entities and policies of central, or Federal
governments. However, concern was expressed over the policies
of state and local governments. This is particularly important in countries such as the U.S., where a considerable
amount of government procurement is on a state and local level
and where some states had enacted local "Buy-American" laws.
However, it was also recognized that central authorities in
federalist type governments might be unable to enforce
procurement regulations on autonomous local and regional
authorities. Nevertheless, a compromise was reached by which
the signatories agreed to inform local governments of the new
procurement rules and the overall objectives of liberalizing
international trade that could benefit exporters in these
regions.

4.   LDCs

From the beginning it was recognized that the LDCs, if
they were to accept a code on government procurement, would
have to be given special allowances. This was predicated upon
the lengthy discussions held by the OECD in this area which
anticipated special treatment for LDCs.[26]

5.   Tender Procedures

The differences in procurement practices in various countries made it crucial to agree on a common terminology for
tender procedures. In the OECD negotiations the U.S. draft
text defined two types of tenders, "public" (formal bidding)
and "informal" (negotiated or sole-sourced).[27] However, other
parties favored a tri-partite system with open, selective and
single tenders. These are defined in detail in the agreement
itself, which will be discussed _infra_.[28] Generally, entities
are expected to use open tenders (all interested parties may
bid) or selective tenders (suppliers invited to do so may bid
-- invitation policies being otherwise consistent with the
Code). Single tendering procedures (entity contacts indivi-

---

[26] See GATT, Draft OECD Instrument on Government Procurement
Purchasing Policies, Procedures, and Practices, GATT Doc.
MIN/NTM/W/81 art. VI, para. 1/2 (Jan. 1977).

[27] See U.S. Delegation Note, OECD, Working Party of the Trade
Committee, Government Procurement, OECD Doc. TFD/TD/521, at 1
(Feb. 1969).

[28] See Code on Government Procurement, _infra_, art. V, para. 1.

dual suppliers) are restricted.   Tendering policies are subject to non-discrimination and national treatment.

6.   Dispute Settlement Mechanisms

Procedures for settlement of disputes involving government procurement were the subject of extended debate.   It was agreed that there should be a mechanism to oversee the dispute settlement procedures and a Committee on Government Procurement was established to facilitate this.   The anticipated framework was that parties would first attempt to settle disputes through bilateral negotiations, and if this failed then they would turn to a GATT mechanism.   The discussions focused around the establishment of panels which would provide findings of fact to a larger committee that would resolve the dispute.

E.   Import Licensing

A subgroup on import licensing was established in 1975, and the first meeting was held in April, 1975.   The subgroup had authority to negotiate both quantitative restrictions and import licensing.   The subgroup began with discussions of the two ad referendum texts drafted prior to the Tokyo Round and data provided in questionnaires.   The subgroup made little progress, particularly in its earlier meetings, and failed to narrow the divergence of views held by various subgroup members.   Among the more difficult issues was the question of automatic licensing since viewpoints were particularly divergent.   Automatic licenses are those approved routinely, compared to those licenses linked to quantitative restrictions whose approvals are limited.   Although the latter is obviously much more of a trade barrier, there was strong feeling on the part of many that automatic licenses created a significant barrier to trade since they created a bureaucratic structure that could become arbitrarily administered. Some countries felt that all automatic licenses should be eliminated.   Others felt they served a useful purpose for monitoring of imports, particularly those of a sensitive nature.   As in other areas discussed previously, there was also a difference of views as to whether any agreement should apply to both agricultural and industrial products or only to industrial products.

Midway through the discussions, the subgroup began to make more progress.   Meetings were held in 1977 and 1978 with informal consultations occuring in between.   By July, 1978 a draft text was produced; and in December, 1978 a draft agreement on import licensing procedures was offered.   The final text was transmitted by the subgroup to the Trade Negotiations Committee in April, 1979.

F.   Safeguards

Safeguard measures provided one of the more difficult areas of negotiations, and the most significant area that failed to result in an agreement. This was undoubtedly due to both the complexity of the issues and the divergent views of the parties, particularly since the developing countries saw safeguard measures as a major obstacle to their freer entry into markets of developed countries. The developed countries wanted to strengthen safeguard measures, arguing that trade could more easily be liberalized and tariffs cut if countries could be assured of adequate and effective safeguards or "escape" mechanisms; if import penetration became too great and injury resulted.

Perhaps the key issue in safeguard negotiations was "selectivity". As discussed earlier, traditionally, actions under Article XIX of the GATT had to be "non-discriminatory" or otherwise treat all importing nations equally. This often caused practical problems where the real cause of market disruption was one country, e.g. a developed nation, but a safeguard duty had to be imposed on all countries, including many LDCs that were only marginally able to compete with developed countries. This, sometimes, had the undesirable effect of actually limiting competition by driving out smaller nations in the process of penalizing larger ones. This shotgun approach of safeguard mechanisms proved to be a major source of concern.

Negotiations on safeguards began late. It was not until early 1978 that negotiations began in earnest. Perhaps because of the controversial nature of the safeguards negotiations, the parties preferred to begin on more positive areas such as tariff cutting. When negotiations began in earnest in 1978, the subgroup had before it an agenda of issues that had been culled from its earlier meetings. These included:

1.   Selectivity
2.   Mandatory use of adjustment assistance[29]
3.   Whether safeguard duties should be regulated to provide specific rates relating to the degree of penetration.
4.   Whether safeguard measures should be imposed only within certain time limits.

---

[29] Adjustment assistance is a process whereby direct monetary aid in the form of grants and loans or retraining is directly provided to workers whose jobs are lost by imports, or to injured companies for retooling, modernization, etc. Liberal trade commentators view this as a more meaningful and direct way to deal with import impacted workers and industries. Unions and others (although beneficiaries) often refer to it derisively as "burial insurance".

5.   Definition of injury and market disruption.

During 1976, many proposals were offered which provided
that any new safeguard mechanisms should include special
provisions for LDCs.   In essence, the LDCs felt that safeguard
measures taken by developed countries should not include them
unless a specific examination was made through a GATT mechanism that indicated any exemption was impractical or un-
warranted. Also suggested were differential standards for
defining such concepts as injury as applied to developing
countries.   In June, 1978, a group of developed countries
tabled a draft text that was diverged considerably from the
position of the LDCs, expressed in 1976. On the selectivity
issue, many developed countries particularly the Nordics and
the EEC, favored an approach of selective actions against
individual countries, with an ex post facto review by a GATT
committee. Others felt that GATT review should come prior to
any selective imposition of safeguard measures.   A third
group, which included the many LDCs favored application of the
MFN non-discrimination principles. These views were not
necessarily in the best interest of the very least developed
countries in Africa, Central and South America and the Carib-
bean, which further complicated the agreement process.
    The developed countries made a concerted effort to obtain
the views of the LDCs on safeguard issues. In July, 1978, the
U.S. and Japan met with five of the advanced LDCs to exchange
views and to encourage their participation in negotiations.
The LDCs had previously presented a paper opposing selectivity
and the U.S. and Japan urged them to negotiate on this issue.
The feeling was that the EEC would not accept a safeguard code
without some selectivity.   India, acting as spokesman for
LDCs, indicated it could not accept the EEC position even if
it meant no safeguards agreement. The general feeling of the
LDCs was that there was nothing to be gained by them in
accepting selectivity.   This was especially prevalent among
the advanced LDCs such as Brazil and Mexico. The idea of some
"compensation" in return for the selectivity was raised by the
LDCs. On July 26, 1978, the EEC had its own meeting with the
LDCs.   The LDCs indicated that they were not opposed to all
negotiations on selectivity but only to the EEC version which
would allow unilateral provisional action. This was viewed as
a sign of some progress on the selectivity issue.   The U.S.
favored a form of "consensual selectivity" as compared to the
EEC's unilateral selectivity. The U.S. objective was to
persuade the EEC that consensual selectivity was sufficient
and to moderate its position, which was unacceptable to the
LDCs.
    Texts on individual points were submitted by the U.S.,
Japan, Canada, the EEC, and the Nordic countries. Selectivity
was the key issue of disagreement. The U.S. position was that
MFN application of safeguard measures should be the norm with

no prior GATT review unless requested by a signatory. However, a party by agreement with another party could restrict imports from that party on a selective basis. If a bilateral agreement on a selective application of safeguard measures could not be reached, the matter could be referred to a committee of signatories. If no agreement was reached, selective action could still be taken with prior approval of the GATT committee and measures were applied on a non-discriminatory basis as between countries to which the measures were selectively applied. Some socially oriented developed countries such as the Nordics proposed a "social clause" which would link adjustment measures to the degree of an exporting nation's compliance with fair labor standards as promulgated by the International Labor Organization.

The definition of injury was also a serious area of disagreement. While the standard of "serious injury" was generally accepted, parties (particularly LDCs and developed nations) disagreed as to the proper threshold for triggering such a finding.

When the Trade Negotiations Committee met in April, 1979, negotiations had reached an impasse; it was agreed that the safeguards groups should continue to meet with the objective of reaching an agreement by July 15, 1979.   However, no agreement was reached. In order to provide readers with some guidance as to the areas discussed and provisional drafts, attached in the Appendix with the text of various Codes, is a draft safeguard code circulated in December, 1978.

The safeguards area continues to be a major negotiating issue. In January of 1982, U.S. Trade Representative Brock, in a speech in Davos, Switzerland, called for a new round of trade negotiations to be mapped out in the November, 1982 GATT Ministerial meeting. One goal of these negotiations, according to Ambassador Brock, was the negotiation of an international Safeguards Code.[30] Later, in March, 1982, the administration announced its goals for the GATT Ministerial meeting. Brock told the Senate Finance Committee, and Trade Sub-committee, that the U.S. will "push for an immediate negotiation of both an important safeguards code and an anti-counterfeit code".[31] Brock indicated that the Safeguards Code, in the U.S. view, should "exercise discipline over the actions nations take to protect producers. These actions the United States believes should be subject to international surveillance and phase out over prescribed time intervals".[32]

---

[30] Journal of Commerce, Jan. 25, 1982, at 4A.

[31] Id. at 1A (Mar. 2, 1982).

[32] Id.

G.   Agriculture

Although agricultural negotiations could be considered as
part of the negotiations on tariffs, subsidies, or other
areas, there are a number of reasons to treat them separately.
First, the MTN participants treated agricultural issues as a
separate negotiating theater. Second, the agricultural
negotiations contained many non-tariff issues as well, and,
the topic is of sufficient importance to warrant separate
treatment.
The initial preparatory work on agriculture focused on
dairy products, cereals, meats, vegetable oils, fruits and
vegetables, tobacco and wine. Attention was, at first,
focused on tariffs and quantitative restrictions and later
into such areas as health and sanitary regulations. Various
differences existed in ideas as to how negotiations should
proceed. Some favored negotiations only on tariffs, while
others felt the focus should be on codes of conduct, such as
health regulations or export and pricing policies. The
negotiating strategy of the U.S. was to seek increased export
opportunities and stability through trading rules and consultative arrangements. Tariff concessions were sought on
products of greater export potential for U.S. products such as
tobacco, meats, vegetable oils, fruits, soybeans, rice and
cotton.[33]
The agriculture group was formally established in
February, 1975. Later in the year three subgroups were also
established; one on grains, one on meat, and the third on
dairy products. These areas were considered the most important, and involved the largest amount of trade. Other
products of less general importance were taken up later.
Little progress, however, was made until 1977. Much of this
was due to the continuing antipathy on agricultural issues
between the U.S. and the European Community, which have been
discussed briefly earlier, and will be discussed in further
detail. Japan indicated little enthusiasm for liberalizing
agriculture trade.[34] The work of the subgroups had largely
been limited to consultations among various countries, which
were later communicated to other members. While ideas were
exchanged, positions remained solidified, and little substantive negotiating progress took place. Movement began to occur
in July, 1977. The Agriculture Group began an offer and
request approach to cover both tariff and non-tariff barriers.
Requests were generally not to be directed to LDCs except in a
limited manner of noting export interests. This was a

---

[33] Bergland (former Secretary of Agriculture), Agriculture, Law
& Pol'y Int'l Bus. 257, 258 (1980).

[34] Background and Status of Multilateral Trade Negotiations
Before the Subcomm. on Trade of the House Comm. on Ways &
Means, 94th Cong., 1st. Sess. 38-39 (1975).

concession to the LDCs' desire for special treatment. By 1978, over seventy countries submitted requests and initial negotiating offers. The specific subgroups also continued their work described below:

1.   Dairy Products

Early talks were of a technical nature since little progress on substance could be reached. Dairy products caused unusually difficult problems due to the wide existence of subsidies and price supports. Agreement on minimum prices for certain products had also been negotiated on a multilateral level.

Late in 1977, two proposals were put forth on dairy products, one by New Zealand and the other by the EEC. These proposals led to a draft arrangement which would form the basis of future proposals. However, since great concern was given to such issues as safeguards and standards, the dairy subgroup had to await action on these areas by other specific subgroups. It was not clear at first whether the dairy and other agricultural agreements would have their own provisions in these areas. In 1978, however, the full group decided that the Code on Standards would be applicable to agriculture and that separate provisions on health, sanitary and veterinary standards would not need to be drafted. The arrangement was viewed as a general agreement to which specific protocols on special problems could be added. Protocols originally included such areas as maximum and minimum prices, although in 1978 the protocol on maximum prices was dropped. By April, 1979, a text of an arrangement was submitted to the Trade Negotiations Committee along with certain amendments proposed by various members and various interpretive declarations.

2.   Grains

The grains subgroup initially focused on four products -- wheat, corn, barley, and sorghum. The main focus was on issues relating to the stabilization of prices and markets, differential treatment for LDCs and liberalization of trade. The work of the grain subgroup was slowed by the existence of outside commodities arrangements such as the activities of the International Wheat Council.[35]

A conference was held in 1977 to negotiate a new agreement to replace the International Wheat Agreement, which was due to expire in July, 1979. Thus, the grain subgroup did not meet during this time period except informally. In March,

---

[35] Commodities including grains had been the subject of a number of international agreements.

1979, the old International Wheat Agreement was extended until
July 1, 1981.

3.   Bovine Meats

This subgroup was organized in May, 1975, but did not
make much progress until mid-July, 1977. The group examined
trade barriers in each country and analyzed the nature of the
world meat trade. Proposals dealt with the liberalization of
trade, special treatment for LDCs and methods of cooperation
and concerted action. The EEC tabled a proposal on a multilateral framework agreement on bovine meat. Later the GATT
secretariat prepared a text that incorporated some of the
EEC's concepts which were the subject of discussion and
revision in 1977 and 1978. The draft agreement or arrangement
was finally submitted to the Trade Negotiations Committee in
April, 1979 after many of the more controversial points had
been worked out. These included agreements that codes on
standards, safeguards and subsidies would apply to the
arrangement without the need for separate provisions in these
areas in the arrangement itself.

4.   General Agricultural Issues

Because of the complexity of agricultural issues, some
participants felt that a broader agreement of general application incorporating certain fundamental principles was desirable. A proposal to create an international agriculture
consultative council was made in 1978 and efforts were made to
reach a "framework" agreement on agriculture but without
success.

5.   Tropical Products

As noted earlier, tropical products were a topic of
special interest at the MTN, largely due to the importance
they held for the LDCs. It was an area where negotiations
began early and yielded some progress. Prior to the beginning
of the MTN, the GATT Special Group on Trade in Tropical
Products had stressed the problem and provided basic materials
to begin negotiations. Various procedures were established for
submission of offers and requests in 1977 and 1978. Certain
offers and concessions were also reached ouside of the MTN
structure and were actually implemented while the MTN was

continuing. A major issue was tariff differences between raw and semi-processed tropical products.[36]

H.   Framework for the Conduct of World Trade

In addition to the specific substantive areas discussed previously, negotiations took place to establish a legal framework for future world trading. A special "framework" group was established for this purpose which was proposed by Brazil and came into existence in late 1976. The group investigated many areas including emergency balance of payment measures, consultation and dispute settlement measures under the GATT, and re-evaluated such traditional GATT concepts as MFN (Most Favored Nation) treatment whereby concessions made under GATT auspices are made equally to all nations as to the most favored nation within the GATT auspices. Other questions particularly relating to the problems of LDCs were also addressed. LDCs were concerned that preferences such as GSP (Generalized System of Preferences) whereby certain tariff benefits were made available only to developing countries required waivers from the GATT because they violated GATT rules on MFN.

In the balance of payments area, countries were permitted under the existing GATT rules to use quantitative restrictions (import quotas) for balance of payment purposes. Consultations were required under rules set out in Article XII and Article XVIII, Paragraph 12(b). However, the system had not functioned perfectly. Many countries used other measures for balance of payment reasons other than quotas. For example, the U.S. had imposed a 10% import surcharge for balance of payment reasons under the Nixon administration which had incurred the ire of many of its trading partners. Some felt that these types of measures should be incorporated into the GATT rules and consultative and surveillance mechanisms established. In 1978, a draft declaration on Trade Measures Taken for Balance of Payments Purposes was tabled by the GATT secretariat.

Negotiations on consultative and dispute settlement measures revolved upon such issues as whether dispute settlements should be mandatory upon the submission of a complaint. The LDCs as a rule felt that GATT dispute settlement mechanisms should be strengthened, including mandatory rulings and sanctions for non-compliance. In mid-1978, the secretariat tabled a draft "Understanding regarding Notification, Consultation, Dispute Settlement and Surveillance" that formed the basis of further negotiations. After various modifications, it was agreed to in early 1979.

---

36 See **MTN** Studies, supra note 7, at 38.

GATT rules on the issue of trade restrictions affecting exports was also one of the issues proposed by Brazilians. The U.S. had a specific interest in this issue along with the balance of payments and dispute settlement issue.[37] Another important goal of the U.S. was to link special treatment for LDCs such as tariff preferences to a system of graduation whereby "developing countries would accept greater obligations under the GATT as their economic situations improve".[38]

I.   Civil Aircraft Code

A Civil Aircraft Code was introduced as a topic late in the MTN. It was based on a U.S. proposal to eliminate tariffs and non-tariff barriers on civil aircraft. Serious negotiations had begun at the Bonn Summit and included such issues as government directed procurement, off-sets, subsidies, standards and quantitative restrictions that overlapped other MTN topics. The U.S. industry, that supplied 85% of all commercial jet aircraft in the world, favored a complete elimination of tariffs and easing of procurement regulations. The U.S. goal was to seek an open market for trade in civil aircraft by binding duty free or low tariff rates due to fear of protectionist measures from Japan, the EEC and Canada, in return for elimination of the 5% U.S. duty.[39] At first it was thought that this might be accomplished solely through tariff negotiations. However, it became clear that non-tariff barriers that limited market access was also a problem for the U.S.[40] Many of these non-tariff barriers dealt with issues such as subsidization and export credits which were interrelated to the subsidies code negotiations, while others dealt with government procurement policies that were interrelated to the negotiations on a government procurement code.

The U.S. negotiating position was first developed by an advisory committee which developed a declaration of policy in 1978.[41] In October, 1978, the U.S. submitted a draft proposal which called for immediate elimination of all customs duties on commercial (civil) aircraft and parts and prohibited certain enumerated non-tariff barriers such as discriminatory governmental certifications and regulations, quotas, government financing of private development, government directed

---

37 Twenty-third Annual Report of the President of the United States on the Trade Agreement Program, 33 (1978) [hereinafter cited at Twenty-third Annual Report].

38 Id.

39 Id. at 35.

40 See American and Foreign Practices in the Financing of Large Commercial Aircraft Sales Before the Subcomm. on Trade of the House Comm. on Ways & Means, 95th Cong., 1st Sess. 61-62 (1978).

41 Id. at 10-21.

procurement practices and other practices.[42] It was the goal of the U.S. negotiators to link tariff and non-tariff issues in one package.[43] Other delegations were more concerned with the elimination of tariffs.   Some countries favored permitting subsidies to the extent they were necessary to produce aircraft competitive with those made in the U.S.

The logic behind this was that aircraft production is highly capital intensive, giving an inherent disadvantage to smaller nations with limited home markets. For these nations to compete at all, they must rely on governmental aid to bring them to at least an equal footing with the well-established and financed U.S. industry. This, it was argued, was not an unfair advantage but only fair and equal competition. The U.S. had to and was willing to accept different degrees of governmental involvement in other countries[44] but wanted more rules and disciplines as to conduct and governmental activities.   Success was greatest in the areas of government procurement and standards but the key issue of export financing was not resolved.

J.   Commercial Counterfeiting

The U.S. initiated commercial counterfeiting as a topic for negotiation in late June, 1978. It was hoped, even at this late date, that this topic could be included as part of the Tokyo Round. The U.S. sought an agreement against international counterfeiting of industrial and intellectual property, particularly trademarks. The U.S. sought an agreement which would improve economic sanctions against counterfeit goods. The substantive questions of whether the intellectual property at issue is protectable was left to national law and no uniform standards were sought.   The initial U.S. proposal dealt only with trademarks and trade names. Other countries favored expanding the proposed code to include other areas such as designs. The U.S. negotiating objective was to gain acceptance of the basic principle that the parties to a counterfeit transaction should be deprived of the economic benefits of the transaction.[45] The original U.S. proposal required forefeiture of the goods. Other proposals included only the forefeiture of a bond equal to the value of the goods or re-exportation of the offending merchandise[46] in

---

42 For a more detailed discussion of the topic by the actual U.S. negotiator, see Piper, Unique Sectoral Agreement Establishes Free Trade Framework, Law & Pol'y Int'l Bus. 221, 223 (1980).

43 Id. at 233.

44 Id.

45 See Twenty-third Annual Report, supra note 37, at 35.

46 Id.

order that any counterfeiting code not become a non-tariff barrier. Procedural safeguards, appeals, consultations, and dispute settlement mechanisms were also proposed. No agreement was reached in 1978 due largely to disagreement as to the degree of flexibility each signatory should have in determining whether merchandise is counterfeit and how sanctions should be imposed.[47] Progress was made in 1979 although no agreement was reached in time to be included in the MTN package. In July, 1979, the U.S. and the EEC reached agreement on a draft text,[48] but other countries had still not accepted it. The draft required either confiscation of the goods or other measures to deter the counterfeiting. The draft applied only to trademarks but was capable of being expanded to other products.

K.   Antidumping Code Amendments

An amended antidumping code[49] was attached to the Proces-Verbal submitted to the Trade Negotiations Committee. The LDCs had a particular amendment that was also submitted which provided that because of the unique situation of LDCs, the value for determining whether goods from an LDC are being dumped should be determined by a comparison of the export price from the developing country with the price of a like product when exported to a third country. Participants finally agreed on a revision to the Code which harmonized many of the provisions dealing with injury, imposition of duties and other matters, with those of the Code on Subsidies. Compromises were reached on a number of issues with the LDCs This included a recognition that for LDCs, the base for calculating dumping margins could be the price of comparable exports to third countries or the cost of production, rather than simply the price that the product is exported to the country alleging dumping. The revised Antidumping Code became effective on January 1, 1980.[50]

---

[47] Id.

[48] Twenty-fourth Annual Report of the President of the United States on the Trade Agreement Program, 72 (1979).

[49] The antidumping code was negotiated during the Kennedy Round and was one of the few non-tariff measures dealt with in that Round. Seventeen countries and the EEC are parties to the agreement. It is officially referred to as the "Agreement on Implementation of Article VI of the General Agreement."

[50] GATT, Activities in 1979, GATT/1980-2, at 25-26.

Chapter 3

THE RESULTS OF THE MTN

This chapter will analyze the concrete results obtained during the MTN. The texts of the actual codes are attached in their entirety in the Appendix. Each code will be analyzed and discussed along with the results of the tariff negotiations. In a later section, specific United States implementing legislation will be discussed along with the reaction in the U.S. Congress and among other countries.

OVERVIEW OF MTN RESULTS

On April 12, 1979, trade negotiators from forty-one countries, including nineteen LDCs agreed upon the final results of the Tokyo Round. The participating countries accounted for more than 90% of the world's trade. By most objective standards, the MTN must be viewed as a success, perhaps the most successful of the seven rounds of multilateral trade negotiations conducted since World War II. For the first time, previously insurmountable obstacles of non-tariff barriers to trade were discussed and to a large extent dismantled. These were not simple issues but politically and emotionally charged areas involving heretofore sacrosanct governmental prerogatives such as procurement and product standards. Moreover, tariff reductions averaging 33% on an aggregate basis of total trade between the participating nations were approved. These reductions, largely to be phased in over eight to ten years, represent substantial tariff concessions in many sensitive areas. If there was a failure in the MTN, it was primarily the failure to complete negotiations on safeguards and counterfeiting. However, the ground work for codes in these areas has been laid. The MTN package was approved by participating delegations on an ad referendum basis. They then had to be finally approved by each participating government or entity (e.g., the EEC). In the case of the United States, a specified process for approval was set

out in the Trade Act of 1974 which authorized U.S. participation in trade negotiations.

TARIFF NEGOTIATIONS

The results of the tariff negotiations are perhaps the
most difficult to quantify. These were negotiations covering
tens of thousands of product categories. Some negotiations
were bilateral, others multilateral, but in the end, all
concessions were extended to all participants in keeping with
the most-favored nation principle. It is very difficult to
analyze the impact of tariff concessions in terms of the exact
amount of trade which will be affected. The negotiations
themselves assessed the value of tariff cuts based on a
comparision of the average level of duties before the negotiations and the duties agreed upon. Tariff negotiations
resulted in two agreements. The first, the "Geneva (1979)
Protocol to the General Agreement on Tariffs and Trade" was
opened for signature on July 11, 1979. Attached to the
protocol were schedules of concessions setting out tariff
cutting commitments made by Argentina, Austria, Canada,
Czechoslovakia, EEC, Finland, Hungary, Iceland, Jamaica,
Japan, New Zealand, Norway, Romania, South Africa, Spain,
Sweden, Switzerland, United States and Yugoslavia.
    The second agreement was entitled the "Protocol Supple-
mentary to the Geneva (1979) Protocol to the General Agreement
on Tariffs and Trade", and was opened to signature on November
22, 1979. This supplementary protocol included additional
tariff concessions not completed by July, 1979. This supplementary protocol was of principal importance because it
contained tariff concessions by the LDCs. Schedules of
concessions were submitted by Australia, Brazil, Canada,
Chile, Dominican Republic, Egypt, EEC, Haiti, India, Indo-
nesia, Israel, Ivory Coast, Korea, Malaysia, Pakistan, Peru,
Singapore, Spain, Uraguay and Zaire. Most concessions were to
be implemented in equal annual increments beginning January 1,
1980 with the full concessions to be accomplished by January
1, 1987. However, there were exceptions for the U.S. concessions for certain sensitive products, such as steel, textiles
and apparel, that did not begin until January 1, 1982 and were
to be accomplished in six stages.
    According to official GATT documents, the total value of
trade affected by concessions was $155 billion. Concessions
by the EEC, Austria, U.S., Canada, Japan, Finland, Norway,
Sweden and Switzerland covered imports valued at $141 billion,
of which $14 billion were in agriculture and $125 billion in
industrial products.[1] The weighted average on industrial

---

[1] GATT, The Tokyo Round of Multilateral Trade Negotiations II --
     Supplementary Report, GATT/1980, at 6 (Jan. 1980).

tariffs will thus decline from 7.0% to 4.7%. Concessions by
developed countries covered 27,000 tariff terms representing
about three-quarters of all dutiable tariff headings and
subheadings.[2] The MTN reductions were greater on finished
manufacturing goods than on semi-manufactured goods, and
lowest on primary or raw materials since many of these
products were already duty-free or at low tariff rates.[3]

The biggest cuts in the industrial sector were in
non-electrical machinery, minerals, wood products and chemicals. Several charts supplied by the GATT indicating the
nature and depth of tariff cuts appear in the Appendix. The
total average tariff cuts by the industrial countries were
about 33-1/3%. This has been argued by some to be insignificant since a 30% cut in a tariff of 10% over eight years would
reduce the import price by less than 0.4 of 1% a year.[4] The
tariff cutting approach ultimately adopted was the Swiss
formula expressed basically as follows:

$$Y = \frac{AX}{A + X}$$

Y = resulting reduced duty rate
X = initial rate of duty applied
A = agreed upon co-effort

This formula reduces higher tariffs by a greater proportion
than lower tariffs thus tending to harmonize rates. The EEC,
Australia and the Scandinavian countries used a co-efficient
of sixteen, while the U.S., Japan and Switzerland used a
co-efficient of fourteen. The smaller the co-efficient, the
greater the tariff reduction. Some countries utilized
different formulas. In practice, U.S. tariffs were reduced by
an average of 32%, those of the EEC by 27%, and Japan by 50%.[5]
The U.S., which had the lowest overall duty rates prior to the
MTN, will continue to have the lowest duty rates after the MTN
concessions are fully implemented, although the percentage
reductions by the EEC and Canada were larger.[6]

It is somewhat more difficult to assess the quantitative
value of tariff cuts to the LDCs since some of the cuts were
on products that at the time were not exported in great
quantities due to high duties in the developed countries.
Moreover, some of the LDC products already received duty-free

---

[2] Id. at 30.
[3] Id. at 32.
[4] U.S. International Trade Commission, Operation of the Trade
Agreements Program, 31st Report, U.S.I.T.C. Pub. No. 1121, at
32-25 (1980).
[5] Id. at 37.
[6] Id.

treatment under GSP and did not benefit from additional tariff concessions.[7]

From the U.S. viewpoint, important concessions of export interest were gained in the following areas:

1.   Agricultural exports including meat to Europe, Japan, Canada and some LDCs.
2.   Tobacco exports to Europe, Canada and Australia.
3.   Fruit and vegetable exports to Europe, Japan and some LDCs.
4.   Wine exports to Canada and Japan.
5.   Oilseed exports to Europe, Japan, Canada and some LDCs.
6.   Nut exports to Europe, Japan and some LDCs.
7.   Reduction of Canadian tariffs on paper, computers, photographic equipment and aerospace machinery.
8.   Substantial reductions in Japanese tariffs on computers, color film, paper and semi-conductors.
9.   Substantial overall reductions in Japanese and EEC duties.[8]

It was estimated that MTN tariff reductions would increase annual U.S. exports by $3.3 billion and U.S. imports by $2.6 billion over an eight year period.   This was expected by the U.S. to lead to a $700 million improvement in its balance of trade.[9]   The U.S. goals in the industrial product tariff negotiations, as summarized by the United States Trade Representative, were to maximize tariff reductions by its trading partners in sectors of the greatest export potential, while minimizing U.S. tariff concessions on items where domestic industries were endangered by import competition.[10] The U.S. had specific goals as to individual trading partners. These included: (1) a reduction in tariff preferences granted by the EEC; (2) a reduction in certain high Japanese duties on items of high export interest to the U.S.; (3) reduction or elimination of large disparities between U.S. and Canadian tariffs; and (4) greater tariff discipline by the LDCs, including binding commitments not to raise tariffs.[11]

---

7   A discussion of Generalized System of Preferences (GSP) is beyond the scope of this book.   A recent discussion of the United States GSP System can be found in Glick, The General-ized System of Preferences: Yesterday, Today and Tomorrow, 30 Fed. Bar J. 284 (May 1983).

8   U.S. Department of State, MTN, Current Policy 56 (revised), 4 (Ap. 1979).

9   Operation of the Trade Agreements Program, supra note 4, at 38.

10   Twenty-fourth Annual Report of the President of the United States on the Trade Agreement Program, 51 (1979).

11   Id.

The extent to which these goals were fully achieved is the subject of varied opinions. The tables attached in the Appendix illustrate the industrial tariff concessions made by the United States, EEC, Canada, Japan and certain other industrialized nations on key product areas. Because of the separate treatment of industrial and agricultural products, and the differences in the results, these areas will be discussed separately.

A. U.S. -- EEC Industrial Tariff Cutting Results

As to industrial products, both the U.S. and the EEC cut tariffs representing about 35% of their bilateral trade. The range of cuts for U.S. products by the EEC was from 4.7% to 7.2%. Particular areas of gains for the U.S. involved electrical machinery, certain chemicals, paper items, printing machinery, scientific instruments, photographic equipment, and certain machine tools. Among the key areas of U.S. concessions to the EEC were reductions on leather, glassware, textile, chemical and machinery items.[12]

B. U.S. -- Canada Industrial Tariff Cutting Results

Prior to negotiations, Canadian duties were significantly higher than those of the U.S. As a result of the MTN, this disparity was decreased. The MTN resulted in an average reduction in Canadian tariffs of 42%, lowering the average tariff from about 11% to a little over 6%.[13] A major concession granted by Canada was exemption of a wide range of machinery from its "machinery program" that generally was dutiable at 15% and now has a duty-free status. This trade was valued at over $500 million prior to the MTN. The U.S. also obtained concessions on paper, wood products, photographic equipment, computers and scientific instruments, many of the same products for which concessions were obtained from the EEC. The major U.S. concessions to Canada extended duty-free treatment on agricultural machinery and parts, and reduced tariffs on certain machinery, non-ferrous metals and paper.

C. U.S. -- Japan Industrial Tariff Cutting Results

As a result of the MTN, Japan cut its statutory tariffs on industrial items by an average of 62%, with the average duty rate dropping from 6.2% to 2.3%. The U.S. was successful

---

12 Id. at 52, 63.

13 Id. at 63.

in obtaining reductions on key items of export interest such
as photographic film, computers, semi-conductors, automobiles,
paper and electrical machinery, which previously had high
tariff rates. For example, average tariffs in the automotive
sector would drop by 83%.[14] The U.S. granted concessions to
Japan on optical goods, scientific instruments, dyes and
woolen fabrics.

D.   Industrial Tariff Cuts With Other European Nations

The U.S. made concessions on such areas of interest to
other industrialized nations as Swiss watches, vodka from
Finland and magnesium from Norway.   The U.S., in turn,
received concessions on such items as chemicals, plastics,
autos, alcoholic beverages and scientific instruments.[15]

E.   Industrial Tariff Cuts With
      Non-European Developed Nations

The U.S. also engaged in bilateral tariff concessions
with such countries as Australia, New Zealand and South Africa
in the industrial area.   Australia made concessions on
computers, plastics, construction machinery and equipment, and
scientific instruments.   U.S. concessions were largely
agricultural and will be discussed later. New Zealand made
tariff concessions on chemicals, chemical compounds and
medical equipment. South Africa made concessions benefiting
U.S. exports of tools, earth-moving equipment and protein
derivatives. The U.S. reduced duties on diamonds, tanning
extracts and metal scraps.[16]

F.   Industrial Tariff Cuts With LDCs

The U.S. made concessions to LDCs on industrial products
which included electrical equipment, carpets, paper products
and light industrial goods. LDC concessions included reductions on industrial and agricultural chemicals, computers,
instruments, agricultural and industrial machinery, paper
products, air conditioning equipment, aircraft and oil
drilling equipment.[17]
In the area of agricultural negotiations, the U.S.
achieved overall tariff reductions on some $4 billion of U.S.
agricultural products (based on 1976 export levels). The

---

14 Id. at 63-64.
15 Id. at 64.
16 Id. at 69-70.
17 Id. at 70-71.

actual results would probably be greater since exports would
be expected to increase from 1976 levels as a result of the
lower duties. This represented about 16% of U.S. agricultural
exports. Products of particular importance to the U.S. for
which concessions were obtained were soybeans, fruits and
fruit juices, almonds, tobacco, beef, pork and turkey. The
U.S. made concessions involving $2.6 billion in agricultural
products (based on 1976 import levels).[18]

G.   U.S. -- EEC Agricultural Tariff Cutting Results

It is fair to say that agricultural tariff cutting by the
EEC was one of the most important and difficult areas for U.S.
tariff negotiations. The EEC Common Agricultural Policy had
long been a major obstacle in improving trade relations. While
many of these problems still exist, particularly relating to
export subsidies, the significance of the MTN tariff cuts
should not be minimized. The major concessions by the Community involved beef, tobacco, rice, poultry, and certain fresh
and canned fruits. The major U.S. concessions involved quotas
on cheese and removal of certain retaliatory duties invoked as
a result of the "Chicken War",[19] and elimination of the wine
gallon method of duty assessment; which will be discussed
below. The EEC, which is the largest export market for U.S.
tobacco, made concessions which reduced duties by one-third on
certain more expensive U.S. tobaccos. The concession on high
quality beef involved both a quota and duty, and was expected
to increase U.S. exports by $60 million annually. Other
technical changes were made in duty calculations on turkeys,
turkey meat and rice, which benefited the U.S. The EEC also
made tariff cuts on U.S. whiskey, particularly bourbon, and on
thirteen fish items including salmon, lobster, eel, hake and
crabs. The main U.S. concession was to increase the EEC quota
allocation on cheese, which particularly benefited Swiss,
Edam, Gouda and Blue-mold cheeses.[20]

---

[18] Id. at 65.
[19] The "Chicken War" resulted from the EEC's barriers against
poultry. The U.S. retaliated by raising duties on grain,
trucks, and other products, which were of importance to
France, Germany, and the Netherlands. For a detailed discussion, see J. Evans, The Kennedy Round in American Trade
Policy -- The Twilight of the GATT, 173-80 (1971).
[20] Twenty-fourth Annual Report of the President, supra note 10,
at 66-67.

H.   U.S. -- Canada Agricultural Tariff Cutting Results

In the value of trade involved (based on pre-MTN 1976 levels), the U.S. granted Canada $350 million in agricultural concessions and received $600 million. Efforts were made to harmonize or equalize duties on various products including live cattle, corn, barley, pork, bourbon, rum and potatoes. Canada reduced its tariffs on orange juice, vegetable oils, tobacco and fish. The U.S. agreed to reduce its duty on Canadian whiskey.[21]

I.   U.S. -- Japan Agricultural Tariff Cutting Results

Probably the largest concession made by Japan to the U.S. in the agricultural area involved soybeans. Japanese tariff reductions averaged about 18% and included such products as pork, grapefruits and lemons. Japan also bound its tariff rates on other items, notably soybeans. Quotas on beef were expanded, as were those on fresh oranges. Both of these are areas in which the U.S. is a prime exporter. Japan also raised its quota on concentrated orange juice and grapefruit juice. Together, these items (oranges, orange juice and grapefruit juice) were expected to increase 1983 U.S. exports by approximately $40 million. Japan also agreed to reduce duties on over twenty-five other fruit and vegetable products, including grapes, avocados and almonds. Japan also agreed to lower its high duty on U.S. bourbon and its duty on wine. Japan also made significant concessions valued at over $200 million on imports of U.S. fish. Japan did not seek concessions from the U.S. on agricultural products except fish.[22]

J.   Results of Agricultural Tariff Cuts
      With Other European Nations

The Nordic nations made tariff cuts largely related to fruits and vegetables. Norway made concessions valued at $5 million, Sweden at $4 million and Finland at $21 million. In addition to fruits and vegetables, Finland cut duties on rice and orange juice, and Norway on turkey rolls. Finland and Sweden cut their duties on U.S. bourbon whiskey and on crabs in airtight containers. U.S. concessions included a reduction on smoked sardines principally supplied by Norway and lowered quotas on certain cheeses produced in all three countries.[23]

Switzerland made concessions valued at $14 million. Particularly important were quota concessions on high quality

---

21 Id. at 67-68.

22 Id. at 65-66.

23 Id. at 68.

beef. The Swiss duty on almonds was eliminated and the tariff on rice reduced. The U.S., in return, established a quota for imports of cheeses.[24] Austria granted concessions valued at about $3 million involving beef, almonds and fruits. U.S. concessions were valued at $16 million.

K. Agricultural Trade Concessions
With Non-European Developed Nations

Because of the largely agricultural nature of their economies, tariff concessions in agricultural areas were of particular importance to Australia and New Zealand. Seventy-five percent of U.S. concessions to Australia involved beef, a major Australian export. This included a duty reduction of one cent per pound on beef and technical changes in the U.S. meat import law. The U.S. also granted Australia a 60% tariff reduction on raw wool. Quotas were also established for cheese and chocolate. Australia granted concessions on tobacco, reducing the duty from $1.18 to $.47 per kilogram.

Principal U.S. tariff concessions to New Zealand involved wool, lamb, beef, veal, butter and cheeses. New Zealand granted concessions on tobacco, rice, citrus products, almonds, apples and pears.

South Africa agreed to eliminate its duties on almonds and horses and reduce those on tallow. U.S. concessions were principally industrial.[25]

L. Agricultural Tariff Cuts With LDCs

The U.S. concluded bilateral agreements with twenty-eight LDCs, many of whom principally exported agricultural products and raw materials. Principal concessions involved canned beef, edible oils, canned fruits and vegetables, and cigar tobacco. Prior to the MTN, approximately 40% of U.S. agricultural products had no duty and the average tariff was only 4%. With the MTN reductions, the average duty on agricultural imports from LDCs will be 2.6%. LDC concessions on agricultural products included soybean products, tallow, fresh fruits and nuts, and poultry.

Of particular interest to LDCs were tariff actions taken by the industrialized countries on "tropical products", which included improvements in duty-free treatment under various GSP (Generalized System of Preferences) programs. This resulted in an overall reduction of MFN rates on tropical products of 13% including 34% on coffee, tea and cocoa; 39% on spices; and 33%

---

24 Id.
25 Id. at 69-70.

on miscellaneous animal products.[26] Two-thirds of all dutiable agricultural exports of the LDCs will be affected by either GSP concessions or MFN tariff cuts valued at approximately $14 billion. Tariff cuts from LDCs amounted to only about 25% of the agricultural concessions granted to the U.S. Almost all of these came from Taiwan, Mexico, the Philippines, Korea and India. Since the concessions from Mexico (as well as those to Mexico) were conditional on Mexico joining the GATT, these concessions were never implemented.[27]

CODE ON SUBSIDIES

One of the major accomplishments of the Tokyo Round was the negotiation of a code on subsidies and countervailing duties, officially known as the "Agreement on Interpretation and Application of Articles VI, XVI, XXIII of the General Agreement on Tariffs and Trade"[28]. The main features of the agreement, as described by the GATT Director General

> include the coverage of both industrial and primary (e.g., agricultural) products in an agreement designed to insure that the use of subsidies does not adversely affect or prejudice the interests of any signatory to the agreement and that the imposition of countervailing duties do not unjustifiably impede international trade. The agreement establishes an international framework of rights and obligations in using subsidies and in invoking countervailing measures against them and imposes a system of surveillance and dispute settlement to hold each country accountable for its activities.[29]

Because of the importance of this Code, a section by section analysis of the code appears in the Appendix.[30] A brief summary of the major provisions will be set out here.

---

[26] GATT, Supplementary Report, supra note 1, at 37.

[27] Operation of the Trade Agreements Program, supra note 4 at 41.

[28] GATT Doc. MTN/NTM/W/236 [hereinafter referred to as the Code on Subsidies]. The full text appears in the Appendix.

[29] See GATT, Supplementary Report, supra note 1, at 37.

[30] This anlaysis was prepared by the U.S. International Trade Commission at the request of the United States Senate Committee on Finance, and appeared in MTN Studies 6, pt. 1, Committee Print, 96th Cong., 1st Sess., CP 96-27, at 103-227 (Aug. 1979).

A.   Subsidies

     Article XVI of the GATT does not prohibit subsidies but
imposes certain conditions on the use of subsidies. In the
Code on Subsidies an effort was made to further define these
conditions and to impose limitations on the use of subsidies.
The Code distinguishes between export subsidies and domestic
subsidies.   Export subsidies are prohibited on industrial and
mineral products (known as non-primary products), except for
special exemptions granted to LDC's.   These had already been
severely restricted under GATT Article XVI, Paragraph 4, but
had not effectively been eliminated.   Under Part II, Article
9, Paragraph 1 of the Code, these subsidies were clearly
prohibited ("signatories shall not grant export subsidies on
products other than certain primary products").
     Although export subsidies are not defined, an illustra-
tive list of export subsidies is attached to the Code as an
annex.   This annex provides twelve examples of practices that
would be considered export subsidies.   For example, item (a)
lists "the provision by governments of direct subsidies to a
firm or an industry contingent on export performance".   The
complete list appears in the Appendix.   As to primary products, principally agricultural, the Code, following Article
XVI:35, provides that direct or indirect export subsidies on
certain primary products are prohibited if granted "in a
manner which results in the signatory granting such subsidy
having more than an equitable share of world export trade in
such product, account being taken of the share of the signatories in trade in the product concerned during a previous
representative period".[31] The concept of "more than an equitable share of world export trade" is defined to include any
case in which "the effect of an export subsidy granted by a
signatory is to displace the exports of another signatory
bearing in mind the developments on world markets".[32] At
least to some of the U.S. negotiators, this distinction
between primary and non-primary products made little sense,
but was largely included as a compromise to permit participation by the EEC, whose common agricultural policy depends on
export subsidies.   It was noted by two of the negotiators that
"the politics of this issue were such that no other result was
possible".[33] Some hypothetical examples of export subsidies,
as provided and interpreted by the U.S.   Commerce Department
appear below:

---

[31] Code on Subsidies, supra note 28, at pt. II, art. 10, para.
    1.
[32] Id. at para. 2(a).
[33] Rivers & Greenwald, The Negotiations of a Code on Subsidies
    and Countervailing Measures: Bridging Fundamental Policy
    Differences, 2 Law & Pol'y Int'l Bus. 1447, 1447 (1979).

Example A:
In October, 1972, the Government of the Thalline Republic
enacted the "Machinery Export Promotion Act" enabling the
payment of direct government-to-industry grants designed
to foster the development and expansion of Thalline
machinery exports.   The Act provides for government
grants to exporters equal to 20% of a company's annual
incremental earnings that can be attributed to export
sales of machinery. Thus, if a Thalline company earned
$10 million from machinery exports in 1973 and $15
million in 1974, it would be eligible for a government
grant of $1 million in 1975 based on the increment in its
1974 earnings over those realized during 1973.

Comment: The "Machinery Export Promotion Act" is an
export subsidy of a type prohibited by the Subsidies
Code. In its "Illustrative List of Export Subsidies",
the Code includes "(a) The provision by governments of
direct subsidies to a firm or an industry contingent upon
export performance".

Example B:
The copper industry in Nargon is totally owned and
operated by the Nargon Government. Prior to 1975,
government-run Nargon Copper employed a uniform pricing
system for the copper it sold to domestic and international consumers of the metal. In 1975, however, the
President of Nargon issued Administrative Decree No. 27,
which authorized a 10% discount in the price of copper
sold to copper consuming firms in the country who agreed
to a five-year commitment whereby they would export at
least one-third of their total production of goods
incorporating copper.

Comment: Administrative Decree No. 27 is an export
subsidy of a type prohibited by the Subsidies Code.   In
its "Illustrative List of export Subsidies", the Code
includes "(d) The delivery by governments or their
agencies of imported or domestic products or services for
use in the production of exported goods, on terms or
conditions more favorable than for delivery of like or
directly competitive products or services for use in the
production of goods for domestic consumption, if (in the
case of products) such terms or conditions are more
favorable than those commercially available on world
markets to its exporters."

Example C:
Corporate income taxes in the Saturnine States are
assessed at a rate of 45% of a company's profits.
Currently, the Saturnine States Parliament is considering

action on a bill that would retain solely from domestic sales while reducing the rate of taxation for companies active in export markets.   Specifically, the bill proposes to lower the rate of corporate income tax to 20% of profits for that portion of a company's profits attributed to export sales.

Comment: The bill under consideration would provide for an export subsidy of a type prohibited by the Subsidies Code.   In its "Illustrative List of Export Subsidies," the Code includes "(e) The full or partial exemption, remission, or deferral specifically related to exports, of direct taxes or social welfare charges paid or payable to industrial or commercial enterprises."

Note: Unlike Examples A and B (above) the hypothetical bill in this example would not necessarily be in violation of the Subsidies Code where its benefits were realized by an exporter of primary products (aside from primary minerals).   In such a case, the Code status of the program would depend on its impact on the exports of a given primary product from the Saturnine States.[34]

Domestic subsidies, those not directed towards export activity, are also covered in the Code.   Part II, Article 11, Paragraph 1 recognizes that domestic subsidies are widely used as important instruments to promote social and economic policy objectives.   These objectives include employment, research and development and elimination of socio-economic disadvantages in particular regions.   The signatories indicate that they do not intend to restrict the right of parties to use domestic subsidies to achieve these goals.   However, signatories imposing domestic subsidies are required to take into account their potential adverse effects on trade.[35] Certain particular domestic subsidy practices that may have an adverse effect on trade and production of other signatories are listed, including government financing of commercial enterprises, subscription to their equity capital, government performed or financial services such as utilities and supply distribution, and government financial research and development.[36] The Code's provisions on domestic subsidies are not as strong as some would have preferred, but it is a significant first step in the recognition by signatories that domestic subsidies can have a trade distorting impact.   Some hypothetical examples of

---

[34] U.S. Department of Commerce, The Tokyo Round Trade Agreements: Subsidies and Countervailing Measures, vol. 1, at 28 (May 1980).

[35] Code on Subsidies, supra note 28, pt. II, art. 11, para. 2.

[36] Id. at para. 3.

domestic subsidies are included in the following hypotheticals provided by the U.S. Department of Commerce.

Unlike the examples given for export subsidies in the preceeding section, no attempt is made in this section to portray a hypothetical subsidy as a violation of the Subsidies Code. Rather, this section is directed at illustrating the type of international trade effects that might flow form the use of domestic subsidies that may or may not results in an international dispute or a counter-vailing duty action.

Example A:
In 1978, the Dorf Turbine Company announced its intention to build a $50 million turbine plant to serve the market in two neighboring countries, Nargon and the Saturnine States. Initially, the company was undecided as to which country would be more suitable for the location of the new plant since neither country imposed tariffs on turbines and the economic situation was comparable for both nations. Several other turbine manufacturers also were operating at the time in both countries.

In early 1979, the Governor of Elysia, one of the 31 states of the Saturnine States, requested a meeting with the Chairman of the Board of Dorf. The Governor promised that if Dorf would locate the plant in Elysia, the state would provide the company with free land and would exempt the company from state income taxes for 10 years. In May 1979, Dorf accepted the Elysian offer and by January 1981, the plant was in full-scale operation. About one-half of the plant's production was marketed in Nargon.

In mid-1983, Spindown Turbines Ltd. of Nargon petitioned for a countervailing duty investigation on the grounds that subsidized imports of turbines originating in Dorf's Elysian plant were causing injury to the turbine industry in Nargon. Eleven months later, Nargon authorities announced their determination that the subsidized turbines had been found to be causing injury to the turbine industry and imposed countervailing duties on all imports of turbines originating in the Dorf plant.

Comment: In this example, a domestic subsidy (in the form of free land and relief from corporate incomes taxes) was provided not by a central government of a country but by a subsidiary state government within the country. In all probability, Elysian authorities were less interested in the international trade impact of the subsidy than they were with fostering new investment within the state.   Nonetheless, because subsidized exports of turbines to Nargon caused injury to the turbine industry in that country, Nargon found it necessary to impose countervailing duties on the products in question.

Example B:
One of the Thalline Republic's principal exports to Nargon is computers.   Prior to the Tokyo Round of Multilateral Trade Negotiations, the Nargon tariff on computers stood at 10% ad valorem.   In the trade negotiations, Thalline negotiators were able to secure a concession from Nargon providing for the elimination of the 10% duty as of January 1, 1980.   In exchange for this concession, the Thalline Republic eliminated the import duty on small aircraft -- a concession of principal interest to Nargon.   Both sides expected that the tariff concessions would have the effect of fostering increased international trade in the products concerned.

In April, 1982, the Nargon Science Council published a report stating that the country was rapidly becoming an importer of high-technology products.   The report warned that unless the Government took steps to foster innovation in Nargon industry, the nation's economy and international terms of trade would suffer a severe deterioration.   Acting on the basis of the report, the Nargon Parliament passed the Research and Development Act of 1982, which provided for government funding of qualified R&D expenditures by private industry.   The annual budget for the new program was set at $500 million, with 20% of this amount earmarked for R&D in the country's small computer industry.

By mid-1986, a Nargon company, Cylon Data Incorporated, had achieved a major technological breakthrough in computer design that made possible significant reductions in the price for mainframe computers.   Cylon had been assisted in this effort by grants made to the company under the 1982 Act.   Beginning in 1987, imports of computers from the Thalline Republic began to fall off as consumers switched to the less expensive models produced domestically.   The decline in computer imports continued in 1988 and 1989.

In the Tokyo Round, the Thalline Republic and Nargon became signatories to the Subsidies Code.   Taking advantage of this fact, Thalline officials claimed in 1989 that Nargon had granted domestic subsidies inconsistently with the Code's provisions in that the R&D

subsidies to the computer industry had import substitution effects that nullified or impaired the benefits to
Thalline exporters of the Nargon tariff concession on
computers. The dispute went unresolved to the Code's
Committee of Signatories, where, after consideration of
the report of the panel, the Committee authorized the
Thalline Republic to withdraw its tariff concession on
small aircraft, which had benefitted Nargon.

Comment: The Subsidies Code requires signatories to
seek to avoid causing, through the use of any subsidy,
nullification or impairment of the benefits accruing
directly or indirectly to another signatory under the
General Agreement on Tariffs and Trade. A tariff
concession clearly falls within this category of benefits. Further, the Code indicates that nullification or
impairment may be demonstrated by the effects of the
subsidy in displacing or impeding the imports of like
products into the market of the subsidizing country. In
our hypothetical example, the Nargon subsidy had effects
that met both of the above tests.[37]

B.   Consultations and Dispute Settlement

The Code provides for a committee to handle disputes. The
committee meets twice yearly in Geneva but can meet more
often. If a mutually acceptable solution cannot be reached
following a certain period after a request for consultations,
any signatory party to the consultation may refer the dispute
to the committee. The committee may authorize countermeasures
if its recommendations are not followed. While this authority
already exists under Article XXIII of the GATT, the Code
transfers this authority from the GATT Council to the Committee on Signatories and imposes strict time limits.[38]

C.   Imposition of Countervailing Duties

Countervailing duties enable an industry in a country
affected by subsidized imports to counteract any injury caused
by the subsidies by imposing a duty equal to the value of the
net subsidy. This self-help provision obviates the need for
use of the consultation and dispute settlement procedures. The
Code does provide rules as to when countervailing duties may
be imposed in Part I, Article 4. This section leaves the

---

[37] The Tokyo Round Trade Agreements: Subsidies and Countervailing Measures, supra note 34, at 30-31.

[38] GATT, The Tokyo Round of Multilateral Trade Negotiations,
supra note 1, at 132.

decision on whether to impose countervailing duties and the amount imposed to authorities of the importing signatory country.[39] However, the Code states that it is desirable that the imposition of countervailing duties be permissive rather than mandatory and that the duty be less than the total amount of the subsidy if such lesser duty would be adequate to remove the injury. However, it is made clear that the duty may not exceed the amount of the subsidy. The Code provides that countervailing duties should be levied on a non-discriminatory basis on all sources of the product found to be subsidized and to be causing injury, although provisions are made to exempt those who have renounced the subsidy or made undertakings as permitted under the Code. These undertakings are set out in Part I, Article 4, Paragraph 5(a) and include agreements by the exporting country to eliminate, limit or control the effects of such subsidy and agreements by exporters to raise their prices to eliminate injury.[40] Where such undertakings are given, the Code permits verification procedures and provides for imposition of duties where undertakings are violated.

The Code permits the imposition of provisional measures while the investigation is being conducted. Such provisional measures, which generally involve the payment of estimated duties or the posting of a bond, can only be imposed after a preliminary positive finding. The Code provides that provisional measures should not be applied unless authorities concerned determine they are necessary to prevent injury being caused during the period of investigation.[41]

The Code permits duties provisionally withheld during the period of investigation to be forfeited upon a final injury determination.[42] This retroactive application of countervailing duties is limited to the amount of the preliminary duty or cash deposit. So if the final duty is higher than the preliminary duty, only an amount equal to the preliminary duty is forfeited. If the final duty is less than the preliminary duty, however, the difference must be refunded to the ex-

---

[39] Code on Subsidies, supra note 28, pt. I, art. 4, para. 1.

[40] Under U.S. implementing legislation, an investigation can also be suspended where at least 85% of the exporters agree to forego the subsidies in question.

[41] Under the U.S. countervailing duty law, provisional duties are always required after a preliminary affirmative determination. No specific provision is made for authorities to determine on a case-by-case basis that they are necessary to prevent injury.

[42] The U.S. law links the forfeiture of the preliminary duties to the final affirmative determination, not to a final finding of injury since preliminary duties are forfeited even in cases not requiring an injury determination. Again, the U.S. law appears to depart from the literal provisions of the Code.

porter.[43] The Code also provides, in what is deemed "critical circumstances", where irreparable injury might result because of massive imports in a relatively short period of time, for retroactive imposition of duties for as much as ninety days prior to application of the provisional measures.[44]

An important accomplishment of the Code was to define for the first time the standards to be used in determining the existence of injury. The Code provides that an injury determination shall involve an objective examination of both the volume of subsidized imports and their effect on prices in the domestic market for like products and the impact of these imports on domestic producers.[45] Specific standards are set out to determine the volume of subsidized imports, e.g., whether there has been a significant increase in the subsidized imports either in absolute terms or relative to domestic production or consumption. In regard to the effect on prices, the Code provides that domestic authorities shall consider whether there has been price undercutting, significant price depression or significant prevention of price increases that might otherwise have occurred.[46] Standards for determining the impact on the domestic industry include actual and potential decline in production, sales, market shares, productivity, return on investments, utilization of capacity, effects on domestic prices, cash flow, inventories, employment, wages, growth, the ability to raise capital and, in the case of agriculture, any increased burden on government support programs.[47]

The Code also provides that there must be a link or nexus between the subsidized imports and the injury. For example, other factors, such as the volume and prices of non-subsidized imports, contraction in demand and changes in patterns of consumption, may be causing the injury rather than subsidized imports.[48] In such a case a countervailing duty should not be imposed.

The term "domestic industry" is defined in the Code to apply to domestic producers of like products, not including producers who are related to the exporters or importers of the allegedly subsidized goods.[49] Injury can be found under the Code even where a majority of the total domestic industry is

---

[43] See Code on Subsidies, supra note 28, pt. I, art. 5, para. 6.
[44] This provision appears in U.S. law, but has not frequently been used.
[45] Code on Subsidies, supra, note 28, pt. I, art. 6, para. 1. The term "like product" is defined to mean not just identical products but also those with "characteristics closely resembling those of the product under consideration". Id. at n.1.
[46] Id. at para. 2.
[47] Id. at para. 3.
[48] Id. at para. 4 n.3.
[49] Id. at para. 5.

not injured, if there is a concentration of subsidized imports
into an isolated market such as a particular region where all
or almost all of the producers in that sub-market are being
injured.[50] In such cases, the Code provides for the imposition
of countervailing duties only on products consigned for
shipment into such sub-markets.[51] If the constitutional law of
the importing country does not permit the selective importation of a countervailing duty, then the authorities in that
country must permit exporters in question to cease exporting
at subsidized prices to the area concerned.[52]

D.   United States Implementing Legislation

The 1979 Trade Agreements Act implements the provisions
of the Subsidies Code by amending the Tariff Act of 1930.
Title III applies to imports from signatory countries, while §
303 of the Tariff Act of 1930, as amended, applies to non-
signatories. In actions under the U.S. countervailing duty
law, non-signatories are not entitled to an injury determination except in the case of duty-free goods. Under § 303, all
duty-free goods are entitled to an injury test. However, the
U.S. has interpreted § 303 as requiring an injury test only in
regard to duty-free goods from countries to which the U.S. has
an "international obligation", namely GATT members. This
interpretation has recently been used to deny an injury test
to duty-free goods from Mexico, a non-GATT, non-Code signatory.[53]
There are actually two remedies under U.S. law against
subsidized imports. One of these is the countervailing duty
law, and the other is § 301 of the Trade Act of 1974, as
amended by § 901 of the Trade Agreements Act of 1979. While
it is beyond the scope of this book to devote an extensive
discussion to the implementing legislation of any one country,
the importance of the United States as a major trading nation
which regularly implements these code provisions warrants some
discussion.

E.   U. S. Countervailing Duty Law

Under U.S. law, a countervailing duty investigation is
generally initiated by the filing of a petition with the U.S.

---

50 Id. at para. 7.
51 Id. at para. 8.
52 Id.
53 See Toy Balloons Investigation, 46 Fed. Reg. 31,698 (1980).
   This case and other countervailing duty cases from Mexico are
   discussed in L. Glick, "Legal Aspects of U.S.-Mexico Trade" in
   Doing Business in Mexico, C.34 at 110 (1983).

Commerce Department by an "interested party", who can be a
manufacturer, producer or wholesaler of a like product in the
U.S., a labor union or a trade association. In the case of
countries entitled to an injury determination under the Code,
a petition must be filed simultaneously with the United States
International Trade Commission (ITC) . The Commerce Department can also initiate investigations on its own without a
petition, but this is rarely done.[54]

These petitions must contain specified information about
the U.S. domestic industry, the product, the alleged subsidies
and the alleged injury. The Commerce Department reviews the
petition as to sufficiency and if found sufficient, institutes
an investigation within twenty days. The U.S. International
Trade Commission then has forty-five days to make a preliminary determination as to whether there is a reasonable
indication of injury. If the ITC finds a reasonable likelihood of injury, the Commerce Department investigation continues, otherwise both investigations are terminated. This is
a new procedure which was added in the 1979 Trade Agreement
Act to protect foreign companies from a long and costly
investigation by the Commerce Department in cases where there
is clearly no injury. In practice, the ITC has found a
reasonable indication of injury in most of the cases it
reviews.[55] After the initial ITC investigation, the Commerce
Department continues its investigation until it makes a
preliminary determination, due eighty-five days from the date
of initiation.[56]

As discussed earlier under the Code provisions, if the
decision is affirmative, entries during the remaining period
of investigation must post an estimated countervailing duty or
enter under bond. The ITC also begins a final injury investigation at this point in time. If the Commerce Department
determination is negative, the investigation is ended.   If
the determination is affirmative, the Commerce Department has
another seventy-five days to reach its final determination.
This may include the holding of a public hearing, if requested, and generally involves a verification trip by
Commerce personnel to the country of exportation to inspect
both governmental and industry records. If the final countervailing duty order is negative, the case is ended, entries are
liquidated and duty deposits refunded. If it is affirmative,
Commerce must await a final injury determination by the ITC
prior to issuing its final order. Countervailing duties are
applied to all imports of the subject goods from the country

---

[54] For applicable regulations, see 19 C.F.R. § 355.26.

[55] For an exception, see Certain Commuter Aircraft from France
and Italy, Inv. Nos. 701-TA-74, 701-TA-175, U.S.I.T.C. Pub.
No. 1269 (1982).

[56] This can be extended to 150 days if a case is extraordinarily
complicated.

investigated, whether or not the exporters and importers of these goods were represented by counsel or participated in the proceedings before the Commerce Department and the ITC. Thus, the order is essentially in rem in nature. The Commerce Department rules do, however, provide for exclusion of individual exporters who, within thirty days of the date of institution of an investigation, supply information to prove that they do not receive the subsidies alleged.[57] An annual review is held to determine the nature and extent of receipt of subsidies and the amount of the countervailing duty can be adjusted upwards or downwards. Moreover, individual exporters who can prove non-receipt of the subsidies can be given a zero rate during the annual review.

F.   Enforcement of United States
      Rights Under Section 301

Cases under § 301 of the Trade Act of 1974 as amended by § 901 of the Trade Agreements Act of 1979 are decided by the President and his trade representative. They are usually instituted by the filing of a petition with the Office of the U.S. Trade Representative.[58] The petition must allege that a subsidy practice in a foreign country has an adverse effect on trade in the U.S. market. Section 301 is not limited to direct subsidies on products, but can include other discriminatory actions or policies which in some way restrict U.S. commerce. This could include laws or policies relating to investments, insurance, etc.

The petition is considered by the U.S. Trade Representative's § 301 Committee, composed of representatives of various government agencies. Within forty-five days from receipt of a petition, the Committee must decide whether to initiate an investigation. Under § 301, the investigation is less formal and more subject to policy considerations. Consultations are held with the foreign government involved in an effort to resolve the problem through diplomatic means. Moreover, under § 301, the President may submit the dispute to a GATT panel for fact finding and recommendations. While the counter-vailing duty law also provides for consultations, use of consultations and GATT dispute settlement mechanisms are more common in cases under § 301. The time limits under § 301 vary depending on the type of case. The final action is taken by

---

[57] See 19. C.F.R. § 355.38. In practice, the Commerce Department has not been following this regulation fully. It will not often exclude an individual exporter from a case, but will grant him a zero rate of duty if he and his government certify non-receipt of the subsidies under investigation. This makes the exporter subject to successive annual reviews.

[58] See 15 C.F.R. § 2006.

the President. One distinct advantage of § 301 is that it can aid U.S. exporters in bringing actions against subsidies that are causing injury in third countries where the U.S. company competes with the subsidized product.[59] The countervailing duty law is limited to subsidies causing injury to a U.S. domestic industry. Often this can result in retaliatory measures against an entirely different product as a method of putting pressure on the subsidizing nation.

CODE ON GOVERNMENT PROCUREMENT

The Code on Government Procurement[60] was a major step in opening up the large government purchasing market to increased worldwide competition. Many countries, largely for political reasons, but sometimes for legitimate defense and security purposes, often restrict government purchases to domestic firms or impose unrealistic requirements that all but eliminate foreign participation. This forecloses a large segment of potential international commerce. For example, the U.S. estimated that the Code on Government Procurement could open as much as $20 billion a year in foreign government purchases now closed to the U.S.[61] It is estimated that the U.S. opened up approximately $12.5 billion of its government procurement market.[62] However, as a result of limitations on governmental entities included by other countries, the U.S. eliminated certain major government entities from coverage. These include the Department of Transportation, Department of Energy, the Department of Interior Bureau of Reclamation, Army Corps of Engineers, the Tennessee Valley Authority (TVA), certain portions of the Government Services Administration (GSA) and certain quasi-governmental organizations, including Amtrak and Conrail (passenger and freight train organizations), Comsat (operator of communications satellites) and the U.S. Postal Service.[63] Also excluded by the U.S. from coverage by the Agreement are most defense related purchases, including arms, ammunition, war materials and "procurements indispens-

---

[59] For example, in the Great Plains Wheat, Inc. case, U.S. wheat exporters alleged that they were injured by EEC subsidies on wheat in third markets where they compete.

[60] GATT Doc. MIN/NTM/W/211/Rev. 2 (Ap. 11, 1979) [hereinafter cited as Code on Government Procurement]. The text appears in the Appendix.

[61] Current Policy 56, supra note 8, at 3.

[62] Twenty-fourth Annual Report of the President, supra note 10, at 43.

[63] Trade Agreements Act of 1979, 96th Cong., 1st Sess. 466 (Statement of Administrative Action). See also, Operation of the Trade Agreements Program, 30th Report, U.S.I.T.C. Pub. No. 1021, at 52 (1979).

able for national security or national defense purposes",[64]
construction contracts, purchases by state and local governments even if using federal funds, small business and minority
business set aside programs, and Department of Agriculture
purchases under farm support programs.[65] Also categorically
excluded from coverage under the Code is the government
purchase of services, except when such services are incidental
to sale of the products.[66] This has become an issue of
increased importance in the 80's, as trade in services has
become a major unregulated area of world trade both in the
public and private sectors. It was hoped that the November,
1982 GATT Ministerial meeting would effectively deal with this
problem, but it did not. Another limitation of the Code is
that it covers only contracts valued over a certain amount;
thus eliminating access to many smaller contracts that are
more frequent in smaller and developing countries.[67]

Despite these limitations, the Government Procurement
Code contained many innovations. Since much of the de facto
discrimination in government purchasing is due to the secret
and often complex nature of government procurement policies, a
major emphasis was on opening these practices to public
disclosure and scrutiny through a policy generally referred to
as "transparency".

Thus, the largest part of the Code is devoted to establishing rules to ensure that government procurement practices
are "...applied openly so that all will be aware that the
procurement process is carried out in a fair and equitable
manner".[68] The Code rules are also designed to discourage
discrimination. At each stage of the government procurement
process, specific rules exist on drafting of specifications
for goods to be purchased, on advertising of prospective
purchases, on the time allocated for submission of bids, on
the qualification of suppliers, on the opening and evaluation
of bids, on the award of contracts and on hearings and

---

[64] Statement of Administrative Action, supra note 63, at 466.
[65] Id.
[66] Id. at 465; Code on Government Procurement, supra note 60, at
art. I, para. 1(a).
[67] Statement of Administrative Action, supra note 63, at 465. The
threshold amount was set at 150,000 Special Drawing Rights,
which are currency equivalent units of the International
Monetary Fund and equivalent to about $190,000 in 1979.
Parties are exhorted to "consider" the application of the Code
to contracts under this amount. See Code on Government
Procurement, supra note 60, at art. I, para. 1(b) n.2.
[68] Executive Summary of President Jimmy Carter, contained in
letter dated Jan. 4, 1979 to Hon. Thomas P. O'Neill, Speaker
of the House of Representatives and to Hon. Walter Mondale,
President of the Senate. 44 Fed. Reg. 1,939 (1979).

appeals of disputes.[69] Also included are international dispute
settlement procedures.[70] However, the Code provisions fall far
short of providing for complete open competition in government
procurement.

For example, while open purchasing procedures, where all
interested parties may bid, are provided for and encouraged,
selective procedures allowing governments to invite bids from
selected suppliers is permitted, and even single source
tenders from one supplier are permitted under certain circumstances,[71] such as purchase of research prototypes, purchase of
patented products, or reasons of "extreme urgency".[72] Nevertheless, the Code is a considerable improvement over the
vacuum that existed before. Although complete open competition in government procurement is not accomplished, openness
in the procedures for such competition have been successfully
established. For example, the Code requires that bids be
awarded to the lowest bidder or, if not the lowest bidder,
then the most responsive bidder in terms of the "specific
evaluation criteria set forth in the notices or tender
documentation".[73] Thus, governments can no longer reject bids
based on undisclosed criteria.

The Code also recognizes the special needs of the LDCs.
Code benefits are available generally only for goods originating in signatory countries. The Code provides, however,
that benefits under the Code can be provided to non-Code
signatory LDCs[74] with respect to products originating in those
countries. LDCs may request, and the developed countries shall
provide, assistance to LDCs in submitting tenders, selecting
products to bid on and complying with technical regulations
and standards.[75]

The Code is largely self-policing. However, a bilateral
consultation process is provided for. In addition, a multilateral dispute settlement mechanism under the GATT is also
available, after conciliatory efforts have failed.

The Trade Agreements Act of 1979 approved the Agreement
on Government Procurement on behalf of the United States but
with the proviso that the President must determine that all,
or all but one, of the major industrial countries also accept
the Agreement and he determines that acceptance by that
country is not essential to the operation of the Agreement and

---

69 Id.; see also Code on Government Procurement, supra note 60,
   at arts. IV and V.
70 Code on Government Procurement, supra note 60, at art. VII.
71 Id. at art. V.
72 Id. at para. 15.
73 Id. at para. 14(f).
74 Id. at art. III, para.11.
75 Id. at para. 12.

if certain other conditions are met.[76] On December 23, 1980,
the U.S. Trade Representative, under authority delegated by
the President, certified that each major industrial country
had accepted the Agreement, and that negotiations with the
major industrial countries concerning entity coverage had been
satisfactorily fulfilled, thus satisfying the conditions of §
2 of the Trade Agreements Act.[77] On December 31, 1980, the
President signed Executive Order 12260, which provided for the
implementation of the Agreement on Government Procurement.[78]
The Executive Order set out in an Annex a list of federal
agencies to which the Agreement would apply. Some fifty-three
agencies were listed. Authority to interpret the Agreement
was delegated to the U.S. Trade Representative. The U.S.
Trade Representative was also authorized to determine the
value of 150,000 Special Drawing Rights for purposes of
exempting small contracts. On January 1, 1981, the U.S. Trade
Representative issued an interpretative determination pursuant
to Executive Order 12188, finding that 150,000 Special Drawing
Rights was equivalent to $196,000.[79] The determination also
listed those countries that have become parties to the
Agreement and will provide reciprocal benefits to the U.S.
Also listed were twenty-six LDCs, which, under § 301(b)(4) of
the Trade Agreements Act, are entitled to the benefits of the
Act without assuming reciprocal obligations. The determination
waived provisions of U.S. law, regulation, practice or
procedure which would result in treatment less favorable for
any of the countries that are covered under benefits of the
Code.[80] The determination prohibited U.S. executive agencies
from procuring any products from countries not designated as
eligible under § 301(b). This order was pursuant to § 302 of
the Trade Agreements Act and was designed as a lever to
"encourage" other countries to sign the Agreement. However,
to soften the harsh effects of this rule, the implementation
of this prohibition was deferred until January 1, 1983 for all

---

[76] See Trade Agreements Act of 1979 § 2(b)(3), 19 U.S.C. § 2503
(b)(3) (1979).   This provision applied to a number of other
codes as well.

[77] See 45 Fed. Reg. 86,605 (1980).

[78] 46 Fed. Reg. 1,653 (1981). The text of the Executive Order
appears in the Appendix to this book.

[79] Id. at 1,657.

[80] Although the determination by the U.S. Trade Representative
only lists countries that have signed the Agreement and LDCs
to whom the benefits of the Agreement apply without signature,
§ 301(a) of the Trade Agreements Act also provides coverage to
non-signatory countries, other than major industrial countries, that have assumed the obligations of the Agreement and
will provide the opportunities under the Agreement to U.S.
products.

countries except major industrial countries (i.e., members of the EEC, Japan and Canada). Pursuant to the Executive Order and the determination of the U.S. Trade Representative, various federal agencies issued revised regulations to complement the provisions of the Agreement.[81]

A.   Success of the Code on Government Procurement

Although there is no doubt that the Government Procurement Code has been an improvement over the previous vacuum in regulation of international government procurement, the results of the agreement are still unclear. As recently as June 9, 1982, U.S. Trade Representative William E. Brock III told the Senate Finance Committee, Sub-committee on Trade, that the "jury is still out" as to the success of the Agreement.[82] Brock noted that from "a strict technical standpoint" he was generally satisfied with implementation of the Agreement by foreign countries, but that the "acid test" for the Agreement is the commercial results and that this could not yet be judged,[83] even though the Code had been in effect for a year and a half at the time. Brock did note, for example, that in 1981, over 1400 Code-covered bidding opportunities were published by other signatory nations and 700 were published through June, 1982. He did not know, however, how many of these 2100 opportunities had been bid on or won by U.S. firms.

Brock noted as one problem area, disagreement as to whether leasing transactions were covered by the Code.[84] He also noted that in 1981, the Italian government was not fully implementing the Code.[85] The U.S. protested to the Code Committee in Geneva and the problem was resolved. Also of concern was the EEC's method of determining the Code threshold for coverage. Brock felt that the EEC was improperly reducing the number of EEC purchases covered by the Code and the U.S. has pursued this through bilateral talks and through the Code Committee.[86]

---

[81] See, for example, Temporary Procurement Regulations issued by the General Services Administration which handles a large portion of U.S. government purchases. 46 Fed. Reg. 3,589 (1981).

[82] Statement of Ambassador William E. Brock III, U.S. Trade Representative Before the Subcomm. on Trade of the Senate Comm. on Finance, at 1 (June 9, 1982).

[83] Id.

[84] Id. at 5.

[85] Id. at 6.

[86] Id. The EEC had apparently been excluding the value of the value-added tax in computing the threshold value.

Progress in opening government procurement has been slow. Some areas have proceeded more quickly than others. For example, although not required under the Code, Japan, through a bilateral agreement with the U.S., has opened up procurement of its huge Nippon Telegraph and Telephone company to U.S. bidders. Japan is the only foreign country that has opened up sales of its telecommunications entity to foreign bidding following the procedures of the Government Procurement Code.[87]

On the other fronts, protectionism has continued to dominate. For example, among states and local governments not covered by the Code, local buy-American or buy-local laws have proliferated. For example, on March 20, 1981, shortly after U.S. implementation of the Code, Virginia passed a law to prohibit state projects from purchasing foreign steel over the protests of the Japanese Government and the U.S. State Department.[88] Some thirty six U.S. states have restrictive procurement laws of some nature discriminating against foreign purchases. Opening up government procurement to the state and local levels is one of the trade issues that must be dealt with in the future.

CODE ON CUSTOMS VALUATION (AGREEMENT ON
IMPLEMENTATION OF ARTICLE VII OF THE GATT)

Customs valuation is one of the least glamourous areas covered by the MTN Codes, but potentially one of the most important. Customs value is utilized for assessment of duties based on value (ad valorem) – a method largely followed by the U.S. and other countries. Where values are artificially calculated, duties can be adversely affected, creating a non-tariff barrier. For example, some countries have utilized an "official" value that has no relation to actual value. This value is usually larger than the actual value and is a restriction on the free entry of goods. Customs value can also be important for computing border taxes and administering licenses and import quotas. Customs valuation methods have been covered in Articles II, VII and X of the GATT. However, these rules are not all-inclusive and leave great leeway to GATT members in determining customs value. For example, countries with valuation methods that pre-dated the GATT were "grandfathered", even if inconsistent with the GATT as permitted by the Protocol of Provisional Application.

Because of differences between the developed and developing countries that could not be resolved, two texts of the Customs Valuation Code were opened for signature in April, 1979. The main difference was the support by developing countries of certain special rules for developing countries,

---

87 Id. at 8.
88 Washington Post, June 14, 1981, at F1.

including a more flexible definition of "related persons", up
to a ten year delay in application of the Code to developing
countries and other provisions.[89] Eventually, by November,
1979, a compromise text was worked out through a Protocol to
the Agreement on Implementation of Article VII of the GATT.
The Protocol provided for the parties to give "sympathetic
consideration" to a request by a developing country for a
delay of up to five years in implementation, and an agreement
to study the problem of definition of related persons as it
applies to sole agents and distributors if practical problems
arise in developing countries in connection with this area.
Developing countries were also allowed to maintain, on a
limited basis, certain "minimum values". Certain other special
provisions were included, including the deletion of a provision in the main text (Article 1.2 (b)(iv)), requiring
Customs officials to accept the transaction value in a sale
between related persons if the importer had demonstrated that
this value closely approximated the transaction value in sales
between unrelated persons of identical goods.[90]

A.   Description of the Agreement and
      Its Effect on Existing Practices

The Customs Valuation Code sets out five methods to
calculate customs value. One is a primary method to be
favored, and the other four are secondary methods to be used
when the primary method is inappropriate. Prior to the Code,
countries had many different methods, often applied arbitrarily. The U.S., for example, had nine different methods
including one, called the American Selling Price, used
largely on chemicals, that was highly controversial since it
was based on the U.S. price of domestically produced goods,
rather than the value of the imported product.
The methods of valuation under the Code are set out
below:

1.   Transaction Value

This is the primary and favored method of valuation. The
transaction value is the price actually paid or payable for

---

[89] See GATT, Supplementary Report, supra note 1, at 136.
[90] For a complete discussion of the Protocol, see id. at 9. See
     also S. 3020, Cong. Rec. 10,835 (1980) (statement of Senator
     Abraham Ribikoff, co-sponsor (with senator Roth) of the U.S.
     legislation to implement the Protocol). U.S. business groups
     generally supported the Protocol. See, e.g., Testimony of
     the Joint Industry Group, U.S. Chamber of Commerce Before the
     Subcomm. on International Trade of the Senate Comm. on Finance
     (Ap. 2, 1980).

the goods, with the addition of certain costs and expenses incurred that are not included in the price, such as brokerage commissions, packing costs and royalties.

Also included in the value are "assists", which are assets that the buyer provides to the seller at no cost or at a cost below the actual value, which would tend to reduce the price of the imported good. The Code allows assists to be included in value if they are tangible (furnishing of materials, tools, dies, engineering and design work).[91] Transaction value is generally used unless Customs finds one of several circumstances:

> (a) Restrictions on the disposition or use of the merchandise are placed on the buyers by the sellers other than restrictions imposed by law, which limit the geographical area of resale or do not substantially affect the value of the merchandise.
> (b) The sale or price of the goods is subject to conditions or considerations for which value cannot be determined.
> (c) The seller receives part of the proceeds of the sale or use of the imported goods unless an adjustment to transaction value can be made.
> (d) When the buyer and seller are related and the relationship affects the price of the goods so as to make transaction value unacceptable.[92]

If transaction value is rejected for one of the above methods, a secondary method of valuation is used - the transaction value of identical or similar merchandise.

2.   Transaction Value of Identical Merchandise

Under this method of valuation, the customs value is determined by looking at the value of identical merchandise exported to the same country of importation on or about the same time as the exportation of the merchandise being appraised.[93]

Problems arise under this method when sales of identical goods are at different commercial levels or substantially different quantities. In such a case, if sufficient information exists, adjustments to the value are permitted.

---

91 The term "assist" is defined in § 201(a) of the Trade Agreements Act of 1979, 19 U.S.C. § 1401a(h)(1)(A), which amended § 402(h) of the Tariff Act of 1930.

92 Trade Agreements Act of 1979 § 201(a), 19 U.S.C. § 1401a (b)(2)(B), amending 19 U.S.C. § 1401a.

93 Id. at 19 U.S.C. § 1401a(c).

3.   Transaction Value of Similar Merchandise

Where both the primary and secondary methods of valuation are inappropriate, a third method is used. Under this method, the transaction value of similar merchandise is used, largely following the same rules and adjustments as with the second method described above.

4.   Deductive Value

If none of the above three methods can be used, Customs may apply a deductive value unless the importer requests the use of computed value, which will be discussed below. This method bases the customs value on the unit price at which the imported article, or similar or identical imported articles, are resold in the greatest aggregate quantity, in the country of importation, at or about the same time as the goods being appraised, in the same condition as imported, to an unrelated buyer. The unit price can be the price at the first commercial level of importation or after further processing, subject to certain restrictions. The price is then subject to certain adjustments for commissions, costs of transportation and insurance, customs duties and federal taxes related to importation and where further processing is involved, the value-added by such further processing.[94]

5.   Computed Value

The last method, computed value, is similar to the old U.S. method of appraisal known as constructed value. Value is calculated by determining costs of material and manufacture, profit and expenses, assists, and packaging costs.

6.   Alternate Methods

If none of the previously discussed methods are appro-priate, Customs may use any of the above methods "reasonably adjusted to the extent necessary to arrive at a value". However, certain methods of valuation are strictly prohibited, such as the use of the selling price of merchandise produced in the U.S. (the old and much critized American Selling Price); the foreign value of the merchandise and other methods including those that are considered "arbitrary or fictitious".

The Customs Valuation Code is probably one of the most complex and difficult codes to understand, particularly for those not already conversant with customs valuation. As to the U.S. Customs Valuation System, certain helpful examples and interpretative notes were published by U.S. Customs that

---

[94] Id. at § 1401a(d).

are of assistance.[95] U.S. Customs also produced a helpful set
of questions and answers relating to the changes in U.S. law
under the Code. The complete text of this document appears in
the Appendix to this book.

CODE ON TECHNICAL BARRIERS TO TRADE (STANDARDS CODE)

Perhaps even more technical than the Customs Valuation
Code, but equally important to freer world trade, is the Code
on Technical Barriers to Trade, sometimes referred to as the
"Standards Code". The goal was to remove artificial barriers
to trade that exist due to different standards and technical
requirements that exist in various countries. For example,
the failure of the United States to utilize the metric system
has resulted in barriers to exports of U.S. equipment and
machinery.
    The Standards Code covers all aspects of product stan-
dards and certifications including agricultural and industrial
products.[96] The Code covers both governmental and private
bodies which promulgate regulations and standards. However,
signatories to the Agreement are obligated to comply with the
Agreement only as to "central governments". Parties, however,
must use their best efforts to obtain compliance by local
governments and private parties.[97] Article 4 of the Code
provides that "Parties shall take such reasonable measures as
may be available to them to ensure that non-governmental
bodies within their territories comply with the provisions of
Article 2...In addition, Parties shall not take measures which
have the effect of, directly or indirectly, requiring or
encouraging such non-governmental bodies to act in a manner
inconsistent with any of the provisions of Article 2".[98] The
U.S. has carried out this requirement in its implementing
legislation by providing that "...no State agency and no
private person should engage in any standards-related activity
that creates unnecessary obstacles to the foreign commerce of
the United States".[99] However, the U.S. law also provides that
no standards-related activity of any private person, federal

---

[95] 45 Fed Reg. 20,912 (1982). An excellent comparison of the
      Code provisions with the previous U.S. valuation system, the
      Brussells definition of value and the Canadian systems is
      contained in MTN Studies 6, pt. 2, supra note 30, at IV-XV,
      62-80.
[96] Id., pt. 3, at 9.
[97] Id. at 10. In the U.S., there are estimated to be 10,000
      federal standards, 100,000 state and local standards, and
      25,000 standards promulgated by private bodies. Id. at 13.
[98] Agreement on Technical Barriers to Trade, art. 4. See
      Appendix for full text.
[99] Trade Agreements Act of 1979 § 403(a), 19 U.S.C. § 2533(a).

or state agency shall be deemed to constitute an unnecessary obstacle to the foreign commerce of the United States if the demonstrable purpose of the standards-related activity is to achieve a legitimate domestic objective including, but not limited to, the protection of legitimate health or safety, essential security, environmental or consumer interest, if such activity does not operate to exclude imported products and which fully meet the objectives of such activity.[100]

Thus, it can be said that the area of standards promulgated by non-central governments and private groups is one that was not completely resolved and could be the source of future problems due to the less than mandatory nature of the application of the Code to these bodies. It is likely, at least under U.S. law, that the Federal Government could override standards promulgated by state and local governments if it so desired, under the Supremacy Clause of the U.S. Constitution, which allows the Federal Government to pre-empt the state and local governments.[101]

Non-governmental bodies provide perhaps even a greater problem. In the U.S., for example, many product standards are established by such independent private organizations as Underwriters Laboratories and the American Society for Testing Materials. These organizations have not traditionally been subject to federal regulation. These organizations, while independent and having high standards of integrity, are comprised of U.S. scientists and technical personnel, often drawn from private industry and not necessarily concerned with international obligations of the U.S. Similar organizations exist in other industrialized countries. It is perhaps too early to judge compliance with the Code by non-governmental bodies.

One disturbing possibility that could lead to evasion of Code principles is the possible delegation by central governments, covered by mandatory Code provisions, to non-governmental bodies obligated only to use best efforts. The Code does prohibit signatories from taking efforts which directly or indirectly require or encourage such non-governmental bodies from acting in a manner inconsistent with the Code. This, however, would not prohibit the delegation or abdication by central government of standards promulgation obligations to independent bodies over which they could exercise no control.[102]

---

[100] Id. at § 401, 19 U.S.C. § 2531.

[101] See, e.g., the National Traffic and Motor Vehicle Safety Act, 15 U.S.C. § 1381, et seq, which prohibits the enforcement of state standards that differ from federal standards. Such provisions are necessary lest automakers be faced with the difficult task of modifying vehicles to conform with different safety standards in every state.

[102] Agreement on Technical Barriers to Trade, art. 6.

A.   Obligations of Central Governments

For the reasons set forth above, it is easier to evaluate the effectiveness of the Code by looking at the mandatory obligations imposed on the central governments which signed the Code. A number of specific requirements that must be followed by central governments are set out in Article 5 of the Code. These include:

(1)   Imported products must be accepted for testing under conditions "no less favorable" than those accorded to like domestic products or comparable imported products.

(2)   Testing methods for imported products must be "no more complex or less expeditious" than those applied to domestic products or comparable imported products.

(3)   Fees charged for testing imported products must be "equitable" in relation to fees charged for testing similar domestic and imported products.

(4)   Test results must be made available to the exporter or importer if requested.

(5)   The location of testing facilities and the selection of samples for testing shall not be such as to cause "unnecessary inconvenience for importers or exporters".

(6)   Imported products shall be given the same privileges of confidentiality as those accorded to domestic products.

Central governments are also required, "whenever possible", to recognize test results and certifications issued by equivalent certifying and testing agencies in foreign countries,[103] even when such test results may differ from their own, if they are satisfied with the methods of testing employed by the foreign body.

B.   Publication and Comment on
Proposed standards and Certifications

Central governments are also required to adopt certain standards and permit openness in these standards and certification procedures. This includes publication of proposed standards and certification requirements sufficiently in advance to permit foreign suppliers to become informed of the procedures, notification to the GATT Secretariat of the products to be covered, and the objective of the proposed standards or certification, provision of copies of proposed

---

[103] Id. at art. 5.2.

standards and certifications on a non-discriminatory basis,
and allowance of a reasonable period for comments by foreign
entities on proposed requirements and to take such comments
into account.[104]

However, the above steps can be circumvented when there
are "urgent problems of safety, health, environmental protection or national security" that require prompt action. In
such cases, immediate notification to other parties through
the GATT Secretariat is still required, although publication
can be disposed with. Moreover, copies of the proposed
standards must still be provided along with an opportunity for
comment and consideration of such comments.[105]

C.   Information Sources

In another effort to ensure openness and transparency in
standards settings, central governments are also required to
set up information agencies where other parties can obtain
data on standards, including information on standards set by
non-central governments and private groups.[106] The United
States has implemented this through the establishment of a
standards information center in the Department of Commerce.[107]

D.   Use of International Standards

One important objective of the Code was to encourage
parties to follow internationally recognized standards promulgated by multi-partite bodies. Parties are urged "wherever
practicable" to cooperate in the preparation of international
standards and to formulate international certification systems
and participate in them.[108] U.S. implementing legislation
provides that federal agencies, in developing standards,
"shall take into consideration international standards and
shall, if appropriate, base the standards on international

---

104 Id. at arts. 2.5, 7.3. Technical standards or regulations
need only be subject to the notification procedures in art.
2.5 if: (a) a relevant international standard does not exist;
(b) the proposed standard or regulation is not substantially
the same as the international standard, and if the standard or
regulation would have "a significant effect on trade of other
Parties". Id. at art. 2.5
105 Id. at arts. 2.6, 7.4.
106 Id. at art. 10.
107 Trade Agreements Act of 1979 § 414, 19 U.S.C. § 2544.
108 Agreement on Technical Barriers to Trade, arts. 2.3, 9.

standards".[109] Further, situations where international standards may not be appropriate are enumerated, and include:

(1) national security requirements;
(2) the prevention of deceptive practices;
(3) protection of human health and safety, animal or
     plant life or health, or the environment;
(4) fundamental climatic or other geographical factors;
     and
(5) fundamental technological problems.[110]

This language closely parallels the language in the Code
at Article 2.2, that requires parties to use relevant international standards, or parts of them where they exist or
completion is imminent, except where inappropriate. The Code
then specifies inter alia the same five standards set out in
the U.S. law. However, the use of the words " inter alia"
indicates that this list is illustrative only and the parties
could develop other circumstances where use of international
standards might be "inappropriate".[111] Thus, it appears that a
party would have wide discretion in interpreting what is
deemed inappropriate.[112] Moreover, while some of the enumerated
circumstances are relatively clear, others are not.   For
example, the prevention of deceptive practices is a broad and
encompassing term.[113]
Protection of human health, safety, animal or plant life
or health, or the environment are also broad terms which could
allow the use of standards higher than existing international
standards.[114] Fundamental climatic and other geographical
factors are not defined, but could include such examples as
requiring certain articles to withstand extreme cold if the
country applying the standard was located in an area of

---

109 Trade Agreements Act of 1979 § 402(2)(A), 19 U.S.C. § 2532
    (2)(A).
110 Id. at § 402(2)(B)(i), 19 U.S.C. § 2532(2)(B)(i).
111 See MTN Studies 6, pt. 3, supra note 30, at 70-71.
112 Id. at 71.
113 The analysis of the Agreement by the U.S. International Trade
    Commission gave as examples of deceptive practices standards
    of labeling which do not adequately state the intended scope
    or limitations of the product or standards not up to date with
    existing technology. Id. However, the U.S. International
    Trade Commission, under its own deceptive trade practices
    statute, § 337 (19 U.S.C. § 1337), has considered as unfair or
    deceptive trade practices violations of the U.S. patent,
    copyright, and trademark law, as well as common law passing
    off, misappropriation of trade secrets and false designation
    of origin.
114 Id.

extremely cold temperatures.[115] Fundamental technical problems also are undefined and quite broad. An example would be requirements for levels of electrical voltage that could uniformly be used in a country's electrical wiring system without requiring rewiring.[116]

E.   Specific Provisions Relating to Developing Countries

The Standards Code has a number of provisions specifically directed towards the LDCs. These appear in several places. Article 11, dealing with technical assistance to other parties, provides for advice on the preparation of technical regulations especially to the developing countries.[117] Article 11.5 similarly provides that "Parties shall, if requested, advise other Parties, especially the developing countries, and shall grant them technical assistance on mutually agreed terms and conditions regarding the steps that should be taken by their producers, if they wish to take part in certification systems operated by governmental or non-governmental bodies within the territory of the Party receiving the request".[118] Furthermore, Article 12 is completely devoted to special and differential treatment of developing countries. This treatment includes giving special attention to the "special development, financial and trade needs of developing countries".[119] The parties recognize that "developing countries should not be expected to use international standards as a basis for their technical regulations or standards, including test methods, which are not appropriate to their development, financial and trade needs".[120] Article 12 also provides that LDCs should be ensured representative participation in international standardizing bodies,[121] and that such bodies shall consider preparing standards on products of special interest to the LDCs.[122] Of particular importance are the provisions of Article 12.8 that permit, for limited time periods, a complete waiver of obligations under the Code, for a particular LDC that requests it.

---

115 Id. at 72.
116 Id.
117 Agreement on Technical Barriers to Trade, art. 11.1
118 Id. at art. 11.5.
119 Id. at art. 12.2.
120 Id. at art. 12.4.
121 Id. at art. 12.5.
122 Id. at art. 12.6.

F.   Enforcement and Dispute Settlement

The Code has specific provisions for enforcement and resolution of disputes. A Committee on Technical Barriers to Trade was established. This Committee is empowered, if bilateral attempts at settlement fail, to meet at the request of a party to investigate a dispute.[123] The dispute settlement procedure involves several tiers and is somewhat complex. The Committee, if it cannot mediate the dispute successfully within three months, can appoint a technical group to make findings of fact and recommendations. If this is unsuccessful, the dispute can be submitted to a panel comprised of knowledgeable governmental officials. The panel, which can develop its own procedures, essentially performs the same task as the technical group, i.e., fact finding and recommendations.[124]

After an investigation is complete and a final recommendation is made, the party to which the recommendation is made must promptly notify the Committee in writing if it "considers itself unable to implement" the recommendation.[125] The Committee is then empowered to take certain actions in the nature of sanctions.[126] This may involve authorizing other parties to the Code to suspend their obligations under the Code as to the recalcitrant party. These sanctions are apparently limited to supervision of obligations under the Standards Code and do not affect other obligations.[127]

The U.S. has implemented this dispute settlement procedure by providing for the Interagency Trade Policy Staff Committee to review and consider any adverse findings against the U.S. by one of the GATT mechanisms.[128] The Committee could recommend enforcement action or appropriate legislation.[129]

CODE ON IMPORT LICENSING PROCEDURES

A form of non-tariff barrier that is prevalent in many countries is the import license. While licensing procedures may often have legitimate goals, they are often used as a thinly veiled form of quota. Some countries, such as Mexico (a non-GATT member), have extensive import licensing requirements. In fact, at the time Mexico was considering GATT accession, this was a major issue raised by the developed

123 Id. at art. 13, 14.
124 Id. at art. 14.14 - 14.18, Annex 3.
125 Id. at art. 14.20.
126 Id. at art. 14.21.
127 See MTN Studies 6, pt. 3, supra note 30, at 133.
128 Trade Agreements Act of 1979 § 424(a), 19 U.S.C. § 2554(a).
129 See Statement of Administrative Action, supra note 63, at 490-91.

countries as a precondition to Mexican membership. The goal of the Agreement on Import Licensing Procedures was not so much to abolish these license requirements, but to streamline the administration of these procedures to reduce unnecessary red tape, which itself has often become a non-tariff barrier. As expressed by former U.S. President Carter in his transmittal message to Congress on the MTN Agreements:

> Its purpose [is] to simplify and harmonize to the greatest extent possible the procedures which importers must follow in obtaining an import license, so that these procedures do not themselves constitute an unnecessary obstacle to international trade.[130]

The Agreement consists of a preamble and five articles. Article I contains the general provisions which define import licensing as "administrative procedures used for the operation of import licensing regimes requiring the submission of an application or other documentation (other than that required for customs purposes) to the relevant administrative body as a prior condition for importation into the customs territory of the importing country".[131]

The general provisions also provide that parties must ensure that their administrative procedures used in connection with import licensing must be in conformity with the GATT[132] with a view toward preventing trade distortions that may arise from inappropriate operation of those procedures.[133] Consistent with the goal of the agreement to prevent import licenses from being used in a discriminatory manner, rather than to prohibit them, Article I provides that import licensing procedures "shall be neutral in application and administered in a fair and equitable manner".[134]

In an effort to promote this fairness and neutrality the Agreement further provides that the publication of procedures for submission of applications and the lists of products subject to the licensing requirement,[135] as well as any changes in import licensing rules or products covered, be "promptly published". In an effort to eliminate unnecessary burdens on importers, the Agreement requires that application forms and procedures for import licenses must be "as simple as possible".[136] An important part of these procedures is the

---

[130] Letter from President Jimmy Carter, supra note 68, at 1941.
[131] Agreement on Import Licensing Procedures (see Appendix), art. I, para. 1.
[132] Article XI of the GATT already covers this topic and prohibits import licenses, but has not been effectively enforced.
[133] Agreement on Import Licensing Procedures, art. I, para 2.
[134] Id. at para. 3.
[135] Id. at para. 4.
[136] Id. at para. 5, 6.

requirement that applicants should only be required to deal
with one administrative body to obtain their licenses . To
eliminate possible abuses by licensing authorities, the Code
provides that applications cannot be refused due to minor
documentation errors and errors of a grave nature are to be
dealt with mildly when there is no proof of fraudulent intent
or gross negligence.[137]

A.   Automatic Licensing Procedures

Article 2 of the Code deals with automatic import licensing. Automatic import licensing is defined as import licensing where approval is freely granted. These systems, in
theory, are designed to monitor and control imports rather
than restrict them.   However, like most administrative
procedures, it is subject to abuse and can be a non-tariff
barrier.   To this end, the Code provides that automatic
licensing procedures shall not be administered in a manner
which restricts imports.[138] While not approving the need for
such automatic license procedures, the Code recognizes that
they may be necessary and they may be maintained so long as
the underlying circumstances that gave rise to their introduction still exist or the purposes of the licensing procedure
cannot be accomplished in a more appropriate way.[139]
The Code further provides for equal treatment and
non-discrimination in granting licenses[140] and that applications
can be submitted on any working day and should be approved
"immediately upon receipt", but in no case in longer than ten
working days.[141]
The U.S. has traditionally favored the elimination of all
automatic import licensing procedures.[142] The U.S. was also
concerned that the mere recognition of automatic licensing
procedures in the Code might legitimize them and make it more
difficult to eventually eliminate them.[143]

B.   Non-Automatic Licensing Procedures

This section is designed to cover, in addition to those
items set out in the general provisions, rules governing

---

[137] Id. at para. 7.
[138] Id. at art. 2, para. 2(a).
[139] Id. at para. 2(b).
[140] Id. at para. 2(c).
[141] Id. at paras. 2(d), (e).
[142] Office of U.S. Special Trade Representative, Trade Policy
Staff Committee, Code of Conduct on Automatic Import Licensing, Doc. 78-76 (June 26, 1978).
[143] MTN Studies 6, pt. 2, supra note 30, at 302.

non-automatic licensing procedures. These often take the form
of quotas, which are technically prohibited by Article XI of
the GATT.   The Code attempts to prevent the procedures in
administering quotas from becoming a barrier in addition to
the quota itself.[144] Parties are required to provide or request
all relevant information relating to the restrictions and to
publish the amount of quotas allocated among supplying
countries.[145] Discrimination among applicants is prohibited,
and rejected applicants must receive upon request the reasons
for their rejection and be given a right to an appeal or
review of the decision.[146]

However, the Code does provide that in granting new
licenses, the parties shall give "special consideration" to
importers from developing countries particularly those from
the least developed countries.[147]

Dispute settlements under the Code are handled under
existing procedures in Articles XXII and XXIII of the GATT.
While the Code was a significant step forward, it did not deal
with all outstanding problems in this area.   For example, it
is somewhat unclear whether agricultural commodities and bilateral export restraint agreements are intended to be
included within the coverage of the agreement.[148] The U.S.
position is that in absence of any provision excluding
agricultural products, they are deemed to be included.   The
Swiss have supported this interpretation, but the EEC has, in
principle, taken the position that agricultural products are
not covered, but in practice has applied it to agricultural
products on at least one occasion.[149]

As to bilateral export restraint agreements (so called
voluntary restraint agreements) which have existed for steel,
automobiles and other products, there is also a question as to
whether they are subject to the provisions of the Code.   The
U.S. International Trade Commission in its analysis of the
Code, included that it is "at least arguable" that it does.[150]

C.   Application to States and Local Governments

There is a significant question as to whether the provisions of the Code are binding on state and local governments
in federal systems. While this question was dealt with in the
Code on Government Procurement, it was not specifically
covered by the Code on Import Licensing.   The question of

144 Agreement on Import Licensing Procedures, art. 3(a).
145 Id. at arts. 3(b), (c).
146 Id. at art. 3(f).
147 Id. at art. 3(1).
148 MTN Studies 6, pt. 2, supra note 30, at 300.
149 Id. at 303.
150 Id.

federal preemption is one that apparently has not been definitively decided and in analyzing the Agreement, the U.S. International Trade Commission took no position and raised the question that such areas as alcohol and tobacco that have long been regulated by the states, might not be subject to the Code.[151]

D.   Effective Date

The Code became effective on January 1, 1980 for the United States, Canada, the EEC, New Zealand, Norway, South Africa, Sweden and Switzerland. Argentina, Austria, Chile, Finland and Japan signed the Code subject to ratification of conditions attached.[152] All of these countries except Argentina had ratified the Agreement by November, 1981. In addition, Hungary, India, Pakistan, Philippines and Romania have signed, and Yugoslavia signed subject to ratification.[153]

CODE ON CIVIL AIRCRAFT

The United States, Japan, the EEC, Canada and Sweden were the impetus behind negotiations for a civil aircraft agreement. The U.S. set out certain issues that it felt needed to be addressed. These included:

(1)   The elimination of duties on aircraft and equipment;
(2)   Buy-national policies;
(3)   Governmental conditions placed on foreign purchases, such as co-production;
(4)   Financing;
(5)   Restrictive standards and certification rules;
(6)   Government aid and subsidies.[154]

The Civil Aircraft Agreement was unique in that it was the only industrial sector for which a specific agreement was reached as part of the MTN. The reasons for this are not certain except that both the U.S. and the EEC strongly felt that significant barriers existed to their exports of aircraft, thus providing a convergence of interest among two of the largest participants that did not exist in other sectoral

---

[151] Id. at 307. The ITC notes that federal law has noted the valid exercise of state police powers even in the area of foreign commerce. See 46 U.S.C. § 97.

[152] Twenty-Fourth Annual Report of the President, supra note 10, at 46.

[153] See GATT Doc. L/4914/Rev. 3/Add. 7.

[154] U.S.International Trade Commission, Operation of the Trade Agreements Program, 30th Report, supra note 63, at 54.

areas. As a sectoral agreement, the Civil Aircraft Agreement covers and makes more specific provisions relating to standards, subsidies and government procurement already covered in other omnibus codes.

The Agreement covers all civil aircraft, and their engines, parts, components or sub-assemblies. Also included are ground flight simulators.[155] The signatories agreed to most of the points set out by the U.S., referred to above as described below.

A.   Customs Duties

The signatories agreed to eliminate all customs duties on civil aircraft and their parts, including duty on the value of repairs made abroad.

B.   Technical Barriers to Trade

The Civil Aircraft Code reaffirms the applicability of the Code on Technical Barriers to Trade in civil aircraft and the Code was specifically acknowledged as being applicable to aircraft certification, operation and maintenance requirements.[156]

C.   Government Procurement and Sales Related Inducements

The Agreement prohibits governmental action to require airlines or aircraft manufacturers to procure civil aircraft from any particular source.[157] Governments are prohibited from exerting "unreasonable pressure" on the companies as well. The effect of this language is somewhat unclear since it would appear to authorize the exertion of "reasonable" pressures which certainly would fly against the spirit of the Code. "Unreasonable" was not defined because it was not possible to obtain international agreement on the definition. However, "reasonable pressures" might be considered to be efforts of government officials on the Board of Government-Owned Airlines to further their own best interests in procurement decisions. An unreasonable activity would be the participation in a "buy-national" policy.[158] Discrimination against suppliers is prohibited as are "inducements" by governments to purchase their aircraft. For example, the offering of landing rights

---

[155] Civil Aircraft Agreement, art. 1.1.
[156] Id. at art. 3.1.
[157] Id. at art. 4.2.
[158] See Testimony of Dr. W. Stephen Piper, coordinator of Aerospace Trade Policy, Office of U.S. Trade Representative Before the Subcomm. on Transportation, Aviation and Communications of the House Comm. on Science and Aviation, at 5 (1979).

or sale of nuclear fuel processing plants linked to purchases of aircraft would be prohibited by the Agreement, thus eliminating political linkages.[159]

D.   Trade Restrictions

Quantitative restrictions such as import quotas may be imposed only in a manner consistent with the GATT. Import licensing or monitoring systems consistent with the GATT are permitted.[160]

E.   Subsidies

The Agreement refers to the Subsidies Code and reaffirms the applicability of that Code to civil aircraft. Specific provisions are added concerning the methods of pricing civil aircraft, that are designed to counteract subsidization. Unfortunately, due to parallel negotiations under the auspices of the OECD, the Code failed to deal with the important question of export credit financing parameters.[161]

F.   Applicability to Non-Central Governments

While the Code is not binding on state and local governments, it provides that signatory central governments may not require or encourage local governments and non-governmental bodies to take actions inconsistent with the Code.[162]

The Agreement is enforced and monitored by a Committee on Trade in Civil Aircraft. The Committee can review Code-related disputes upon the request of a signatory.[163] Attached to the Agreement as an Annex was a list of items for which duty-free treatment is to be incorporated. Implementation of the Code required only modest changes in U.S. laws and regulations, primarily the elimination of certain tariffs and an amendment to the Buy America Act.[164] This was accomplished in Title VI of the Trade Agreements Act of 1979 and was implemented through certain changes in U.S. Customs regulations in January, 1980.[165]

---

[159] Civil Aircraft Agreement, art. 4.4; see also Testimony of Dr. Piper, supra note 158, at 6.

[160] Civil Aircraft Agreement, art. 5.

[161] Id. at arts. 6.1, 6.2; see also Testimony of Dr. Piper, supra note 158, at 7.

[162] Civil Aircraft Agreement, art. 7.1.

[163] Id. at art. 8.

[164] Statement of Administrative Action, supra note 63, at 505.

[165] 45 Fed. Reg. 1633 (1980).

The U.S. retained the ability to impose internal taxes,
such as sales taxes on civil aircraft, and the provisions of
the antidumping and countervailing duty laws are still applicable.[166] U.S. acceptance and implementation of the Agreement was
conditioned on the acceptance of the Agreement by the major
industrial countries, Canada, the EEC, Japan and Sweden.
However, once implemented, the U.S. granted unconditional Most
Favored Nation treatment to all countries. Nevertheless, the
President has the power to withdraw or terminate duty-free
treatment as to any country that has not met its obligations
to the U.S. under the Agreement without granting adequate
compensation.[167] The Aircraft Agreement became effective on
January 1, 1980. As of August, 1982, seventeen countries and
the EEC had accepted The Civil Aircraft Agreement (these
included a number of indiviudual EEC member states that signed
individually for jurisdictional reasons, since certain EEC
member states exert independent authority in the aviation
area). Three countries, Egypt, Greece and Italy, had signed
the Code subject to ratification.[168]

From a substantive viewpoint, it is possible to view the
Civil Aircraft Agreement as having accomplished little more
than restating and affirming many of the principles of other
substantive agreements, such as the Agreement on Government
Procurement, Subsidies and Standards. While it did result in
the elimination of duties on civil aircraft, these duties had
already been eliminated in some countries or were quite low,
as in the United States, where the duty was 5% ad valorem.
Nevertheless, the Civil Aircraft Agreement set the precedent
for future sectoral agreements. In fact, during the negotiations of the Civil Aircraft Agreement, reference was made to
the possibility that the Aircraft Agreement could be a precedent for other sectoral agreements.[169]

AGRICULTURAL AGREEMENTS

In conjunction with the Multilateral Trade Negotiations,
a number of agricultural agreements were negotiated, both on a
bilateral and multilateral basis. These largely dealt with
the many non-tariff aspects of international agricultural
trade that often result in serious barriers such as quotas.
The agricultural agreements were numerous and often quite

---

166 Id.
167 Id. at 506; The Trade Agreements Act of 1979 § 601(b).
168 See GATT Doc. L/4914/Rev.5/Add 9.
169 This observation was made by Dr. W. Stephen Piper, the chief
    U.S. negotiator for the Agreement on Civil Aircraft, in a
    paper entitled "Unique Sectoral Agreement Establishes Free
    Trade Framework: A History of the MTN Agreement on Trade in
    Civil Aircraft", at 17.

technical and cannot be completely discussed in this work.
Major breakthroughs in protectionist agricultural trade
policies were not obtained.[170] However, a number of significant
multilateral agreements dealing with world agricultural
problems were completed. These will be discussed below.

A.   International Dairy Arrangement

World trade in dairy products has been a particular
problem area due to unstable prices and severe competition.
The objective of the International Dairy Arrangement (IDA) was
to expand and liberalize world trade in dairy products under
stable market conditions.[171]
The Arrangement covers such products as fresh and
preserved milk and cream, butter, cheese, curd, and casein.[172]
The IDA establishes an International Dairy Council that may
expand coverage of the Agreement to other dairy products. The
Council also acts as an information gathering body and the
participants agree to submit to the Council information
required for it to monitor and assess the overall situation in
the world market.[173] This data includes production, consumption, prices, stocks and trade. If the Council finds that "a
serious market disequilibrium" or a threat of such disequilibrium exists, which affects or may affect international
trade, the Council will proceed to identify possible solutions
for consideration by the signatories.[174] The Council also acts
as a conciliatory mechanism to resolve disputes between
participants.[175] In cases involving disequilibrium and potential actions, the Council is required when "feasible and
appropriate" to take into account the special and more
favorable treatment to be given to developing countries.[176]
Certain provisions regarding the uses of dairy products for
foreign aid purposes are also included.
The Arrangement entered into force on January 1, 1980,
and replaced the arrangement concerning certain dairy products, which entered into force on May 14, 1970, and the
protocol relating to milk fat, which entered into force on May
11, 1973, for participants in those two agreements.[177] No
implementing legislation in the U.S. was required.   The

---

170 MTN Studies 6, supra note 30, CP-96-12, at III (June,1979).
171 Twenty-fourth Annual Report of the President , supra note 10,
    at 49.   IDA, art. I.   (See Appendix for full text of the
    Agreement.)
172 IDA, art. II.
173 Id. at art. III.
174 Id. at art. IV, para. 2.
175 Id. at art. IV, para. 6.
176 Id. at art. IV, para. 4.
177 Id. at art. VIII, paras. 1 (d), 3.

Arrangement had an initial duration of three years and is automatically extended for further three year periods unless the Council decides otherwise at least eighty days prior to the expiration date.[178] There are currently eighteen participants in the Arrangement.[179] In addition, there are three protocols to the Arrangement that fix minimum export prices . However, signatories to the Arrangement need not sign each protocol. These protocols are as follows:

1.   Protocol Regarding Certain Milk Powders

This Protocol covers milk powder and cream powder and sets minimum export prices for skimmed milk powder ($425 per metric ton), whole milk powder ($725 per metric ton), and buttermilk powder ($425 per metric ton). These minimum prices are subject to review once a year based on such factors as the costs faced by producers, economic factors in the world market, the need to maintain a long-term minimum return to the most economic producers, the need to maintain stability of supply and to ensure acceptable prices to consumers, the current market situation, and the need to improve the relationship between the levels of the minimum prices and dairy support levels in the major producing participant countries.[180] Minimum price levels need not be adhered to for imports and exports of skimmed milk powder and buttermilk powder used for animal feed, provided advance notice is given and adequate measures exist to ensure the utilization of the imports for these purposes.[181] Similarly, non-commercial transactions for relief and charitable purposes are exempted.[182]

2.   Protocol Regarding Milk Fat

This Protocol covers anhydrous milk fat and butter and establishes minimum prices of $1100 per metric ton for anhydrous milk fat and $925 per metric ton for butter.[183] These prices are subject to review and modification. Non-commercial transactions for relief and charitable purposes are exempted.[184] However, no exemption for sales of animal feeds exists.

---

[178] Id. at art. VIII, para. 4.
[179] GATT Doc. L/4914/Rev.5/Add. 9.
[180] Protocol Regarding Certain Milk Powders, pt. Two, art. 3, para.3(b).
[181] Id. at para. 5.
[182] Id. at Para. 8.
[183] Protocol Regarding Milk Fat, pt. Two, art. 3, para. 2(b).
[184] Id. at para. 7.

3.   Protocol Regarding Certain Cheeses

This Protocol covers only certain types of cheeses, those with a fat content in dry matter, by weight, greater than or equal to 45%, dry matter content by weight, greater than or equal to 50%.[185] Its provisions are generally similar to the Protocols on Certain Milk Powders and Milk Fat. A minimum price level is established at $800 per metric ton,[186] which is subject to review and adjustment. Sales for relief and charitable purposes are exempted.[187] A special exception is also made for exports of "small quantities of natural un-processed cheese which would be below normal export quality as a result of deterioration or production faults".[188] Advance notification of such sales is required.

B.   Arrangement Regarding Bovine Meats

The purpose of the Arrangement Regarding Bovine Meats is to promote the expansion, greater liberalization and stability of the international meat and livestock market by facilitating the progressive dismantling of obstacles and restrictions to world trade in bovine meats and large animals.[189] Participants agreed to regularly monitor and assess world market situations and report to an International Meat Council.[190] This includes data on consumption, prices, stocks and trade and information on domestic trade policies and measures.[191] The Council, if it finds a "serious imbalance or a threat thereof in the inter-national meat market, may identify for consideration by governments, possible solutions to remedy the situation consistent with the principles and rules of GATT.[192] The Council operates by a consensus.[193] In taking any such action, special and favorable consideration is to be given to the needs of the LDCs where "feasible and appropriate".[194]

Since the Council is composed of all participants in the Arrangement,[195] it is unclear how easily any consensus can be reached. A consensus is reached only if no member of the Council formally objects and is tantamount to unanimous approval.[196] The Arrangement entered into force on January 1,

---

185 Protocol Regarding Certain Cheese, pt.One, art. 1, para.1.
186 Id. at pt. Two, art. 3, para. 2(b).
187 Id. at para. 7.
188 Id. at pt. Three, art. 7, para. 2.
189 This Arrangement covers beef, veal and live cattle.
190 Arrangement Regarding Bovine Meat, pt. One, art. III, para.1.
191 Id. at para. 3.
192 Id. at para. 2.
193 Id.
194 Id. para. 4.
195 Id. at pt. Two, art. V, para. 1.
196 Id. at para. 3.

1980, and there were twenty-three signatories as of July 1, 1982.[197] The Bovine Meat Arrangement does not contain provisions establishing minimum prices. The Arrangement remains in force for three years and is automatically extended for successive three year periods unless the Council acts at least eighty days prior to the expiration date.[198] No legislative changes were required in U.S. law to implement the Arrangement.

C.   Bilateral Agricultural Agreements

As part of the MTN negotiations numerous bilateral agreements covering agricultural products were negotiated. These were much more specific and detailed than the multilateral agreements discussed above. Some of the more important of these, dealing with non-tariff measures, will be summarized below:

1.   Agreements Between the U.S. and the European Communities on Cheeses

The U.S. agreed to remove certain cheeses from quotas, including Stilton, Roquefort, and others.   Quotas were established for a number of other cheeses, including cheddar and swiss.[199] The EEC could continue subsidies for cheeses only if the subsidies do not result in prices for cheeses below the wholesale market level of like U.S. cheese.[200] If subsidies are applied in this manner, the U.S. will not impose countervailing duties on these cheeses. If not, the U.S. is permitted to take retaliatory action after consultations.[201]

The actions include the imposition of fees or the denial of entry[202] by the U.S. President, upon the advice of the Secretary of Agriculture. The fee imposed may not exceed the amount of the subsidy and is designed to ensure that the duty paid wholesale price of the imported article will not be less than the domestic wholesale market price of similar articles produced in the United States.[203] In this regard, it does not differ greatly from countervailing duties that are waived for

---

[197] GATT Doc. L/4914/Rev.5/Add.9.

[198] Arrangement Regarding Bovine Meat, pt. Three, art. VI, para. 4.

[199] Arrangement Between the U.S. and the European Economic Community Concerning Cheeses, para. 1, Annex I.

[200] Id. at para. 3.

[201] Id. at para. 4.

[202] The Trade Agreements Act of 1979 § 702(b), (d), 19 U.S.C. § 1202.

[203] Id. at § 702(d)(1)(A).

cheese imports. However, there are certain differences between the provisions of this law and the operations of the countervailing duty law that will be discussed infra.

2.   Agreement Between the U.S. and the EEC on Poultry

This Agreement, accomplished through an exchange of letters, resulted in the EEC modifying its method of calculating prices and duties on turkey parts. The EEC tariff on uncooked seasoned turkey meat was bound and provided for consultations if U.S. exports of turkey meat exceeded the level of 1977 and 1978.[204]

3.   Agreement Between the U.S. and the EEC on Rice

Also by means of an exchange of letters, the U.S. and the EEC agreed that as of september 1, 1979 and September 1, 1980, the EEC would reduce its threshold price for long grain rice to the level of the threshold price for round grain rice and maintain the existing duty classification on parboiled rice.[205]

4.   Agreement Between the U.S. and the EEC Concerning High Quality Beef

In this Agreement, consisting of an exchange of letters, the EEC agreed to establish a quota of 10,000 metric tons of high quality beef with an ad valorem duty of 20%. Consultations were provided for in 1983 to consult about the possibility of further expansion in trade in high quality beef.[206]

5.   Agreement Between the U.S. and the EEC Concerning Fresh, Chilled and Frozen Beef

The U.S. and the EEC agreed by exchange of letters for the U.S. to allow 5,000 metric tons of fresh, chilled or frozen beef from the EEC to be imported, and to consult in 1983 about the possibility of expanding trade in this area.[207]

---

204 Agreements Reached in the Tokyo Round of the Multilateral Trade Negotiations, Message from the President of the United States, 96th Cong., 1st Sess. 423 (1979) [hereinafter Message from the President].
205 Id. at 424.
206 Id. at 425.
207 Id. at 427.

6.   Agreement Between the U.S. and Switzerland Concerning Cheeses

By an exchange of letters dated April 12, 1979, the U.S. and Switzerland approved an arrangement on cheeses negotiated as part of the MTN. Under this Arrangement, the U.S. agreed to bind the quota levels for various categories of cheeses from Switzerland. The Swiss affirmed that it was their intention not to allow Swiss exports to undercut the levels of wholesale prices of like cheeses in selected major American cities by means of subsidies.[208]

7.   Agreement Between Switzerland and the U.S. Concerning Trade in Beef

Switzerland also agreed as a result of the MTN to open its market by granting minimum import licenses for fresh, frozen and chilled beef up to 2,000 tons per year. Certain specific cuts of beef were enumerated as qualifying for these licenses.[209]

8.   Agreement Between the U. S. and Austria Concerning Agricultural Products

In return for securing access to the U.S. market for Austrian cheeses, Austria granted to the U.S. certain concessions relating to certain U.S. agricultural exports to Austria. The U.S. agreed to modify its import system so that certain Austrian cheeses would not be subject to quotas. Quota levels for certain other types of cheeses were bound. Total quota levels were set at 7,850 metric tons. Austria agreed not to grant governmental subsidies in a manner which would result in the price of Austrian cheeses falling below the wholesale prices of like U.S. domestic cheeses. It was understood that any governmental subsidies inconsistent with this would be subject to countervailing duties. Austria, in return, permitted U.S. imports of fresh and chilled high quality beef under quotas of 300 metric tons for the first year, to increase to 600 metric tons over an eight year period. The quota applies to portioned steaks and tenderloins. Austria also granted certain concessional rates of duty on poultry, nuts, and dried fruit.[210]

---

208 Id. at 437.
209 Id. at 442.
210 Id. at 465.

9.   Agreement Between the U.S. and Finland
      Concerning Cheeses

The Agreement with Finland concerning cheeses was similar
to those that the U.S. negotiated with other countries.   The
U.S. agreed to allow certain types of cheeses to be imported
without quotas and bound the quotas on others.   Total quota
imports from Finland was fixed at 10,500 metric tons.   Finland
agreed that it would not grant subsidies to its cheese exports
in a manner so as to result in a price of cheese below the
wholesale prices of similar U.S. cheeses, or otherwise it
would be subject to countervailing duties.[211]

10.   Agreement Between the U.S. and Argentina

On March 7, 1979, the U.S. and Argentina, through a
Memorandum of Understanding, set out mutual trade concessions
granted.   These went beyond agricultural products.   However,
of interest for discussion in this section was the U.S. undertaking to establish a quota level of 4,456 metric tons for
certain cheeses exported from Argentina and duty concessions
on Argentine beef in airtight containers.   Argentina made
tariff concessions on certain U.S. agricultural products,
notably a 50% duty reduction on apples.[212]

11.   Agreement Between the U.S. and Australia

The U.S. and Australia agreed to tariff concessions on a
number of products.   In the agricultural area, the U.S. agreed
to a quota on worldwide meat imports which (fresh, chilled or
frozen beef, veal, mutton and goat meats) was established at
1.2 billion pounds a year, or 1.3 billion pounds when voluntary restraint agreements were in effect, and base quotas
calculated under the U.S. meat import law were above 1.2
billion.   The U.S. also agreed to provide minimum levels of
imports for Australian cheeses totalling 4,100 tons and for
chocolate crumb totalling 2,000 tons.[213] The U.S. further
agreed to pursue efforts to find an expeditious settlement to
the outstanding countervailing duty order on Australian
butter.

---

211 Id. at 491.
212 Id. at 499.
213 Id. at 507.

12.   Agreement Between the U.S. and Israel

The U.S. and Israel reached a bilateral accord on a number of tariff concessions including agricultural products. The U.S. provided a minimum cheese import quota of 750 metric tons and made tariff cuts on products of interest to Israel, such as citrus fruits, dates, etc. Israel made concessions to the U.S., including the duty free admission of live bovine animals and flour of oil seeds.[214]

13.   Agreement Between the U.S. and Iceland

Through an exchange of letters in May, 1979, the U.S. and Iceland confirmed agreements reached in Geneva relating to certain agricultural products. The U.S. granted an import quota of 623 tons to Icelandic cheeses and Iceland made tariff concessions on U.S. apples, dried fruits and fruit juices. By a separate letter dated June 12, 1979, the Government of Iceland agreed that if it should grant subsidies to cheese exports, these payments will be provided in such a way so as not to result in the sale of Icelandic cheeses in the U.S. below the wholesale prices of U.S. domestic cheeses.[215]

14.   Agreement with Portugal

By an exchange of letters in June, 1979, the U.S. and Portugal reached an agreement relating to cheeses and meats. The U.S. provided an additional cheese quota allocation to Portugal of 350 metric tons, bringing their total quota to 581 metric tons. Portugal agreed to the price assurances relating to subsidies similar to those in the other agreements discussed above. Portugal established a special quota for U.S. high quality beef and bound a tariff rate for this.[216]

15.   Agreement Between the U. S. and Canada Concerning Cheeses

On June 15, 1979, the U.S. agreed to admit certain Canadian cheeses without quota and fixed a quota of 2,044 metric tons on other cheeses. Canada agreed to certain price undertakings if it provided subsidies to cheese exports.[217] The U.S. agreed to notify Canada and enter into consultations before taking counteraction.

---

214 Id. at 523.
215 Id. at 545.
216 Id. at 553.
217 Id. at 564.

16. Agreement Between the U.S. and Norway
     Concerning Cheeses

On May 17, 1979, the U.S. and Norway entered into an
agreement covering cheeses. Certain cheeses, such as sheep
and goats milk cheeses and soft-ripened cows milk cheeses in
retail packages, were admitted free from quotas, while quota
levels on other types of cheeses were bound at 7,200 metric
tons. Norway agreed to price undertakings relating to any
subsidies it might grant to cheese exports, and a compliance
mechanism was established to provide for consultations and an
opportunity for Norway to take remedial actions. The U.S.,
unlike in certain other agreements, specifically agreed not to
take countervailing duty action against Norwegian cheese
exports so long as the stated price conditions were met.
Through the mandatory consultation mechanism, that did not
appear in most other bilateral agreements, the likelihood of
unilateral U.S. counteraction against Norway was diminshed,
since Norway would have the opportunity to take remedial
action.[218]

17. Agreement Between the U.S. and Sweden
     Concerning Cheeses

Under this Agreement, signed on June 13, 1979, the U.S.
bound quota levels for Swedish cheese at 1,350. Unlike most
other cheese agreements, there was no provision for non-quota
imports. The provisions as to pricing, subsidies and consultations were similar to those in the U.S. agreement with
Norway.[219]

18. Agreement Between the U.S. and New Zealand

On May 21, 1979, the U.S. and New Zealand entered into a
bilateral agreement covering both agricultural and industrial
products. New Zealand offered tariff concessions on rice and
certain fresh fruits (permitting duty-free entry), bacon, ham,
sausage, cereal flours, turkey, canned meats and tobacco. The
U.S. offered concessions on lamb meat, milk, cream, butter,
cheddar cheeses, beef and veal, lamb and mutton (admitted
duty-free), certain fresh cherries and rasberries. New
Zealand also agreed to grant exemption from import licenses
for prepared or preserved turkey and from new licenses for

---

[218] Id. at 572. Such consultative provisions appeared in the
     Agreement with Canada, but in less explicit terms. It did not
     appear, for example, in the agreements with Finland, Iceland
     and Portugal.
[219] Id. at 579

almonds and rice in retail packs. Allocations were also
increased for fish fillets, crustaceans, specialty flowers,
soya bean meal and flour, and canned and preserved meats and
nuts. The U.S. agreed to a minimum global quota for fresh,
chilled or frozen beef, veal, mutton (excluding lamb) and goat
meat of 1.2 billion pounds. This will be increased to 1.3
billion pounds when voluntary restraint agreements are in
effect or when the base quota under the U..S meat import law
is above this level.   The U.S. agreed to bind New Zealand
cheese quotas at 17,422 metric tons and to provide New Zealand
a "nominal" quota for chocolate crumb, to allow New Zealand to
participate in prospective shortfalls in the utilization of
quotas of other countries.[220]

D.   Changes in U.S. Law Required for Implementing Various Agricultural Agreements

1.   Cheese

U.S. quotas on cheese totalled 111,000 metric tons, an
increase of only 15,000 metric tons over the 1978 level. The
main change was to place all cheeses under quota except
certain types less competitive with domestic cheeses (e.g.,
sheep and goat's milk cheeses).   This increased the total
amount of cheeses covered by quotas from approximately 50% to
85%.[221] Secondly, the U.S. agreed to permit some level of
subsidization of cheese exports without the automatic imposition of countervailing duties, in exchange for a commitment
not to undercut U.S. wholesale prices.

To implement these agreements, the President had to
proclaim these quotas under Section 22 of the Agricultural
Adjustment Act of 1933. (7 U.S.C. § 624).[222] It was provided
that the 111,000 level could not be increased except through
the normal procedures of the Agricultural Adjustment Act,
requiring hearings, findings and recommendations by the
International Trade Commission unless the Secretary of
Agriculture finds extraordinary circumstances.[223] U.S. legislation, as discussed previously, also authorized the imposition
of fees on subsidized cheese exports found to be sold below
the wholesale U.S. prices or the prohibition of the entry of
such cheeses.   Such action can be taken by the President after
he receives findings from the Secretary of Agriculture.[224] A
list of prohibited subsidies is published each year.[225] The

---

[220] Id. at 447.
[221] Statement of Administrative Action, supra note 63, at 511.
[222] Trade Agreements Act of 1979 § 701(a), 19 U.S.C. § 1202.
[223] Id. at § 701(b).
[224] Id. at § 702(b).
[225] Id. at § 702(a).

Secretary must make his findings within thirty days from the date of receipt of a complaint[226] and publish his findings within five days.[227] Foreign governments are then notified and if within fifteen days they do not agree to eliminate the subsidy or increase the U.S. wholesale price to an acceptable level, then the Secretary of Agriculture shall recommend to the President the imposition of a fee or the prohibition of entry.[228] The U.S. President must then act within seven days.[229]

What is significant about these provisions is that, unlike the U.S. countervailing duty law, administrative action is extremely quick. Moreover, unlike the countervailing duty law, which only permits the imposition of additional duties, the provisions in Title VII permit the complete prohibition of entry, a remedy that appears in only a few other U.S. laws.[230] Thus, a powerful and effective substitute to the counter-vailing duty law was established for dealing with subsidized cheese exports. At the same time, the countervailing duty law was made specifically inapplicable to cheese products covered by bilateral agreements with price undercutting commitments. This was hardly a boon to the cheese exporting countries which generally would have been entitled to an injury determination prior to the imposition of a countervailing duty, which they did not receive under Title VII.[231]

The Department of Agriculture has issued regulations for issuing import licenses and quota allocations,[232] and for implementing the complaint procedure where price undercuttings are alleged.[233]

2.   Meat

The Agreement reached by the U.S. regarding meat pro-ducts, required amendment to the Meat Import Law of 1964. The amendments contained in § 704 of the Trade Agreements Act of 1979 established a 1.2 billion pound minimum quota level for all countries on an MFN basis.[234] Also, certain new tariff classifications were created for several categories of meat products. U.S. meat imports will still be subject to volun-tary restraint agreements negotiated pursuant to § 204 of the Agricultural Adjustment Act of 1956.

---

226 Id. at § 702(b)(2).
227 Id. at § 702(c).
228 Id. at § 702(c)(3).
229 Id. at § 702(d).
230 See for example, Section 337 of the Tariff Act of 1930, 19 U.S.C. § 1337.
231 See discussion of Code on Subsidies, supra notes 28-59 and accompanying text.
232 7 C.F.R. §§ 6.20-6.32.
233 7 C.F.R. § 6.40.
234 Trade Agreements Act of 1979 § 704(b).

3.   Chocolate Crumb

The U.S. agreed to increase quotas for chocolate crumb. A special quota was established for Australia and New Zealand, neither of which had allocations at that time.[235]

4.   Alcoholic Beverages

Although not strictly an agricultural product, alcoholic beverages were an important item in the Multilateral Trade Negotiations. Most of the emphasis was on the U.S. system of assessing excise taxes and customs duties. Under this system, known as the "wine gallon method", the U.S. assessed taxes and duties on imported spirits on all bottles containing less than one gallon, as if they were 100 proof. In most cases, proofs were considerably less, so the imported products paid an artificially high duty and excise tax. Domestic producers generally only paid excise tax on the "proof gallon" method, based on actual proofage, since they could control the time the assessment was made to ensure that the spirits were in containers holding more than one gallon. This was a classic non-tariff barrier which, although neutral on its face, clearly was utilized to give preference to the domestic producers. This was a particular area of concern among the major exporters of alcoholic beverages to the U.S., Canada and the EEC.

The U.S. agreed to give up the wine gallon method of assessment, and in return received various concessions from other countries. For example, the EEC, in an exchange of letters, agreed to "do everything within is competence to obtain the elimination of those measures in the member states which result in discrimination against U.S. distilled spirits".[236] Finland agreed that its state alcohol monopoly would continue to stock U.S. brands of bourbon and reduce the customs duty, and stock two additional whiskies and one additional wine from the U.S.[237] The abolition of the wine gallon method was accompanied by numerous changes in the laws dealing with distilled spirits and will not be discussed here in detail. The full text can be found in Title VII of the Trade Agreements Act of 1979. The most significant provisions relating to tariff treatment are set out in Sections 851 to 856, which repeal the wine gallon method of assessment.

---

[235] Trade Agreements Act of 1979 § 703, 19 U.S.C. § 1202.
[236] Message from the President, supra note 204, at 429.
[237] See letter dated April 12, 1979 from Permanent Mission of Finland in Geneva to the Head of the U.S. Delegation.

However, the new rates proposed are equivalent to both the duty and excise tax, thus denying imports the benefit of any duty reduction from the elimination of the wine gallon method.[238] However, Section 855 allows the President to proclaim a lower rate whenever he "determines that adequate reciprocal concessions have been received therefor under a trade agreement".[239]

Thus, for those countries not granting reciprocal revisions to the United States, the new tariffs were increased so as to be equal to the revenue protection provided under the old wine gallon method.[240] Among the countries that originally offered inadequate compensation necessitating a duty increase were Jamaica, Peru, Israel, Mexico, Spain, and Trinidad and Tobago. Implementation of the changes discussed above required considerable changes in U.S. laws. Tax changes were made in the "Distilled Spirits Tax Revision Act of 1979" which was incorporated as subtitle A of Title VIII of the Trade Agreements Act of 1979. Subtitle B of Title VIII of the Trade Agreements Act implemented the tariff changes.

THE GROUP FRAMEWORK AGREEMENT

The Group Framework Agreement did not receive as much publicity as the various substantive codes. Nevertheless, it was one of the most significant accomplishments of the MTN and dealt with many important issues which did not fit under one of the other negotiating topics. One of the principal motivations behind the Group Framework was the desire of the LDCs to institutionalize the concept of differential treatment for them. However, the developed nations also saw the need for a framework agreement to deal with many of the problems that increasingly plagued trade relations in the 1970's, such as export controls and import surcharges for Balance of Payments purposes.

Another important area of concern was the effectiveness (or lack of effectiveness) of the GATT dispute settlement mechanisms. The U.S. generally favored greater GATT enforcement powers, while other countries, particularly LDCs which sometimes deviated from GATT rules, preferred a less effective enforcement role for the GATT.[241]

---

[238] Trade Agreements Act of 1979 at § 852, 19 U.S.C. § 1202; Statement of Administrative Action, supra note 63, at 530.
[239] Trade Agreements Act of 1979 at § 855(a), 19 U.S.C. § 1202.
[240] MTN Studies 6, pt. 4, supra note 30, at 238.
[241] Id. at 144-45. The text of the Group Framework Agreement appears in Doc. MTN FR/W/20 Rev.2, and is set out in the Appendix.

A.   Differential and More Favorable Treatment,
      Reciprocity And Fuller Participation of
      Developing Countries   (Points 1 and 4)

The issue of differential treatment for developing
countries was of major concern to the LDCs and one of their
prime goals in the Tokyo Round. Indeed, the Tokyo Declaration
itself, which led to the MTN, clearly stated that the developing countries do not expect reciprocity for commitments
made by them in the negotiations to reduce or remove tariff
and trade barriers to the LDCs. The LDCs were not expected to
make contributions "...inconsistent with their individual
development, financial and trade needs...", and it was recognized that special and more favorable treatment to the LDCs
would be given where "feasible and appropriate".[242]
The broad objectives set out in the Tokyo Declaration
were refined and implemented in points 1 and 4 of the Group
Framework Agreement. The first paragraph of this section
(sometimes referred to as the Enabling Clause) provides the
legal basis for differential treatment by recognizing that
special treatment to the LDCs can be given notwithstanding the
non-discrimination provisions in Article I of the GATT.[243]
However, despite this broad legal basis for discriminatory
treatment, the actual circumstances in which such discrimination is permitted is limited to four specific categories:

(1)   Preferential tariff treatment (duty-free entry)
       provided by the Generalized System of Pre-
       ferences (GSP).[244]

(2)   More favorable treatment afforded in the
       numerous   GATT   codes   on   non-tariff
       barriers.

(3)   Regional or global arrangements among LDCs to
       reduce or eliminate tariffs and NTBs among
       themselves.

(4)   Special treatment for the least developed among
       the developing countries in the context of any
       general or specific measures favoring developed
       countries.[245]

It was noted that these four types of special treatment
for LDCs were the only ones generally authorized by the Group

---

[242] See Tokyo Declaration, GATT Doc. MTN (73)(1), para. 5, the
text of which is set out in the Appendix.

[243] Group Framework Agreement, supra note 241, at para. 1.

[244] Many developed countries have established GSP plans, including
the U.S. For a recent discussion of the U.S. program, see
Glick, The Generalized System of Preferences - Yesterday,
Today and Tomorrow, 30 Fed. B. New & J. 284 (May 1983). This
proviso formally recognizes GSP and replaces the GATT waiver
of June 25, 1971.

[245] Group Framework Agreement, supra note 241, at para 2.

Framework Agreement, but that contracting parties could
consider other proposals for differential and more favorable
treatment on an ad hoc basis.[246]

In addition to setting out the circumstances where
differential and preferential treatment may be legitimately
granted to the LDCs, this section also sets out three limitations on use of preferential treatment. It is provided that
such treatment shall:

> (1) Be designed to facilitate and promote the trade
>   of LDCs and not to raise barriers to the trade
>   of other countries;
> (2) Shall not constitute an impediment to the
>   reduction or elimination of tariffs and other
>   restrictions to trade on an MFN basis; and
> (3) If necessary, be modified to "respond posi-
>   tively to the development, financial and trade
>   needs of LDCs".[247]

This last provision also provides part of the basis for
the concept of graduation, whereby preferential benefits
accorded to LDCs can be withdrawn or modified as those LDCs
develop to the point where they "graduate" from the need for
special assistance. This is made more specific in Paragraph
7, to be discussed infra.

Paragraph 4 of this section provides that before a party
takes any action to introduce, modify or withdraw an arrange
ment under this section, it must notify the other contracting
parties and provide them with all the information they "may
deem appropriate" to this action. In addition, parties must
provide "adequate opportunity" for prompt consultations with
other parties as to "any difficulty or matter that may arise".
While the aims of this paragraph are beneficial, the use of
such terms as "may deem appropriate" and "adequate opportunity" creates sufficient ambiguity that could render the
implementation of these provisions less than completely
effective.[248]

Paragraph 5 of this section reiterates and elaborates
upon the language contained in Paragraph 5 of the Tokyo
Declaration. It sets out that the developed countries do not
expect reciprocity for commitments made by them in trade
negotiations with the LDCs, and the developed countries agree
not to seek concessions that are inconsistent with the
development, financial and trade needs of the LDCs.[249] Paragraph
6 further expands on this concept by requiring the developed

---

246 Id. at n.**
247 Id. at para. 3.
248 Id. at para 4.
249 Id. at para. 5. This paragraph essentially reaffirms Para-
     graph 8 of Article XXXVI of the GATT. See also Interpretive
     Note to Article XXXVI, GATT Annex I, Ad Article XXXVI. It is
     unclear whether it actually adds anything new.

countries to "exercise the utmost restraint" in seeking concessions from the LDCs and reiterates the standard set out in Paragraph 5 that the LDCs shall not be expected to make concessions or contributions that are inconsistent with their particular problems and situations.

Paragraph 7 sets out in detail the graduation concept referred to in Paragraph 3(c). This was a provision strongly urged by the United States.[250] The provision, while less than explicit, indicates that the LDCs "expect" that their capacity to make contributions or negotiated concessions would improve with the "progressive development of their economies and improvement of their trade situation", and they "would accordingly expect" to participate more fully in the framework of rights and obligations under the GATT.[251] This "graduation" clause was extremely important to the developed countries that conditioned their support for the enabling clause "on a commitment by developing countries to assume fuller GATT obligations in line with their development progress and recognition that benefits of special treatment would be phased out as that economic progress is made".[252]

Most recently the U.S. has implemented the graduation policy in connection with its administration of the GSP Program in the U.S. Starting with a recommendation in the President's five year report on the GSP program, the Office of U.S. Special Trade Representative has implemented a policy of removing products from GSP on a selective, non-MFN basis for those countries that have reached a sufficient level of development to become competitive in that product.[253]

Paragraph 9 does little more than again restate the principles set out in Paragraphs 5 and 6. Paragraph 9 requires the parties to collaborate in arrangements for review of the operation of the provisions of this section.

B.   Draft Declaration on Trade Measures Taken for
      Balance-of-Payment Purposes (Point 2A)

This provision is designed to permit various trade measures for limited balance-of-payments purposes. It expands upon provisions already in the GATT permitting quantitative restrictions (quotas) for balance-of-payments purposes in certain circumstances. The question of utilization of quanti-

---

250 See MTN Studies 6, pt. 4, supra note 30, at 165.
251 Group Framework Agreement, supra note 241, at para. 7.
252 Executive Office of the President, Office of Special Trade Representative, Framework, (GATT Reform) Release No. G-6 (May 2, 1976).
253 For a complete discussion of how graduation is being implemented in the U.S. GSP program and plans for the future, see Glick, supra note 244.

tative restrictions under the GATT is a complex one. Article
XI contains a general prohibition on quantitative restric-
tions, Article XII contains certain general exceptions, while
Article XVIII:B provides special rules for developing nations.
Article XII permits quantitative restrictions under the
following conditions:

>   (1)   In order to safeguard a country's extended
>   financial position and balance-of-payments;
>   (2)   But only to the extent necessary:
>   (a) to forestall the imminent threat of, or to
>   stop, a serious decline in its monetary re-
>   serves; or
>   (b) in the case of a contracting party with
>   very low monetary reserves, to achieve a
>   reasonable rate of increase in its reserves.[254]

Article XVIII applies similar conditions to LDCs, except
that the requirement for an "imminent" threat is deleted.
When quantitative restrictions are imposed under the GATT,
they must be implemented on an MFN basis.[255] Two exceptions to
this are permitted: first, when the IMF approves such
restrictions as being equivalent to exchange controls; and
second, if the GATT determines that only a small portion of
trade is affected and the benefits of the quantitative
restrictions "substantially outweigh" any injury.[256] Certain
mandatory consultations are also required. While the GATT
permitted quantitative restrictions and provided rules and
regulations to restrict and regulate those restrictions, there
was no coverage of other devices used to accomplish similar
results, such as import surcharges. Surcharges had generally
not been permitted under the GATT since they are inconsistent
with the binding of duty rates.[257]The importance of dealing
with this issue became increasingly important after the United
States, invoking the Trading with the Enemy Act, imposed a 10%
import surcharge in 1971. Other countries had also used
similar measures, which, while technically illegal under the
GATT, were on occasion given waivers. This led to the desire
by a number of countries to formalize and legalize non-
quantitative restriction measures to deal with balance-of-
payments problems.

The first part of Point 2A is the Preamble that states
general principles governing use of trade measures for
balance-of-payments purposes. The Preamble notes that the
contracting parties are "convinced" that restrictive trade
measures are, in general, an inefficient means to maintain or
restore balance-of-payments equilibrium. Nevertheless, it is
noted that these measures are being used, including methods

---

254 See GATT, art. XII.
255 See GATT, art. XIII.
256 See GATT, art. XIV.
257 See GATT, art. II.

other than quantitative restrictions, and that they should be avoided by the developed countries "to the maximum extent possible". One important portion of the Preamble is the reaffirmation that restrictive import measures taken for balance-of-payments purposes should not be used for the purpose of protecting one particular industry or sector.

The operative provisions of Point 2A provide certain conditions to the use of restrictive import measures in addition to those provided under existing GATT provisions. These restrictions are as follows:

> (1) In applying restrictive import measures, parties must comply with GATT rules and "give preference" to restrictive measures that have "the least disruptive effect on trade". LDCs would also look at their particular developmental problems in deciding what measures to impose;
>
> (2) Parties should avoid the simultaneous application of more than one type of restrictive measure; and
>
> (3) "Whenever practicable", the parties shall publicly announce a time schedule for the removal of the measures.[258]

It is further provided that developed countries, in implementing restrictive import measures permitted under this section, take into account the "export interests" of the LDCs and may even exempt certain products of the LDCs from any surcharge or other measure.[259] This is another departure from the general rule of non-discrimination in the implementation of restrictive measures and creates yet another exception to GATT Article XIII. Its inclusion is no doubt a recognition of the increasing pressures applied by the LDCs, particularly in the context of negotiating the Group Framework Agreement.

Point 2A also imposes a requirement upon the parties to notify the GATT of all actions taken to introduce or increase restrictive import measures taken for balance-of-payments purposes by themselves or other parties.[260] Any such restric-

---

[258]Group Framework Agreement, supra note 241, at Point 2A, para. 1. It is further provided that these provisions are not intended to modify the substantive provisions of the GATT. If this is the case, then it has been suggested that the imposition of surcharges could contravene GATT Article II. This limitation, proposed by those that were opposed to any legalization of surcharges and similar measures compromises the effectiveness of this entire portion of the Agreement. See MTN Studies 6, pt. 4, supra note 30, at 181.

[259] Group Framework Agreement, supra note 241, at Point 2A, para. 2.

[260] Id. at para. 3. Such notification is not required prior to the introduction or increase of the measures.

tive import measures taken for balance-of-payments purposes
are subject to consultations under the auspices of the GATT
Committee on Balance-of-Payments Restrictions.[261] This Committee must contain a balanced cross-section of members and
precise rules are set out for the consultation procedures.
Many of these rules simply incorporate existing GATT procedures.

These procedures are fairly elaborate and provide for a
more quasi-judicial type of proceeding than perhaps some of
the parties may have desired. For example, the GATT Secretariat plays an important role and prepares a factual background
paper which it submits to the Committee, after the consulting
contracting party has had an opportunity to review it.[262] The
Committee, in turn, must present a quasi-legal report to the
Council that essentially must include findings of fact,
conclusions of law and the rationale therefore. This tended
to make these decisions less arbitrary and political, and to
encourage more recognition of these consultations as having a
precedential value, which, while falling short of stare
decisis, does lend more predictability to these determinations.[263] Further evidence of the quasi-legal role of the
Committee is that it is also charged with determining whether
a restrictive import measure is inconsistent with the provisions of GATT Article XII, XVIII:B or Point 2A of the
Agreement.[264]

C.   Safeguard Action for
      Development Purposes (Point 2B)

As will be discussed infra, safeguard actions, or actions
taken to alleviate increased imports causing injury, were a
topic of much discussion at the MTN, but one which in general
must be listed among the MTN failures. In fact, to this date,
there has been a failure to negotiate a GATT safeguard code.
Nevertheless, at least for purposes of the Group Framework
Agreement, at least a limited accord was reached on the use of
safeguard measures for developmental purposes. Existing GATT
Article XVIII already permitted developing nations to institute restrictive trade measures for the purposes of aiding the
establishment of certain industries considered vital. However,
such actions are subject to consultations and require GATT
approval. The purpose of Point 2B was to liberalize these
procedures for the benefit of the LDCs.

Point 2B recognizes that the LDCs may need to go beyond
taking measures for the establishment of particular indus-

---

[261]Id. at para. 4.
[262]Id. at para. 7.
[263]Id. at para. 11.
[264]Id. at para. 13.

tries, as set out in Article XVIII of the GATT, and may need to take import action to further "development of new or the modification or extension of existing production structures".[265] The rights of LDCs to take action under Sections A and C of Article XVIII are reiterated, but with "additional flexibility provided". The LDCs are permitted, from the provisions of Section A and Paragraphs 14, 15, 17 and 18 of Section C, "to the extent necessary for introducing the measures contemplated on a provisional basis immediately after notification".[266] Both the existing procedures under Sections A and C require prior GATT approval before the LDC can act. In Section A, the LDC can raise tariffs for the purpose of promoting the establishment of a particular industry "with a view to raising the general standard of living of its people".[267] However, this cannot be done unless the other contracting parties authorize such an increase.

Under Section C, an LDC may use measures necessary to promote a particular industry, but only after finding that governmental assistance is necessary and that there are no practicable alternatives consistent with the GATT. The LDC, prior to taking action, must notify the GATT and delay any action for thirty to ninety days. Consultations may be required, particularly where the proposed action has the effect of reducing a previous concession. If consultations are unsuccessful, affected parties may retaliate by suspending substantially equivalent concessions.[268] Point 2B recognizes that there may be unusual circumstances where an LDC might have difficulties in delaying implementation of measures permitted under Sections A and C of Article XVIII if it is required to comply with the notice/consultation/approval provisions contained therein, and permits deviation from these requirements, but only to the extent necessary to introduce measures contemplated on a provisional basis. Notification is still required, but the measures can be implemented immediately.[269]

Moreover, it is at least inferred that consultations may still be required after implementation of the measures.[270] LDCs are also required to follow the non-discrimination provisions in Article XVIII.

---

[265] Group Framework Agreement, supra note 241, at Point 2A, para. 1.

[266] Id. at para. 2.

[267] GATT, art. XVIII:7(a).

[268] GATT, art. XVIII:2.

[269] Group Framework Agreement, supra note 241, at Point 2B, para. 2.

[270] MTN Studies 6, pt. 4, supra note 30, at 191.

D. Draft Understanding Regarding Notification,
    Consultation, Dispute Settlement and
    Surveillance (Point 3)

The purpose of Point 3 is to clarify procedures for GATT consultation and enforcement procedures. Much of Point 3 is a reaffirmation of existing principles and exhortations to take voluntary actions to improve upon existing procedures. For example, contracting parties "should endeavor" to give notice in advance of implementing measures[271]and to "undertake" to respond to requests for consultations promptly and to conclude consultations expeditiously.[272]

As to resolution of disputes, certain improvements are set out relating to establishment of panels to assist in dispute settlement, choice of panel members, opportunity to be heard by such panels, and procedural operations of panels. No attempt was made to introduce structural changes in the existing GATT dispute settlement mechanisms.[273] At least some commentators believe that the GATT dispute settlement mechanisms have been ineffective due to a number of factors. These include the lack of a clear definition of the concept of "nullification and impairment" contained in Article XXIII, lack of personnel and resources, ineffective operation of GATT panels, lack of definition of the types of questions for which dispute settlement should be used, and other reasons.[274] To a large extent, these problems were not resolved by the MTN, although specific and sometimes more effective dispute settlement procedures were adopted as part of the individual MTN Codes.

Moreover, the U.S. negotiators themselves indicated that Point 3B contained "perhaps the most significant agreement in the framework package for the United States..."[275] The U.S. believed that "this agreement contains several important features which should improve our ability to manage trade disputes in the GATT".[276] Among the benefits cited were strengthening of notification obligations, codification of the traditional GATT practice of according review by an impartial panel and other procedural provisions to prevent abuse of process.[277]

Finally, Point 3 contains certain provisions relating to surveillance of developments in world trading and technical assistance for LDCs to assist them in compliance with the

[271]Group Framework Agreement, supra note 241, at Point 3, p.1.
[272] Id. at 2.
[273]MTN Studies 6, pt. 4, supra note 30, at 212.
[274]Id. at 211-12.
[275]Twenty-fourth Annual Report, supra note 10, at 47.
[276] Id.
[277] Id.

agreement.[278] Also appended to the Agreement is an annex containing the "agreed description of the customary practice of the GATT in the field of dispute settlement".

E.   Understanding Regarding Export Restrictions and Charges (Point 5)

The final section of the Group Framework Agreement dealt with the area of export restrictions and charges. The objective of this section was to bring export measures under a discipline comparable to those affecting imports.[279] However, Point 5 basically does little more than restate "existing GATT provisions relating to export restrictions and charges" that are contained in an attached annex and to agree to future reassessment of these provisions. This was far less than the United States had sought.[280] In fact, one of the U.S. mandates in the Trade Act of 1974 that provided negotiating authority was for the President to negotiate on the question of export controls.[281] In analyzing the existing GATT provisions on export restrictions, U.S. analysts observed that the GATT provisions have been criticized because of the large number of exceptions that render prohibitions meaningless, and because of the lack of effective dispute settlement mechanisms that make enforcement impossible.[282]

THE ANTIDUMPING CODE AMENDMENTS – THE AGREEMENT ON IMPLEMENTATION OF ARTICLE VI OF THE GATT

The proces-verbal issued on April 12, 1979, listed two separate texts of amendments to the antidumping code, which had originally been negotiated as part of the Kennedy Round.[283] One of these texts was submitted by the LDCs and dealt with a question of particular importance to them, the determination of price for products exported by LDCs for purposes of calculating whether sales at less than fair value are taking place. Certain understandings were reached during the negotiations that enabled the LDCs to withdraw their text and to allow for one text to be signed by the parties.[284] These understandings included a recognition that special economic conditions in the

---

[278]Group Framework Agreement, supra note 241, at Point 3, p.7.
[279]Framework, supra note 252, at 3.
[280]See generally MTN Studies 6, pt. 4, supra note 30, at 224.
[281]Trade Act of 1974 § 121(a)(7).
[282]MTN Studies 6, pt. 4, supra note 30, at 226.
[283]See MTN/NTM/W/232 Add.1/Rev.1, Add.2 and Corr.1 and MTN/NTM/ W/232, Add.1/Rev.1, Add.2 and Corr. 1 as amended by MTN/NTM/ W/241/Rev.1.
[284]See GATT, Supplementary Report, supra note 1, at 11.

LDCs might affect home market prices and that export prices might be below home market prices.

Normally a good indication of dumping is when the export price to the country bringing the dumping action is less than the price in the home market. This is _prima facie_ evidence of less than fair value sales. Certain adjustments are permitted to the prices to permit various costs, such as advertising, shipping, etc. and "circumstances of sale", to be taken into consideration, in determining whether warranties are included in both sales or if a difference in quantities would justify the price differential. The LDCs argued that when special economic conditions in their home market affect prices in the domestic market, then the home market price is not always a valid indication of dumping. The LDCs favored a comparison of the export price of the product in one market (i.e., the country of investigation) to export prices in third markets, or with the cost of production plus certain allowances for costs and profits.[285] The LDCs were also permitted on a case-by-case basis, to receive certain limited exceptions from the Code in recognition that there might be difficulty in adopting their legislation consistent with the Code.

One of the main functions of the Code was to conform the previously negotiated Antidumping Code with the newly nego-tiated Code on Subsidies.[286] This resulted in numerous substan-tive changes in the Antidumping Code and required extensive legislative changes in many countries including the U.S. A complete discussion of antidumping is beyond the scope of this book. Moreover, many of the procedural changes are identical to those discussed in connection with the Subsidies Code, _supra_. Among the more significant changes were those re-quiring greater transparency or openness in the conduct of antidumping investigations, the placing of a one year time limit on investigations and a detailed description of how material injury to a domestic industry should be determined.[287] Dumping has been a continual source of friction and concern in international trade, particularly due to what has been perceived by other countries as the vigorous enforcement by the U.S.

Antidumping had been regulated by the GATT from its inception. Article VI of the GATT prohibited dumping if it causes or threatens to cause material injury to an established industry or materially retards the establishment of a domestic industry.[288] The U.S., however, was not obligated to follow the provisions of Article VI since it was inconsistent with existing U.S. law, and under the "Grandfather Clause", protec-

285 Id.
286 Twenty-fourth Annual Report of the President, _supra_ note 10, at 42.
287 Id.
288 GATT, art. VI.

tion of the Protocol of Provisional Application,[289] the U.S. was able to apply a different and less demanding injury test which permitted the finding of injury in almost any case where there was minimal injury. In 1967, the Antidumping Code was signed by eighteen countries, including the United States. However, there was serious opposition to the Code in the U.S. Congress, which was concerned that it diluted the effectiveness of the U.S. antidumping law, particularly relating to the concept of material injury. Congressional approval was finally obtained, but only with the specific proviso that the U.S. Antidumping Act of 1921 was to have supremacy over the Code Provisions. In addition, any conflicts between the two were to be resolved in favor of the U.S. law and the U.S. would take into account the provisions of the Code "only insofar as they are consistent with the Antidumping Act, 1981" as applied by the administering agency.[290]

The 1979 Code, which was adopted by the U.S. and implemented in the Trade Agreements Act of 1979, provides definitions and explanations of some of the key terms used in antidumping investigations, such as injury and industry. For example, Article 3 provides that a determination of injury shall be based on positive evidence and involve an objective analysis of both the volume of the dumped imports and their effect on prices in the domestic market for like products and the consequent impact of these imports on domestic producers of such products.[291]

In looking at the volume of imports, the investigating authorities are to consider whether "there has been a significant increase in dumped imports, either in absolute terms or relative to production or consumption in the importing country".[292] With regard to prices, they shall consider "whether there has been a significant price undercutting by the dumped imports as compared with the price of a like product of the importing country, or whether the effect of such imports is otherwise to depress prices to a significant degree or prevent price increases, which otherwise would have occurred, to a significant degree".[293]

One important change in the Antidumping Code of 1979 was the elimination of the requirement in the 1967 Code that the dumped imports be demonstrably the principal cause of injury

---

[289] See Protocol of Provisional Application of the General Agreement on Tariffs and Trade, 55 U.N.T.S. 308, para. 1(b) (Oct. 30, 1947).

[290] See Act of Oct. 24, 1968, Pub.L.No. 90-634, § 201(a), 82 Stat.1347 (1968).

[291] Antidumping Code, art. 3, para. 1.

[292] Id. at art. 3, para. 2.

[293] Id.

to the domestic industry.[294] However, injury must still be
material.[295] Adoption of the 1979 Code by the U.S. meant that
the U.S., for the first time, had to change its domestic laws
to require material injury.[296]

Industry is defined in Article 4,[297] including special
circumstances involving related producers. Also, conditions
are set out where there may be an industry consisting of a
geographical submarket. In such cases, injury may be found to
exist "even when a major portion of the total domestic
industry is not injured", provided that the dumped products
are concentrated in an isolated market and are causing injury
to producers of "all or almost all" of the production within
the submarket.[298] In such cases, where a submarket is used as
the industry, dumping duties can only be assessed on production consigned for final consumption in that submarket, unless
the constitutional laws of the importing country do not permit
the imposition of levies in such a manner. In such cases, the
dumping duty may be levied on all importers of the product if
the exporters are given the opportunity to cease exporting at
dumped prices to the areas concerned, and adequate assurances
of this are not received and such duties cannot be levied on
specific producers who supply the areas in question. As a
result of the Code provisions on industry, the U.S. law for
the first time contained a definition of injury. This definition is substantially similar to the Code provision.[299]

The other significant changes brought about by the 1979
Antidumping Code deal with administrative matters such as time
periods and procedures for investigations. These largely
parallel those of the Subsidies Code, supra. For example, the
Code provides for simultaneous consideration and investigation
of dumping and injury and the conclusion of investigations in
one year.[300]

---

294 Agreement on Implementation of Article VI of the General
   Agreement on Tariffs and Trade, 19 U.S.T. 4348, art. 3(a)
   (June 30, 1967).
295 Antidumping Code, art. 3 n.2 defines injury to mean, "material injury to a domestic industry or material retardation of
   the establishment of such an industry..."
296 Trade Agreements Act of 1979 § 101, Amending the Tariff Act
   of 1930 § 717(7)(A) defines the term "material injury" as
   "harm which is not inconsequential, immaterial or unimpor-
   tant".
297 Antidumping Code, art. 4, para. 1.
298 Domestic industry is defined in the Code as referring to
   "the domestic producers as a whole of the life products or
   to those of them whose collective output of the products
   constitutes a major proportion of the total domestic production of those products".
299 See Trade Agreements Act of 1979 § 101, amending the Tariff Act of 1930 § 771 (4)(A).
300 Antidumping Code, art. 5, paras. 3, 5.

Chapter 4

THE FAILURES OF MTN – THE CODES THAT ALMOST WERE

While the word "failure" of course denotes certain
subjective judgmental factors, it is not used herein with the
intention of diminishing the many accomplishments of the MTN.
However, certain areas of negotiation, whether due to complexity, the late stage at which they were tabled, or controversial subject matters, did not bear fruit. Most of these
areas are still under discussion, and agreement might still
emerge in the future. The two significant areas where no
substantive agreements were reached were Safeguards and
Commercial Counterfeiting, each of which shall be discussed
below.

PROPOSED SAFEGUARDS CODE

The Tokyo Declaration included a call to include an
"examination of the adequacy of the multilateral safeguard
system..."[1] Safeguard measures are designed to allow for
sanctioned forms of trade restrictions where they are needed
to offset harm resulting from increased import penetration,
often caused by tariff concessions.

Some of the history of the negotiations is briefly
discussed in Chapter 2, Section F. The present status of the
Safeguard negotiations will be discussed in the succeeding
chapter on post-MTN activities. The discussion herein will
focus on the provisions of the draft Safeguard text to provide
background for the concepts that were discussed and considered, albeit never adopted.

Moreover, additional details about the negotiation
process and the reasons behind the failure to reach agreement
will be provided. This is useful not only as a tool to
learning why the Safeguards Agreement was not adopted, but
also as a prologue to the problems faced in the present and

---

[1] Tokyo Declaration, GATT Doc. MIN (73)(1), para. 3(d).

future in attempting to successfully negotiate a code on safeguards.

A.   Summary and Analysis of the Draft Safeguards Code

On June 22, 1978, a Draft Integrated Text on Safeguards was circulated at the request of certain developed countries.[2] Although this draft was later amended by the Nordic countries,[3] it will be the principal focus of our discussion. The draft was circulated with the disclaimer that it was an "informal working paper drafted with a view to facilitating further consideration of this subject...   It does not commit any delegation to all or any part of the text, nor does it prejudice in any way the negotiating position of any delegation in any area of the MTN..."[4] This language was intended to allow the U.S. and the six other developing countries that proposed the draft to circulate it for discussion without binding their positions. The seven countries known informally as "Group of 7"[5] had met on a number of occasions to form this Integrated Text that resulted from individual texts that had been submitted by the U.S. EEC, Japan, Canada and the Nordic countries. This effort began on April 28, May 1, and May 2, 1978.   The early efforts at producing an integrated text resulted in a rather long, "bracket-laden" draft that preserved more of the individual position than integrated them, but this was recognized as a sin qua non for further refinement.

The draft code was characterized as an agreement to implement Article XIX of the GATT, rather than as an amendment to it.   GATT Article XIX authorizes a contracting party to suspend, modify or withdraw tariff concessions or impose import restrictions on a most-favored-nation basis if a product is being imported in such increased quantities so as to cause or threaten to cause serious injury to a domestic industry producing like or directly competitive products. A country must give advance notice of any actions taken pursuant to GATT Article XIX and consult with the other parties that would be affected before or immediately after taking such action. Parties affected by safeguard actions can request compensation in the form of a substantially equivalent concession, and if an agreement as to such concession is not reached, unilateral retaliation in the form of suspending a substantially equivalent concession is permitted. The purpose of the Code from the U.S. viewpoint was apparently twofold:

---

2   See MTN/56/W/39, a copy of which appears in the Appendix.
3   MTN/56/W/40.
4   Draft Integrated Text on Safeguards, at 1.
5   U.S., EEC, Japan, Canada, Switzerland, Australia, and the Nordic countries.

first, to examine the coverage of Article XIX; and second, to require that all countries taking Article XIX actions meet certain minimum procedural standards.[6] The U.S. had implemented Article XIX primarily in Section 201 of the Trade Act of 1974, known as the "Escape Clause".[7]   Only three countries, the U.S., Canada and Australia, have regularly undertaken safeguard investigations and these countries have accounted for over two-thirds of the Article XIX actions.[8]

The Draft Integrated Text consisted of General Provisions and nine chapters. The General Provisions essentially require that signatories agree not to take any safeguard actions except through and in conformance with Article XIX. The term "safeguard action" , however, is not defined in the Code, making this General Provision somewhat illusory.[9]   This requirement is also without prejudice to rights permitted under other GATT provisions, protocols and arrangements.[10] Some LDCs had sought to have the General Provisions contain language concerning adjustment assistance. While the U.S., EEC and Japan indicated they might consider some mention of the subject, they opposed any linkage between adjustment assistance and safeguard measures. Chapter 1 of the Draft Integrated Codes sets forth criteria for invocation of safeguard measures, and contains many important substantive provisions. However, as will be seen from an analysis, many of the key terms were bracketed alternatives, for which no consensus had been reached.

Chapter 1 provides that safeguard action can only follow a determination by domestic authorities that imports of a particular product are causing or threatening to cause serious injury to domestic producers of like or directly competitive products. Also included in brackets is a language that would require such injury only to [a[major][significant] part of all] domestic producers. Use of this bracketed language would, of course, make injury determinations more difficult,

---

6   U.S. International Trade Commission, Preliminary Draft Legal Analysis on Safeguards Code, GC-B-265, at i (Oct. 19, 1978) [hereinafter USITC Analysis]. This analysis was largely based on the June 22, 1978 Integrated Text, but contains some modifications from later drafts.

7   The escape clause was first implemented in the Trade Agreements Extension Act of 1951 § 7.

8   USITC Analysis, supra note 6, at 6.

9   The U.S. considered lack of definition of the terms "safeguard action" or "safeguard measure" as a weakness of the Code. Id. at G.n.1. The original U.S. draft code submitted in September, 1977, did contain a defintion. Id. at 15.

10   Draft Integrated Text on Safeguards, at 1. Footnote 1 to the General Provision notes that some delegations believe it will be necessary to identify these other protocols, arrangements and agreements prior to final acceptance of the text.

particularly if the standard to be adopted was that of a major part of all domestic producers. This was of particular concern to the U.S., which felt that the use of "major part" could limit the flexibility the U.S.I.T.C. has under its existing authority.[11] The U.S. statute speaks in terms of injury to a "substantial portion" of the domestic industry. This presumably is somewhere in between "significant" and " major", but even the use of "significant" would create contention and probably require a change in U.S. domestic law.

Chapter 1, Paragraph 1 continues on to require any such injury determination to be made only when "...imports have increased in such quantities, or in such relative quantities, and under such conditions demonstrably as to [account for the principal] cause [of] serious inujury sustained or demonstrably likely to be sustained by domestic producers."[12] Certain LDCs, notably India and Brazil, opposed the concept of injury due to relative increases and argued that only absolute increases be actionable. However, the U.S. and Canada pointed out that the interpretative history of Article XIX already recognized relative increases as a basis for safeguard relief.[13] Moreover, certain LDCs, such as India, supported the bracketed language requiring that the increased imports be the principal cause of serious injury. The U.S. position was that if the principal cause language was adopted, the Code would never be approved by the U.S. Congress.

There is no requirement that increased imports be the principal cause of serious injury, either in U.S. law or GATT Article XIX. U.S. law uses the term "substantial cause of serious injury".[14] This obviously requires a lower degree of causation[15] and is more beneficial to domestic producers. Chapter 1, Paragraph 1 further requires that the determination in all cases shall be made on the basis of positive findings of fact and not on mere conjecture or remote or hypothetical possibility. As to threat of injury, this must be proven to be "clearly imminent". These provisions would tend to require more rigid criteria and more formal proceedings before a safeguard action could be taken. This might be particularly true for countries other than the U.S. that do not already have formalized administrative procedures. The"clearly imminent" standard would tighten the formal criteria for relief in a way that does not presently exist either in GATT Article XIX or in U.S. law.[16]

Interestingly, the provisions on injury in the proposed code omitted any requirement that there must be a showing that

---

11 Draft Integrated Text on Safeguards, at 26-27.
12 Id. at ch. 1, para. 1.
13 This information is based on reports of discussions.
14 Trade Act of 1974 § 201(b)(1).
15 See id. at § 201(b)(4).
16 USITC Analysis, supra note 6, at 30.

imports increased as a result of concessions made in tariff negotiations. This requirement exists in Article XIX and existed in the U.S. law prior to the 1974 Trade Agreements Act. To many, the only rationale for safeguard actions is when a linkage can be made between increased imports and the results of tariff concessions. Otherwise, safeguard measures are little more than a license to increase duties whenever imports increase for any reason and injury results. Paragraphs 2, 3 and 4 of Chapter 1 are essentially footnotes to Paragraph 1, which expands on concepts contained therein.[17] Of particular interest is Paragraph 3, which is entirely in brackets. Subparagraph "a" of Paragraph 3 would provide that domestic producers, who are also importers would not be included in the domestic industry for purposes of a safeguards investigation. This provision, if adopted, would require a revision in U.S. law that allows a domestic producer who also imports, to be treated as part of the domestic industry, as to its domestic production.[18] Paragraph 4, also bracketed, expands on the concept of principal cause and was reportedly completely unacceptable to U.S. negotiators.[19]

Chapter 2 is labelled "Conditions" and describes the manner in which safeguard measures are to be imposed. One of the principal aims of this chapter was to impose some time limits on safeguard relief. This time period is left blank in the draft.[20] The EEC, during negotiations, proposed a short initial period of one to two years, with extensions subject to international review. The draft text presently simply requires that the safeguard action shall remain in force only so long as it is necessary in order to prevent or remedy serious injury to domestic producers. U.S. law currently permits a maximum of five years relief with one three-year extension.[21] Chapter 2 would also require the progressive liberalization of safeguard measures, during the period they are in effect, to encourage adjustment by domestic producers. Another proposed restriction in Chapter 2 would be to require that the level of imports under the safeguard relief not be lower than the level in a previous representative period, such as a twelve-month period terminating a certain number of months prior to the time the safeguard investigation was initiated. This would minimize the problems caused to affected exporters, importers and consumers.

Chapter 3 covers response to safeguard measures and contains two alternative texts. It deals with the important issue of retaliation. Alternative I would provide that if safeguard measures were imposed in accordance with the rules

---

17 Id. at 32.
18 See Trade Act of 1974 § 201(b)(3)(A).
19 USITC Analysis, supra note 6, at 35.
20 Draft Integrated Text on Safeguards, ch. 2, para. 1(b).
21 Trade Act of 1974 § 203(h).

of the proposed code, retaliation might not be needed. The controversy was whether retaliation should be optional or prohibited in such circumstances. Three bracketed alternatives are included whereby the affected signatory [shall] [should normally] or [may] refrain from retaliation. This is obviously a crucial issue. The LDCs generally favored retaining the right to retaliation, while recognizing that if it is agreed that a safeguard action complied with the Code, the exporting signatory would refrain from retaliation, but at a later date, if the safeguard action has had a serious effect on their interests, retaliation would be permitted. This provision, while at first reading appears to be a compromise provision, contains the requirement that there must be an agreement that the safeguard actions meet the Code criteria. This essentially gives the affected party a control over whether the new retaliation provision applies and makes this provision nugatory. The provisions on serious adverse effect have much the same effect, unless this decision were to be made by a multipartite body under the GATT.

    Chapter 4, entitled "Nature of Safeguard Action" begins with a note to the effect that this chapter does not reflect the views of all delegations which participated in drafting the other chapters and "substantially more discussion" will be required. This chapter deals with the highly controversial issue of selectivity, which was probably the largest single source of disagreement in the safeguards negotiations. Selectivity refers to the right to impose safeguard measures on a selective basis, that is, only against those countries that are the greatest cause of the injury. Historically, safeguard investigations involve imports from many countries and if the criteria for relief is found, then the duty increase is imposed on a most-favored-nation, non-discriminatory basis. Many have argued that this is unfair in that it tends to penalize nations that may have only been a minor contributor to market disruption. Safeguard investigations, some argue, should be treated like countervailing duty or antidumping investigations where individual countries may be singled out. Obviously, countries that might be the true targets of safeguard investigations have the most to fear about selectivity. This was reflected in the negotiating history. For example, in the first plurilateral safeguard meeting held, Japan announced that it could not discuss selectivity at the present stage of negotiations in a plurilateral setting. The Nordic countries responded by saying that safeguard negotiations could not proceed unless selectivity was discussed. Privately, however, the Japanese were willing to discuss selectivity, and even prepared their own text which was discussed with the U.S. and others. Private bilateral meetings between the U.S. and Japan occurred on numerous occasions to discuss selectivity. The Japanese position was that MFN should still remain the general prin-

ciple and be departed from only in well defined and exceptional circumstances. A country invoking selectivity must show
clearly unusual circumstances justifying selective action
according to the Japanese viewpoint.   In addition, the
Japanese felt that selectivity should only be applied with the
exporter's consent, except that it might be applied under
certain circumstances on a non-conferred basis.[22] There was
also substantial opposition to selectivity among the LDCs.
Their principal fear was that the developed countries would
use selectivity as a price related measure against the LDCs.
For example, Brazil was afraid that selectivity would encourage open protectionist moves against countries whose
prices were more competitive. Pakistan called selectivity a
"heresy" which, by definition, was unfair and inequitable.

India, Egypt and Korea believed that selectivity was
aimed at low cost goods and, therefore, penalized efficiency.
Mexico felt that if selectivity was adopted, it would be
better for it not to join the GATT. Many LDCs pointed to the
selectivity provisions in the multifibre arrangement as an
example of how selectivity has worked to the detriment of the
LDCs.   At the other end of the spectrum, such developed
contries as the Nordics argued that selectivity was an
indispensible element for them to participate in a safeguard
code, and that selectivity should be the general rule and MFN
applications utilized only in cases where a particular source
of injurious imports cannot be utilized. The EEC supported
selectivity and tried to respond to the objections of the LDCs
by noting that it was better to have open selective actions
subject to GATT surveillance than what exists now, where many
countries "get around" MFN. Switzerland seemed to favor the
Japanese approach with MFN as the general rule, but selectivity permitted in certain tightly controlled circumstances.

The U.S. position was that MFN should still be the basic
principal and the issue was whether to permit selectivity as
an exception to MTN and under what circumstances. The U.S.
stressed that selectivity was not the major issue to them,
but rather improvement in transparency and overall discipline
of the safeguards system. The U.S. has traditionally been
ambivalent about the selectivity issue. The U.S. has engaged
in selectivity in the form of orderly marketing agreements
negotiated bilaterally as an alternative to multilateral
safeguard relief taken under the "escape clause" on an MFN
basis. However, the cornerstone of this has always been the
consent or agreement of the exporter. While the U.S. seemed
to feel that the consensual approach was the best one, it
recognized the strong EEC position in favor of non-consensual
selectivity and acknowledged that if there were to be an
effective safeguards agreement which included the major

---

[22] The foregoing is based on accounts of a meeting between the
Japanese and U.S. safeguard negotiators.

countries and the EEC, that some form of selectivity was going to be required which went beyond the consensual approach. The U.S. believed that some compromise on selectivity was needed if a safeguards agreement were to be reached and felt that if no safeguards agreement were negotiated, the world situation would be likely to deteriorate due to domestic pressures for selective action.[23]

This substantial divergence of views was the reason that the Draft Integrated Text could not include a definitive provision on selectivity and was prefaced by the note disclaiming any consensus as to the proposed provisions contained therein. Nevertheless, to even reach the point where provisions on selectivity could be included at all in the draft text must be regarded as a significant accomplishment.

Chapter 4 provides that, in general, safeguard measures are to be applied on a "global" (MFN) basis. However, under certain delineated circumstances, safeguard measures could be applied on a selective basis.[24] These circumstances must be "unusual and exceptional" where it is clearly established that serious injury or a threat thereof exists and where such injury "is caused by sharp and substantial increases of imports from one or a limited number of countries and the effects of imports from other sources are regarded as being negligible".[25] An additional requirement, contained in brackets, is that such imports causing serious injury must be "clearly distinguished from other imports of a particular product".[26] Under such circumstances, an importing signatory may apply safeguard measures on a selective basis provided measures are applied equitably among the imports causing serious injury. However, bracketed language provides that selective action can be undertaken only "by agreement with the exporting signatory..."[27] A footnote indicates that consultations must proceed any action,[28] and Paragraph 3 describes the procedures for consultations.

Also contained in Chapter 4 as bracketed language is a provision linked with earlier bracketed language requiring exporter agreement prior to selective action. This provision, contained in Paragraph 4, provides that, in seeking agreements with exporting signatories to impose selective measures, the terms of such measures should normally be more liberal than those permitted in Chapter 2 and that compensation shall be offered.[29] The offering of more liberal terms as an inducement

---

23 The foregoing is based on accounts of a meeting on safeguards between the U.S., Pakistan, Hong Kong, Korea and Brazil.
24 Draft Integrated Text on Safeguards, ch. 4, para. 1.
25 Id. at para 2. Quoted language is in brackets.
26 Id.
27 Id.
28 Id. at 6, para. 2 n.1.
29 Id. at para. 4.

to accepting selective action appears to be a constructive approach to encouraging agreement on selective measures, assuming that exporter agreement eventually becomes a provision of the final agreement. A note to this section would also provide that in cases of selective safeguard action, a shorter duration of the relief would be appropriate.

Paragraph 5 provides that when selective safeguard measures are taken on a consensual basis, and if those measures place the exporting country in a disadvantageous position in relation to other exporting countries not subject to the safeguard relief, then consultations may be requested and held. If no satisfactory solution is reached as a result of consultations, the exporting signatory may withdraw the agreement.[30] Paragraphs 6, 7 and 8 contain two alternative texts describing how actions can be taken. Consultations held prior to the institution of relief (described in Paragraph 3) are unsuccessful. One alternative would permit unilateral action if consultations do not result in an agreement within a reasonable time and where critical circumstances exist. The other alternative would provide for referral to the Committee on Safeguard Measures, if an impasse in consultations is reached. The Committee would follow certain established procedures and utilize a number of criteria, set out in Paragraph 6, in making its determination. If the Committee approves the safeguard action, and if no agreement has been reached, the importing signatory is permitted to implement selective safeguard measures. There are also provisions which confirm the rights of exporting signatories who are the subject of safeguard action to "suspend substantially equivalent concessions or other obligations under the GATT".[31]

A special section labeled Chapter 4 bis deals with the troublesome area of export restraints. These usually take the form of what are sometimes called Voluntary Restraint Agreements (VRAs), which are often negotiated as an alternative to unilateral safeguard measures. This subchapter, which appears in brackets, would limit such agreements by providing that they may not be entered into if they circumvent the obligations and responsibilities imposed by the Code and the Article by restricting exportations of a particular product for the purpose of protecting from import competition domestic producers of a like or directly competitive product in the territory of any other party to the agreement.[32] The U.S. supported this concept since, although it frequently encouraged VRAs resulting from U.S. escape clause actions, the U.S. has been adversely affected by actions taken by other nations in third markets. For example, it is argued that Japanese voluntary restraints on steel exports to Europe may

---

30 Id. at para. 5.
31 Id. at 9, ch. 4, para. 10.
32 Id. ch. 4bn, para. 1.

have put increased pressure on the U.S. market.[33] U.S. orderly
marketing agreements entered into after an escape clause
agreement under § 201 were not thought to be in violation of
Chapter 4 bis because they are negotiated after proceedings
which were consistent with the "responsibilities and obligations resulting for importers" under Chapter 4 bis.   VRAs
negotiated under the provisions of the meat import law,
however, were considered to be in violation.[34]

Chapter 5 deals with the areas of notification and
consultation.   Article XIX:2 of the GATT already requires a
contracting party to notify other parties "as far in advance
as practicable" before instituting safeguard action, and to
provide an opportunity for consultations prior to any action.
However, in "critical circumstances", safeguard actions may be
imposed without prior consultations, provided that consultations are held immediately thereafter.   Chapter 5 expands upon
these basic concepts. Paragraph 1 provides for written notice
in advance of implementation of proposed safeguard actions,
with bracketed language providing for a specific number of
days' notice.   Other bracketed language would spell out the
information that should be contained in such notice.[35] Paragraph 2 requires consultations with signatories that have a
substantial interest as exporters of the product concerned.
Bracketed language would expand this to those signatories
whose trade interests are likely to be substantially affected.
This would mean that even non-exporting nations would have a
right to consultations if they could show that they would be
prejudiced by such action.   This could conceivably occur where
Country A brings an action against imports from Countries B
and C.   Country D, which does not export the product, but
imports it, could be concerned that any action closing off the
market in Country A, would result in increased pressure on the
market in Country D if Countries B and C divert their efforts
from A's market to D's.

Bracketed language in Paragraph 2 would require consultations to begin within thirty days from the date of notification. Bracketed Paragraph 3 provides for convening the
Safeguards Committee to consult with any parties that request
such a consultation.   Bracketed language would require such
consultations within fifteen days after written notification.[36]
Paragraphs 4 and 5 repeat provisions in Article XIX:3 of the
GATT pertaining to interim implementation of safeguard
procedures pending final outcome of consultations in certain
circumstances. Article 6 provides further details on actions
taken on a provisional basis due to critical circumstances.

---

[33] See USITC Analysis, supra note 6, at 59.
[34] Id. at 61.
[35] Draft Integrated Text on Safeguards, ch. 5, para. 1.
[36] Id. at ch. 5, para. 3.

Notification and consultation procedures would also be applied to requests for extension of safeguard relief.[37] Notification can be made by any signatory and once made, adequate opportunity for prompt consultations are to be afforded.[38] Paragraph 11 provides for a bill of particulars that would have to be provided by the signatory implementing a safeguard action.[39]

Chapter 6 deals with the issues of surveillance and dispute settlement. It provides for the establishment of a Committee on Safeguard Measures which would act as the surveillance and enforcement mechanism. Among its duties would be to review all outstanding safeguard measures at least once a year. Each signatory with a safeguard measure in force would be required, once a year, to submit a written report to the Committee explaining why the safeguard measure is still necessary and what progress is being made towards its removal.[40]

The Committee would convene to hear complaints by any signatory, but only after an effort at bilateral consultations was made. Two alternative provisions were proposed whereby the Committee could appoint a panel of experts. The first alternative simply provides for the establishment of a panel upon request for the purpose of making findings which will assist the Committee with its recommendations and rulings. The second alternative elaborates in considerable detail how such a panel would work. Particularly, the panel would report on whether a safeguard action by one signatory had met the criteria and conditions of the agreement and also whether such action may have damaged the export interest of another signatory.[41] It is further provided that any safeguard action found not to be in conformity with the criteria and conditions of this Agreement shall be modified or terminated to conform with the Agreement,[42] and that compensation shall be offered by a signatory who takes safeguard actions found not to be in conformity with the Code.[43]

Provisions are contained for the panel's recommendations which would permit the suspension of obligations to be self-executing if these recommendations are not acted upon by the Committee within a certain time period; a sixty day period is suggested in bracketed language.[44] It is clear that alternative II provides a highly organized and probably effective dispute settlement mechanism. However, it may prove

---

[37] Id. at ch. 5, para. 8.
[38] Id. at para. 10.
[39] Id. at para. 11. A footnote to this Paragraph notes that inclusion of the provision is "to be considered later".
[40] Id. at ch. 6, para. 2.
[41] Id. at ch. 6, Alternative II, para. 7.
[42] Id. at para. 8.
[43] Id. at para. 10.
[44] Id. at para. 11.

too "legalistic" for those who prefer to see the GATT dispute
settlement mechanisms from becoming overly formal and judicial
in character.

Chapter 7, entitled Domestic Procedures, also sets out
two alternative approaches, both bracketed. The purpose of
Chapter 7 is to ensure that each code signatory adopts
procedures for making safeguard determinations that are
transparent and consistent with traditional concepts of due
process. This does not now exist in all countries. Even in
the U.S. where hearings under § 201 are public, there is
lacking a great deal of what might be termed procedural due
process. For example, the author's experience in § 201
proceedings has indicated that the U.S.I.T.C. will generally
allow Congressional and other public officials to testify at
the public hearing, but will not permit attorneys for parties
(generally the importers) to cross-examine them. Thus, a
domestic complainant can prepare all types of factual and
opinion testimony to be given to a Congressman to deliver, and
it will go into the record without opportunity to be tested
for validity by cross-examination. Also, unlike cases under
other statutes where attorneys for the parties can see
confidential data under administrative protective orders, data
submitted by complainants in § 201 cases is often confidential
and cannot be seen even by attorneys for importers who have to
defend against it. This is especially true if the complainant
consists of a single company that comprises the entire
domestic industry. Under certain past ITC chairmen, the time
for presentations and cross-examinations in § 201 proceedings
has been severely limited, often bordering on a denial of a
meaningful opportunity to present one's case. Thus, it could
be argued that even the U.S. procedures have considerable room
for improvement in terms of due process.

The Code Alternative I, as in the preceeding Chapter, is
a shorter, more general statement than that contained in
Alternative II. Alternative I merely calls for established
procedures, and uses such vague and unenforceable terms as
"adequate public notice". One rather dubious limitation in
Alternative I is that the entity making the safeguard decision
would only be required to publish a report of its determination if it were affirmative (i.e., granting relief). It would
seem to be in the best interests of promoting certainty and
understanding of the grounds and criteria for safeguard relief
for all decisions to be published.[45] Alternative II provides a
more thorough procedural framework for the conduct of safeguard investigations including a requirement that evidence of
serious injury must be present to support the initiation of an
investigation. The use of the word "evidence" denotes a more
formal legal approach that would require at least a quasi-
judicial analysis of the facts alleged, even prior to initia-

---

[45] Id. at ch. 7, paras. 1, 2.

tion of the investigation. Also, a requirement for specific notice to exporters with a substantial interest is provided.[46] Alternative II also provides that "all" interested parties shall be afforded the opportunity to present "all evidence" they consider useful.[47] This rather broad language could even result in procedural reforms in the U.S., where the proceedings, although open, are often subject to various limitations in the presentation of viewpoints. For example, it is not uncommon at the prehearing conference held prior to a § 201 or § 203 hearing for the U.S.I.T.C. chairman to require all foreign respondents to be restricted to a certain time period for their cases, often a matter of a few hours, forcing them to allocate their time between many parties and generally tending to limit the presentation of the fullest case.

This is motivated largely by the ITC's desire to move their schedule along rapidly, but it often imposes unfair restrictions on the parties. Also, the use of the word "evidence" in Alternative II evokes a higher, more judicial standard than now exists in most countries, including the U.S., where much of the material utilized by the ITC in making its determinations would not qualify as "evidence" as that term is construed by scholars and courts. Alternative II provides for submission of information on a confidential basis, but it does not deal with the due process problem discussed above that can result in parties being completely in the dark as to the basis for their opponent's case. Alternative II would also limit the institution of a new investigation on the same subject, unless one year had elapsed since the previous determination, except where good reason is determined to exist.[48]

Consistent with other MTN codes that contain special provisions for LDCs, the Draft Integrated Text contains a chapter focusing on developing countries. Those provisions, entirely in brackets, provide for special treatment for LDCs in safeguard measures. Signatories would "make particular efforts" to refrain from imposing safeguard measures on imports of particular products of special interest to LDCs. Where such measures are imposed, they would be limited to "the minimum feasible in extent and duration".[49] Where an LDC is covered by a safeguard action and is a small supplier or new entrant to the market, action taken should permit continued market access with moderate growth on terms more favorable than those afforded to other affected parties.

These provisions would provide substantial benefits to the LDCs, but would also be a serious departure from MFN principles. It is indeed ironic that the LDCs that generally

---

[46] Id. at ch. 7, Alternative II, para. 2.
[47] Id. at para. 3.
[48] Id. at para. 5.
[49] Id. at ch. 8, para. 1.

opposed the concept of selectivity because it would permit
measures directly against them which are   inconsistent with
MFN principles, at the same time seek benefits that are to be
applied selectively to LDCs. Serious questions about the legal
soundness of the Code would certainly be raised if selectivity
was not permitted in implementing safeguard measures while at
the same time allowed LDCs to receive "terms more favorable
than those accorded to other affected parties".[50] Moreover,
since it is very often the LDCs who are the source of low
price imports that result in injury and are the basis for
safeguard relief, it could be argued that any substantial
limitation on the ability to apply safeguard measures against
offending LDCs could severely cripple the effectiveness of the
Code. If this language is adopted, it could also result in
significant changes in U.S. law. For example, the U.S. escape
clause measure permits the removal of benefits under the
Generalized System of Preferences (GSP) for articles that are
the subject of escape clause relief. Since GSP, by definition, applies only to developing countries, this provision
probably would be found to be inconsistent with at least the
intent of Chapter 8 of the Code.[51]

The last chapter of the Draft Integrated Text contains
various miscellaneous provisions. The thrust of Chapter 9 is
to provide a sunset provision for safeguard measures. Those
in conformity with the Code shall be terminated within a
specific number of years (left blank in the draft), although
they may be extended in accordance with the provisions for
extension in Chapter 2 of the Draft Integrated Text.[52] Non-
complying safeguard measures would have to be terminated
within one year after the Code comes into force, unless they
are modified to be in conformity with the Code.[53] One problem
with the implementation of the provision is the use of the
term"safeguard measure", which, as pointed out earlier, is
undefined.

It is likely that voluntary restraint agreements not in
conformity with the Code (e.g., not based on injury determinations) would have to be terminated.[54] Finally, Chapter 9
provides for each signatory to notify the Safeguards Committee
of its legislation, regulations and procedures adopted to
implement the agreement and prompt notification must be given
of any future changes.[55] A note to Chapter 9 indicates that
consideration should be given to including provisions governing the use of automatic licensing and similar surveillance
measures for safeguard related purposes.

---

[50] Id.
[51] See § 203(F)(2) of the Trade Act of 1974.
[52] Draft Integrated Text on Safeguards.
[53] Id. at ch. 9, para.1.
[54] See USITC Analysis, supra note 6, at 83.
[55] Draft Integrated Text on Safeguards, ch. 9, para. 3.

CONCLUSION

More recent negotiations relating to safeguards have still not yielded results. In assessing the results as of the end of the Tokyo Round, a number of conclusions can be reached. By the end of the Tokyo Round, most countries had come to accept selectivity as "a working hypothesis".[56] The important outstanding issue relating to selectivity was whether such actions should be taken only with the agreement of the affected party or after a prior determination by the Safeguard Committee. Certain industrialized countries, on the other hand, favored unilateral selective action, especially in critical circumstances.[57]

COMMERCIAL COUNTERFEITING CODE

Serious efforts to negotiate a code on commercial counterfeiting were initiated by the United States at a very late stage of the MTN. The purpose of the Code would be to regulate the problem of imported goods bearing false trade-marks. This has been an increasing problem in the U.S. and other countries. Although U.S. law has procedures to combat such activities,[58] the United States and the EEC reached an ad referendum agreement on a text in mid-1980,[59] but other countries had still expressed disagreement on a number of major points, particularly the definition of counterfeiting.[60] The main elements of the U.S. proposal would be to require economic sanctions against counterfeit imports. The question of trademark coverage and validity would not be covered in the Code, but would be determined by the domestic laws of each importing nation. The exact coverage of the Agreement was an issue of some disagreement. The original U.S. proposal covered only trademarks or trade names. Other proposals have suggested the expansion of coverage to include designs and models. Some elements also favored the inclusion of copy-

---

[56] GATT, Activities in 1980, GATT/1981-1, at 14.

[57] Id.

[58] For example, the U.S. Customs laws permit seizure of goods that violate U.S. registered trademarks and copyrights (19 U.S.C. § 1526) and § 337 of the Tariff Act of 1930 (19 U.S.C. § 1337) permits exclusion of goods imported by use of unfair acts or unfair methods of competition, but requires a finding of injury. See e.g., Glick, Section 337 of the Tariff Act of 1930 - A Trade Remedy For All Seasons, 29 Fed. B. News & J. 31 (1982).

[59] See MTN/NTM/W/225.

[60] See U.S. International Trade Commission, Operation of the Trade Agreements Program, 31st Report, U.S.I.T.C. Pub. No. 1121, at 56 (1980).

rights. The U.S. negotiating objective was to gain acceptance of the basic principle that the parties to a counterfeit transaction (i.e., exporter and importer) be deprived of the economic benefit of the transaction. The initial U.S. proposal required forfeiture of the counterfeit goods.[61] Others favored permitting the re-export of the counterfeit goods, which, while adding an extra cost to the perpetrators, would conceivably permit resale in the home market or perhaps re-exportation to non-Code signatory countries with weak or ineffective domestic trademark laws. The U.S. sought inclusion of various procedural safeguards that would prevent the Agreement from operating as a non-tariff barrier. Further discussion of recent developments in the area of the commercial counterfeiting code will be discussed in succeeding chapters.

In September, 1982, the United States, the EEC, Japan and Canada held further discussions on the Counterfeiting Code and came up with a new draft test which has been circulated by the GATT. However, many LDCs have resisted GATT efforts to pursue discussions on a counterfeiting code and have indicated their belief that the World Intellectual Property Organization is the proper entity to continue these discussions.[62]

---

[61] See Twenty-third Annual Report of the President of the United States on the Trade Agreements Program, 35-36 (1978).   U.S. law already provides for such sanctions. See Customs Procedural Reform and Simplification Act of 1978 § 211.

[62] U.S. International Trade Commission, Operation of the Trade Agreements Program, 34th Report, U.S.I.T.C. Pub. No. 1414, (1983).

Chapter 5

THE AFTERMATH OF THE MTN - IMPLEMENTATION AND RESULTS

U.S. IMPLEMENTATION OF THE MTN PACKAGE

As discussed previously, many of the MTN Codes required substantive changes in U.S. law. These were carried out in the Trade Agreements Act of 1979. Many of the substantive changes in U.S. laws have already been discussed. Extensive public hearings were held and testimony received before various committees of the U.S. Congress.[1] While a diversity of views was presented and there was much discussion and lobbying at the Committee level, there was considerable concern in Congress that the MTN package would open many doors to other countries' imports to the U.S. without assisting U.S. exports.[2] While the trade committees in the House and the Senate considered changes in the U.S. trade laws, the Senate Committee on Banking, Housing and Urban Affairs, for example, heard testimony on the implications of the Tokyo Round on U.S. exports.[3]

Some even predicted that Congress would not approve the MTN package. This was due to several controversies that coincided with considerations of the MTN legislation, particularly involving Belgian steel and Japanese television imports.[4] The MTN implementing legislation provided a forum for many of those in the U.S. Congress who were concerned that the U.S. government officials were lax in enforcing existing

---

[1] See, e.g., Multilateral Trade Negotiations Implementing Legislation, Before the Subcomm. on Trade of the House Ways and Means Comm., 96th Cong., 1st Sess. (1979).

[2] See, e.g., Strauss's Next Hurdle - The Hill, Bus. Wk. 32 (Jan. 15, 1979).

[3] See Hearings Before the Senate Subcomm. on International Financing of the Comm. on Banking, Housing and Urban Affairs, 96th Cong., 1st Sess. (1979).

[4] Why Congress Might Squash the Trade Pact, Bus. Wk. 37-38 (Feb. 12, 1979).

import laws and that some reorganization of trade functions
was needed. The U.S. had a record trade deficit in 1978 and
the attitude in Congress was more towards protecting domestic
industry than liberalizing U.S. trade.[5] There was heavy
criticism of what many viewed as the lack of enforcement of
the U.S. antidumping and countervailing duty laws by the U.S.
Treasury Department.[6] There was considerable discussion both
of removing these functions from Treasury, which was ultimately done, and for uniting all trade enforcement and policy
decisions in one agency, which has yet to be accomplished.

For example, there were reports that Senator William
Roth, the ranking minority member of the Senate Finance
Committee, Subcommittee on Trade, threatened to "hold the new
multilateral trade agreement for ransom until President Carter
creates a separate Department of Trade".[7] Influential
senators such as Ribicoff and the then majority leader Robert
Byrd, both supported creation of a new trade department.[8]
Another controversial issue had to do with waiver of countervailing duties enforcement while the trade agreement was being
ratified. The President was previously given authority to
waive enforcement of countervailing duties during the MTN
negotiations to supposedly create a more congenial atmosphere
for talks with our trading partners. This authority expired
on January 2, 1979 and the EEC warned the U.S. that it might
not approve the trade agreement package unless the waiver was
extended. This issue gave increased leverage to protectionists in Congress.[9]

Another powerful force was the U.S. textile lobby and its
supporters who pushed for exempting textiles from tariff cuts.
This effort, led by Congressman Kenneth Holland and Senator
Ernest Hollings, both from South Carolina, a leading textile
state, caused considerable concern by U.S. negotiators who
attempted to forestall these efforts through promises of aid
and assistance to the U.S. textile industry.[10] Meanwhile, U.S.
trade negotiators praised the package as "the most significant
trade negotiation ever conducted on behalf of this nation".[11]
However, U.S. Trade Representative Strauss was quoted as
saying that "there is no significant opposition" in Congress

---

5   "Controntation in Congress Over Carter's Trade Pact", N.Y.
    Times, Feb. 11, 1979, at v.
6   Id.
7   "Trade Pact Delay Threatened", Washington Post, May 17, 1979,
    at col. 1.
8   See, e.g., The Trade Tangle Gets Knottier, Bus. Wk. (Jan. 29,
    1979).
9   Id.
10 Id.
11 "Carter Sends Congress New Trade Agreement", Washington Post,
    June 19, 1979, at col. 1.

to the new trade act.[12] Perhaps Ambassador Strauss was encouraged by the special provisions contained in the Trade Act of 1974 that provided for rapid consideration of the trade package by Congress without amendments.[13] While this did prevent a "christmas tree" approach of numerous diluting or "pork barrel" type amendments, it tended to put the entire package in jeopardy, rather than simply portions of it, and resulted in the "hostage" strategy discussed above where Congressmen who could not amend the bill sought other legislation or concessions as the quid pro quo for approval of the pact.

The Trade Agreement's implementing legislation was introduced as S. 1376 in the Senate and H.R.4537 in the House. Prior to introduction of this legislation, the Administration had submitted a draft bill and accompanying statement of administrative action[14] and a series of hearings were held. On May 24, 1979, the two trade committees, the Senate Finance Committee and the House Ways and Means Committee issued a joint press release with their recommendations for implementing legislation, noting that the members had completed consultations with the Administration on legislation to implement the MTN and that differences between the House and Senate had been resolved at joint meetings held May 21 through May 23, 1979.[15]

Despite all of the controversy and posturing, when the bill was finally brought for vote, the results were overwhelmingly in support of the Administration bill. For example, the vote in the House of Representatives was 395 to 7 in favor.[16] However, this lopsided vote does not necessarily reflect the extent of concern that existed in Congress over the MTN package, particularly over the extent that U.S. businesses would benefit. The approval of the package was due in large part to the intensive lobbying efforts of the Administration, particularly in convincing members of Congress that U.S. exports would be positively affected by the codes. For example, Ambassador Alonzo McDonald, Deputy Special Trade Representative, told a Congressional committee that:

---

[12] Id.

[13] Title I of the 1974 Trade Act provides for automatic discharge of the trade package from committee after forty-five days if not reported, and a vote in each house within fifteen days after the bill was reported. A "closed rule" prohibiting amendment was included. See S. Rep. No. 1298, 93d Cong., 2d Sess. 22.

[14] Trade Agreements Act of 1979, 96th Cong., 1st Sess. (Statement of Administrative Action).

[15] Senate Comm. on Finance, House Comm. on Ways & Means, Joint Press Release No. 1 (May 24, 1979).

[16] 125 Cong. Rec. 92, 5690-94 (1979).

> I believe that the Tokyo Round results are
> potentially the most significant development
> in international trade since the establishment
> of the GATT over 30 years ago. The United
> States can look forward to important benefits,
> both short and long term, including major new
> opportunities for export growth across a wide
> spectrum of our industrial and agricultural
> sectors.[17]

McDonald predicted that the Government Procurement Code would open up $20 billion in new markets for U.S. producers where they had been systematically excluded in the past resulting in an annual U.S. increase in exports of $ 1.3 to $2.3 billion.[18] The Standards Code was praised as a method of significantly reducing the possibility that standards would be used to keep out U.S. products.[19]

On the topic of the Subsidies Code, McDonald seemed to tread carefully, pointing out that the Code would stop unfair subsidization by competitors of the U.S., but would still permit the U.S. to maintain such politically popular subsidy programs as the Domestic International Sales Corporation Program (DISC) and subsidized loans for export sales through the Export-Import Bank. In addition, he suggested that legislation to permit U.S. export trading companies would not be prevented.[20] In fact, during questioning by Subcommittee Chairman Stevenson, McDonald emphasized that the U.S. trade negotiators were careful "to preserve to ourselves as much latitude as we thought would be reasonable", including the preservation of U.S. export credits and guarantees, and commodity credit corporation credits for agricultural exports.[21] In fact, McDonald noted that as far as export promotion activities were concerned, the U.S. was "free to provide whatever reasonable help we think appropriate..."[22]

Also crucial in winning support for the trade package was the willingness of the Administration to succumb to Congressional pressures for a reorganization of U.S. foreign trade functions. James T. McIntyre, Jr., Director of the White House Office of Management and Budget outlined the Administration plan to a Congressional subcommittee on August 1,

---

[17] See Hearings on the Implications of the Tokyo Round Agreement on U.S. Exports Before the Subcomm. on International Finance of the Senate Comm. on Banking, Housing and Urban Affairs, 96th Cong., 1st Sess. 1-2 (1979) (Testimony of Ambassador Alonzo L. McDonald).

[18] Id. at 3.

[19] Id.

[20] Id.

[21] Id. at 10, 11.

[22] Id. at 11.

1979,[23] characterizing the Administration's reorganization plan as designed to prepare the Federal Government for "aggressive enforcement of the MTN Code" and to "improve our export promotion activities".[24] McIntyre admitted that "the trade machinery we now have cannot do this job effectively".[25] He pointed out that trade functions were located in eight departments and agencies, with loose coordination through committees. However, what was lacking was "a central authority capable of planning our trade strategy and assuring its implementation".[26]

The Administration's proposal consisted of a plan to "strengthen and centralize function of the Office of Special Trade Representative, which would be renamed the Office of United States Trade Representative. The proposal also planned to give added responsibility to the Department of Commerce, which would be renamed the Department of Trade and Commerce, and the creation of a new Undersecretary of Trade thereunder. An expanded role for the Interagency Trade Policy Committee was also envisioned.[27] The plan would not shift any responsibilities for agricultural trade out of the Agriculture Department or affect the operations of such autonomous agencies as the Export-Import Bank.[28]

Many of these planned changes have, in fact, been accomplished by Reorganization Plan No. 3 of 1979.[29] Administration and enforcement of the antidumping, countervailing duty and national security import laws was transferred from the Treasury Department to the Commerce Department, as were the commercial attaches previously in the State Department. Although the name of the Department of Commerce was not changed, significant internal reorganizations occurred, including the creation of an Undersecretary of Trade. Other proposals, such as a plan to transfer unfair trade practice cases under § 337 of the Tariff Act of 1930[30] from the U.S. International Trade Commission to the Department of Commerce, were never implemented. As will be discussed _infra_ in the section on recent developments, this plan has not satisfied

---

[23] See Statement of James T. McIntyre, Jr., Director, Office of Management and Budget Before the Subcomm. on Legislation and National Security of the House Comm. on Government Operations, (Aug. 1, 1979).

[24] Id. at 1.

[25] Id. at 4.

[26] Id. at 5.

[27] Id.

[28] Id. at 6.

[29] White House Press Release to U.S. Congress, Sept. 25, 1979.

[30] 19 U.S.C. § 1337. For a discusison of the operation of this trade law, see Glick, Section 337 of the Tariff Act of 1930 - A Trade Relief Measure for all Seasons, 29 Fed. B. News and J. 31 (1982).

many critics who still are urging a Department of Trade. At
the time of this writing, proposals for additional reorganization of the trade structure were pending.

WORLDWIDE IMPLEMENTAITON AND POST MTN ACTIVITIES
RELATING TO SPECIFIC CODES

A.   Subsidies
One of the busiest post MTN implementation areas has
concerned subsidies and countervailing duties. The Committee
on Subsidies and Countervailing Duties held five formal
meetings and several informal meetings in 1980. One item of
particular importance was the procedure for handling commitments of LDCs under Article 14, Paragraph 5 of the Code to
reduce or eliminate export subsidies when they are inconsistent with the country's competitive or development needs.
Although the language of Article 14, Paragraph 5 is not
mandatory, the U.S. has taken the position that it will not
grant the benefits of the Subsidies Code to LDCs that do not
make such commitments.[31] The Committee adopted a procedure
whereby such commitments would be noted by the Committee,
without being formally approved or accepted, through informal
examinations and consultations between the parties.[32] The
prevailing view appeared to be that there were unilateral and
voluntary commitments under the language of Article 14,
Paragraph 5, and that the Committee, therefore, should not be
in the position of approving or disapproving them.
In 1980, such commitments were notified by Brazil, Korea,
Pakistan and Uruguay.[33] However, India, although signing the
agreement, announced that it would not enter into any commitment under Article 14, Paragraph 5. In response to this, the
United States announced that it would not apply the Code to
India in accordance with Article 19, Paragraph 9,[34] and
proceeded to apply a countervailing duty to industrial
fasteners from India without applying the Code provisions,
particularly the injury test.[35] At the Committee's meeting in
October, 1980, India requested the Committee to examine the
U.S. action. India argued that commitment under Article 14,
Paragraph 5 was voluntary and that it was improper for the
U.S. to use the provisions in Article 19, Paragraph 9 to
coerce such commitments. India also argued that the U.S. did
not even follow the proper procedures in invoking Article 19,

---

[31] U.S. International Trade Commission, Operation of the Trade
Agreements Program, 32d Report, U.S.I.T.C. Pub. No. 1307, at
5-7 (1982).

[32] Id. at 58.

[33] Id.

[34] Id.

[35] See note 1, supra.

Paragraph 9.[36] India even asked the entire GATT council to convene a panel to consider the questions involved pursuant to Article XXIII of the GATT. Such a panel was convened on November 10, 1980. The issue was debated at the December, 1980 meeting of the Committee on Subsidies and Countervailing Measures, but was not resolved.[37] However, in September, 1981, the U.S. agreed to apply the provisions of the Code to India in exchange for a commitment from India to restrict the use of its export subsidy program.[38] India therefore asked that the GATT panel be terminated.[39]

The Committee on Subsidies and Countervailing Measures also met to consider a number of technical questions. One of these questions was the definition of "related parties", a term used frequently in both the subsidies and antidumping codes.[40] As a result of this effort, a definition of related parties was developed and adopted by both the subsidies and dumping committees.[41] A relationship was found to exist when 1) one of the parties directly or indirectly controls the other; 2) both parties are directly or indirectly controlled by a third person; or 3) together the parties directly or indirectly control a third person that is substantially benefiting from the imports.[42] Another group of experts was established to consider how to calculate the amount of an export subsidy,[43] some progress had been made on this.[44]

Other issues dealt with by the Subsidies and Countervailing Measures Committee was the need for better and more objective reporting of new subsidies under GATT Article XVI.[45] One area of considerable disagreement involved the United States DISC program (Domestic International Sales Corporation). Several countries believed this was an export subsidy.[46]

Four GATT panels had been established to examine the U.S. DISC program along with tax practices of certain other nations. The DISC provides that special export sales corpora-

---

[36] Operation of the Trade Agreements Program, 32d Report, supra note 31, at 58.

[37] Id. See also GATT Focus, 2 (Feb.- Mar. 1981).

[38] U.S. International Trade Commission, Operation of the Trade Agreements Program, 33d Report, U.S.I.T.C. Pub. No. 1308, at 65 (1981).

[39] GATT, Activities in 1981, GATT/1982-1, at 51.

[40] Id. at 10.

[41] Id.

[42] Operation of the Trade Agreements Program, 33d Report, supra note 38, at 65 n.1.

[43] Id. at 65.

[44] GATT Focus, 4 (Nov. 1982).

[45] Report of April 28, 1983 Meeting, in GATT Focus, 2 (June 1982).

[46] Id.

tions may be established in the U.S. to stimulate exports
through partial tax deferrals on export income. The EEC, in a
draft submitted to the GATT Council, requested that the
Council recommend that the United States "take appropriate
action without delay to bring the DISC legislation into
conformity with the provisions of GATT".[47] The U.S. indicated
that it could not agree to adopt the draft decision. The U.S.
pointed out that although the investigative panels did find
some inconsistencies between the DISC and U.S. obligations
under Article XV:4, the panelists also came to the same
conclusion with respect to certain practices of France,
Belgium and the Netherlands.[48] The U.S. believed the DISC was
in conformity with the GATT and that the decisions of the
panel were incorrect. The U.S. relied on a December, 1981
"understanding" that provided that activities located outside
the territory of an exporting country need not be subject to
taxation and should not be regarded as export activities under
Article XVI:4.[49] Other countries indicated that they did not
consider this understanding as an acceptance of the DISC
system.[50] Interestingly, France and certain other European
countries took the position that their tax incentive systems
were, in fact, acceptable under the 1981 understanding, while
the U.S. DISC was not.

     At a subsequent Council meeting, the original draft
decision was withdrawn by the EEC and a stronger one substituted which would "authorize the European community to suspend
the application of tariff concessions or other GATT obligations to the United States at an appropriate level to be
determined".[51] After consultations were held, a majority of
the Council indicated that the U.S. should take appropriate
action to bring its DISC legislation into conformity with the
GATT. In October, 1982, the U.S. informed the GATT Council
that it intended to submit legislation to Congress that would
amend the DISC in certain ways to address the concerns
expressed by the GATT Council.[52] This was undoubtedly motivated by the fact that the U.S. had little support at the
GATT Council on the DISC issue and stood "virtually alone".[53]
Also, the U.S. was anxious to remove this sore point in
U.S.-EEC relations, which had recently worsened as a result of
recent actions taken against EEC steel makers.[54] The U.S.

---

[47] GATT, Activities in 1983, (GATT/1983-2), at 65.
[48] Id.
[49] Id. at 65-66, 466 n.1.
[50] Id. at 66.
[51] Id. at 66-67.
[52] Id. at 67.
[53] Lee, "Washington Isolated on Defense of DISC", Journal of
    Commerce, Sept. 23, 1982, at 4A.
[54] "Brock Offers Substitute for DISC Plan", Washington Post, July
    28, 1982, at D7.

Trade Representative therefore proposed to eliminate the DISC tax deferral but would give an exemption to U.S. exporters on income received from foreign operations in an amount equal to what the exporter had paid under DISC.[55] However, this proposal did not meet with unified support in the government. For example, officials in Treasury have suggested a complete abolition of the DISC and increased support in other areas, such as the Export-Import Bank.[56]

A number of GATT panels have been established to investigate other areas of contention relating to subsidies and countervailing duties. One panel was established in January, 1982 to examine a complaint cited by the U.S. against EEC subsidies on exports of wheat flour. Another was set up in June, 1982 based on a U.S. charge that EEC was subsidizing certain types of pasta. These panels gave their reports at the meetings of the Committee on Subsidies and Countervailing Measures held on May 9, 1983 and June 9 - 10, 1983. These were the first reports by panels set up under the dispute settlement procedures of Article 18 of the Subsidies Code.[57] Concerning the pasta products, a majority of the panel found the EEC subsidies to be inconsistent with Article 9 of the Code.[58] The decision on wheat flour was less clear cut. Since this was a primary product, Article 10 of the Code required a finding that subsidies resulted in the EEC "having more than an equitable share" of the trade in this product. The panel was unable to reach this conclusion, partially because the concept of "more than an equitable share" was not well defined under the Code. The panel indicated that U.S. commercial interests may well have been hurt by these subsidies.[59]

At the May 18-19, 1983 panel meeting, another panel was set up, this time at the request of the EEC, to examine U.S. sales of one million tons of wheat flour to Egypt.[60] It is apparent that one of the main conflict areas relating to subsidies has been between the U.S. and the EEC involving agricultural matters. This will be discussed further in the section on post-MTN agricultural issues.

---

55 Id.

56 "Administration in Wrangle over Tax Break for Major Exporters", Washington Post, Dec. 9, 1982, at E3. On August 4, 1983, two bills were introduced to revise DISC, S. 1804 and H.R. 38100. As of the date of this writing, no action had been taken on either bill.

57 GATT Focus, 4 (June-July 1983).

58 Id.

59 Id.

60 Id.

B.   Government Procurement

As of late 1981, U.S. officials had been "reasonably
satisfied with the Code". In 1981, over one thousand notices
of proposed purchases were published by other code signatories, of which over 450 were from the EEC, over 350 from
Japan and 75 from Canada, which represented new export
opportunities for the U.S. The U.S. has indicated that it
believes that other Code signatories have adopted "all
necessary changes in their procurement laws and practices".[61]
However, U.S. officials believe that there have been a number
of problems with Code implementation. For example, the U.S.
found that almost 50% of the EEC's notices of bidding opportunities did not provide the required thirty days for response. Other problems related to the EEC's method of
calculating whether a contract falls below the Code's threshold for coverage.[62]

One major accomplishment for the U.S. enabled by the Code
was an agreement with Japan opening up the huge Nippon
Telephone & Telegraph (NTT) Company to foreign vendors — a
market estimated to be $3.3 billion. This was accomplished
by an exchange of letters in December, 1980. NTT revised its
procurement practices, published specifications in English and
prepared English translations of documents. The NTT agreement
is particularly significant since Japan was the only foreign
country to agree to open its telecommunications entity to
foreign sales under the Procurement Code. Actual sales
through the end of 1981 were only $3.5 million, consisting
mostly of off-the-shelf items rather than the high technology equipment the U.S. is most interested in selling. Part
of this was apparently due to the fact that U.S. firms did not
bid on a large number of NTT contracts.[63] A notable success
was Motorola's eight million dollar contract to deliver 45,000
telephone pagers and to submit a prototype mobile phone.[64]
However, these sales were insignificant compared to the fifty

---

[61] Hearings on U.S. Trade Policy Before the Subcomm. on Trade of
the House Comm. on Ways and Means, 95th Cong., 1st Sess. 149
(Testimony of W. Douglas Newkirk, Assistant U.S. Trade
Representative for GATT Affairs).

[62] Id.

[63] See Public Oversight Hearing on the Operation of the Govern-
ment Procurement Code and Related Agreement Before the
Subcomm. on International Trade of the Senate Comm. on
Finance, 9-10 (1982) (Statement of Ambassador William E.
Brock, III).

[64] Id. at 11.

million dollar purchase by American Telephone and Telegraph from the Japanese in 1981.[65]

One area of disagreement between the U.S. and certain other Code signatories is the U.S. position that leasing transactions are covered by the Code.[66] In 1981, the U.S. also found that Italian government officials were not fully implementing the law and dispatched a negotiating team to Rome and Geneva.[67] The U.S. has also initiated efforts to expand the Code to cover heavy electrical and transportation equipment[68] and formal renegotiation of the Code is provided for in the Code itself, to begin no later than December 31, 1983.

As far as U.S. implementation of the Code, § 301 of the Trade Agreements Act of 1979 gave the U.S. President the power to waive government laws and regulations that discriminate against foreign vendors. However, this applies only to purchases covered by the Agreement and excludes arms, construction contracts, certain defense items, and purchases by certain exempted agencies. Thus, the discriminatory Buy American Act[69] that requires government purchases of U.S. products unless the imported products are from 6 to 12% cheaper (50% for Department of Defense contracts), can still be applied to many types of purchases. For code products, Buy American waivers can be obtained for products of designated countries, including all least developed countries and countries that provide reciprocal benefits to the U.S. Various implementing laws have been promulgated.[70] Moreover, state and local governments that have been exempt from the Code have been increasingly active in imposing their own restrictions. For example, the State of Virginia passed a law in March, 1981 to keep state projects from using Japanese steel. The government of Japan protested and even the U.S. State Department sent a letter to Virginia explaining that this law would violate the spirit of the Government Procurement Code.[71] Virginia, nevertheless, enacted the law which grants a 10% preference to American-made steel in all public works projects exceeding 50%. Similar legislation has been passed in Maryland but was defeated in New York, Iowa and Washington. A total of thirty-six states have some form of restrictive procurement law. However, such sentiments are not unique to the U.S. For example, in Europe, Japanese automobile manufacturers threatened to pull out of the Geneva International Auto

---

[65] Id. at 12 (Statement of Lionel Olmer, Undersecretary for International Trade, United States Department of Commerce).
[66] Id. at 5 (Brock Statement).
[67] Id. at 6.
[68] Id. at 8 (Olmer Statement).
[69] Buy American Act, 41 U.S.C. § 10a, et seq.
[70] See 46 Fed. Reg. 21,194 (1981).
[71] "Protectionist States Waging A Battle to 'Buy American'", Washington Post, June 14, 1981, at F1.

Motor Show because of signs urging Europeans to save jobs by
purchasing European vehicles.[72] Advertisements urging consumers to buy only locally made goods have been appearing
both in the U.S. and in Europe.[73] At a July 27, 1983 meeting
of a U.S. textile industry and labor coalition, a "Buy
American" campaign for clothing was launched, which included
special labelling of U.S. products. Related to this was a
bill introduced by textile advocate Senator Strom Thurmond
(S.1816) that would require " Made In America" labels on all
domestic clothing and more prominent country of origin marking
for imported clothing.[74]

Despite these nationalistic activities, it appears that
overall progress has been made in opening up government procurement activities. The GATT Committee on Government
Procurement has continued to meet and discuss such areas as
inclusion of taxes and customs duties in the minimum value of
procurement contracts and the inclusion of leasing arrangements under the Code.[75] In March, 1981, GATT also published
lists of purchasing agencies or entities covered by the
Agreement.[76] In accordance with Article IX:6(b) of the Code,
negotiations are to be undertaken to broaden and improve the
Agreement not later than the end of the third year from the
date it entered into force. Among the topics to be considered
in this review, which will begin during the Committee's
November, 1983 meeting, will be expanding coverage of the
Code to include service contracts, and expanding the entities
covered.[77]

As far as disputes under the Code, a panel has been
established at the request of the United States to examine the
practices of the EEC in excluding the value added tax in determining the value of a contract for purposes of computing
whether the threshold of code coverage has been triggered.

C.   Customs Valuation

Since the Customs Valuation Agreement did not enter into
force until January 1, 1981, there has been less time to
evaluate its success. However, the U.S. and the EEC have
applied the Code since July 1, 1980. As of August 13, 1982,
seventeen countries, including the EEC member states, had

---

[72] "'Buy European' Speech Snarls Geneva Auto Show", Wall St. J.,
     Mar. 5, 1982, at 33.
[73] "Ads Aim at Arresting Imports", Journal of Commerce, Dec. 18,
     1980, at 1.
[74] 8 U.S. Import Weekly (BNA) 779-80 (Aug. 17, 1983).
[75] See Activities in 1981, supra note 39, at 11.
[76] Agreement on Government Procurement, Annexes I-III (1981).
[77] GATT Focus, 3 (July-Aug. 1983).

accepted the Code[78] and two more had signed it subject to ratification. U.S. experience with implementation of the Agreement has been quite good[79] and the number of disputed valuation decisions in the U.S. has decreased.[80]

The committee established to administer the Customs Valuation Code met for the first time on January 13, 1981 mainly to discuss procedural matters and future work. The signatories also exchanged information on legislation for implementing the Code.[81] A second meeting of the committee was held on May 5, 1981. A number of countries made policy statements expressing hope that other countries would soon accede to the Code. An exchange of views on the implementation of the code was given and data on various valuation methods used was exchanged.[82] The possibility of amending the Code to cover certain areas, such as treatment of interest for deferred payments and evaluation of computer software, were discussed at the May 4 - 5, 1982 meeting.[83] At the November 10 - 11, 1982 meeting, the committee reviewed the first two years of implementation and concluded that the Agreement has been operating satisfactorily and that the parties recognize the new valuation systems as having resulted "in uniform, fair and greatly simplified procedures for valuation of imported products".[84] The Committee indicated that most countries have been using the transaction value method of valuation for practically all transactions. The Committee also noted as an indication of the satisfactory operation of the Agreement that there had been no consultations under Article 19 of the Code and no recourse to the dispute settlement procedures under Article 20.[85]

However, this does not mean that there have not been any disagreements over the interpretation and operation of the Agreement. For example, Canada has complained that the transportation costs of its products after they enter the U.S. were sometimes included in the value of the goods. The Canadian government has requested that U.S. Customs authorities adjust the price of Canadian imports to exclude from dutiable value freight charges incurred after the goods arrive in the U.S.[86] There has also been some discussion about various countries' implementing legislation. Some concern was expressed over the Finnish legislation that appeared to some signatories to be

---

[78] GATT Doc. L/4914/Rev.5/Add.9.
[79] Statement of W. Douglas Newkirk, supra note 61, at 150.
[80] Id.
[81] GATT Focus, 1 (Feb.- Mar. 1981).
[82] Id. at 4 (June 1981).
[83] Id. at 4 (June 1982).
[84] Id. at 4 (Jan. - Feb. 1983).
[85] Id.
[86] Operation of the Trade Agreements Program, 33d Report, supra note 38, at 61.

somewhat vague and that might permit the use of minimum customs values. The Finns denied this and defended their broad language as necessary to provide flexibility.[87]

D.   Technical Barriers to Trade

The U.S. has indicated that there have been relatively few problems in implementing the Code on Technical Barriers to Trade (Standards Code).[88] Although there were some delays at implementation, this has been overcome. Numerous notifications of standards have been made. The GATT Committee on Technical Barriers to Trade undertook a study on private standardizing and certifying bodies,[89] and examined such issues as notification procedures, technical assistance to developing countries, and regional standardization activities.[90] The standards area has not been subject to as many controversies as, for example, the area of subsidies and contervailing duties, and the GATT Committee itself concluded as of October, 1982 that "in general the Agreement had operated satisfactorily".[91] This does not mean there have been no areas of disagreement. For example, one issue discussed was whether the Standards Code applied to processes and production methods (PPMs) used to make the product, as opposed only to the end product itself. The U.S. has taken the position that PPMs qualify as standards under the Code, while the EEC disagrees with this interpretation. The issue was highlighted when the EEC required the use of poultry chilling systems not commonly used in the United States, and gave domestic and foreign suppliers different time limits to meet this requirement.[92] The EEC claims these types of activities are not covered by the Code. The Committee requested all signatories to submit examples of PPMs in other countries that create trade barriers.

Another issue concerned the use of regional standardizing and certifying bodies. The U.S. was concerned that such bodies might be outside the reach of the Code.[93]

---

87 Id.
88 Statement of W. Douglas Newkirk, supra note 61, at 150.
89 Activities in 1981, supra note 39, at 11.
90 GATT Focus, 4 (Nov. 1981).
91 GATT, Activities in 1982, at B2.
92 Operation of the Trade Agreements Program, 33d Report, supra note 38, at 72.
93 Id.

E.   Import Licensing Procedures

The Committee on Import Licensing met twice in 1981. There were no licensing disputes but the activities consisted largely of consultations on procedural matters and information sharing. The Committee had already begun to compile information on the licensing activities of each signatory.[94] The Committee adopted procedures to require that all signatories notify the Committee of all aspects of its licensing system which will then form the basis of a bi-annual review.[95] At least during the first year and a half the U.S. found no major difficulties with the implementation of the Code.[96]

F.   Civil Aircraft

The Committee on Civil Aircraft has met a number of times to consider a variety of issues. A subcommittee was also established to examine the implementation of duty-free treatment for aircrafts and aircraft parts, to consider a proposal for more uniform statistical reporting and to consider a list of products that might be added to coverage of the Agreement.[97] At the committee meeting held on December 16-17, 1981, the Committee discussed how the signatories planned to implement the Agreement and the legal basis used by signatories for defining "military aircraft", which is excluded from coverage of the Agreement. While this might seem like a simple issue given U.S. standards of separation of military and civil functions, it is not necessarily true in other countries. Thus, for example, the question arose whether the Italian "Carabinieri" was a civilian entity covered by the Agreement or an exempted military entity. The Committee met on June 18, 1981 and examined questions relating to products that might be included under the coverage of the Code. Among the proposals to extend the Agreement was one which would expand the Agreement to include all aircraft parts, since about 5% of traded parts are now excluded. Another proposal would require that all signatories provide data on the extent to which they subsidize aircraft research, development, production and purchase.[98]

Another important topic discussed at the June 18, 1983 meeting dealt with export credits, since many governments were

---

94 Id. at 62.
95 Statement of W. Douglas Newkirk, supra note 61, at 150.
96 Id.
97 Operation of the Trade Agreements Program, 33d Report, supra note 38, at 59; Activities in 1981, supra note 39, at 12; GATT Focus, 2 (Feb. - Mar. 1981).
98 Operation of the Trade Agreements Program, 33d Report, supra note 38, at 59.

providing low interest export financing.[99] The issue received
further discussion at the October 28-30, 1983 meeting, where
the U.S. indicated that it considered this issue as one of
utmost concern and was prepared to avail itself of GATT
mechanisms to deal with this problem.[100] This had become a
sensitive political issue in the U.S., where the aircraft
industry, that had traditionally dominated the world, was
losing sales to foreign aircraft that came with attractive
financing packages. Of particular concern was the marketing
of the airbus, produced by a European consortium. The airbus
was the first foreign aircraft manufactured to break into the
U.S. market with a sale of twenty-five planes to Eastern
Airlines in 1978. More significantly, the airbus cut into
Boeing's overseas market. In May, 1982, Boeing's president
wrote to the U.S. Secretary of Commerce calling for an
investigation of export financing for the airbus and greater
government financial aid for U.S. aircraft exporters.[101] Other
U.S. producers of smaller aircraft have brought countervailing
duty petitions relating to foreign subsidized aircraft. One
of these brought by a still-on-the-drawing board U.S. manufacturer, involved a commuter aircraft manufactured jointly by
Aerospatiale in France, and Aeritalia in Italy. The ITC
dismissed the case after a preliminary finding of no injury.[102]
Another case was brought by Fairchild Swearingen Corp. to
impose countervailing duties on Brazilian aircraft. Fairchild
alleged numerous subsidies on the development, manufacture and
exportation of the Brazilian plane, including preferential
financing at 9% compared to the rate in the U.S. of 18 to
22%.[103] The ITC, however, also rejected Fairchild's petitions.[104]

Fairchild has appealed this decision to the U.S. Court of
International Trade.[105] This question will undoubtedly continue
to be an important one in the United States.

Other issues affecting trade in civil aircraft relate to
the quota system applied by Japan. This was discussed at the
October, 1983 committee meeting. Japan maintains an import
licensing requirement on civil aircraft that other countries

---

99 Id.; GATT Focus, 4 (July - Aug. 1981).
100 GATT Focus, 4 (Nov. 1981).
101 "Boeing Asks Government Aid in Countering Foreign Competition", Washington Post, July 1, 1982, at A6.
102 Certain Commuter Aircraft from France and Italy, U.S.I.T.C.
Pub. No. 1269 (1982).
103 "Fairchild Petitions for U.S. Duties Against Brazilian
Commuter Plane", Journal of Commerce, Aug. 17, 1982, at 2A.
104 Certain Commuter Aircraft from Brazil, U.S.I.T.C. Pub. No.
1291 (1982).
105 "Fairchild Asks Reversal of Trade Ruling", Washington Post,
Nov. 11, 1982, at 7.

consider to be a non-tariff barrier.[106] At the March 17, 1982 meeting of the Committee, Japan announced that it had withdrawn civil aircraft from the list of imports under quota.[107] In October, 1982, the Committee met to begin discussions on a review of the agreement with a view towards broadening it and improving it, pursuant to Article 8.3 of the Agreement, which mandates such a review by the end of the third year from entry into force of the Agreement.[108]

The Committee also discussed the possibility of eliminating customs duties on civil aircraft repairs.[109] This is covered under Article 2.1.2. It was eventually decided that duties on repairs should be eliminated only on certain products enumerated in an annex to the Agreement.[110] A consensus also appears to have emerged to extend the list of products covered to include sixteen new tariff headings.[111]

G.   Antidumping

The Committee on Antidumping Practices has been quite active since the amendments to the Code have been accepted as part of the MTN. It works jointly with the Committee on Subsidies and Countervailing Measure to develop a definition of"related parties".[112] One early activity of the Committee was to deal with the practice of "basic price systems". Such systems, often referred to as "trigger price" mechanisms, are designed to establish a predetermined level when imports may be considered to be less than fair value sales. The Committee developed certain guidelines for avoiding the proliferation of these systems and stated that basic price systems should not be used to provide the basis for any antidumping investigation. While special monitoring systems may be used, they may not be substituted for carrying out a full antidumping investigation in accordance with the procedures of the Code.[113]

Other individual disputes were considered by the Committee, including a charge by the U.S. that the EEC had

---

[106] Operation of the Trade Agreements Program, 33d Report, supra note 38, at 59.
[107] GATT Focus, 2 (Ap. - May 1982).
[108] Id. at 4 (Nov. 1982).
[109] Id.
[110] Id. (June - July 1983).
[111] Id.
[112] See discussion of the work of the Committee on Subsidies and Countervailing Measures, supra notes 31-60 and accompanying text.
[113] GATT Focus, 3 (Ap. 1981).

initiated an investigation on bed linen without sufficient evidence.[114]

H.   Agriculture

The agricultural area overlaps with a number of separate codes, as well as with tariff related measures. It has been an area of considerable concern in world trade since the MTN was completed. In fact, a large number of the GATT Council dispute settlement meetings have focused on agricultural problems. Some of the more significant disputes are discussed below:

1.   EEC/Canada - Imports of Beef

Canada filed a complaint against the EEC relating to a tariff rate quota[115] maintained by the EEC on imports of high quality beef. The EEC regulations permitted imports of up to ten thousand tons of grain-fed beef, described as beef graded by the U.S. Department of Agriculture - "choice" or "prime". An annex to the regulation stated that the USDA was the only agency with authority to issue such certificates. Canada considered this regulation discriminatory and in violation of Articles I and II of the GATT. The GATT panel agreed and the Council adopted the report in March, 1981.[116]

2.   EEC - Sugar

Brazil and Australia expressed their concern over sugar export refunds granted by the EEC. A working group was set up to review this situation.[117] In April, 1982, a group of ten GATT sugar producing nations submitted a joint request for consultations with the EEC on sugar. The ten countries accused the EEC of maintaining internal support prices on sugar far exceeding world market prices which had stimulated a dramatic growth in EEC sugar production and exportable surpluses. This surplus, it was alleged, was disposed of with the assistance of subsidies so as to expand the EEC's share of world trade and depress world prices.[118] Consultations were requested and held.

---

[114] Operation of the Trade Agreements Program, 33d Report, supra note 38, at 67.

[115] A tariff rate quota imposes de facto quantitative restrictions by raising the tariff duty progressively as the quantity of imports increases.

[116] Activities in 1981, supra note 39, at 43-44.

[117] Id. at 45-46.

[118] Activities in 1982, supra note 91, at 56-57.

3.   Japanese Restraints On Tobacco

In 1979, the U.S. filed a complaint about Japanese restrictions on imports of tobacco.[119] The U.S. alleged a variety of discriminatory practices on behalf of the Japanese state tobacco trading monopoly that resulted in discrimination against exports from the U.S.   Bilateral consultations were not successful and the U.S. sought recourse under GATT Article XXIII. A panel was set up in February, 1980.   In the interim, the U.S. and Japan reached a bilateral solution and the complaint was withdrawn.[120]

4.   Spain/Brazil - Unroasted Coffee

In January, 1980, Brazil complained that a change in Spain's tariffs on unroasted coffee was discriminatory against Brazil. The panel found the charge discriminatory and not in conformity with Article I:1, resulting in an impairment of benefits to Brazil under Article XXIV of the GATT.   The Council adopted the report and in December, 1981, Spain announced that it would give equal treatment to coffee from Brazil.[121]

5.   Spain/U.S. - Soybean Oil

The U.S. filed a complaint against Spanish measures that restricted the sale of soybean oil which the U.S. claimed impaired concessions on imports of soybeans.   Spain is a large producer of competing olive oil, as well as soybean oil.   The Spanish authorities argued that once the soybeans were imported and made into oil, they became a domestic product not subject to GATT regulation.   The panel agreed that sale in Spain of soybean oil made in Spain was a domestic matter outside the scope of the GATT.   Nevertheless, the panel did find that Spain's activities could have the effect of displacing exports of U.S. soybean oil to traditional markets, possibly nullifying benefits under Article XXIII.   Because of conflicting views in the report, it was never adopted by the Council.[122]

---

[119] GATT, Activities in 1979, GATT 1980/2, at 79-81.

[120] GATT Activities in 1981, supra note 39, at 46.

[121] Id. at 48.

[122] Id. at 48-49; Operation of the Trade Agreements Program, 33d Report, supra note 38, at 51-52.

6.   U.S./EEC - Canned Peaches, Pears and Raisins

In March, 1982, the U.S. asked the council to set up a panel to examine EEC subsidies on canned peaches, pears and raisins. A panel was set up to study this matter.[123]

7.   U.S./EEC - Citrus Products

In June, 1982, the U.S., in connection with action taken under § 301 of the Trade Act of 1974, notified GATT that the EEC was granting tariff preference on imports of nine citrus products from certain Mediterranean countries that violated the non-discrimination provisions of Article I. A panel was set up to study this issue in November, 1982.[124]

8.   U.S. Agricultural Adjustment Act

The Council, at the request of New Zealand, set up a working party to investigate the waiver granted by the GATT in 1955 of U.S. obligations under GATT Articles II and XI, that permitted the U.S. to take certain actions under § 22 of the U.S. Agricultural Adjustment Act. New Zealand questioned whether it was the purpose of the 1955 waiver to permit the U.S. to permanently take action in derogation of GATT Article XI.[125]

9.   EEC Sugar Export Subsidies

Many GATT sugar exporting countries have claimed that the EEC has more than an equitable share of the world market due to its subsidization of sugar exports. This, it was claimed, nullified and impaired the rights of other countries under Article XXIII of the GATT.   On June 15, 1982, the EEC agreed to hold bilateral consultations on this issue.[126]

Tensions in the agricultural area have been particularly high between the U.S. and the EEC. The U.S. has continuously criticized the EEC farm policy, known as the Common Agricultural Policy (CAP), which maintains high support prices for many of its agricultural products and subsidizes exports of surplus products, which are then, often sold below world prices and undercut U.S. prices. The CAP has worked success-

---

[123] Activities in 1982, supra note 91, at 54.

[124] Id. at 54-55.

[125] Id. at 77.

[126] U.S. International Trade Commission, Operation of the Trade Agreements Program, 34th Report, U.S.I.T.C. Pub. No. 1414, at 45 (1983).

fully to increase EEC exports of many products including wheat, sugar and poultry.   In reaction, the U.S., which supports farm prices but does not subsidize exports, threatened to impose U.S. export subsidies.   Proposals considered ranged from outright subsidies, such as are used in the EEC, to low interest loans for purchasers of U.S. exports. In fact, on October 20, 1982, the U.S. announced a program of subsidized below-market financing available for U.S. agricultural exports to LDCs.[127] In January, 1983, the U.S. sold a million tons of wheat flour to Egypt below world prices in retaliation against the CAP. The EEC complained to the GATT that this sale was in violation of GATT rules and asked for $30 million in compensation. The attempts at conciliation have failed and an arbitration panel has been established.[128] Agricultural problems were an important issue at the November, 1982 GATT Ministerial meeting in Geneva, and will be discussed infra.

Another U.S.-EEC area of dispute involves corn glutten feed. The EEC had agreed during the Kennedy Round to bind its duties on this product at a zero or low duty rate. The EEC imports of corn glutten feed from the U.S. have increased to the point where the EEC imports 75% of total U.S. output. The EEC has expressed concern that these imports are displacing consumption of domestically grown grain and in April, 1982, the EEC Commission threatened to apply a tariff rate quota on corn glutton imports exceeding three million tons (the level of 1981 U.S. exports).[129]

In March, 1983, the U.S. Senate Agricultural Committee indicated support for legislation setting out a package of subsidies to expand U.S. farm exports.   These included mandatory exports of subsidized U.S. dairy products, subsidized interest rates and products, offering of free government-owned commodities to goad foreign countries as an inducement to buy U.S. products.[130]

On June 22 and 23, 1983, the U.S. and the EEC began a series of meetings on agricultural issues. Shortly before these meetings, the EEC announced that it would seek renegotiation of tariffs on certain sensitive farm products including soya, tapioca and corn-glutton feed. In August, 1981, the EEC announced proposals which would virtually end the EEC system of unlimited price supports. While this would end artifically high prices in the EEC and possibly leave a

---

[127] See "U.S. - EEC Flour Dispute to be Referred to GATT", Journal of Commerce, May 19, 1983, at AJ5A.

[128] Id. at 129-30.

[129] Id. at 130-31.

[130] See S.822; Agricultural Export Equity and Market Expansion Act of 1983 and S. Rep. No. 27, 98th Cong., 1st Sess. (1983). See also, "Farm Export Subsidy Backed by Hill Unit", Washington Post, Mar. 3, 1983, at col. 1.

smaller surplus to export, it would not eliminate direct export subsidies that are a major source of U.S. concern.[131]

10. U.S/Japan Agricultural Issue

Japan is the largest export market for U.S. farm products, and agriculture is the largest U.S. export to Japan. Japan has restricted U.S. imports with quotas on some twenty-two agricultural and fishery items.[132] Japan, like the EEC, also maintains price supports and import restrictions that hamper U.S. exports Bilateral consultations between the U.S. and Japan were held in April 1982, and again in October 1982. The U.S. demanded elimination of Japanese quotas on beef and citrus by 1984 which was rejected by Japan.[133] Further talks were held in July, 1983 concerning Japanese import controls on thirteen products, shortly after the U.S. filed formal charges against Japanese agricultural practices with the GATT.[134] Discussions were continued in meetings held in September, 1983.

11. Arrangement Regarding Bovine Meat

The International Meat Council, composed of two representatives from each signatory to the Arrangement, has met on a number of occasions since the Agreement went into force in January, 1980. The Council has discussed various papers submitted relating to issues of competition and costs in the beef industry.[135] Although no official changes have been made in the Agreement, trade problems in beef have continued. As a result of high levels of exports from Australia and New Zealand to the U.S., voluntary restraint agreements were negotiated in October, 1982.[136]

12. International Dairy Arrangement

The International Dairy Products Council, and its three subcommittees on milk powders, milk fat and cheese, have met on a number of occasions. In 1982, the Council, in accordance

---

[131] See "EC Plans Subsidy Cuts in Farming", Journal of Commerce, Aug. 1, 1983, at A1.

[132] Operation of the Trade Agreements Program, 34th Report, supra note 126, at 176.

[133] Id. at 178.

[134] "U.S. - Japan Farm Talks Due to Open Monday", Journal of Commerce, July 7, 1983 at 1A.

[135] See GATT, The World Market for Bovine Meat (Jan. 1983).

[136] Operation of the Trade Agreements Program, 34th Report, supra note 126, at 269.

with the provisions of the Arrangement, evaluated the functioning of the Arrangement and the world market situation.[137]

I.   Safeguards

The Committee on Safeguards has continued to meet. On
April 15, 1981, the Committee agreed to intensify its
efforts,[138] and reported to the council on June 11, 1981.[139] At
the November, 1981 GATT Session of the Contracting Parties,
the Director General reported that "the situation is still
deadlocked..." It was not until the July, 1982 meeting that a
consensus had emerged on some principles and objectives of a
GATT safeguards agreement. These included the following
concepts:

(1) That safeguard measures would be temporary and of an
exceptional nature;
(2) Procedures for applying safeguard measures would be
defined; and
(3) Transparency of the measures would be insured.[140]
Further discussions of safeguards measures took place at the
November, 1982 GATT Ministerial meeting, which will be
discussed infra.

---

137 See GATT, World Trade for Dairy Products (Nov. 1982).
138 GATT Focus, 3 (May 1981).
139 Id. at 1 (July - Aug. 1981).
140 Id. at 1 (Sept. - Oct. 1982).

Chapter 6

THE GATT MINISTERIAL MEETING
NOVEMBER, 1982

The GATT Ministerial meeting of November, 1982 was seen by many as a vehicle to regain the momentum in solving outstanding world trading problems that had been lost shortly after conclusion of the MTN. The idea for the GATT Ministerial meeting was first raised at the Ministerial meeting of the Organization for Economic Cooperation and Development in June, 1981.[1] Later that month, the GATT consultative group of eighteen endorsed the concept that was later suggested at the July Ottawa summit and the Cancun summit meeting in October, 1981. The final decision to convene the Ministerial was made at the annual meeting of the contracting parties on November 23-25, 1981.[2] This was the first time in almost ten years that the contracting parties deemed it necessary to convene a meeting at such a high level.[3] The need for the Ministerial level meeting was the result of an increase in protectionist pressures and measures implemented as a result of the downturn in the world economy.[4] The U.S. looked at the GATT Ministerial meeting as "a pivotal opportunity to embark on an effort to improve the rules and countries' adherence to them, as well as to undertake a work program to extend GATT disciplines in new areas".[5] The U.S. rejected the concept that the Ministerial should function merely as "a ceremonial confirmation of the status quo".[6] He noted that the "Government of

---

[1] See Testimony of Ambassador William E. Brock, U.S. Trade Representative, Before the Subcomm. for International Trade of the Senate Finance Comm., at 11 (Mar. 1, 1982) [hereinafter "Brock Testimony"].

[2] Id.

[3] U.S. International Trade Commission, Operation of the Trade Agreements Program, 34th Report, U.S.I.T.C. Pub. No. 1414, at 14 (1983).

[4] Id.

[5] Brock Testimony, supra note 1, at 5.

[6] Id.

the United States is committed to further trade liberalization".[7] Brock stated that the U.S. objectives for the GATT
Ministerial were to: (1) strengthen the GATT institution; (2)
resist protectionism; (3) provide a forum for discussion of
developing country trade issues; and (4) to launch a program
of trade liberalization in the 1980's.[8]
    Specific issues that the U.S. proposed to discuss
included the following:

A.   Completion of Unfinished GATT Negotiations

1.   Safeguards Code
The U.S. considered this to be one of the most important
objectives of the GATT Ministerial. The U.S. would like a
code that covers all actions that have the effect of protecting domestic producers from injury as a result of competition from imported products. A central problem from the
U.S. viewpoint was how to deal with the "gray areas", e.g.,
voluntary restraint agreements (VRAs) and orderly marketing
agreements (OMAs).[9]
2.   Counterfeit Code
The U.S. hoped that the ministers would be in a position
to approve a final agreement that could be opened for signature, but was unclear whether the LDCs would permit this.[10]

B.   Issues Relating to Established Work Programs

1.   Government Procurement Code
The U.S. sought negotiation of extended entity coverage
under the Code as envisioned in Article IX (6)(b)[11] of the
Government Procurement Code.
2.   Standards Code
Triennial review of the Code as provided for in Article
15.9 of the Standards Code.[12]
3.   Civil Aircraft Code
Further netogiations as provided for in Article 8.9 of
the Civil Aircraft Code.[13]

---

[7]   Id.
[8]   Id. at 6.
[9]   See U.S.T.R., U.S. Objectives for the GATT Ministerial
      Meeting, at 1 (Nov. 24-27, 1978) [hereinafter "U.S. Objec-
      tives"].
[10] Id. at 2; Brock Testimony, supra note 1, at 7.
[11] Brock Testimony, supra note 1, at 7.
[12] Id.
[13] Id.

4.   Tariff Adjustment

Tariff adjustment resulting from the adoption of the harmonized system of tariff nomenclature.[14]

C.   Emerging Issues that Require Decision As to Future Work Programs

1.   Trade in Services

Trade in services, as opposed to goods, has never been covered by the GATT.   This would include such areas as insurance and banking where discriminatory practice have been increasingly prevalant. The U.S. sought to achieve a commitment to undertake a detailed work program on trade in service backed by a formal statement of the ministers that this was an important problem.   The U.S. hoped that the Ministerial would identify the objectives of such a program with some specificity and establish a general time frame for completion.[15] The fundamentals of the work program would include: (a) documentation and analysis of barriers to international trade in services, including the problem of market access; and   (b) examination of basic GATT principles and procedures to trade in service.[16]

2.   Trade Related Investment Issues

The U.S. proposed that the GATT for the first time review international investment issues including an inventory of restrictive practices and an analysis of how GATT rules could be strengthened to cover these practices.   This would include the area of performance requirements.[17]

3.   Trade in High Technology Goods

The U.S. saw increasing opportunities for exports of high technology goods as a critical issue in future U.S. trade relations.   The U.S. believed that barriers to trade, investment and flow of technology impeded this.[18] The proposed work program in this area would include: (a) a study of policies and practices that affect high technology trade; (b) an examination of existing barriers and distortions to trade in high technology areas and how these are presently dealt with under GATT and MTN codes; and (c) recommendations on specific

---

[14] Id.

[15] Id. at 8.

[16] U.S. Objectives, supra note 9, at 3.

[17] Brock Testimony, supra note 1, at 8; U.S. Objectives, supra note 9, at 4.

[18] Brock Testimony, supra note 1, at 9.

steps needed including proposed modification of existing rules.[19]

D.   Agricultural Trade Issues

The U.S. saw as an important goal for the Ministerial, the improvement of GATT rules covering the agricultural sector.   This particularly would be directed towards more discipline on the use of subsidies.[20] This could include a standstill agreement on agricultural subsidies followed by a gradual phasing out over a number of years.[21]

E.   LDCs

The U.S. indicated its intent to carry out President Reagan's pledge at the Cancun summit by calling on the GATT to seriously consider trade issues of importance to the LDCs. The U.S. has explored the concept of a special GATT round of nego- tiations between LDCs and developed countries. Special LDC tariff rates would be established below the MTN level but above the GSP (zero) level. The LDCs, in return would under- take increased steps to liberalize their own markets.[22]

The GATT Council entrusted preparations for the Minis- terial to a Preparatory Committee (Prepcom), which first met in December, 1981 and met monthly thereafter until November, 1982, during which time various countries submitted agenda proposals.[23]

In its earlier meetings, the Committee considered a catalog of topics prepared by the Secretariat.   Substantive work was begun at the third Prepcom meeting on February 9, 1983. Efforts to narrow the original catalog of topics were made.[24] By April, 1982, a concensus had emerged on the structure of the document to be submitted to the ministers. The document was to consist of three parts: (1) a declara- tion or political undertaking; (2) substantive decisions giving effect to the declaration; and (3) subjects requiring future examination.[25] The declaration was to set out the problems facing the world trading community and to also contain a reaffirmation by the contracting parties to abide by the GATT disciplines and to seek necessary solutions to world

---

[19] U.S. Objectives, supra note 9, at 3.

[20] Id. at 1.

[21] Id.

[22] Id. at 2.

[23] Operation of the Trade Agreements Program, 34th Report, supra note 3, at 14.

[24] See GATT Focus, 1 (Feb. 1982).

[25] Id. at 1 (June 1982).

trade problems. The second part, dealing with substantive
decisions, would give effect to the political declaration.
This could be either specific solutions to certain problems or
guidelines for solutions with particular time limits. The
third part, dealing with subjects to be further examined
would provide for specific studies with definite time limits.[26]
    Various topics were organized into these three areas and
several drafts were prepared and circulated. Various GATT
bodies also proposed agenda items and took responsibility for
various areas. For example, the "Group of 18" was given
special responsibility for agricultural issues, the Committee
on Trade and Development worked on issues relating to trade
liberalization benefiting the LDCs, and the Committee on
Tariff Concessions worked on two topics -- adoption of a harmonized commodity restriction and tariff escalation.[27]
However, as the date of the meeting approached, it became
apparent that the level of disagreement on inclusion of
various topics would require the GATT Council to seek lower
common denominators if anything positive were to come from
the meeting. In its November, 1972 official newsletter, the
GATT noted that:

> [t]here are still many points of disagreement and
> the general feeling is that the text [of the
> Ministerial declaration] will have to be simplified
> considerably. While everyone agrees on the need to
> arrive at a political commitment to combat pro-
> tectionism and disintegration of the multilateral
> trading system, opinions differ as to the factors to
> be held responsible and the strength of the remedies
> applied.[28]

    Outsiders also began to doubt whether any significant
agreement could be reached at the Ministerial due largely to
the world recession which had stimulated "protectionistic
reflexes".[29] Others predicted the demise of the GATT if the
Ministerial were to produce nothing substantial. One economist predicted that:

> the GATT system is in no shape to deal with the
> intensified economic stagnation that would follow a
> further collapse of the concensus for reasonably
> free-trade that has prevailed in most capitalistic

---

26 Id. at 3 (July - Aug. 1982).
27 Id. at 4.
28 Id. at 1 (Nov. 1982).
29 "Trouble in the GATT", Financial Times, Oct. 26, 1982.

industrial countries during the past 40 years. The institution's pillars are flaking.[30]

In view of increasing protectionistic pressures, many delegations felt the time was wrong for any bold new GATT initiatives.[31] The EEC, for example, advocated that the Ministerial should largely focus on a recommitment by members to refrain from activities inconsistent with the GATT. Others questioned whether the GATT was the proper forum for certain topics and suggested future action by WIPO and the OECD as alternative forums. As late as ten days before the meeting, the draft text of the ministerial document remained in dispute.[32]

THE MINISTERIAL MEETING

Due to the wide divergence of views and the need to reach some agreement lest the meeting be deemed a failure and the credibility of the GATT threatened, the Ministerial had to be extended beyond its original scheduled period.[33] The U.S. delegation was openly disappointed in the outcome of the Ministerial, and two topics of major concern to the U.S. were not included in the Ministerial declaration at all. The topics were trade in high technology goods and investment issues.[34] U.S. Trade Representative Brock was quoted as giving the results of the Ministerial "a grade of C".[35] The Ministerial ended with the issuance of the Ministerial Declaration, the text of which is set out in the Appendix. Some of the principal features are discussed below.

A.   Political Statement

The Ministerial declaration begins with the stark and candid admission that "...the multilateral trading system, of which the General Agreement is the legal foundation, is seriously endangered".[36] It was further recognized that due to the "current crisis in the world economy...protectionist pressures on governments have multipled, disregard of GATT

---

[30] Protection from Protectionists, The Economist (July 31, 1982).

[31] Operation of the Trade Agreements Program, 34th Report, supra note 3, at 16.

[32] Id.

[33] Id. at 20.

[34] Id.

[35] Id.

[36] Ministerial Declaration, Political Statement, at para. 1.

disciplines has increased and certain shortcomings in the GATT system have been accentuated".[37]

The Declaration went on to criticize specific forms of protectionistic practices, such as import restrictions, particularly those applied outside of GATT disciplines, subsidies for production and exports, and restrictive trade measures applied for non-economic reasons.[38] Disagreement over safeguard measures and the degree of liberalization in agricultural trade were cited. The statement criticized restrictions on trade in textiles and clothing imposed by the multilateral arrangement which is outside of, and "in major derogation from", the GATT.[39]

The political statement ends with a schedule of general and specific commitments couched in terms of resisting "protectionist pressures in the formulation and implementation of national trade policy" and to refrain from taking or maintaining any measures inconsistent with GATT.[40] Specific areas included a commitment to "abstain from taking restrictive trade measures for reasons of a non-economic character, not consistent with the general agreement",[41] to ensure special treatment for LDCs,[42] and by improving GATT disciplines on agricultural trade, including improving market access.[43]

B.   Safeguards

The contracting parties agreed that there was a need for improved and more efficient safeguard systems. A proposed code was envisioned that would contain provisions on transparency, coverage, objective criteria for action, temporary nature of actions, compensation and retaliation, and notification and dispute settlement. It was further agreed that a subsidies code would be drawn up by the Council for adoption by the contracting parties by the summer of 1983 session.[44] This has yet to occur. Conspicuously absent was any statement on the issue of selectivity, clearly one of the issues that has prevented the conclusion of any code to date.

---

[37] Id.
[38] Id. at para. 3.
[39] Id. at para. 4.
[40] Id. at para. 7.
[41] Id. at para. 7(iii).
[42] Id. at para. 7(iv)(b).
[43] Id. at para. 7 (v).
[44] Ministerial Declaration, Safeguards, at paras. 2, 3.

C.   LDCs

A number of steps were agreed upon relating to the LDCs. These appeared to be mostly reaffirmations of pre-existing goals and commitments, rather than any novel or dramatic breakthroughs. The parties instructed the Committee on Trade and Development to consult with contracting parties concerning their obligations to LDCs under Part IV of the GATT and to improve programs for GSP and MFN treatment of products of "particular export interest to developing countries".[45] Action in these and other areas were agreed to be reviewed at the GATT 1984 session.

D.   Dispute Settlement Procedures

Here again, the parties largely agreed to reaffirm their commitment made in the MTN Group Framework Agreement, discussed _supra_. They did agree that while no further changes in the framework itself were needed, there was room for more effective use of existing mechanisms. For example, the parties agreed that if a dispute is not resolved through initial consultations, the "good offices of the Director-General", or someone selected by him, could be asked for confidential conciliation.[46] Other agreements concerned procedures when time limits for establishment of a panel cannot be met,[47] cooperation of the parties in providing experts to serve on panels and the payment of such experts,[48] assistance to panels from the GATT Secretariat,[49] and various guidelines for the functioning of the panels.[50] Provisions were made for periodic review by the GATT Council of recommendations and rulings by the contracting parties and reports by the parties themselves on their implementation of such rulings and recommendations.[51] It was clarified that the contracting parties' action could include a recommendation for compensatory adjustment with respect to other products or an authorization for suspension of concessions or obligations.[52]

---

[45] Ministerial Declaration, GATT Rules and Activities Relating to Developing Countries, at paras. 1-3.

[46] Ministerial Declaration, Dispute Settlement Procedures, at para. (i).

[47] Id. at para. (ii).

[48] Id. at para. (iii).

[49] Id. at para. (iv).

[50] Id. at paras. (v)-(vii).

[51] Id. at para. (viii).

[52] Id. at para. (ix).

The parties also agreed to avoid obstructing the dispute settlement process, but without any prejudice to other rights under the GATT.[53]

E.   Trade in Agriculture

Although substantive gains in resolving the myriad agricultural related problems were absent, the parties did at least make progress from a procedural point of view in the creation of a GATT Committee on Trade and Agriculture, open to all parties, which would work towards a greater liberalization of trade in agricultural products.[54] The Committee was charged with examining such issues as market access and competition, including subsidies and other forms of assistance.[55]

F.   Tropical Products

The parties agreed to continue work aimed towards the liberalization of trade in tropical products (including processed and semi-processed products).[56]

G.   Quantitative Restrictions and Other
Non-Tariff Measures

In this area, a special group was created to review existing quantitative restrictions and non-tariff trade measures, the grounds on which they are maintained, and their conformity with provisions of the GATT. The goal of this process is to achieve elimination of those measures not in conformity with GATT mandates or, alternatively, to bring these measures into conformity.[57]

H.   Tariffs

The parties agreed to give "prompt attention" to the problem of escalation of tariffs on products with increased processing, with a view toward "elimination or reduction" of such escalation. Attention was also given to work on a harmonized tariff nomenclature system. While the GATT endorsed prompt introduction of such a system, it was agreed that such

53 Id. at para. (x).
54 Ministerial Declaration, Trade in Agriculture, at para.4.
55 Id. at para. 1.
56 Ministerial Declaration, Tropical Products.
57 Ministerial Declaration, Quantitative Restrictions and Non-Tariff Measures, at para. 1.

a system would not impair existing concessions or change the general level of duties.[58]

I.   MTN Agreements

The parties agreed to review the operation of the MTN Agreements and Arrangements to determine their adequacy and effectiveness.[59]

J.   Export Credits for Capital Goods

The parties recommended that special attention be given to relevant credit provisions, including specific terms and conditions, in order to facilitate the expansion of developing countries' imports of capital goods, consistent with their trade and development needs.[60]

K.   Textiles and Clothing

In order to implement the concern over non-GATT restrictions on textile trade expressed in the Political Statement, the parties agreed to carry out on a priority basis a study of world trade in textiles and clothing, particularly the prospects for LDCs and the impact of such existing restraints as the Multifiber Arrangement (MFA). The goal was to examine the possibilities of trade liberalization in the textiles and clothing areas, including the possibility of full application of GATT disciplines.

L.   Trade in Services

Despite the strong interest of the U.S. and certain other parties in this area, the sole action at the Ministerial meeting was to recommend to the parties "with an interest in services of different types to undertake, as far as it is able, national examination of the issues in this sector".[61] The parties were also invited to exchange information among themselves "through relevant international organizations", such as GATT, and at the 1984 session, the parties would consider "whether any multilateral action in these matters is

---

[58] Ministerial Declaration, Tariffs, at para. 2.
[59] Ministerial Declaration, MTN Agreements and Arrangements.
[60] Ministerial Declaration, Export Credits for Capital Goods, at paras. 1, 2.
[61] Ministerial Declaration, Trade in Services, at para. 1.

appropriate and desirable".[62] The quoted language indicates the extremely weak and non-committal nature of the ministers' interest in this question. One could almost argue that this language was worse than none at all. For example, recommending that parties "with an interest in services" examine these issues, could well be interpreted as an indication that the ministers did not feel that this was an issue in which a large number of parties had an interest. The language as to future consideration as to whether multilateral action is "appropriate and desirable", indicates a reluctance of the ministers to make any commitment to even review the area of Trade in Services at the 1984 session. Undoubtedly, this was the cause of some of the disappointment expressed by the U.S. and others over the lack of success of the Ministerial.

A number of other areas were specifically covered in the Ministerial Declaration. These included instructions to the Council to examine the question of counterfeit goods and to consult with the World International Property Organization to clarify the jurisdictional issues involved.[63] Furthermore, the ministers decided that the contracting parties should notify the GATT of goods produced and exported which are banned by that country's local authorities for health and safety reasons.[64] Also included were recommendations to examine special problems with regard to trade in certain natural resource products, including: (a)   non-ferrous metals and minerals; (b)   forestry products; and (c) fish and fisheries products;[65] and   to consult with the International Monetary Fund on the possibility of a study of the effects of erratic fluctuations in exchange rates on international trade[66] and to study dual pricing practices and rules of origin.[67]

THE AFTERMATH OF THE MINISTERIAL

Shortly after the Ministerial meeting, U.S. Trade Representative Brock was reported to have commented that he would give the Ministerial a grade of "C", and   maybe a "C+" depending on how things developed. Some would agree with this assessment. Others might suggest that a more appropriate grade would be an "incomplete". Other descriptions of the Ministerial range from a "wash out" to a "modest achieve-

---

62 Id. at para. 3.

63 Ministerial Declaration, Trade in Counterfeit Goods, at para. 21.

64 Ministerial Declaration, Export of Domestically Produced Goods.

65 Ministerial Declaration, Export.

66 Ministerial Declaration, Exchange Rate Fluctuations and Their Effect on Trade.

67 Ministerial Declaration, Dual Pricing and Rules of Origin.

ment".[68] Naturally, such appraisements are subjective and depend both on one's point of view and expectations from the meeting. Criticism of the ministerial naturally led to criticism of the GATT. Some delegates wondered out loud if GATT was capable of handling the novel and complex problems of the 80's. For example, Senator Grassley, who attended the meeting, commented on the floor of the Senate:

> During last week's meeting of GATT in Geneva, it became apparent to me that GATT either cannot or will not handle the difficult and complex areas of non-tariff barriers, export subsidies, import licensing, trade in services, investments and high technology.[69]

Other countries were equally critical. The Australian delegation called the Ministerial Declaration meaningless and refused to sign it.[70] LDCs, such as members of the Organization of American States, found the failure to reach agreement on agricultural subsidies by the EEC a "serious shortcoming".[71] Others were not so delicate in their appraisals. U.S. Senator William Proxmire, a more vocal member of the U.S. Senate, commented that "the GATT is done, fini, kaput"[72] and even officials in the U.S. Trade Representative's office have admitted that they are exploring non-GATT forums and bilateral approaches to resolving problems.

The GATT, itself, did not accept these predictions of doom. It referred to the Ministerial session as "a stand against protectionism, and priorities for future activity".[73] At its January 26, 1983 meeting, the GATT Council approved the first set of measures to put into effect the decisions of the GATT Ministerial and the subsequent actions by the Council on November 29, 1983. The Council established procedural

---

68 See After GATT: A Code for a Domestic Economic and Trade Summit, Cong. Rec. S.13,625 (1982). Senate Finance Committee Chairman Dole commented that he was "greatly disturbed" by the GATT Ministerial, and that the GATT's viability "may have been called into serious question". Senator Roth, also a member of the Finance Committee, called the GATT a "paper mouse", that is virtually useless in settling trade disputes. See "Senators Question Viability of GATT", Journal of Commerce, Jan. 4, 1983, at 5A.

69 Cong. Rec., supra note 68, at 13,625.

70 Organization of American States, 7 OAS-CECON Trade News 3 (Dec. 1982).

71 Id.

72 Proxmire Calls GATT "Kaput" and USTR Official Talks of Alternative Approaches, U.S. Import Weekly (BNA) 89596 (Sept. 14, 1983).

73 GATT Focus, 1 (Dec. 1982).

arrangements to begin implementing the various programs listed
in the Declaration. Several new bodies were set up, including
a Committee on Trade in Agriculture, which held its first
meeting in March, 1983, and a Group on Quantitative Restrictions and other Non-Tariff Measures, which also met in March,
1983.[74] The Council, at its January, 1983 meeting, observed
that the Ministerial Declaration "has strengthened its
responsibilities for dispute settlement".[75] Progress has been
made in the work of the several committees. For example, the
Committee on Trade in Agriculture requested participants to
provide information on subsidy programs by June 15, 1983.[76] The
Quantitative Restriction Group began the first stage of its
work in assembling documentation on various quantitative
restrictions and non-tariff measures now in operation.[77]
Discussions on safeguards have also been continuing, but in an
informal group. This was to avoid the formal rhetoric and
restatement of positions that had characterized the regular
meetings. On July 12, 1983, the Chairman of the GATT Council
made a progress report on these discussions. It is clear, he
reported, that the scope of safeguard measures being used
extended far beyond Article XIX of the GATT and included
various bilateral arrangements, such as orderly marketing
agreements, voluntary restraint agreements, surveillance
systems, price undertakings and export forecasts. Also,
industry-to-industry agreements not clearly involving government and unilateral actions were frequently taken. These
non-GATT measures were found to be more frequently used than
those under GATT Article XIX and were frequently used as
substitutes for other actions permitted under GATT Article VI
(countervailing duties and antidumping). The informal group
has focused on answering the following questions about
safeguard measures taken:

-    What was the precise nature of the action?

-    What were the reasons that led to taking such
     action?

-    What were the reasons that led exporting countries
     to accept them?

-    What were the reasons why Article XIX action had not
     been taken?

---

[74] See id. at 1 (Jan. - Feb. 1983).
[75] Id.
[76] Id. at 1 (Mar. - Ap. 1983).
[77] Id. at 1 (Ap. - May 1983).

   -    What were the effects of the actions, including
        on trade of third countries?

   -    What could be said about the phasing out of the
        action, including any problems that needed to
        be dealt with and how multilateral disciplines
        could be established?[78]

As noted above, conclusions about the success or failure
of the Ministerial varied in accordance with various parties
expectations. Those that expected resolution of major trade
problems were disappointed. Those with less ambitious predictions were often satisfied. For example, Roy Denman, the
EEC's Chief Representative at the GATT, in a signed opinion
piece in the Washington Post eleven days before the meeting,
noted that "we need first to avoid exaggerated expectations...[The] GATT meeting cannot in three days...produce a
new heaven and a new earth..."[79] Even some U.S. observers with
more modest expectations seemed satisfied with the Ministerial
results.
        One leading economist was quoted as saying, "the minis-
terial conference accomplished what any sophisticated person
could have expected it to do - make a beginning toward the
negotiations of some key issues in the next few years."[80] Even
experienced trade negotiators such as former Assistant
Secretary of State and USTR official Robert Hormats, found
that the Ministerial made progress toward making the GATT
dispute settlement mechanism work better, and that there was a
serious attempt to work out a better safeguard mechanism.[81]
What is clear is that the failure of the Ministerial to live
up to the expectations of some, has served to weaken the
stature of the GATT, place increased pressure on the GATT to
perform, and encourage forum shopping by dissatisfied parties
who feel other international bodies such as the OECD, WIPO, or
UNCTAD may hold the key to unlocking the morass of trade
problems that has seemed to, at least temporarily, paralyze
the GATT.
        Indeed, it appears that some of the other trade forums
are hungrily awaiting the demise of the GATT in a not unpreda-
tory fashion. For example, the United Nations Conference on
Trade and Development (UNCTAD) blamed GATT for "the deterioration of the world trading system" and suggested that GATT be
"scrapped and replaced by an improved legal framework for

---

78 Id. at 4 (July - Aug. 1983).
79 "What's GATT Mommy", Washington Post, Nov. 11, 1982, at A27.
80 "GATT Talks: 3 Score Cards," N. Y. Times, Dec. 1, 1982, at D2
    (quoting Lawrence B. Krause of the Brookings Institution).
81 Id.

international trade."[82] This undoubtedly reflects the rivalry
for more power in the international trade arena between UNCTAD
and the OECD, where LDCs and communist countries have a larger
share of power, and the GATT, which is often viewed as
dominated by a small group of industrialized nations. The
final hands in this high stakes game for control over the
world trading system is still to be played, and for the time
being at least, the GATT must still be viewed as the dominant
factor in the world trading regime.

---

[82] "U.N. Agency Report Raises Some Eyebrows by Blaming GATT for
World Trade Problems," Wall St. J., Sept. 7, 1982, at 30.

Chapter 7

CURRENT ISSUES IN WORLD TRADE

While the focus of this book is the Multilateral Trade
Negotiations in 1979, and not a review of all world trade
issues to date, it is difficult to look at the MTN in a
vacuum. Indeed, when this book was begun, the depth and
breadth of the problems that face the world trading community
in the Orwellian year of 1984 could not be fully comprehended.
I cannot hope to do justice to all of these current issues
without perhaps turning this work into a multi-volume treatise. Nevertheless, I shall try to cover a number of current
issues that set the stage for trade in the last decade of the
Twentieth Century.

THE JAPANESE CHALLENGE - CAN THE WEST MEET IT?

No discussions of current issues in world trade would be
complete without some discussion and recognition of the
phenomena of Japanese industrial productivity and dominance in
the world export market. The western superpowers watched
first with amusement and then with dismay as the Japanese
emerged from the ashes of the Empirial era, from the literal
Armageddon of Hiroshima, to what many would say is the world's
leading industrial nation. How did this happen? Can it
continue? What can the West learn from this lesson? I can
only hope to touch on the answers to these frequently raised,
but infrequently answered, questions.

What is clear is that Japan, through a studied dedication
to productivity, quality and export acumen, has become a
symbol of affordable quality goods, causing serious self-
examination of the American tradition of leadership in quality
and excellence. Some would argue that the Japanese phenomena
was facilitated, indeed precipitated, by the massive post-war
aid provided by the U.S. which enabled Japan to rebuild a
modern technological industrial base that soon overshadowed
many U.S. industries that had not modernized since the

industrial revolution. Surely there is some truth to this.
But money alone cannot turn a semi-feudal agricultural country
into a technological dynamo. If this were true, we might be
seeing mini-Japans all over Africa, Asia and Latin America.
Rather, it appears to be a particular devotion to industrial
productivity, almost as a religious phenomena, that has
created the Japanese challenge. Moreover, the interaction of
government and private industry has created a monolithic
trading entity, sometimes bitterly referred to as "Japan
Incorporated", unparalleled in the West. Such agencies as
JETRO, the Japan External Trade Organization, and MITI, the
Ministry of Trade and Industry, have enabled Japan to speak
with one voice, and compete with a unified determination that
has been impossible with the pluralistic structure of the
U.S. government, with its competing centers of power.

The success of Japan, at least until recently, has
spurred little desire in the West to emulate their system.
Rather, the Japanese challenge has been met with thinly veiled
racial epithets and less thinly veiled attacks at the one-way
nature of Japanese trade. This is not hard to understand. It
is difficult for U.S. industry leaders, used to years of
dominance in world markets, to politely watch Japanese
delegations visiting the U.S. to assist our industries in
becoming more productive and educate us on how to export. The
U.S., long an exporter of technical assistance and aid in the
battle to win men's minds in the war against Soviet Communism
is not used to receiving aid missions from foreign nations.
Moreover, despite its many praiseworthy successes, the
Japanese have managed to keep their home market one of the
world's most impenetrable, through devices ranging from high
tariffs to byzantine health and safety regulations. Western
exporters who have superior products for which there is a
demand in the Japanese market often give up in dismay at the
almost insurmountable task of selling in Japan. This, more
than any other factor, has led to bitter anti-Japanese
sentiment and cries of reciprocity that often sound like the
trumpets forwarning a trade war that could easily be unleashed.

Surely, if a trade war with Japan were to be unleashed,
there would have been no better climate than the period in
the late ' 70's and early ' 80's, when the MTN was being
negotiated. For example, in 1978, the U.S. trade deficit with
Japan reached a record $11.6 billion, contracting to $8.7
billion in 1979 and widening to $9.9 billion in 1980.[1] Such
large deficits were economically and politically unacceptable
to the U.S.

In November, 1980, by an overwhelming margin of 363 to 2,
the U.S. House of Representatives adopted a resolution

---

[1]   Japan Economic Institute, Yearbook of U.S.-Japan Economic
Relations in 1980 , 44.

protesting the large imbalance in U.S.-Japanese trade,[2] and urged Japan to assume a greater sense of responsibility for the trade deficit. The resolution noted that this large trade imbalance contributed to controversies between the two nations and eroded support among American workers and industries for an open trading system. The resolution charged that Japanese trade barriers and practices restricted or prevented the sale of American beef, citrus products , lumber, leather, tobacco and telecommunications equipment. In June, 1980, the United Auto Workers filed an historic petition with the U.S.I.T.C. seeking a five year duty increase on Japanese cars and trucks under § 201 of the Trade Act of 1974. This case could well have been the first shot fired in an all out U.S.-Japan trade war. Only the 3-2 decision by the U.S.I.T.C. finding no injury saved a major confrontation.[3]

Nevertheless, the actions in the Congress and the automobile case, undoubtedly communicated to the Japanese the seriousness of U.S. intentions and resulted in some major initiatives by the Japanese. A panel of Japanese trading experts was established to advise MITI on Japan's barriers to imports.[4] An import stimulation plan was developed.[5] A cabinet-level council was set up to develop an emergency package to reduce Japan's trade surplus.[6] In November, 1982, President Reagan made a formal request to the Japanese government that they eliminate tariffs on twenty-nine items. This demand was rejected by the Japanese on the ground that a unilateral tariff cut for the U.S. would cause problems under the GATT.[7] However, in December, 1981, after two days of trade talks, Japan made an official pledge to open its markets.[8] In late December, Japan agreed to abolish some non-tariff barriers and in January, 1982, considered further action.[9] Late in January, the Japanese proposed reducing or eliminating some sixty-seven non-tariff barriers compiled from a list of ninety-nine submitted by trading partners. These changes dealt with such areas as stringent customs, product

---

[2] See H. Con. Res. 376, 96th Cong., 2d Sess., 121. Cong. Rec. 10,710 (1980).
[3] See U.S.I.T.C. Pub. No. 1008 (1980).
[4] "Japanese to Study Barriers to Imports", Journal of Commerce, Aug. 21, 1981, at 13.
[5] "Japan Seeks to Increase Imports", Journal of Commerce, Oct. 29, 1981, at 14.
[6] "Japan Acts to Cut Trade Imbalances", Journal of Commerce, Nov. 2, 1981, at 1A.
[7] "U.S. Demands Rejected by Japanese", Journal of Commerce, Nov. 19, 1981, at 1A.
[8] "Japan Vows to Open Up Trade Doors", Journal of Commerce, Dec. 11, 1981, at 1A.
[9] "Japanese Push to Dismantle Barriers to Imports", Journal of Commerce, Jan. 7, 1982, at 1A.

standards and testing requirements.[10] In April, 1982, Japan implemented, one year earlier than required, tariff cuts on 1,653 products agreed to in the Tokyo Round, a move reportedly opposed by many groups in Japan.[11] Also, a number of substantive reforms were made, according to the Director General of Japanese Customs and Tariff Bureau, Koichi Kakimazu. These included:

1.   Adoption of a customs procedure similar to the "immediate entry" procedure in the U.S., allowing goods to be released from Customs prior to assessment.
2.   Simplified Customs examination procedures.
3.   Reduction in import documentation requirements.
4.   Reduction in the number of goods physically inspected by Customs.
5.   Creation of a centralized classification center in Tokyo to ensure more uniform classification of imports. This is similar to a procedure adopted by U.S. Customs. In addition, an office of Trade Ombudsman was established out of the Prime Minister's office to process grievences about Japanese trade barriers.[12]

In a further move to offset the aftermath of protectionist pressures arising out of the automobile escape clause case and proposed legislation to impose automobile import quotas, in April, 1981 Japan announced a plan to "voluntarily" limit Japanese auto exports to the U.S. to 1.7 million per year, a 6 or 7% reduction from levels in 1980.[13] Since restrictions on exports to the U.S. only left more Japanese cars to be sold in other nations, Canada and the EEC pressured Japan for similar restraints. In June, 1982, Japan announced voluntary restraints on automobile exports to Canada, a reduction of about 6% from 1980 levels.[14] Official U.S. Commerce Department data for 1981 showed an 11% decrease in automobile imports for 1981, with a 4.1% decrease for Japanese autos.[15] At the same time, there were indications that some Japanese firms might shift production to the U.S.

---

10 "Japan Plans Cutback in Trade Bars", Washington Post, Jan. 27, 1982, at 27.

11 "Japan Working to Ease Access Market", Journal of Commerce, May 17, 1982, at 4A.

12 Id. An excellent analysis of Japanese trade barriers and proposed changes appears in a study issued by the U.S. Trade Representative in November, 1982, entitled "Japanese Barriers to U.S. Trade and Recent Japanese Government Trade Negotiations."

13 "Tokyo Plan Would Limit Car Exports", Journal of Commerce, Ap. 20, 1981, at 1.

14 U.S. Import Weekly (BNA) 12 (June 10, 1981).

15 ITA, U.S. Department of Commerce News, 82-27.

Indeed, the Chairman of Ford Motor Company, Philip Caldwell, invited the Japanese to build production plants in the U.S.[16] Toyota responded with reports that it might build a plant in the U.S.,[17] and Nissan, the manufacturer of Datsun, announced plans to build a $500 million plant in Tennessee for production of small trucks.[18]

The future of the voluntary restraints is uncertain. The Japanese government, due to pressure from their domestic manufacturers and the upswing in U.S. automobile production,[19] has indicated that it wants to terminate the restraints in March, 1984.[20] However, in late August, 1983, the Japanese government appeared to moderate its position and indicated that an extension of the restraints might be considered.[21] At the same time, legislation imposing global quotas on imports of certain motor vehicles is being drafted by the House Energy and Commerce Committee Chairman, John Dingell. The proposed bill would reportedly limit imports to 15% of the U.S. market.[22] This was believed to be a response to the uncertain Japanese position on extension of the voluntary restraints. Other legislation, referred to as "local content legislation", that would require automobiles sold in the U.S. to contain a certain portion of domestically produced materials (H.R. 1231), was pending in Congress at the time of this writing.

All of this does not portray a particularly bright picture for advocates of freer trade. On the contrary, there is increased evidence of activities both in the U.S. and abroad that are inconsistent with basic GATT principles. The increased use of "voluntary" restraints backed up by likelihood of the legislative action if not adopted is the very type of activity that concerns many people in GATT, and which has prevented any consensus on a new safeguards code. In the context of U.S.-Japanese relations, it is clear that Japan is aware of the growing disenchantment in the U.S., with its relatively closed market; and Japan has responded, although reluctantly, with some admirable initiatives . The U.S., on the other hand, has begun to recognize that there are many

---

[16] "Caldwell Asks Japan to Shift Share of Auto Output to U.S.", Washington Post, Feb. 20, 1982, at D8.

[17] "Toyota May Build U.S. Plant", Journal of Commerce, Feb. 17, 1982, at A1.

[18] "Nissan Answers U.S. Critics With $500 Million Plant", Journal of Commerce, Feb. 17, 1982, at 3A.

[19] "Big 3 Auto Sales Surge Another 40.1%", Journal of Commerce, Aug. 16, 1983, at 1A.

[20] "Japan Won't Extend U.S. Auto Sales Limits", Journal of Commerce, July 1, 1983, at 1A.

[21] "Japanese May Extend Auto Curbs", Journal of Commerce, Aug. 29, 1983, at 1A.

[22] U.S. Import Weekly (BNA) 938 (Sept. 21, 1983).

lessons to be learned from the Japanese success experience, and the Japanese challenge has, more than any other single force, launched a renaissance in rethinking of U.S. policies toward manufacturing, production and trade, and the relationship between the government and private industry. This has manifested itself most vividly in the current pre-occupation in the U.S. over the need for an "industrial policy".

INDUSTRIAL POLICY - 1984

The concept of an industrial policy is somewhat akin to strategic planning used by private corporations. It involves the use of centralized planning to direct capital and labor to the sectors which the country can develop most successfully. As noted by one recent commentator, "of all the industrial nations only Japan has an industrial policy generally recognized as successful".[23] This has been accomplished by centralized economic planning backed by the power of the government to enforce its planning decisions on industry, through such devices as licensing of technology, and control over capital. For example, most industrial borrowing in Japan is controlled by twelve banks whose reserves are controlled by a centralized authority. MITI has considerable influence as to which sectors are to receive additional capital. If the U.S. were to adopt such procedures, private industry would have to be prepared for a great deal more governmental intervention. There are many ironies that the U.S., in 1984, is considering such moves, setting aside the obvious Orwellian fears predicted for 1984 of "big government" and "big brother". For example, it is ironic that the Reagan laissez-faire, pro-business government would be seriously considering such quasi-socialistic concepts as centralized planning and government control of industry to focus its resources for the benefit of an overall industrial plan that will promote the commonweal. Indeed, except in time of war, it has been impossible to focus U.S. industrial resources towards one central purpose that overrides the internecine warfare that is prevalent in our free enterprise economy. One wonders whether the U.S. government is willing to compromise the freedom of individual businesses to produce what they want, when they want, in order to make the U.S. industrially more competitive as a nation. Perhaps freedom is more valuable in the U.S. than industrial success. The next decade will undoubtedly reveal whether 1984 will become the start of major change in U.S. policy towards the industrial sector.

---

23 "Industrial Policy: Learning from the Japanese", Journal of Commerce, Sept. 23, 1983, at 4A.

U.S. EXPORT POLICY

Another lesson that the U.S. appears to have learned from the Japanese is that success in exporting is not accidental. It is the result of careful planning and strong government support. The U.S. has responded to this challenge by re-thinking many of the barriers to greater exports. One of these barriers is the strong U.S. antitrust laws which limit the ability of U.S. industries to cooperate in pooling technology and in working together to penetrate foreign markets.   To alleviate this problem, the U.S. has enacted export trading company legislation to permit the type of trading consortiums prevalent in Japan.[24] This legislation, while too new to be evaluated, offers increased U.S. alterna-tives to the Japan, Inc. so feared and revered in world markets.   Increased emphasis has also been given in the U.S. Commerce Department to increasing export opportunities for U.S. companies.   This was partially accomplished in the Trade Agreements Act of 1979, which created the U.S. Commercial Service under the Commerce Department to replace foreign commercial attaches previously under the auspices of the U.S. State Department. This, it was believed, would emphasize the role of U.S. attaches abroad in locating and fostering export opportunities for U.S. businesses.

TRADE REORGANIZATION

Another area of recent activity in the U.S., which is also at least in part a response to the Japanese, is Trade Reorganization. As discussed earlier, there has been in-creasing pressure, in the Congress and elsewhere, for the U.S. to consolidate and unify its various trade functions in one super-agency. The reasons behind this vary.   Some believe that the U.S. cannot speak with one voice on trade matters when various policy and enforcement functions are divided[25] among different agencies. Others favor reorganization to

---

[24] See Export Trading Companies Act of 1982, Pub. L. No. 97-290. Actually, U.S. companies have been permitted to do this since 1918 under the Webb-Pomerene Act, 15 U.S.C. §§ 61-65. That Act exempted associations engaged solely in export trade from certain provisions of the antitrust laws. However, the law was not greatly utilized due to its failure to cover service industries and because the vagueness of its antitrust exemp-tions which created uncertainties.

[25] President Reagan, in a closed circuit speech to U.S. Chamber of Commerce members in 42 cities, stated that creation of a cabinet level trade agency would let both "U.S. business and the world know we speak with one voice" in the trade field. Washington Post, May 11, 1983, at D7.

solidify functions in a particular agency that they feel might best carry out certain objectives. For example, the earlier transfer of antidumping and countervailing duty functions from Treasury to Commerce was favored by some who viewed Commerce as more aggressive in the enforcement areas. Certainly, the success of Japan's MITI has been a role model which many in the U.S. would like to follow. At least one experienced commentator has viewed the proposed U.S. Department of International Trade and Industry (DITI) as a direct response to Japan's MITI.[26]

The plan, announced in May, 1983, would essentially merge the Office of U.S. Trade Representative with the Department of Commerce's International Trade Administration. Some reports indicated that the Export-Import Bank and the Overseas Private Investment Corporation might also become part of the super agency. Initial reaction to the plan was mixed. Some sources in the U.S. Trade Representative's Office expressed concern that their elite White House status would be diminished if they were merged with the mammoth Commerce Department. More recent reports were that U.S.T.R. would remain intact as an office within the new department.[27] Also, some current reports indicated that the entire Department of Commerce would be dismantled, with other agencies like the National Oceanic and Atmospheric Administration, becoming separate agencies.[28] Whether a Department of International Trade will ever be created is uncertain at the present time. Whether it will solve the myriad U.S. trade problems is even more speculative. For example, even if the proposed plan were implemented, it would be unlikely to really create a unified trade policy. Agricultural trade matters would still be handled by the Department of Agriculture. Many important trade decisions will still be made by the autonomous U.S. International Trade Commission, and the powerful counter-pressures of the legislative branch will still be prevelant. As with the issue of industrial policy, it is unclear whether the pluralistic U.S. system can adapt to the centralization of decision making and the elimination of competing influences that some see as a necessity to regain U.S. competitiveness in world trade.

---

26 Rowen, "Should we have a DITI to match Japan's MITI", Washington Post, July 17, 1983, at A1. "The Reagan administration in its desperation to do something that will help this country compete with Japan, has proposed the creation of a new Department of International Trade and Industry."

27 U.S. Import Weekly (BNA) 365 (June 8, 1983).

28 Id.

Chapter 8

CONCLUSION

    While the focus of this book has been on the Multilateral
Trade Negotiations, we have tried to place this important
event in world trade development in an historical context. We
have looked at the seeds for the MTN that were planted in the
Kennedy Round, the successes and failures of the MTN, the
implementation of the MTN, the GATT Ministerial, and Post-
Ministerial Trade issues. While any conclusions as to the
place of the MTN in the history of trade negotiations is bound
to be subjective, it is this author's view that the MTN may
well have been the most significant round of trade negotiations in history. This is largely due to the success in
negotiating substantive codes of conduct in the non-tariff
trade barriers area, a task that had never before been
attempted, much less been accomplished.
    The Codes have proven to be largely effective, at least
in dealing with the trade problems prevalent at the time they
were adopted. They were not intended to deal with some of the
current problem areas of trade in services or high technology
products. It is perhaps the great success of the MTN that has
made the 1982 Ministerial meeting appear to be such a dismal
failure to many. Perhaps some had expected a repeat performance of the successes of the Tokyo Round. This was, at least
in hindsight, unrealistic, because the problems faced at the
Ministerial were, to a large degree, more complex than those
faced at the Tokyo Round, and more importantly, because it was
not feasible to accomplish in a one week meeting, what was
accomplished over several years in the Tokyo Round. Moreover,
many of the actors were different, e.g., such forceful
negotiators as former U.S. Trade Representative Strauss were
no longer part of the process. Nevertheless, the perception
exists, and perhaps with some validity that the MTN was the
zenith of the GATT and that the Ministerial was the nadir.
    While it would be an overstatement to link the future of
the GATT to the future of world economic stability, if the
GATT should fail and be deemed obsolete, the effect on world

trade could be significant.   It is uncertain whether such political groups as UNCTAD, with its power spread among many third world and socialist nations, could tackle the complex world trading problems without becoming the stage for socio-political rhetoric that has characterized and, to a large degree, paralyzed the United Nations in recent years.   In this author's opinion, the GATT may not be perfect, but it is the best structure we have for resolution of the world's complex trading problems.   The GATT, although not immune to politics, is removed from the highly charged East-West confrontations that have tended to turn many multi-partite organizations into political debating societies, powerless to effectively tackle complex legal and economic problems.

What is clear is that the 1980's will be a crucial period in world trade and that the future of the non-Communist economic order could well depend on the success or failure of trade policies adopted by the remaining market economies that have been the backbone of the economic and financial stability of the world.

APPENDICES

MINISTERIAL MEETING TOKYO, 12-14 SEPTEMBER 1973

Declaration

1.   The Ministers, having considered the report of the Preparatory Committee
for the Trade Negotiations and having noted that a number of governments have
decided to enter into comprehensive multilateral trade negotiations in the
framework of GATT and that other governments have indicated their intention to
make a decision as soon as possible, declare the negotiations officially open.
Those governments which have decided to negotiate have notified the
Director—General of GATT to this effect, and the Ministers agree that it will be
open to any other government, through a notification to the Director—General, to
participate in the negotiations. The Ministers hope that the negotiations will
involve the active participation of as many countries as possible. They expect
the negotiations to be engaged effectively as rapidly as possible, and that, to
that end, the governments concerned will have such authority as may be required.

2.   The negotiations shall aim to:

- achieve the expansion and ever-greater liberalization of world trade and
improvement in the standard of living and welfare of the people of the
world, objectives which can be achieved, _inter alia_, through the progressive
dismantling of obstacles to trade and the improvement of the international
framework for the conduct of world trade.

- secure additional benefits for the international trade of developing
countries so as to achieve a substantial increase in their foreign
exchange earnings, the diversification of their exports, the acceleration
of the rate of growth of their trade, taking into account their development
needs, an improvement in the possibilities for these countries to participate in the expansion of world trade and a better balance as between
developed and developing countries in the sharing of the advantages
resulting from this expansion, through, in the largest possible measure, a
substantial improvement in the conditions of access for the products of
interest to the developing countries and, wherever appropriate, measures
designed to attain stable, equitable and remunerative prices for primary
products.

To this end, co-ordinated efforts shall be made to solve in an equitable
way the trade problems of all participating countries, taking into account the
specific trade problems of the developing countries.

3. To this end the negotiations should aim, _inter alia_, to:
    (a) conduct negotiations on tariffs by employment of appropriate formulae
         of as general application as possible;
    (b) reduce or eliminate non-tariff measures or, where this is not
         appropriate, to reduce or eliminate their trade restricting or dis-
         torting effects, and to bring such measures under more effective
         international discipline;
    (c) include an examination of the possibilities for the co-ordinated
         reduction or elimination of all barriers to trade in selected sectors
         as a complementary technique;
    (d) include an examination of the adequacy of the multilateral safeguard
         system, considering particularly the modalities of application of
         Article XIX, with a view to furthering trade liberalization and
         preserving its results;
    (e) include, as regards agriculture, an approach to negotiations which,
         while in line with the general objectives of the negotiations, should
         take account of the special characteristics and problems in this
         sector;
    (f) treat tropical products as a special and priority sector.

4. The negotiations shall cover tariffs, non-tariff barriers and other
measures which impede or distort international trade in both industrial and
agricultural products, including tropical products and raw materials, whether
in primary form or at any stage of processing including in particular products
of export interest to developing countries and measures affecting their exports.

5. The negotiations shall be conducted on the basis of the principles of
mutual advantage, mutual commitment and overall reciprocity, while observing
the most-favoured-nation clause, and consistently with the provisions of the
General Agreement relating to such negotiations. Participants shall jointly
endeavour in the negotiations to achieve, by appropriate methods, an overall
balance of advantage at the highest possible level. The developed countries do
not expect reciprocity for commitments made by them in the negotiations to

reduce or remove tariff and other barriers to the trade of developing countries,
i.e.. the developed countries do not expect the developing countries. in the
course of the trade negotiations, to make contributions which are inconsistent
with their individual development, financial and trade needs. The Ministers
recognize the need for special measures to be taken in the negotiations to
assist the developing countries in their efforts to increase their export
earnings and promote their economic development and, where appropriate, for
priority attention to be given to products or areas of interest to developing
countries. They also recognize the importance of maintaining and improving
the Generalized System of Preferences. They further recognize the importance
of the application of differential measures to developing countries in ways
which will provide special and more favourable treatment for them in areas of
the negotiation where this is feasible and appropriate.

6.   The Ministers recognize that the particular situation and problems of the
least developed among the developing countries shall be given special attention,
and stress the need to ensure that these countries receive special treatment in
the context of any general or specific measures taken in favour of the
developing countries during the negotiations.

7.   The policy of liberalizing world trade cannot be carried out successfully
in the absence of parallel efforts to set up a monetary system which shields
the world economy from the shocks and imbalances which have previously occurred.
The Ministers will not lose sight of the fact that the efforts which are to be
made in the trade field imply continuing efforts to maintain orderly conditions
and to establish a durable and equitable monetary system.

The Ministers recognize equally that the new phase in the liberalization
of trade which it is their intention to undertake should facilitate the orderly
functioning of the monetary system.

The Ministers recognize that they should bear these considerations in mind
both at the opening of and throughout the negotiations. Efforts in these two
fields will thus be able to contribute effectively to an improvement of
international economic relations, taking into account the special characteristics of the economies of the developing countries and their problems.

8.   The negotiations shall be considered as one undertaking, the various elements of which shall move forward together.

9.   Support is reaffirmed for the principles, rules and disciplines provided for under the General Agreement.[1] Consideration shall be given to improvements in the international framework for the conduct of world trade which might be desirable in the light of progress in the negotiations and, in this endeavour, care shall be taken to ensure that any measures introduced as a result are consistent with the overall objectives and principles of the trade negotiations and particularly of trade liberalization.

10. A Trade Negotiations Committee is established, with authority, taking into account the present Declaration, inter alia:

   (a) to elaborate and put into effect detailed trade negotiating plans and to establish appropriate negotiating procedures, including special procedures for the negotiations between developed and developing countries;

   (b) to supervise the progress of the negotiations.

The Trade Negotiations Committee shall be open to participating governments.[2] The Trade Negotiations Committee shall hold its opening meeting not later than 1 November 1973.

11. The Ministers intend that the trade negotiations be concluded in 1975.

---

[1]This does not necessarily represent the views of representatives of countries not now parties to the General Agreement.

[2]Including the European Communities.

STATUS OF TOKYO ROUND MTN AGREEMENT SIGNATURES AND ACCEPTANCES
(BY CODE)
AS OF MARCH 1, 1983
(REVISED IN ACCORDANCE WITH GATT DOCUMENT L/4914/REV.6/ADD.2)

	CODE	ACCEPTED	ACCEPTED WITH RESERVATION	SIGNED SUBJECT TO RATIFICATION
A.	TARIFF PROTOCOL	ARGENTINA, AUSTRIA, BELGIUM*, CANADA, CZECHOSLOVAKIA, DENMARK*, EUROPEAN ECONOMIC COMMUNITY, FINLAND, FRANCE*, HUNGARY, ICELAND, IRELAND*, ITALY*, JAMAICA, JAPAN, LUXEMBORG*, NETHERLANDS*, NEW ZEALAND, NORWAY, POLAND, ROMANIA, SOUTH AFRICA, SPAIN, SWEDEN, SWITZERLAND, UNITED KINGDOM*, UNITED STATES, WEST GERMANY*, YUGOSLAVIA		ISRAEL
B.	SUPPLEMENT TO THE TARIFF PROTOCOL	AUSTRALIA, BELGIUM*, BRAZIL, CANADA, CHILE, DOMINICAN REPUBLIC, EUROPEAN ECONOMIC COMMUNITY, HAITI, INDIA, INDONESIA, ISRAEL, IVORY COAST, KOREA, MALAYSIA, PAKISTAN, PERU, SINGAPORE, SPAIN, URUGUAY, ZAIRE		EGYPT
C.	STANDARDS	ARGENTINA, AUSTRIA, BELGIUM*, BRAZIL, CANADA, CHILE, CZECHOSLOVAKIA, DENMARK*, EGYPT, EUROPEAN ECONOMIC COMMUNITY, FINLAND, FRANCE*, GREECE*, HONG KONG, HUNGARY, IRELAND*, ITALY*, JAPAN, KOREA, LUXEMBORG*, NETHERLANDS*, NEW ZEALAND, NORWAY, PAKISTAN, PHILIPPINES, ROMANIA, RWANDA, SINGAPORE, SPAIN, SWEDEN, SWITZERLAND, TUNISIA, UNITED KINGDOM*, UNITED STATES, WEST GERMANY*, YUGOSLAVIA		
D.	PROCUREMENT	AUSTRIA, CANADA, EUROPEAN ECONOMIC COMMUNITY (FOR MEMBER STATES), FINLAND, HONG KONG, JAPAN, NORWAY, SINGAPORE, SWEDEN, SWITZERLAND, UNITED KINGDOM, UNITED STATES		

EC MEMBER STATES SIGN INDIVIDUALLY DUE TO JURISDICTION DIVISIONS
BETWEEN THE EUROPEAN COMMISSION AND THE MEMBER STATES

183

STATUS OF TOKYO ROUND MTN AGREEMENT SIGNATURES AND ACCEPTANCES
(BY CODE)
AS OF MARCH 1, 1983
(REVISED IN ACCORDANCE WITH GATT DOCUMENT L/4914/REV.6/ADD.2)

CODE	ACCEPTED	ACCEPTED WITH RESERVATION	SIGNED SUBJECT TO RATIFICATION
E. SUBSIDIES	AUSTRALIA, AUSTRIA, BRAZIL, CANADA, CHILE, EGYPT, EUROPEAN ECONOMIC COMMUNITY (FOR MEMBER STATES), FINLAND, INDIA, HONG KONG, JAPAN, KOREA, NORWAY, PAKISTAN, SWEDEN, SWITZERLAND, UNITED STATES, URUGUAY, YUGOSLAVIA	NEW ZEALAND, SPAIN	
F. MEAT	ARGENTINA, AUSTRALIA, AUSTRIA, BRAZIL, BULGARIA, CANADA, EUROPEAN ECONOMIC COMMUNITY (FOR MEMBER STATES), FINLAND, HUNGARY, JAPAN, NEW ZEALAND, NORWAY, POLAND, ROMANIA, SOUTH AFRICA, SWEDEN, SWITZERLAND, TUNISIA, UNITED KINGDOM* (RE: BELIZE), UNITED STATES, URUGUAY, YUGOSLAVIA		EGYPT
G. DAIRY	ARGENTINA, AUSTRALIA, AUSTRIA, BULGARIA, EUROPEAN ECONOMIC COMMUNITY (FOR MEMBER STATES), FINLAND, HUNGARY, JAPAN, NEW ZEALAND, NORWAY, POLAND, ROMANIA, SOUTH AFRICA, SWEDEN, SWITZERLAND, UNITED STATES, URUGUAY		EGYPT
H. CUSTOMS	AUSTRIA, EUROPEAN ECONOMIC COMMUNITY (FOR MEMBER STATES), FINLAND, HONG KONG, HUNGARY, JAPAN, NEW ZEALAND, NORWAY, ROMANIA, SPAIN, SWEDEN, SWITZERLAND, UNITED KINGDOM, UNITED STATES, YUGOSLAVIA	ARGENTINA, BRAZIL, CANADA, INDIA, KOREA	
I. CUSTOMS VALUATION PROTOCOL	AUSTRIA, BRAZIL, CANADA, EUROPEAN ECONOMIC COMMUNITY (FOR MEMBER STATES), FINLAND, HONG KONG, HUNGARY, JAPAN, NEW ZEALAND, NORWAY, ROMANIA, SPAIN, SWEDEN, SWITZERLAND, UNITED KINGDOM, UNITED STATES, YUGOSLAVIA	INDIA, KOREA	ARGENTINA

EC MEMBER STATES SIGN INDIVIDUALLY DUE TO JURISDICTION DIVISIONS BETWEEN THE EUROPEAN COMMISSION AND THE MEMBER STATES

STATUS OF TOKYO ROUND MTN AGREEMENT SIGNATURES AND ACCEPTANCES
(BY CODE)
AS OF MARCH 1, 1983
(REVISED IN ACCORDANCE WITH GATT DOCUMENT L/4914/REV.6/ADD.2)

CODE	ACCEPTED	ACCEPTED WITH RESERVATION	SIGNED SUBJECT TO RATIFICATION
J. LICENSING	AUSTRALIA, AUSTRIA, CANADA, CHILE, CZECHOSLOVAKIA, EGYPT, EUROPEAN ECONOMIC COMMUNITY (FOR MEMBER STATES), FINLAND, HONG KONG, HUNGARY, INDIA, JAPAN, NEW ZEALAND, NORWAY, PAKISTAN, ROMANIA, SOUTH AFRICA, SWEDEN, SWITZERLAND, UNITED STATES, YUGOSLAVIA	PHILIPPINES	ARGENTINA
K. AIRCRAFT	AUSTRIA, BELGIUM*, DENMARK*, EUROPEAN ECONOMIC COMMUNITY, FRANCE*, GREECE*, HONG KONG, IRELAND*, ITALY*, JAPAN, LUXEMBORG*, NETHERLANDS*, NORWAY, ROMANIA, SWEDEN, SWITZERLAND, UNITED KINGDOM*, UNITED STATES, WEST GERMANY*	CANADA	EGYPT
L. ANTIDUMPING	AUSTRALIA, AUSTRIA, BRAZIL, CANADA, CZECHOSLOVAKIA, EGYPT, EUROPEAN ECONOMIC COMMUNITY (FOR MEMBER STATES), FINLAND, GREECE, HONG KONG, HUNGARY, INDIA, JAPAN, NORWAY, PAKISTAN, POLAND, ROMANIA, SPAIN, SWEDEN, SWITZERLAND, UNITED KINGDOM, UNITED STATES, YUGOSLAVIA		

EC MEMBER STATES SIGN INDIVIDUALLY DUE TO JURISDICTION DIVISIONS
BETWEEN THE EUROPEAN COMMISSION AND THE MEMBER STATES

GENERAL AGREEMENT ON
TARIFFS AND TRADE

MTN/SG/W/39*
22 June 1978
Special Distribution

Multilateral Trade Negotiations

Group "Safeguards"

Original: English

DRAFT INTEGRATED TEXT ON SAFEGUARDS

(Circulated at the request of several delegations)

Note: This is an informal working paper drafted with a view to facilitating
further consideration of this subject. It does not commit any delegation
to all or any part of the text nor does it prejudice in any way the
negotiating position of any delegation in any area of the MTN. It is
understood that all elements of this text are interrelated and that in
the light of its further evolution, delegations may wish to propose
additional elements or alternative texts.

GENERAL PROVISION

Without prejudice to the rights and obligations of GATT contracting parties
regarding restrictive measures permitted for specified purposes under the terms
of other GATT provisions, protocols, agreements and arrangements negotiated
under GATT auspices[1], signatories undertake not to take safeguard action except
through invocation of Article XIX and in accordance with the following
provisions.

CHAPTER 1 – CRITERIA FOR INVOCATION

1. In the implementation of paragraph 1 of Article XIX, signatories agree that
safeguard action may only follow a determination by the domestic authorities
concerned that imports of a particular product[2] are causing or threatening to
cause serious injury to /a /major/ /significant/ part of all/ domestic producers

---

[1] Some delegations believe that it will be necessary to identify which
"protocols, agreements and arrangements" are referred to, prior to final
acceptance of this text. It has been proposed to add at this point, language
along the following lines: "... and where such rights are explicitly invoked by
reference to specific GATT articles or other provisions ...".

[2] A representative of several contracting parties understands that this
language refers to imports of a particular product into the territory of a
contracting party.

*The present document replaces document MTN/INF/26 circulated on
21 June 1978, the text of which remains unchanged.

of like or directly competitive products. Such a determination shall be
made only when such imports have increased in such quantities, or in such
relative quantities, and under such conditions demonstrably as to /account
for the principal[1]/ cause /of/ serious injury sustained or demonstrably
likely to be sustained by domestic producers. The determination in all
cases shall be made on the basis of positive findings of fact and not on
mere conjecture, or remote or hypothetical possibility; in the case of
a determination of threat of serious injury, those findings shall include
evidence that serious injury, although not yet existing, is clearly
imminent.

2.   Determination of the existence of serious injury or threat thereof,
including the evaluation of the effects of the said imports on the domestic
producers, shall be based on examination of factors having a bearing on
the state of the domestic producers in question, such as: development
and prospects with regard to output, turnover, inventories, market share,
profits, prices, export performance, employment and wages, imports,
utilization of capacity of domestic industry, productivity, and investment
/, as well as the size of the market/. The list is not exhaustive, nor
can any one or several of the factors necessarily give decisive guidance.

/3.[2] (a) The term "domestic producers" shall be interpreted as referring
to the domestic producers as a whole of the like products or the directly
competitive products or to those of them whose collective output of the
products constitutes a /significant/ /major/ proportion of the total
domestic production of those products except that when producers are
importers of the like products or the directly competitive products the
domestic producers shall be interpreted as referring to the rest of the
producers.

      (b) Where two or more countries have reached such a level of
integration that they have characteristics of a single, unified market,
the producers in the entire area of integration shall be taken to be the
producers referred to in sub-paragraph (a)./

/4. The determination of "principal cause" shall be based on an examination of the effect of the said imports on one hand and on the other hand,
all other factors which, individually or in combination, may be adversely
affecting the domestic producers, for example: competition among domestic
producers, contraction in demand due to substitution by other products or
to changes in consumer tastes./

---

[1]See also paragraph 4, determination of "principal cause".

[2]This paragraph is an alternative to the bracketed language beginning
on the fifth line of paragraph 1. It would be for consideration whether
language along the lines of Article 4(a)(ii) of the Anti-dumping Code
should be included.

CHAPTER 2 - CONDITIONS

1.   As a rule safeguard measures should be applied in a manner that is proportionate to the injury caused or threatened to be caused. Therefore, it is agreed that:

   (a) Product coverage of a safeguard action shall be limited to imports of the particular product or products causing or threatening serious injury, although appropriate allowance may be made for dealing with the possibility of circumvention through, for example, minor design or processing changes or incomplete assembly of component parts.

   (b) A safeguard action shall remain in force only so long as it is necessary in order to prevent or remedy serious injury to domestic producers. /At the time it takes a safeguard action, the importing signatory shall stipulate the period of validity of such action. A safeguard action may be extended beyond such period on terms no more restrictive than those obtaining immediately prior to the extension. In no case will the safeguard action and its extension(s) total more than /x/ years./

   (c) /No safeguard actions shall be implemented with respect to any product which was subject to a safeguard action within the preceding /two years/./

   (d) Safeguard measures shall /to the extent feasible/ be progressively liberalized during the period of their application to encourage the adjustment of domestic producers to import competition /and to minimize trade restrictive effects of safeguard actions on exporting signatories/.

   (e) Safeguard measures shall not /normally/ reduce the level of imports below the level in a previous representative period /(i.e. a twelve-month period terminating (...) months preceding the month in which domestic procedures provided for in Chapter 7 are initiated)/.

CHAPTER 3 - RESPONSE TO SAFEGUARD MEASURES

ALTERNATIVE I

1.   /Signatories agree that the right of a contracting party to suspend substantially equivalent concessions or other obligations under Article XIX:3(a) is maintained./ If, /however,/ following the consultations described in Chapter 5, a signatory affected as an exporter of the product concerned to the territory of the signatory taking the safeguard action agrees that the requirements of this Agreement have been met by the latter signatory it /shall/ /may/ refrain from exercising its rights under Article XIX:3(a) of the General Agreement with respect to the suspension of substantially equivalent concessions or other obligations so long as the signatory taking the action continues to comply fully with the requirements of this Agreement.

2.   If the affected signatory does not so agree and exercises those rights, the signatory taking safeguard action may request review of the matter under Chapter 6.

ALTERNATIVE II

/NOTE: Safeguard action which fully meets the criteria and conditions of Article XIX does not, of itself, constitute nullification or impairment of any GATT rights because Article XIX is an integral part of the GATT and part of the context within which other obligations are assumed. Moreover, in most cases where it has been agreed or established that the safeguard action has been applied in a manner that is consistent with the requirements of Article XIX, there will not necessarily be any undue adverse impact on the interests of the exporting countries concerned. However, it is recognized that there may arise situations in which a safeguard action which is fully justified under Article XIX could nevertheless have or could come to have an adverse effect on the interests of the exporting countries concerned in terms of the impact of the action on the overall balance of advantages._/

1. Signatories agree that in considering whether "agreement" in the sense of Article XIX:3(a) is reached they would, in the first instance, examine whether the safeguard action meets the criteria and conditions of Article XIX. If it is agreed or established that the action taken by an importing signatory is fully consistent with the criteria and conditions of Article XIX the exporting signatory concerned will refrain from exercising its rights under Article XIX:3(a) with respect to the suspension of substantially equivalent concessions.

2. At a later point if the exporting signatories concerned consider that, although the safeguard action in question has met the criteria and conditions of Article XIX, that action has nevertheless had a serious adverse effect on their interests, then there would be further consideration of whether there was agreement in the sense of Article XIX:3(a). In these circumstances it is agreed that the exporting signatories would be free to pursue their rights under that Article with respect to the suspension of substantially equivalent concessions. In such a case, however, consideration of "substantially equivalent concessions" would be related to the effect of the measure which has been used by the importing signatory rather than to the amount of the trade covered by the safeguard measure.

/NOTE: In order to make such provisions practical, the ninety-day provision in XIX:3(a) would have to be altered._/

/NOTE: The Committee would then have the thirty days provided for in Article XIX during which it could disapprove, or not disapprove, of the proposed suspension of concessions or other obligations. If the Committee was unable to reach agreement, it would be appropriate to provide for referring the matter to the Panel. In such a situation it would probably be necessary to provide for extension of the thirty-day limit, to allow time for the necessary deliberations, although it would be important to ensure that the procedures worked without undue delay./

3.   It is further agreed that recourse to the provisions of Article XIX:3(a) by an exporting signatory does not limit its right to invoke the general dispute settlement procedures set out in this Agreement with a view to obtaining a finding that the safeguard action at issue is not in conformity with Article XIX, and a recommendation that the signatory taking such action should cease taking such action (or modify such action so as to conform with Article XIX), and should offer such compensation as will offset the damage to the interests of the exporting signatory.

CHAPTER 4 - NATURE OF SAFEGUARD ACTION

NOTE: The text of this Chapter will require substantially more discussion. It does not reflect the views of all delegations which participated in the drafting of the other Chapters of the Draft Integrated Text on Safeguards.

1.   In general, safeguard measures pursuant to this Agreement shall be applied on a global basis without discrimination as between sources of imports. In circumstances described in the following paragraph, safeguard measures may be applied to imports from particular sources in accordance with the provisions of this Chapter. In all cases, the obligations, conditions, criteria, and procedures established in the other Chapters of this Agreement shall be adhered to.

2.   In unusual and exceptional circumstances where it is clearly established that serious injury or threat thereof, as described in Chapter 1, exists /and is caused by sharp and substantial increase of imports from one or a limited number of countries and the effects of imports from other sources are regarded as being negligible,/ /and where imports causing serious injury can be clearly distinguished from other imports of a particular product,/ an importing signatory may /by agreement with the exporting signatory /pursuant to the subsequent paragraphs,/ / apply safeguard measures limited to imports from such particular sources causing serious injury or threat thereof, provided such measures are applied equitably

as amongst imports causing or threatening to cause serious injury. The measures may be taken by either the importing signatory or exporting signatory or both.[1]

3. When seeking agreement with respect to a proposed measure of the kind described in the preceding paragraph, in consultations pursuant to Chapter 5, both signatories shall endeavour to reach a conclusion within a reasonable period of time. It is appropriate for such consultations normally to cover, _inter alia_, factual evidence on injury and source of imports, the terms of the proposed measure in relation to the requirements of Chapter 2 (including level of restriction, period of validity, product coverage, possibility of progressive liberalization of the restriction), and both parties' intentions with respect to offsetting measures or adjustments.

/4. In seeking the agreement of the exporting signatory concerned the importing signatory should normally offer more liberal terms than those provided for in Chapter 2 and alleviate the level of restraint over the period of application, and in order to facilitate agreement, the importing signatory should endeavour to offer sufficient compensation to the exporting signatory subject to the safeguard measures./

/NOTE: Duration of measures.

1. Provisions for maximum duration of safeguard measures (global basis) should be made in this Agreement.

2. In the case of selective application, shorter duration of measures may be appropriate. Differentiation may also be appropriate between cases of consent and non-consent of the exporters involved.

3. This point should be reviewed in conjunction with relevant provisions of the code./

5. Non-global safeguard measures taken under this Chapter should not place the exporting signatory subject to these measures in a disadvantageous position in relation to other exporting countries not subject to these measures. If an exporting signatory which has agreed to safeguard measures pursuant to the preceding paragraphs considers that it is placed in a disadvantageous position in relation to other exporting countries not subject to the said measures, it may request consultation with the importing signatory invoking the said measures at any time throughout the period of application. The importing signatory shall consult with the requesting exporting signatory without delay. If no satisfactory solution is reached as a result of the consultation, the exporting signatory may withdraw the agreement to the said measures.

---

[1]/In adhering to the obligations and procedures specified in this Chapter, signatories further understand that no such measure may be taken without prior consultation as provided in Chapter 5./

6. If the consultations described in paragraph 3 do not result in agreement between the importing signatory and the exporting signatory within a reasonable period of time* and if critical circumstances as defined in Article XIX:2 exist, the importing signatory may proceed to take the action proposed on condition that such action is immediately notified to the Committee which shall review the matter without delay.**

_____
*To allow time for the substantive bilateral discussions which are envisaged in this chapter, this period would normally be of the order of 30 to 60 days.

**Review by the Committee should not prevent continuing consultations, where appropriate, between the signatories mainly concerned with a view to reaching a mutually satisfactory agreement. In such a case the Parties would naturally so inform the Committee.

7. In cases where a unilateral action is thus referred to it, the Committee shall expeditiously consider the matter, in consultation with the parties concerned and shall in particular review the following aspects*:

(a) whether the circumstances which make it appropriate to limit the action to imports from particular sources, have been shown to exist;

(b) whether the action is applied equitably as between imports causing or threatening to cause serious injury;

_____
*In carrying out its review the Committee may wish to establish a Panel. The present language is not intended to exclude this possibility. The review would naturally cover all of the circumstances relating to the action as in the case of any global safeguard measure; but it is suggested, in this case of unilateral selective action, that its attention be directed on a priority basis to the justification for selectivity.

6. If, in consultations described in paragraph 3 agreement on the proposed measure is not reached between the importing signatory and the exporting signatory within a reasonable period of time, /and the existence of critical circumstances is clearly established - where delay would cause damage difficult to repair and invocation without the agreement of the exporting signatory on the proposed measure is necessary -/ the matter may be referred to the Committee on Safeguard Measures which shall examine the matter without delay and shall also assist the parties in seeking a mutually satisfactory solution to the problem.

7. Upon such referral, the Committee shall expeditiously consider the matter and determine the following, along with any recommendations it considers appropriate*:

(a) existence of the circumstances as referred to in paragraph 2;

(b) existence of /critical/ circumstances where /delay would cause damage difficult to repair and/ invocation without the agreement of the exporting signatory on the proposed measure is necessary;

_____
*To assist its consideration of the matter, the Committee shall normally establish a panel of experts which shall be normally required to report its findings within /60/ days. In general the procedures to be followed for Committee Review would be those provided in Chapter 6, paragraph ____ as supplemented by this Chapter.

(c) whether the consultations have sufficiently covered the matters indicated in paragraphs /3 to 5/ above.

The Committee shall endeavour in the course of this review to promote any solution which would be mutually satisfactory to the parties, but in the event that such a solution is not discovered, the Committee shall make such recommendations to the parties as it considers appropriate in the light of the facts, including indications of any appropriate modifications to the measure taken which would make it more acceptable.

8. In cases where the Committee recommends that the importing signatory modify the measure taken or discontinue its selective application, the importing signatory shall to the maximum extent possible comply with such a recommendation or with all those aspects of it which it judges to be feasible. It is understood that where for compelling reasons, an importing signatory decides that such a recommendation cannot be followed, the full right of the exporting signatory immediately to suspend equivalent concessions shall be preserved and the Committee is authorized to approve without delay an appropriate level of retaliation in the light of all the circumstances.

(c) whether the proposed measure is to be applied equitably as amongst imports causing or threatening to cause serious injury;

(d) whether the proposed measure is otherwise in accordance with the obligations, conditions, criteria, and procedures established by this Agreement.

/The Committee in its consideration shall also look into whether the proposed measure is in line with the provisions of paragraph 4./ During the period of the Committee's consideration, the importing signatory may not implement the proposed non-global safeguard measure.

8. Upon /a positive determination/ /approval/ by the Committee, and if no agreement has been reached by that time, the importing signatory may implement the safeguard measure limited to imports from particular sources (which imports are causing serious injury or threat thereof) consistent with the requirements of this Agreement.

9.   If the exporting signatory subject to the safeguard measure provided
for in the preceding paragraph is of the view that the determination made
by the Committee is no longer justified due to·changes in circumstances or
that it is placed in a disadvantageous position due to the subsequent
developments in relation to other exporting countries not subject to the
said measure it may refer the matter to the Committee at any time throughout
the application of the said measure. Upon such referral, the Committee
shall promptly re-examine the said determination and make, where appropriate,
any recommendations it considers necessary.[1]

10. Exporting signatories who are "affected contracting parties" referred
to in Article XIX:3(a) retain the right to suspend substantially equivalent
concessions or other obligations under the GATT as provided in that Article
/and subject to the provisions of Chapter 3/. The "agreement" referred to
in paragraph 2 of this Chapter may include agreement not to exercise those
rights. /Where safeguard measures are taken pursuant to paragraph 8 of this
Chapter, the exporting signatory affected by such measures /may have
recourse to those rights without passage of the thirty-day requirement
provided for in Article XIX:3(a)/ /shall be free to suspend the application
of substantially equivalent concessions or other obligations under the GATT
to the trade of the importing signatory taking the safeguard measure/./

CHAPTER 4 bis

/USE OF EXPORT RESTRAINTS/[2]

/1. Parties to this Agreement, whether importers or exporters, undertake
not to circumvent the responsibilities and obligations resulting for
importers from this Agreement and from Article XIX of the General Agreement
by means of arrangements or undertakings of any kind to restrict the
exportation of a particular product for the purposes of protecting from
import competition domestic producers of a like or directly competitive
product in the territory of any other party to the General Agreement.

2.   Any party which considers that such a restraint agreement or understanding /including those on a non-governmental basis/ has been or may be
entered into which it believes may adversely affect its trade interests may,
pursuant to Chapter 5, request consultations with the government(s) it
considers to be concerned with a view to obtaining clarification of the
matter. If such consultations do not produce a satisfactory outcome, the
matter may be referred to the Committee on Safeguard Measures in accordance
with the provisions of Chapter 6/.

---

[1]It should be recalled that there will also be an annual report to the
Committee by signatories on safeguard measures they are maintaining in
force and an annual review by the Committee of those measures, pursuant to
Chapters 5 and 6.

[2]In the light of the variety of views on this subject, further
substantive discussion will be needed.

CHAPTER 5 - NOTIFICATION, CONSULTATION

1.   Signatories shall, in accordance with paragraph 2 of Article XIX, provide written notice /to reach the CONTRACTING PARTIES/ /at least ___ days/ in advance of the implementation of a proposed safeguard measure under this Agreement giving all relevant particulars /including but not necessarily limited to: a description of the products against which action is proposed, of what action is proposed, the expected date of implementation and for how long the measure is expected to be in effect; and an explanation of why the action is necessary in terms of the criteria set out in Chapter 1/.

2.   The signatory proposing to adopt a safeguard measure shall be prepared to open consultations with the CONTRACTING PARTIES and those signatories that have a substantial interest as exporters of the product concerned /or whose trade interests are likely to be substantially affected/ before the measure is introduced. Consultations requested[1] shall begin as soon as possible and /preferably/ /in any case/ no later than /thirty days/ from the date /of notification/ /the notification has reached the CONTRACTING PARTIES/.

/3. Regarding consultations with the CONTRACTING PARTIES, it is agreed that if any signatory wishes to have the Committee consult with the signatory proposing to take action, the chairman shall, within /15/ days after he has received written notice of such wish, convene the Committee for this purpose./

/4. Where undue delay in beginning or completing these consultations would lead to damage in the importing country which would be difficult to repair, the importing signatory would be permitted to apply the notified measures on an interim basis pending the final outcome of consultations./

5.   Where the procedures indicated above are followed, the provisions of Article XIX:3(a) will apply.

6.   In the "critical circumstances" referred to in Article XIX, measures may be introduced immediately /following notification/ /and shall be notified immediately/. In this case the action taken will be on a provisional basis /with a maximum validity of /60/ /90/ days/ and the signatory taking action shall be prepared to open consultations /immediately/ /as soon as possible/ /within 15 days/ /with the /CONTRACTING PARTIES/ /Committee/ and those signatories referred to in paragraph 2/. In this event the provisions of Article XIX:3(b) will apply, in addition to those of XIX:3(a).[2]

---

[1]It would be for consideration whether there should be a limited period within which requests for consultation on a (proposed) measure could be made.

[2]Applicability of Article XIX:3(a) to "critical circumstances" measures to be examined further.

7. When a signatory implements a safeguard measure it shall promptly notify the Committee of all relevant particulars. It shall subsequently notify the Committee promptly of any significant changes in the way in which the measure is maintained.

8. A signatory considering the extension of an action shall notify the CONTRACTING PARTIES / ___ days/ before its scheduled expiration and afford an opportunity to consult with it, regarding the possible extension, before the original action expires.

/9. Any signatory which considers that any matter affecting the operation of the Agreement has not been notified in accordance with the provisions of this Agreement, may make a request in writing to the Committee that such matter be notified by the signatory or signatories concerned and may itself notify the matter./

/10. Signatories to this Agreement shall accord sympathetic consideration to, and shall afford adequate opportunity for prompt consultation regarding, such representations as may be made by another signatory with respect to any matter affecting the operation of this Agreement./[1]

/11.[2] A signatory implementing a safeguard action, in conducting consultations provided for in the preceding paragraphs, shall present following particulars in writing as far in advance as may be practicable and in any case not later than the first opportunity of the said consultations.

    (a) In case of the consultation provided for in paragraphs 2 /and 3/,

        (i) a product subject to a safeguard action, date of the implementation, duration of the implementation, type and contents of the action.

        (ii) materials to prove the following,

            (a) that serious injury or threat thereof is determined in compliance with the provisions of Chapter 1.

            (b) that the safeguard action is in compliance with the conditions provided for in Chapter 2.

        (iii) other particulars for reference.

---

[1]This provision is analogous to Article XXII:1 of the General Agreement.

[2]Inclusion of this paragraph in this Chapter or elsewhere in this Agreement to be considered later.

(b) In case of the consultations provided for in paragraph 6, materials to prove the existence of critical circumstances where delay would cause damage which it would be difficult to repair in addition to the particulars described in preceding sub-paragraph.

(c) In case of the consultations provided for in paragraph 8,

(i)   period of extension, type and contents of an extended action.

(ii)   reasons to necessitate the extension concerned and sufficient materials to prove the said necessity.

(iii) other particulars for reference.7

CHAPTER 6 - SURVEILLANCE, DISPUTE SETTLEMENT[1]

1.   The signatories to this Agreement request the CONTRACTING PARTIES to establish a Committee on Safeguard Measures composed of the representatives of the signatories of this Agreement. This Committee shall elect its own chairman and shall meet as necessary, within /30/ days of a request, but not less than once a year for the purpose of affording signatories to this Agreement the opportunity of reporting on the application of this Agreement, on the application of safeguard measures under this Agreement, and of consulting on any matters affecting the operation of this Agreement. The Committee shall also review once a year all safeguard measures in force, on the basis of reports submitted by signatories (pursuant to paragraph 2) and of other information available to the Committee. In the discharge of its duties, the Committee may consult with any contracting party to the GATT, and any other entity or person, and may request from any signatory such information as it considers necessary and appropriate.

2.   Any signatory maintaining a safeguard measure in force shall once a year, on a date set by the Committee, submit a written report to the Committee explaining why the measure is still necessary and what progress is being made towards its removal.

/3. Consultations under paragraph 1 of this Chapter or action taken in accordance with paragraphs 5 and 6 shall be without prejudice to Article XXII and XXIII to the General Agreement./

/3. The signatories also request the CONTRACTING PARTIES to confer upon this Committee the functions of the CONTRACTING PARTIES under Article XIX, XXII and XXIII of GATT for all matters arising as a result of the application of this Agreement as between signatories to it./

---

[1] Some delegations suggest that it would be for consideration whether there should be a sub-committee of signatories for, _inter alia_, continuing surveillance and conciliation purposes.

/3. Nothing in this Agreement shall prejudice the rights of contracting parties under Articles XXII and XXIII of the General Agreement with respect to any matter affecting the operation of the General Agreement; except that, with respect to matters arising between signatories to this Agreement or affecting its operation, including possible nullification or impairment of benefits under this Agreement, signatories shall resort to the procedures of this Agreement./

/4. If any signatory should consider that any safeguard measures, or any system of safeguards, is being applied, or instituted, in a manner inconsistent with the provisions of this Agreement, or any benefit accruing to it directly or indirectly under this Agreement, or the GATT, is being nullified or impaired or that the attainment of any objective of this Agreement or the GATT, is being impeded as the result of the manner in which another signatory, or signatories, is, or are, implementing the provisions of this Agreement, it may, with a view to reaching a satisfactory resolution of the matter, make written representations to the other signatory, or signatories, which it considers to be concerned. Each signatory shall accord sympathetic consideration to and afford adequate opportunity for prompt consultation regarding such representation as may be made by another signatory./

5. It will also be open to any signatory to request the Chairman of the Committee on Safeguard Measures to convene a special meeting of the Committee in order to bring to the attention of parties to the Agreement any problem resulting from action or lack of action by a signatory in a particular case which it has not been possible to resolve by means of bilateral consultations. The Committee shall meet within /30/ days of such request.

6. The Committee shall consider the matter and whatever actions may be appropriate to promote solutions to problems which may be brought to its attention in this way.

ALTERNATIVE I

/Including the establishment upon request of a panel of experts acting in their individual capacities to review the matter and make such findings as will assist the Committee in making appropriate recommendations or rulings/.

/NOTE: It will be appropriate to specify in more detail the procedures of this paragraph, in particular the panel procedures, while taking into account the formulation of dispute settlement procedures in other areas of the MTN./

ALTERNATIVE II

/7. The signatories also request the CONTRACTING PARTIES to establish a Panel composed of persons qualified in the fields of trade relations and acting in their individual capacities. The panel members shall be appointed from time to time by the Director-General of GATT in consultation with the Chairman of the Committee. The Panel shall carry out the responsibilities assigned to it under this Agreement and such other functions as may be given to it by the Committee. In the discharge of its responsibilities, the Panel may consult with any contracting party to the GATT or any other entity or person and may request from any signatory such information as it considers necessary and appropriate.

8. Any signatory shall respond promptly and fully to any request by the Panel for such information as the Panel considers necessary and appropriate.

9. If no mutually satisfactory solution is reached by the Committee within /45/ days from the time the matter was referred to it, the Chairman shall, at the request of any of the signatories concerned direct the Panel inter alia to promptly: (i) investigate the matter; (ii) make appropriate efforts to facilitate a mutually satisfactory solution; (iii) make a statement concerning the facts of the matter including whether a safeguard action met the criteria and conditions of this Agreement and whether a safeguard action by one signatory may have damaged the export interests of any signatory or signatories involved in the dispute; and (iv) as appropriate make such recommendations to the Committee as the facts warrant, including whether a given safeguard measure should be modified or terminated and, adjustments to compensate for the loss of benefit, or damage, occasioned by the safeguard action, measure or practice at issue.

10. The signatories agree that any safeguard action found not to be in conformity with the criteria and conditions of this Agreement shall be modified or terminated so as to conform with the Agreement. Signatories further agree that compensation shall be offered by the signatory concerned for damage caused by any safeguard action which has been found not to be in conformity with this Agreement.

11. If the Panel's recommendations are not adopted by the signatories concerned within /60/ days from the time the report has been received by the Committee, the Panel shall, as soon as possible, recommend to the Committee that a signatory or signatories be authorized to suspend the application, to any other signatory or signatories, of such obligations as may be appropriate in the circumstances. If this latter recommendation is not acted on by the Committee within a period of /60/ days, the signatory which the Panel has proposed be authorized to suspend obligations shall then be free to do so.

12. Any recommendation under the above paragraph shall aim at maintaining the balance of rights and obligations at the highest possible level./

CHAPTER 7 - DOMESTIC PROCEDURES

ALTERNATIVE I

/1. Before a safeguard action may be implemented by a signatory, a previously designated governmental entity shall, pursuant to established procedures and within a reasonable period of time, examine the proposals for such action and determine that the requirements of Chapter 1 have been met.

2. In examining the proposal(s), the entity shall provide adequate public notice of the beginning of its examination and the opportunity for importers and any other interested parties to present their views and relevant evidence, in public hearings and otherwise, in order to facilitate the development of the fullest possible information upon which the competent authorities may judge the need for safeguard action. In each case, there shall be published a report of the entity's determination if affirmative, including the factors considered, criteria applied and rationale used in arriving at its conclusions./

ALTERNATIVE II

/1. In arriving at a determination of serious injury, a signatory which intends to take a safeguard action shall follow domestic procedures previously established and made public.

2. Investigation of injury shall normally be initiated upon a request on behalf of the producers affected, supported by evidence of serious injury for the producers concerned. If in special circumstances the importing signatory decides to initiate an investigation without having received such a request, it shall proceed only if it has evidence on serious injury. Once the importing signatory is satisfied that there is sufficient evidence on serious injury and decides to initiate the investigation, it shall notify signatories having a substantial interest as exporters of the product concerned and those known to be concerned thereof and shall, unless there are special reasons against doing so, publish a public note.

3. All interested parties shall be afforded an opportunity to present all evidence that they consider useful in respect to the investigation in question and to express opinions. All information which is provided on a confidential basis shall be treated as strictly confidential by the authorities concerned.

4. The authorities shall notify the governments of exporting signatories and the interested parties of their determination based on the investigation, indicating the reasons thereof and the criteria applied.

5. Except for good reason to be determined to exist, no investigation shall be made with respect to the same subject matter as a previous investigation unless 1 year has elapsed since the determination under paragraph 4 was made./

CHAPTER 8 - DEVELOPING COUNTRIES

/1. Signatories shall, within the terms of the provisions of this Agreement, make particular efforts to refrain from imposing safeguard measures on imports of particular products of special interest to developing country signatories, or, where such measures are imposed, to limit them strictly to the minimum feasible in extent and duration. In particular, measures imposed consistent with the requirements of this Agreement shall normally permit, for any developing country signatories which are small suppliers or new entrants to the market of the product with respect to which action is taken, continued market access with moderate growth on terms more favourable than those accorded to other affected parties.

2. Signatories which are developed countries /reserve the right to no longer/ /may determine after consultation with the affected developing countries that it is no longer appropriate to/ extend differentiated and more favourable treatment under this Article to individual developing country signatories, when such countries, or the relevant sectors within those countries, have achieved substantially higher levels of economic development or the developing country is internationally competitive in the product./

CHAPTER 9 - OTHER PROVISIONS[1]

/1. All safeguard measures maintained pursuant to Article XIX or the General Agreement by a signatory on the date of entry into force of the Agreement for it, shall be terminated no more than ____ years from that date unless extended under provisions of Chapter 2.

2. All other safeguard measures maintained by a signatory shall be notified to the Committee no later than the date of entry into force of the Agreement for that signatory. Such measures shall be terminated no later than one year following entry into force of this Agreement for that signatory unless continued maintenance of the measures is in conformity with this Agreement./

3. Each signatory to this Agreement shall, promptly following the date the Agreement enters into force for it, notify the Committee of its legislation, regulations and administrative procedures to be used in the implementation of this Agreement. Hereinafter, each signatory shall notify promptly the Committee of any change in such legislation, regulations and procedures.

> NOTE: Consideration should be given to /the inclusion in this Agreement of/ provisions governing the use of automatic licensing and similar surveillance measures for safeguard-related purposes.

---

[1]One delegation emphasizes that existing discriminatory bilateral safeguard arrangements should be abolished under a new safeguard system, and that existing discriminatory quantitative restrictions should be eliminated immediately.

Appendix IV

LEGAL INSTRUMENTS

MULTILATERAL TRADE NEGOTIATIONS

GENEVA (1979) PROTOCOL
TO THE GENERAL AGREEMENT ON TARIFFS AND TRADE
(L/4875)

The contracting parties to the General Agreement on Tariffs and Trade and the European Economic Community which participated in the Multilateral Trade Negotiations 1973-79 (hereinafter referred to as "participants"),

Having carried out negotiations pursuant to Article XXVIII bis, Article XXXIII and other relevant provisions of the General Agreement on Tariffs and Trade (hereinafter referred to as "the General Agreement"),

Have, through their representatives, agreed as follows:

1. The schedule of tariff concessions [1] annexed to this Protocol relating to a participant shall become a Schedule to the General Agreement relating to that participant on the day on which this Protocol enters into force for it pursuant to paragraph 5.

2. (*a*) The reductions agreed upon by each participant shall, except as may be otherwise specified in a participant's schedule, be implemented in equal annual rate reductions beginning 1 January 1980 and the total reduction become effective not later than 1 January 1987. A participant which begins rate reductions on 1 July 1980 or on a date between 1 January and 1 July 1980 shall, unless otherwise specified in that participant's schedule, make effective two-eighths of the total reduction to the final rate on that date followed by six equal instalments beginning 1 January 1982. The reduced rate should in each stage be rounded off to the first decimal. The provisions of this paragraph shall not prevent participants from implementing reductions in fewer stages or at earlier dates than indicated above.

(*b*) The implementation of the annexed schedules in accordance with paragraph 2(*a*) above shall, upon request, be subject to multilateral examination by the participants having accepted this Protocol. This would be without prejudice to the rights and obligations of contracting parties under the General Agreement.

---

[1] See page 5 for a list of the Schedules annexed.

3. After the schedule of tariff concessions annexed to this Protocol relating to a participant has become a Schedule to the General Agreement pursuant to the provisions of paragraph 1, such participant shall be free at any time to withhold or to withdraw in whole or in part the concession in such schedule with respect to any product for which the principal supplier is any other participant or any government having negotiated for accession during the Multilateral Trade Negotiations, but the schedule of which, as established in the Multilateral Trade Negotiations, has not yet become a Schedule to the General Agreement. Such action can, however, only be taken after written notice of any such withholding or withdrawal of a concession has been given to the CONTRACTING PARTIES and after consultations have been held, upon request, with any participant or any acceding government, the relevant schedule of tariff concessions relating to which has become a Schedule to the General Agreement and which has a substantial interest in the product involved. Any concessions so withheld or withdrawn shall be applied on and after the day on which the schedule of the participant or the acceding government which has the principal supplying interest becomes a Schedule to the General Agreement.

4. (a) In each case in which paragraph 1(b) and (c) of Article II of the General Agreement refers to the date of that Agreement, the applicable date in respect of each product which is the subject of a concession provided for in a schedule of tariff concessions annexed to this Protocol shall be the date of this Protocol, but without prejudice to any obligations in effect on that date.

(b) For the purpose of the reference in paragraph 6(a) of Article II of the General Agreement to the date of that Agreement, the applicable date in respect of a schedule of tariff concessions annexed to this Protocol shall be the date of this Protocol.

5. (a) This Protocol shall be open for acceptance by participants, by signature or otherwise, until 30 June 1980.

(b) This Protocol shall enter into force on 1 January 1980 for those participants which have accepted it before that date, and for participants accepting after that date, it shall enter into force on the dates of acceptance.

6. This Protocol shall be deposited with the Director-General to the CONTRACTING PARTIES who shall promptly furnish a certified copy thereof and a notification of each acceptance thereof, pursuant to paragraph 5, to each contracting party to the General Agreement and to the European Economic Community.

7. This Protocol shall be registered in accordance with the provisions of Article 102 of the Charter of the United Nations.

Done at Geneva this thirtieth day of June one thousand nine hundred and seventy-nine, in a single copy, in the English and French languages, both texts being authentic. The Schedules annexed hereto are authentic in the English, French and Spanish language as specified in each Schedule.

Schedules annexed

V — Canada	LVII — Yugoslavia
X — Czechoslovakia	LIX — Switzerland
XIII — New Zealand	LXII — Iceland
XIV — Norway	LXIV — Argentina
XVIII — South Africa	LXVI — Jamaica
XX — United States of America	LXIX — Romania
XXIV — Finland	LXXI — Hungary
XXX — Sweden	LXXII
XXXII — Austria	and — European Communities
XXXVIII — Japan	LXXII bis
XLV — Spain	

PROTOCOL SUPPLEMENTARY TO THE GENEVA (1979) PROTOCOL TO THE GENERAL AGREEMENT ON TARIFFS AND TRADE
(L/4812)

The contracting parties to the General Agreement on Tariffs and Trade and the European Economic Community which participated in the Multilateral Trade Negotiations 1973-79 (hereinafter referred to as " participants ").

Considering that a part of the tariff negotiations carried out in the Multilateral Trade Negotiations have been completed subsequent to the establishment of the Geneva (1979) Protocol to the General Agreement on Tariffs and Trade (hereinafter referred to as " the Geneva (1979) Protocol "),

Having agreed to put into effect the results of these negotiations which involve concessions or contributions additional to those included in the schedules annexed to the Geneva (1979) Protocol or which concern concessions or contributions made by participants not having a schedule annexed to that Protocol,

Recognizing that the results of these negotiations also involve some concessions offered in negotiations leading to the establishment of schedules annexed to the Geneva (1979) Protocol,

Having agreed to annex to the General Agreement on Tariffs and Trade the schedules of concessions which it was not possible to include in the Geneva (1979) Protocol,

Have through their representatives agreed as follows:

1.   The schedule of tariff concessions [1] annexed to this Protocol relating to a participant shall become a Schedule to the General Agreement on Tariffs and Trade (hereinafter referred to as " the General Agreement ") relating to that participant on the day on which this Protocol enters into force for it pursuant to paragraph 5.

2.   (*a*) The reductions agreed upon by each participant shall, except as may be otherwise specified in a participant's schedule, be implemented in equal annual rate reductions beginning 1 January 1980 and the total reduction become effective not later than 1 January 1987.   A participant which begins rate reductions on 1 July 1980 or on a date between 1 January and 1 July 1980 shall, unless otherwise specified in that participant's schedule, make effective two-eighths of the total reduction to the final rate on that date followed by six equal instalments beginning 1 January 1982. The reduced rate should in each stage be rounded off to the first decimal. The provisions of this paragraph shall not prevent participants from implementing reductions in fewer stages or at earlier dates than indicated above.

   (*b*) The implementation of the annexed Schedules in accordance with paragraph 2(*a*) above shall, upon request, be subject to multilateral examination by the participants having accepted this Protocol.   This would be without prejudice to the rights and obligations of contracting parties under the General Agreement.

3.   After the schedule of tariff concessions annexed to this Protocol relating to a participant has become a Schedule to the General Agreement pursuant to the provisions of paragraph 1, such participant shall be free at any time to withhold or to withdraw in whole or in part the concession in such schedule with respect to any product for which the principal supplier is any other participant or any government having negotiated for accession during the Multilateral Trade Negotiations, but the schedule of which, as established in the Multilateral Trade Negotiations, has not yet become a Schedule to the General Agreement.   Such action can, however, only be taken after written notice of any such withholding or withdrawal of a concession has been given to the CONTRACTING PARTIES and after consultations have been held, upon request, with any participant or any acceding government, the relevant schedule of tariff concessions relating to which has become a Schedule to the General Agreement and which has a substantial interest in the product involved.   Any concessions so withheld or withdrawn shall be applied as soon as possible and not later than the thirtieth day following the day on which the schedule of the participant or the acceding government

---

[1] See page 7 for a list of the Schedules annexed.

which has the principal supplying interest becomes a Schedule to the General Agreement.

4. (a) In each case in which paragraph 1(b) and (c) of Article II of the General Agreement refers to the date of that Agreement, the applicable date in respect of each product which is the subject of a concession provided for in a schedule of tariff concessions annexed to this Protocol shall be the date of this Protocol, but without prejudice to any obligations in effect on that date.

(b) For the purpose of the reference in paragraph 6(a) of Article II of the General Agreement to the date of that Agreement, the applicable date in respect of a schedule of tariff concessions annexed to this Protocol shall be the date of this Protocol.

5. (a) This Protocol shall be open for acceptance by participants, by signature or otherwise, until 30 June 1980.

(b) This Protocol shall enter into force on 1 January 1980 for those participants which have accepted it on or before that date, and for participants accepting after that date, it shall enter into force on the dates of acceptance.

6. This Protocol shall be deposited with the Director-General to the CONTRACTING PARTIES who shall promptly furnish a certified copy thereof and a notification of each acceptance thereof, pursuant to paragraph 5, to each contracting party to the General Agreement and to the European Economic Community.

7. This Protocol shall be registered in accordance with the provisions of Article 102 of the Charter of the United Nations.

Done at Geneva this twenty-second day of November, one thousand nine hundred and seventy-nine, in a single copy, in the English and French languages, both texts being authentic. The Schedules annexed hereto are authentic in the English, French and Spanish language as specified in each Schedule.

Schedules annexed

I — Australia	XXXIX — Malaysia
III — Brazil	XLII — Israel
V — Canada	XLV — Spain
VII — Chile	LII — Ivory Coast
XII — India	LX — Republic of Korea
XV — Pakistan	LXIII — Egypt
XXI — Indonesia	LXVIII — Zaire
XXIII — Dominican Republic	LXXII — European Economic
XXVI — Haiti	Community
XXXI — Uruguay	LXXIII — Singapore
XXXV — Peru	

Appendix V

TABLE 1 - TARIFF REDUCTION PROFILE[1]
(9 industrial tariffs combined)

Value of imports ($bn)	Initial level of duty					Total dutiable
	1.1-5	5.1-10	10.1-15	15.1-25	over 25	
	38.8	49.8	34.6	18.8	4.0	146.0
Subject to cut:			percentages			
up to 20%	33	8	17	18	51	19
20.1 - 40%	24	53	44	22	17	38
40.1 - 99.9%	11	23	30	41	19	24
100%	15	3	3	1	0	6
no reduction	17	13	6	18	13	13

[1] Taking only those items on which tariff concessions were made.

TABLE 2 - DEPTH OF TARIFF REDUCTIONS AND POST-MTN TARIFF AVERAGES

		All industrial products		Raw materials		Semi-manufactures		Finished manufactures	
		Depth of cut	Tariff average	Depth of cut	Tariff average	Depth of cut	Tariff average	Depth of cut	Tariff average
9 tariffs combined	W	34	4.7	64	0.3	30	4.0	34	6.5
	S	39	6.4	37	1.6	36	6.2	40	7.1
USA	W	31	4.4	77	0.2	33	3.0	29	5.7
	S	44	6.3	45	1.8	39	6.1	46	7.0
Canada	W	38	7.9	69	0.5	30	8.3	39	8.3
	S	42	7.3	48	2.6	44	6.6	40	8.1
Japan	W	49	2.8	67	0.5	30	4.6	52	6.0
	S	42	6.0	45	1.4	36	6.3	45	6.4
EC	W	29	4.7	15	0.2	27	4.2	29	6.9
	S	30	6.4	16	1.6	30	6.2	29	7.0
Austria	W	13	7.8	9	0.8	19	4.7	13	16.1
	S	31	8.1	27	1.9	29	7.3	32	9.1
Finland	W	21	5.5	60	0.3	13	5.9	22	6.1
	S	14	11.4	40	0.5	10	11.7	16	12.0
Norway	W	25	3.2	39	0.0	21	1.4	25	4.2
	S	22	6.7	29	0.9	20	5.4	22	7.8
Sweden	W	28	4.1	21	0.0	38	3.3	26	4.9
	S	20	4.8	27	0.4	15	5.1	22	5.1
Switzerland	W	23	2.3	28	0.2	25	1.2	22	3.1
	S	24	2.9	15	1.5	23	2.8	25	3.0

W: Weighted average   S: Simple average

Source: GATT

TABLE 3 - SECTORIAL TARIFF REDUCTIONS AND POST-MTN AVERAGES

		Depth of cut		Post-MTN averages	
		Weighted	Simple	Weighted	Simple
Wood, pulp, paper and furniture	- Total	40	41	1.7	4.1
	- Raw materials	54	46	0.2	0.7
	- Semi-manufactures	38	41	1.9	3.7
	- Finished manufactures	41	41	4.2	5.1
Textiles and clothing	- Total	19	31	11.8	10.4
	- Raw materials	25	21	0.8	2.9
	- Semi-manufactures	22	30	11.5	9.6
	- Finished manufactures	19	33	16.7	11.8
Leather, rubber, footwear and travel good	- Total	14	30	6.3	7.2
	- Raw materials	80	50	0.0	1.0
	- Semi-manufactures	35	35	4.4	4.5
	- Finished manufactures	11	29	10.2	10.2
Base metals	- Total	31	38	2.7	5.0
	- Raw materials	82	61	0.0	0.2
	- Semi-manufactures	26	34	3.2	4.6
	- Finished manufactures	37	40	5.9	6.1
Chemicals (incl. photographic supplies)	- Total	38	40	5.3	6.2
	- Semi-manufactures	36	39	5.0	6.2
	- Finished manufactures	43	44	6.0	6.2
Transport equipment	- Total	36	35	5.0	6.5
Non-electric machinery	- Total	47	46	4.1	4.4
Electric machinery	- Total	34	42	6.1	5.0
Minerals, precious stones and metals	- Total	43	39	2.2	4.3
	- Raw materials	69	35	0.3	1.4
	- Semi-manufactures	21	39	1.1	3.6
	- Finished manufactures	40	40	6.9	6.5
Manufactured articles n.e.s.	- Total	42	45	5.5	6.0

Source: GATT

AGREEMENT ON INTERPRETATION AND APPLICATION OF ARTICLES VI, XVI AND XXIII OF THE GENERAL AGREEMENT ON TARIFFS AND TRADE

The signatories [1] to this Agreement,

Noting that Ministers on 12-14 September 1973 agreed that the Multilateral Trade Negotiations should, *inter alia*, reduce or eliminate the trade restricting or distorting effects of non-tariff measures, and bring such measures under more effective international discipline,

Recognizing that subsidies are used by governments to promote important objectives of national policy,

Recognizing also that subsidies may have harmful effects on trade and production,

Recognizing that the emphasis of this Agreement should be on the effects of subsidies and that these effects are to be assessed in giving due account to the internal economic situation of the signatories concerned as well as to the state of international economic and monetary relations,

Desiring to ensure that the use of subsidies does not adversely affect or prejudice the interests of any signatory to this Agreement, and that countervailing measures do not unjustifiably impede international trade, and that relief is made available to producers adversely affected by the use of subsidies within an agreed international framework of rights and obligations,

Taking into account the particular trade, development and financial needs of developing countries,

Desiring to apply fully and to interpret the provisions of Articles VI, XVI and XXIII of the General Agreement on Tariffs and Trade [2] (hereinafter referred to as " General Agreement " or " GATT ") only with respect to subsidies and countervailing measures and to elaborate rules for their

---

[1] The term " signatories " is hereinafter used to mean Parties to this Agreement.

[2] Wherever in this Agreement there is reference to " the terms of this Agreement " or the " articles " or " provisions of this Agreement " it shall be taken to mean, as the context requires, the provisions of the General Agreement as interpreted and applied by this Agreement.

application in order to provide greater uniformity and certainty in their implementation,

Desiring to provide for the speedy, effective and equitable resolution of disputes arising under this Agreement,

Have agreed as follows:

PART I

Article 1

Application of Article VI of the General Agreement [1]

Signatories shall take all necessary steps to ensure that the imposition of a countervailing duty [2] on any product of the territory of any signatory imported into the territory of another signatory is in accordance with the provisions of Article VI of the General Agreement and the terms of this Agreement.

Article 2

Domestic procedures and related matters

1.   Countervailing duties may only be imposed pursuant to investigations initiated [3] and conducted in accordance with the provisions of this Article. An investigation to determine the existence, degree and effect of any alleged subsidy shall normally be initiated upon a written request by or on behalf of the industry affected.   The request shall include sufficient evidence of the existence of (*a*) a subsidy and, if possible, its amount, (*b*) injury within the meaning of Article VI of the General Agreement as interpreted by this Agreement [4] and (*c*) a causal link between the subsidized imports and the

---

[1] The provisions of both Part I and Part II of this Agreement may be invoked in parallel: however, with regard to the effects of a particular subsidy in the domestic market of the importing country, only one form of relief (either a countervailing duty or an authorized countermeasure) shall be available.

[2] The term " countervailing duty " shall be understood to mean a special duty levied for the purpose of off-setting any bounty or subsidy bestowed directly or indirectly upon the manufacture, production or export of any merchandise, as provided for in Article VI:3 of the General Agreement.

[3] The term " initiated " as used hereinafter means procedural action by which a signatory formally commences an investigation as provided in paragraph 3 of this Article.

[4] Under this Agreement the term " injury " shall, unless otherwise specified, be taken to mean material injury to a domestic industry, threat of material injury to a domestic industry or material retardation of the establishment of such an industry and shall be interpreted in accordance with the provisions of Article 6.

alleged injury. If in special circumstances the authorities concerned decide to initiate an investigation without having received such a request, they shall proceed only if they have sufficient evidence on all points under (a) to (c) above.

2. Each signatory shall notify the Committee on Subsidies and Countervailing Measures [1] (a) which of its authorities are competent to initiate and conduct investigations referred to in this Article and (b) its domestic procedures governing the initiation and conduct of such investigations.

3. When the investigating authorities are satisfied that there is sufficient evidence to justify initiating an investigation, the signatory or signatories, the products of which are subject to such investigation and the exporters and importers known to the investigating authorities to have an interest therein and the complainants shall be notified and a public notice shall be given. In determining whether to initiate an investigation, the investigating authorities should take into account the position adopted by the affiliates of a complainant party [2] which are resident in the territory of another signatory.

4. Upon initiation of an investigation and thereafter, the evidence of both a subsidy and injury caused thereby should be considered simultaneously. In any event the evidence of both the existence of subsidy and injury shall be considered simultaneously (a) in the decision whether or not to initiate an investigation and (b) thereafter during the course of the investigation, starting on a date not later than the earliest date on which in accordance with the provisions of this Agreement provisional measures may be applied.

5. The public notice referred to in paragraph 3 above shall describe the subsidy practice or practices to be investigated. Each signatory shall ensure that the investigating authorities afford all interested signatories and all interested parties [3] a reasonable opportunity, upon request, to see all relevant information that is not confidential (as indicated in paragraphs 6 and 7 below) and that is used by the investigating authorities in the investigation, and to present in writing, and upon justification orally, their views to the investigating authorities.

6. Any information which is by nature confidential or which is provided on a confidential basis by parties to an investigation shall, upon cause shown, be treated as such by the investigating authorities. Such information

---

[1] As established in Part V of this Agreement and hereinafter referred to as " the Committee ".

[2] For the purpose of this Agreement " party " means any natural or juridical person resident in the territory of any signatory.

[3] Any " interested signatory " or " interested party " shall refer to a signatory or a party economically affected by the subsidy in question.

shall not be disclosed without specific permission of the party submitting it.[1] Parties providing confidential information may be requested to furnish non-confidential summaries thereof. In the event such parties indicate that such information is not susceptible of summary, a statement of reasons why summarization is not possible must be provided.

7. However, if the investigating authorities find that a request for confidentiality is not warranted and if the party requesting confidentiality is unwilling to disclose the information, such authorities may disregard such information unless it can otherwise be demonstrated to their satisfaction that the information is correct.[2]

8. The investigating authorities may carry out investigations in the territory of other signatories as required, provided they have notified in good time the signatory in question and unless the latter objects to the investigation. Further, the investigating authorities may carry out investigations on the premises of a firm and may examine the records of a firm if (a) the firm so agrees and (b) the signatory in question is notified and does not object.

9. In cases in which any interested party or signatory refuses access to, or otherwise does not provide, necessary information within a reasonable period or significantly impedes the investigation, preliminary and final findings[3], affirmative or negative, may be made on the basis of the facts available.

10. The procedures set out above are not intended to prevent the authorities of a signatory from proceeding expeditiously with regard to initiating an investigation, reaching preliminary or final findings, whether affirmative or negative, or from applying provisional or final measures, in accordance with relevant provisions of this Agreement.

11. In cases where products are not imported directly from the country of origin but are exported to the country of importation from an intermediate country, the provisions of this Agreement shall be fully applicable and the transaction or transactions shall, for the purposes of this Agreement, be regarded as having taken place between the country of origin and the country of importation.

12. An investigation shall be terminated when the investigating authorities are satisfied either that no subsidy exists or that the effect of the alleged subsidy on the industry is not such as to cause injury.

---

[1] Signatories are aware that in the territory of certain signatories disclosure pursuant to a narrowly-drawn protective order may be required.

[2] Signatories agree that requests for confidentiality should not be arbitrarily rejected

[3] Because of different terms used under different systems in various countries the term " finding " is hereinafter used to mean a formal decision or determination.

13. An investigation shall not hinder the procedures of customs clearance.

14. Investigations shall, except in special circumstances, be concluded within one year after their initiation.

15. Public notice shall be given of any preliminary or final finding whether affirmative or negative and of the revocation of a finding. In the case of an affirmative finding each such notice shall set forth the findings and conclusions reached on all issues of fact and law considered material by the investigating authorities, and the reasons and basis therefor. In the case of a negative finding each notice shall set forth at least the basic conclusions and a summary of the reasons therefor. All notices of finding shall be forwarded to the signatory or signatories the products of which are subject to such finding and to the exporters known to have an interest therein.

16. Signatories shall report without delay to the Committee all preliminary or final actions taken with respect to countervailing duties. Such reports will be available in the GATT secretariat for inspection by government representatives. The signatories shall also submit, on a semi-annual basis, reports on any countervailing duty actions taken within the preceding six months.

Article 3

Consultations

1. As soon as possible after a request for initiation of an investigation is accepted, and in any event before the initiation of any investigation, signatories the products of which may be subject to such investigation shall be afforded a reasonable opportunity for consultations with the aim of clarifying the situation as to the matters referred to in Article 2, paragraph 1 above and arriving at a mutually agreed solution.

2. Furthermore, throughout the period of investigation, signatories the products of which are the subject of the investigation shall be afforded a reasonable opportunity to continue consultations, with a view to clarifying the factual situation and to arriving at a mutually agreed solution. [1]

3. Without prejudice to the obligation to afford reasonable opportunity for consultation, these provisions regarding consultations are not intended to prevent the authorities of a signatory from proceeding expeditiously

---

[1] It is particularly important, in accordance with the provisions of this paragraph, that no affirmative finding whether preliminary or final be made without reasonable opportunity for consultations having been given. Such consultations may establish the basis for proceeding under the provisions of Part VI of this Agreement.

with regard to initiating the investigation, reaching preliminary or final findings, whether affirmative or negative, or from applying provisional or final measures, in accordance with the provisions of this Agreement.

4. The signatory which intends to initiate any investigation or is conducting such an investigation shall permit, upon request, the signatory or signatories the products of which are subject to such investigation access to non-confidential evidence including the non-confidential summary of confidential data being used for initiating or conducting the investigation.

Article 4

Imposition of countervailing duties

1. The decision whether or not to impose a countervailing duty in cases where all requirements for the imposition have been fulfilled and the decision whether the amount of the countervailing duty to be imposed shall be the full amount of the subsidy or less are decisions to be made by the authorities of the importing signatory. It is desirable that the imposition be permissive in the territory of all signatories and that the duty be less than the total amount of the subsidy if such lesser duty would be adequate to remove the injury to the domestic industry.

2. No countervailing duty shall be levied [1] on any imported product in excess of the amount of the subsidy found to exist, calculated in terms of subsidization per unit of the subsidized and exported product. [2]

3. When a countervailing duty is imposed in respect of any product, such countervailing duty shall be levied, in the appropriate amounts, on a non-discriminatory basis on imports of such product from all sources found to be subsidized and to be causing injury, except as to imports from those sources which have renounced any subsidies in question or from which undertakings under the terms of this Agreement have been accepted.

4. If, after reasonable efforts have been made to complete consultations, a signatory makes a final determination of the existence and amount of the subsidy and that, through the effects of the subsidy, the subsidized imports are causing injury, it may impose a countervailing duty in accordance with the provisions of this section unless the subsidy is withdrawn.

---

[1] As used in this Agreement " levy " shall mean the definitive or final legal assessment or collection of a duty or tax.

[2] An understanding among signatories should be developed setting out the criteria for the calculation of the amount of the subsidy.

5. (*a*) Proceedings may [1] be suspended or terminated without the imposition of provisional measures or countervailing duties, if undertakings are accepted under which:

(i) the government of the exporting country agrees to eliminate or limit the subsidy or take other measures concerning its effects; or

(ii) the exporter agrees to revise its prices so that the investigating authorities are satisfied that the injurious effect of the subsidy is eliminated. Price increases under undertakings shall not be higher than necessary to eliminate the amount of the subsidy. Price undertakings shall not be sought or accepted from exporters unless the importing signatory has first (1) initiated an investigation in accordance with the provisions of Article 2 of this Agreement and (2) obtained the consent of the exporting signatory. Undertakings offered need not be accepted if the authorities of the importing signatory consider their acceptance impractical, for example if the number of actual or potential exporters is too great, or for other reasons.

(*b*) If the undertakings are accepted, the investigation of injury shall nevertheless be completed if the exporting signatory so desires or the importing signatory so decides. In such a case, if a determination of no injury or threat thereof is made, the undertaking shall automatically lapse, except in cases where a determination of no threat of injury is due in large part to the existence of an undertaking; in such cases the authorities concerned may require that an undertaking be maintained for a reasonable period consistent with the provisions of this Agreement.

(*c*) Price undertakings may be suggested by the authorities of the importing signatory, but no exporter shall be forced to enter into such an undertaking. The fact that governments or exporters do not offer such undertakings or do not accept an invitation to do so, shall in no way prejudice the consideration of the case. However, the authorities are free to determine that a threat of injury is more likely to be realized if the subsidized imports continue.

6. Authorities of an importing signatory may require any government or exporter from whom undertakings have been accepted to provide periodically information relevant to the fulfilment of such undertakings, and to permit verification of pertinent data. In case of violation of undertakings, the authorities of the importing signatory may take expeditious

---

[1] The word " may " shall not be interpreted to allow the simultaneous continuation of proceedings with the implementation of price undertakings, except as provided in paragraph 5(*b*) of this Article.

actions under this Agreement in conformity with its provisions which may constitute immediate application of provisional measures using the best information available. In such cases definitive duties may be levied in accordance with this Agreement on goods entered for consumption not more than ninety days before the application of such provisional measures, except that any such retroactive assessment shall not apply to imports entered before the violation of the undertaking.

7.   Undertakings shall not remain in force any longer than countervailing duties could remain in force under this Agreement.   The authorities of an importing signatory shall review the need for the continuation of any undertaking, where warranted, on their own initiative, or if interested exporters or importers of the product in question so request and submit positive information substantiating the need for such review.

8.   Whenever a countervailing duty investigation is suspended or terminated pursuant to the provisions of paragraph 5 above and whenever an undertaking is terminated, this fact shall be officially notified and must be published.   Such notices shall set forth at least the basic conclusions and a summary of the reasons therefor.

9.   A countervailing duty shall remain in force only as long as, and to the extent necessary to counteract the subsidization which is causing injury.   The investigating authorities shall review the need for continued imposition of the duty, where warranted, on their own initiative or if any interested party so requests and submits positive information substantiating the need for review.

Article 5

Provisional measures and retroactivity

1.   Provisional measures may be taken only after a preliminary affirmative finding has been made that a subsidy exists and that there is sufficient evidence of injury as provided for in Article 2, paragraph 1 (*a*) to (*c*). Provisional measures shall not be applied unless the authorities concerned judge that they are necessary to prevent injury being caused during the period of investigation.

2.   Provisional measures may take the form of provisional countervailing duties guaranteed by cash deposits or bonds equal to the amount of the provisionally calculated amount of subsidization.

3.   The imposition of provisional measures shall be limited to as short a period as possible, not exceeding four months.

4.   The relevant provisions of Article 4 shall be followed in the imposition of provisional measures.

5. Where a final finding of injury (but not of a threat thereof or of a material retardation of the establishment of an industry) is made or in the case of a final finding of threat of injury where the effect of the subsidized imports would, in the absence of the provisional measures, have led to a finding of injury, countervailing duties may be levied retroactively for the period for which provisional measures, if any, have been applied.

6. If the definitive countervailing duty is higher than the amount guaranteed by the cash deposit or bond, the difference shall not be collected. If the definitive duty is less than the amount guaranteed by the cash deposit or bond, the excess amount shall be reimbursed or the bond released in an expeditious manner.

7. Except as provided in paragraph 5 above, where a finding of threat of injury or material retardation is made (but no injury has yet occurred) a definitive countervailing duty may be imposed only from the date of the finding of threat of injury or material retardation and any cash deposit made during the period of the application of provisional measures shall be refunded and any bonds released in an expeditious manner.

8. Where a final finding is negative any cash deposit made during the period of the application of provisional measures shall be refunded and any bonds released in an expeditious manner.

9. In critical circumstances where for the subsidized product in question the authorities find that injury which is difficult to repair is caused by massive imports in a relatively short period of a product benefiting from export subsidies paid or bestowed inconsistently with the provisions of the General Agreement and of this Agreement and where it is deemed necessary, in order to preclude the recurrence of such injury, to assess countervailing duties retroactively on those imports, the definitive countervailing duties may be assessed on imports which were entered for consumption not more than ninety days prior to the date of application of provisional measures.

Article 6

Determination of injury

1. A determination of injury [1] for purposes of Article VI of the General Agreement shall involve an objective examination of both (a) the volume of subsidized imports and their effect on prices in the domestic market for

---

[1] Determinations of injury under the criteria set forth in this Article shall be based on positive evidence. In determining threat of injury the investigating authorities, in examining the factors listed in this Article, may take into account the evidence on the nature of the subsidy in question and the trade effects likely to arise therefrom.

like products [1] and (b) the consequent impact of these imports on domestic producers of such products.

2. With regard to volume of subsidized imports the investigating authorities shall consider whether there has been a significant increase in subsidized imports, either in absolute terms or relative to production or consumption in the importing signatory. With regard to the effect of the subsidized imports on prices, the investigating authorities shall consider whether there has been a significant price undercutting by the subsidized imports as compared with the price of a like product of the importing signatory, or whether the effect of such imports is otherwise to depress prices to a significant degree or prevent price increases, which otherwise would have occurred, to a significant degree. No one or several of these factors can necessarily give decisive guidance.

3. The examination of the impact on the domestic industry concerned shall include an evaluation of all relevant economic factors and indices having a bearing on the state of the industry such as actual and potential decline in output, sales, market share, profits, productivity, return on investments, or utilization of capacity; factors affecting domestic prices; actual and potential negative effects on cash flow, inventories, employment, wages, growth, ability to raise capital or investment and, in the case of agriculture, whether there has been an increased burden on Government support programmes. This list is not exhaustive, nor can one or several of these factors necessarily give decisive guidance.

4. It must be demonstrated that the subsidized imports are, through the effects [2] of the subsidy, causing injury within the meaning of this Agreement. There may be other factors [3] which at the same time are injuring the domestic industry, and the injuries caused by other factors must not be attributed to the subsidized imports.

5. In determining injury, the term " domestic industry " shall, except as provided in paragraph 7 below, be interpreted as referring to the domestic producers as a whole of the like products or to those of them whose collective output of the products constitutes a major proportion of the total domestic

---

[1] Throughout this Agreement the term " like product " (" produit similaire ") shall be interpreted to mean a product which is identical, i.e. alike in all respects to the product under consideration or in the absence of such a product, another product which although not alike in all respects, has characteristics closely resembling those of the product under consideration.

[2] As set forth in paragraphs 2 and 3 of this Article.

[3] Such factors can include *inter alia*, the volume and prices of non-subsidized imports of the product in question, contraction in demand or changes in the pattern of consumption, trade restrictive practices of and competition between the foreign and domestic producers, developments in technology and the export performance and productivity of the domestic industry.

production of those products, except that when producers are related [1] to the exporters or importers or are themselves importers of the allegedly subsidized product the industry may be interpreted as referring to the rest of the producers.

6. The effect of the subsidized imports shall be assessed in relation to the domestic production of the like product when available data permit the separate identification of production in terms of such criteria as: the production process, the producers' realization, profits. When the domestic production of the like product has no separate identity in these terms the effects of subsidized imports shall be assessed by the examination of the production of the narrowest group or range of products, which includes the like product, for which the necessary information can be provided.

7. In exceptional circumstances the territory of a signatory may, for the production in question, be divided into two or more competitive markets and the producers within each market may be regarded as a separate industry if (a) the producers within such market sell all or almost all of their production of the product in question in that market, and (b) the demand in that market is not to any substantial degree supplied by producers of the product in question located elsewhere in the territory. In such circumstances injury may be found to exist even where a major portion of the total domestic industry is not injured provided there is a concentration of subsidized imports into such an isolated market and provided further that the subsidized imports are causing injury to the producers of all or almost all of the production within such market.

8. When the industry has been interpreted as referring to the producers in a certain area, as defined in paragraph 7 above, countervailing duties shall be levied only on the products in question consigned for final consumption to that area. When the constitutional law of the importing signatory does not permit the levying of countervailing duties on such a basis, the importing signatory may levy the countervailing duties without limitation, only if (a) the exporters shall have been given an opportunity to cease exporting at subsidized prices to the area concerned or otherwise give assurances pursuant to Article 4, paragraph 5, of this Agreement, and adequate assurances in this regard have not been promptly given, and (b) such duties cannot be levied only on products of specific producers which supply the area in question.

9. Where two or more countries have reached under the provisions of Article XXIV:8(a) of the General Agreement such a level of integration that they have the characteristics of a single, unified market the industry

---

[1] The Committee should develop a definition of the word " related " as used in this paragraph.

in the entire area of integration shall be taken to be the industry referred to in paragraphs 5 to 7 above.

PART II

Article 7

Notification of subsidies [1]

1. Having regard to the provisions of Article XVI:1 of the General Agreement, any signatory may make a written request for information on the nature and extent of any subsidy granted or maintained by another signatory (including any form of income or price support) which operates directly or indirectly to increase exports of any product from or reduce imports of any product into its territory.

2. Signatories so requested shall provide such information as quickly as possible and in a comprehensive manner, and shall be ready, upon request, to provide additional information to the requesting signatory. Any signatory which considers that such information has not been provided may bring the matter to the attention of the Committee.

3. Any interested signatory which considers that any practice of another signatory having the effects of a subsidy has not been notified in accordance with the provisions of Article XVI:1 of the General Agreement may bring the matter to the attention of such other signatory. If the subsidy practice is not thereafter notified promptly, such signatory may itself bring the subsidy practice in question to the notice of the Committee.

Article 8

Subsidies — General provisions

1. Signatories recognize that subsidies are used by governments to promote important objectives of social and economic policy. Signatories also recognize that subsidies may cause adverse effects to the interests of other signatories.

2. Signatories agree not to use export subsidies in a manner inconsistent with the provisions of this Agreement.

---

[1] In this Agreement, the term " subsidies " shall be deemed to include subsidies granted by any government or any public body within the territory of a signatory. However, it is recognized that for signatories with different federal systems of government, there are different divisions of powers. Such signatories accept nonetheless the international consequences that may arise under this Agreement as a result of the granting of subsidies within their territories.

3. Signatories further agree that they shall seek to avoid causing, through the use of any subsidy

(a) injury to the domestic industry of another signatory [1],

(b) nullification or impairment of the benefits accruing directly or indirectly to another signatory under the General Agreement [2], or

(c) serious prejudice to the interests of another signatory. [3]

4. The adverse effects to the interests of another signatory required to demonstrate nullification or impairment [4] or serious prejudice may arise through

(a) the effects of the subsidized imports in the domestic market of the importing signatory,

(b) the effects of the subsidy in displacing or impeding the imports of like products into the market of the subsidizing country, or

(c) the effects of the subsidized exports in displacing [5] the exports of like products of another signatory from a third country market. [6]

Article 9

Export subsidies on products other than certain primary products [7]

1. Signatories shall not grant export subsidies on products other than certain primary products.

---

[1] Injury to the domestic industry is used here in the same sense as it is used in Part I of this Agreement.

[2] Benefits accruing directly or indirectly under the General Agreement include the benefits of tariff concessions bound under Article II of the General Agreement.

[3] Serious prejudice to the interests of another signatory is used in this Agreement in the same sense as it is used in Article XVI:1 of the General Agreement and includes threat of serious prejudice.

[4] Signatories recognize that nullification or impairment of benefits may also arise through the failure of a signatory to carry out its obligations under the General Agreement or this Agreement. Where such failure concerning export subsidies is determined by the Committee to exist, adverse effects may, without prejudice to paragraph 9 of Article 18 below, be presumed to exist. The other signatory will be accorded a reasonable opportunity to rebut this presumption.

[5] The term " displacing " shall be interpreted in a manner which takes into account the trade and development needs of developing countries and in this connection is not intended to fix traditional market shares.

[6] The problem of third country markets so far as certain primary products are concerned is dealt with exclusively under Article 10 below.

[7] For purposes of this Agreement " certain primary products " means the products referred to in Note Ad Article XVI of the General Agreement, Section B, paragraph 2, with the deletion of the words " or any mineral ".

2. The practices listed in points (a) to (l) in the Annex are illustrative of export subsidies.

Article 10

Export subsidies on certain primary products

1. In accordance with the provisions of Article XVI: 3 of the General Agreement, signatories agree not to grant directly or indirectly any export subsidy on certain primary products in a manner which results in the signatory granting such subsidy having more than an equitable share of world export trade in such product, account being taken of the shares of the signatories in trade in the product concerned during a previous representative period, and any special factors which may have affected or may be affecting trade in such product.

2. For purposes of Article XVI: 3 of the General Agreement and paragraph 1 above:

(a) " more than an equitable share of world export trade " shall include any case in which the effect of an export subsidy granted by a signatory is to displace the exports of another signatory bearing in mind the developments on world markets;

(b) with regard to new markets traditional patterns of supply of the product concerned to the world market, region or country, in which the new market is situated shall be taken into account in determining " equitable share of world export trade ";

(c) " a previous representative period " shall normally be the three most recent calendar years in which normal market conditions existed.

3. Signatories further agree not to grant export subsidies on exports of certain primary products to a particular market in a manner which results in prices materially below those of other suppliers to the same market.

Article 11

Subsidies other than export subsidies

1. Signatories recognize that subsidies other than export subsidies are widely used as important instruments for the promotion of social and economic policy objectives and do not intend to restrict the right of signatories to use such subsidies to achieve these and other important policy objectives which they consider desirable. Signatories note that among such objectives are:

(*a*) the elimination of industrial, economic and social disadvantages of specific regions,

(*b*) to facilitate the restructuring, under socially acceptable conditions, of certain sectors, especially where this has become necessary by reason of changes in trade and economic policies, including international agreements resulting in lower barriers to trade,

(*c*) generally to sustain employment and to encourage re-training and change in employment,

(*d*) to encourage research and development programmes, especially in the field of high-technology industries,

(*e*) the implementation of economic programmes and policies to promote the economic and social development of developing countries,

(*f*) redeployment of industry in order to avoid congestion and environmental problems.

2. Signatories recognize, however, that subsidies other than export subsidies, certain objectives and possible form of which are described, respectively, in paragraphs 1 and 3 of this Article, may cause or threaten to cause injury to a domestic industry of another signatory or serious prejudice to the interests of another signatory or may nullify or impair benefits accruing to another signatory under the General Agreement, in particular where such subsidies would adversely affect the conditions of normal competition. Signatories shall therefore seek to avoid causing such effects through the use of subsidies. In particular, signatories, when drawing up their policies and practices in this field, in addition to evaluating the essential internal objectives to be achieved, shall also weigh, as far as practicable, taking account of the nature of the particular case, possible adverse effects on trade. They shall also consider the conditions of world trade, production (e.g. price, capacity utilization etc.) and supply in the product concerned.

3. Signatories recognize that the objectives mentioned in paragraph 1 above may be achieved, *inter alia*, by means of subsidies granted with the aim of giving an advantage to certain enterprises. Examples of possible forms of such subsidies are: government financing of commercial enterprises, including grants, loans or guarantees; government provision or government financed provision of utility, supply distribution and other operational or support services or facilities; government financing of research and development programmes; fiscal incentives; and government subscription to, or provision of, equity capital.

Signatories note that the above form of subsidies are normally granted either regionally or by sector. The enumeration of forms of subsidies set out above is illustrative and non-exhaustive, and reflects these currently granted by a number of signatories to this Agreement.

Signatories recognize, nevertheless, that the enumeration of forms of subsidies set out above should be reviewed periodically and that this should be done, through consultations, in conformity with the spirit of Article XVI:5 of the General Agreement.

4. Signatories recognize further that, without prejudice to their rights under this Agreement, nothing in paragraphs 1-3 above and in particular the enumeration of forms of subsidies creates, in itself, any basis for action under the General Agreement, as interpreted by this Agreement.

Article 12

Consultations

1. Whenever a signatory has reason to believe that an export subsidy is being granted or maintained by another signatory in a manner inconsistent with the provisions of this Agreement, such signatory may request consultations with such other signatory.

2. A request for consultations under paragraph 1 above shall include a statement of available evidence with regard to the existence and nature of the subsidy in question.

3. Whenever a signatory has reason to believe that any subsidy is being granted or maintained by another signatory and that such subsidy either causes injury to its domestic industry, nullification or impairment of benefits accruing to it under the General Agreement, or serious prejudice to its interests, such signatory may request consultations with such other signatory.

4. A request for consultations under paragraph 3 above shall include a statement of available evidence with regard to (a) the existence and nature of the subsidy in question and (b) the injury caused to the domestic industry or, in the case of nullification or impairment, or serious prejudice, the adverse effects caused to the interests of the signatory requesting consultations.

5. Upon request for consultations under paragraph 1 or paragraph 3 above, the signatory believed to be granting or maintaining the subsidy practice in question shall enter into such consultations as quickly as possible. The purpose of the consultations shall be to clarify the facts of the situation and to arrive at a mutually acceptable solution.

Article 13

Conciliation, dispute settlement and authorized countermeasures

1.   If, in the case of consultations under paragraph 1 of Article 12, a mutually acceptable solution has not been reached within thirty days [1] of the request for consultations, any signatory party to such consultations may refer the matter to the Committee for conciliation in accordance with the provisions of Part VI.

2.   If, in the case of consultations under paragraph 3 of Article 12, a mutually acceptable solution has not been reached within sixty days of the request for consultations, any signatory party to such consultations may refer the matter to the Committee for conciliation in accordance with the provisions of Part VI.

3.   If any dispute arising under this Agreement is not resolved as a result of consultations or conciliations, the Committee shall, upon request, review the matter in accordance with the dispute settlement procedures of Part VI.

4.   If, as a result of its review, the Committee concludes that an export subsidy is being granted in a manner inconsistent with the provisions of this Agreement or that a subsidy is being granted or maintained in such a manner as to cause injury, nullification or impairment, or serious prejudice, it shall make such recommendations [2] to the parties as may be appropriate to resolve the issue and, in the event the recommendations are not followed, it may authorize such countermeasures as may be appropriate, taking into account the degree and nature of the adverse effects found to exist, in accordance with the relevant provisions of Part VI.

Part III

Article 14

Developing countries

1.   Signatories recognize that subsidies are an integral part of economic development programmes of developing countries.

---

[1] Any time periods mentioned in this Article and in Article 18 may be extended by mutual agreement.

[2] In making such recommendations, the Committee shall take into account the trade, development and financial needs of developing country signatories.

2.   Accordingly, this Agreement shall not prevent developing country signatories from adopting measures and policies to assist their industries, including those in the export sector. In particular the commitment of Article 9 shall not apply to developing country signatories, subject to the provisions of paragraphs 5 through 8 below.

3.   Developing country signatories agree that export subsidies on their industrial products shall not be used in a manner which causes serious prejudice to the trade or production of another signatory.

4.   There shall be no presumption that export subsidies granted by developing country signatories result in adverse effects, as defined in this Agreement, to the trade or production of another signatory. Such adverse effects shall be demonstrated by positive evidence, through an economic examination of the impact on trade or production of another signatory.

5.   A developing country signatory should endeavour to enter into a commitment [1] to reduce or eliminate export subsidies when the use of such export subsidies is inconsistent with its competitive and development needs.

6.   When a developing country has entered into a commitment to reduce or eliminate export subsidies, as provided in paragraph 5 above, countermeasures pursuant to the provisions of Parts II and VI of this Agreement against any export subsidies of such developing country shall not be authorized for other signatories of this Agreement, provided that the export subsidies in question are in accordance with the terms of the commitment referred to in paragraph 5 above.

7.   With respect to any subsidy, other than an export subsidy, granted by a developing country signatory, action may not be authorized or taken under Parts II and VI of this Agreement, unless nullification or impairment of tariff concessions or other obligations under the General Agreement is found to exist as a result of such subsidy, in such a way as to displace or impede imports of like products into the market of the subsidizing country, or unless injury to domestic industry in the importing market of a signatory occurs in terms of Article VI of the General Agreement, as interpreted and applied by this Agreement.   Signatories recognize that in developing countries, governments may play a large rôle in promoting economic growth and development.   Intervention by such governments in their economy, for example through the practices enumerated in paragraph 3 of Article 11, shall not, *per se*, be considered subsidies.

8.   The Committee shall, upon request by an interested signatory, undertake a review of a specific export subsidy practice of a developing country

---

[1] It is understood that after this Agreement has entered into force, any such proposed commitment shall be notified to the Committee in good time.

signatory to examine the extent to which the practice is in conformity with the objectives of this Agreement. If a developing country has entered into a commitment pursuant to paragraph 5 of this Article, it shall not be subject to such review for the period of that commitment.

9. The Committee shall, upon request by an interested signatory, also undertake similar reviews of measures maintained or taken by developed country signatories under the provisions of this Agreement which affect interests of a developing country signatory.

10. Signatories recognize that the obligations of this Agreement with respect to export subsidies for certain primary products apply to all signatories.

PART IV

Article 15

Special situations

1. In cases of alleged injury caused by imports from a country described in NOTES AND SUPPLEMENTARY PROVISIONS to the General Agreement (Annex I, Article VI, paragraph 1, point 2) the importing signatory may base its procedures and measures either

  (a) on this Agreement, or, alternatively

  (b) on the Agreement on Implementation of Article VI of the General Agreement on Tariffs and Trade.

2. It is understood that in both cases (a) and (b) above the calculation of the margin of dumping or of the amount of the estimated subsidy can be made by comparison of the export price with

  (a) the price at which a like product of a country other than the importing signatory or those mentioned above is sold, or

  (b) the constructed value [1] of a like product in a country other than the importing signatory or those mentioned above.

3. If neither prices nor constructed value as established under (a) or (b) of paragraph 2 above provide an adequate basis for determination of dumping or subsidization then the price in the importing signatory, if necessary duly adjusted to reflect reasonable profits, may be used.

---

[1] Constructed value means cost of production plus a reasonable amount for administration, selling and any other costs and for profits.

4. All calculations under the provisions of paragraphs 2 and 3 above shall be based on prices or costs ruling at the same level of trade, normally at the ex factory level, and in respect of operations made as nearly as possible at the same time. Due allowance shall be made in each case, on its merits, for the difference in conditions and terms of sale or in taxation and for the other differences affecting price comparability, so that the method of comparison applied is appropriate and not unreasonable.

PART V

Article 16

Committee on Subsidies and Countervailing Measures

1. There shall be established under this Agreement a Committee on Subsidies and Countervailing Measures composed of representatives from each of the signatories to this Agreement. The Committee shall elect its own Chairman and shall meet not less than twice a year and otherwise as envisaged by relevant provisions of this Agreement at the request of any signatory. The Committee shall carry out responsibilities as assigned to it under this Agreement or by the signatories and it shall afford signatories the opportunity of consulting on any matters relating to the operation of the Agreement or the furtherance of its objectives. The GATT secretariat shall act as the secretariat to the Committee.

2. The Committee may set up subsidiary bodies as appropriate.

3. In carrying out their functions, the Committee and any subsidiary bodies may consult with and seek information from any source they deem appropriate. However, before the Committee or a subsidiary body seeks such information from a source within the jurisdiction of a signatory, it shall inform the signatory involved.

PART VI

Article 17

Conciliation

1. In cases where matters are referred to the Committee for conciliation failing a mutually agreed solution in consultations under any provision of this Agreement, the Committee shall immediately review the facts involved

and, through its good offices, shall encourage the signatories involved to develop a mutually acceptable solution.[1]

2.   Signatories shall make their best efforts to reach a mutually satisfactory solution throughout the period of conciliation.

3.   Should the matter remain unresolved, notwithstanding efforts at conciliation made under paragraph 2 above, any signatory involved may, thirty days after the request for conciliation, request that a panel be established by the Committee in accordance with the provisions of Article 18 below.

Article 18

Dispute settlement

1.   The Committee shall establish a panel upon request pursuant to paragraph 3 of Article 17.[2]   A panel so established shall review the facts of the matter and, in light of such facts, shall present to the Committee its findings concerning the rights and obligations of the signatories party to the dispute under the relevant provisions of the General Agreement as interpreted and applied by this Agreement.

2.   A panel should be established within thirty days of a request therefor[3] and a panel so established should deliver its findings to the Committee within sixty days after its establishment.

3.   When a panel is to be established, the Chairman of the Committee, after securing the agreement of the signatories concerned, should propose the composition of the panel.   Panels shall be composed of three or five members, preferably governmental, and the composition of panels should not give rise to delays in their establishment.   It is understood that citizens of countries whose governments[4] are parties to the dispute would not be members of the panel concerned with that dispute.

4.   In order to facilitate the constitution of panels, the Chairman of the Committee should maintain an informal indicative list of governmental and

---

[1] In this connexion, the Committee may draw signatories' attention to those cases in which, in its view, there is no reasonable basis supporting the allegations made.

[2] This does not preclude, however, the more rapid establishment of a panel when the Committee so decides, taking into account the urgency of the situation.

[3] The parties to the dispute would respond within a short period of time, i.e. seven working days, to nominations of panel members by the Chairman of the Committee and would not oppose nominations except for compelling reasons.

[4] The term "governments" is understood to mean governments of all member countries in cases of customs unions.

non-governmental persons qualified in the fields of trade relations, economic development, and other matters covered by the General Agreement and this Agreement, who could be available for serving on panels. For this purpose, each signatory would be invited to indicate at the beginning of every year to the Chairman of the Committee the name of one or two persons who would be available for such work.

5. Panel members would serve in their individual capacities and not as government representatives, nor as representatives of any organization. Governments would therefore not give them instructions with regard to matters before a panel. Panel members should be selected with a view to ensuring the independence of the members, a sufficiently diverse background and a wide spectrum of experience.

6. To encourage development of mutually satisfactory solutions between the parties to a dispute and with a view to obtaining their comments, each panel should first submit the descriptive part of its report to the parties concerned, and should subsequently submit to the parties to the dispute its conclusions, or an outline thereof, a reasonable period of time before they are circulated to the Committee.

7. If a mutually satisfactory solution is developed by the parties to a dispute before a panel, any signatory with an interest in the matter has a right to enquire about and be given appropriate information about that solution and a notice outlining the solution that has been reached shall be presented by the panel to the Committee.

8. In cases where the parties to a dispute have failed to come to a satisfactory solution, the panels shall submit a written report to the Committee which should set forth the findings of the panel as to the questions of fact and the application of the relevant provisions of the General Agreement as interpreted and applied by this Agreement and the reasons and bases therefor.

9. The Committee shall consider the panel report as soon as possible and, taking into account the findings contained therein, may make recommendations to the parties with a view to resolving the dispute. If the Committee's recommendations are not followed within a reasonable period, the Committee may authorize appropriate countermeasures (including withdrawal of GATT concessions or obligations) taking into account the nature and degree of the adverse effect found to exist. Committee recommendations should be presented to the parties within thirty days of the receipt of the panel report.

PART VII

Article 19

Final provisions

1. No specific action against a subsidy of another signatory can be taken except in accordance with the provisions of the General Agreement, as interpreted by this Agreement.[1]

Acceptance and accession

2. (*a*) This Agreement shall be open for acceptance, by signature or otherwise, by governments contracting parties to the GATT and by the European Economic Community.

(*b*) This Agreement shall be open for acceptance, by signature or otherwise, by governments having provisionally acceded to the GATT, on terms related to the effective application of rights and obligations under this Agreement, which take into account rights and obligations in the instruments providing for their provisional accession.

(*c*) This Agreement shall be open to accession by any other government on terms, related to the effective application of rights and obligations under this Agreement, to be agreed between that government and the signatories, by the deposit with the Director-General to the CONTRACTING PARTIES to the GATT of an instrument of accession which states the terms so agreed.

(*d*) In regard to acceptance, the provisions of Article XXVI: 5(*a*) and (*b*) of the General Agreement would be applicable.

Reservations

3. Reservations may not be entered in respect of any of the provisions of this Agreement without the consent of the other signatories.

Entry into force

4. This Agreement shall enter into force on 1 January 1980 for the governments [2] which have accepted or acceded to it by that date. For each other

---

[1] This paragraph is not intended to preclude action under other relevant provisions of the General Agreement, where appropriate.

[2] The term " governments " is deemed to include the competent authorities of the European Economic Community.

government it shall enter into force on the thirtieth day following the date of its acceptance or accession to this Agreement.

National legislation

5. (a) Each government accepting or acceding to this Agreement shall take all necessary steps, of a general or particular character, to ensure, not later than the date of entry into force of this Agreement for it, the conformity of its laws, regulations and administrative procedures with the provisions of this Agreement as they may apply to the signatory in question.

   (b) Each signatory shall inform the Committee of any changes in its laws and regulations relevant to this Agreement and in the administration of such laws and regulations.

Review

6. The Committee shall review annually the implementation and operation of this Agreement taking into account the objectives thereof. The Committee shall annually inform the CONTRACTING PARTIES to the GATT of developments during the period covered by such reviews. [1]

Amendments

7. The signatories may amend this Agreement having regard, *inter alia*, to the experience gained in its implementation. Such an amendment, once the signatories have concurred in accordance with procedures established by the Committee, shall not come into force for any signatory until it has been accepted by such signatory.

Withdrawal

8. Any signatory may withdraw from this Agreement. The withdrawal shall take effect upon the expiration of sixty days from the day on which written notice of withdrawal is received by the Director-General to the CONTRACTING PARTIES to the GATT. Any signatory may upon such notification request an immediate meeting of the Committee.

Non-application of this Agreement between particular signatories

9. This Agreement shall not apply as between any two signatories if either of the signatories, at the time either accepts or accedes to this Agreement, does not consent to such application.

---

[1] At the first such review, the Committee shall, in addition to its general review of the operation of the Agreement, offer all interested signatories an opportunity to raise questions and discuss issues concerning specific subsidy practices and the impact on trade, if any, of certain direct tax practices.

Annex

10. The annex to this Agreement constitutes an integral part thereof.

Secretariat

11. This Agreement shall be serviced by the GATT secretariat.

Deposit

12. This Agreement shall be deposited with the Director-General to the CONTRACTING PARTIES to the GATT, who shall promptly furnish to each signatory and each contracting party to the GATT a certified copy thereof and of each amendment thereto pursuant to paragraph 7, and a notification of each acceptance thereof or accession thereto pursuant to paragraph 2, and of each withdrawal therefrom pursuant to paragraph 8 of this Article.

Registration

13. This Agreement shall be registered in accordance with the provisions of Article 102 of the Charter of the United Nations.

Done at Geneva this twelfth day of April nineteen hundred and seventy-nine in a single copy, in the English, French and Spanish languages, each text being authentic.

ANNEX

ILLUSTRATIVE LIST OF EXPORT SUBSIDIES

(a) The provision by governments of direct subsidies to a firm or an industry contingent upon export performance.

(b) Currency retention schemes or any similar practices which involve a bonus on exports.

(c) Internal transport and freight charges on export shipments, provided or mandated by governments, on terms more favourable than for domestic shipments.

(d) The delivery by governments or their agencies of imported or domestic products or services for use in the production of exported goods, on terms or conditions more favourable than for delivery of like or directly competitive products or services for use in the production of goods for domestic consumption, if (in the case of products) such terms or conditions are more favourable than those commercially available on world markets to their exporters.

(e) The full or partial exemption, remission, or deferral specifically related to exports, of direct taxes [1] or social welfare charges paid or payable by industrial or commercial enterprises. [2]

(f) The allowance of special deductions directly related to exports or export performance, over and above those granted in respect of production for domestic consumption, in the calculation of the base on which direct taxes are charged.

(g) The exemption or remission in respect of the production and distribution of exported products, of indirect taxes [1] in excess of those levied in respect of the production and distribution of like products when sold for domestic consumption.

(h) The exemption, remission or deferral of prior stage cumulative indirect taxes [1] on goods or services used in the production of exported products in excess of the exemption, remission or deferral of like prior stage cumulative indirect taxes on goods or services used in the production of like products when sold for domestic consumption; provided, however, that prior stage cumulative indirect taxes may be exempted, remitted or deferred on exported products even when not exempted, remitted or deferred on like products when sold for domestic consumption, if the prior stage cumulative indirect taxes are levied on goods that are physically incorporated (making normal allowance for waste) in the exported product. [3]

(i) The remission or drawback of import charges [1] in excess of those levied on imported goods that are physically incorporated (making normal allowance for waste) in the exported product; provided, however, that in particular cases a firm may use a quantity of home market goods equal to, and having the same quality and characteristics as, the imported goods as a substitute for them in order to benefit from this provision if the import and the corresponding export operations both occur within a reasonable time period, normally not to exceed two years.

(j) The provision by governments (or special institutions controlled by governments) of export credit guarantee or insurance programmes, of insurance or guarantee programmes against increases in the costs of exported products [4] or of exchange risk programmes, at premium rates, which are manifestly inadequate to cover the long-term operating costs and losses of the programmes. [5]

(k) The grant by governments (or special institutions controlled by and/or acting under the authority of governments) of export credits at rates below those which they actually have to pay for the funds so employed (or would have to pay if they borrowed on international capital markets in order to obtain funds of the same maturity and denominated in the same currency as the export credit), or the payment by them of all or part of the costs incurred by exporters or financial institutions in obtaining credits, in so far as they are used to secure a material advantage in the field of export credit terms.

Provided, however, that if a signatory is a party to an international undertaking on official export credits to which at least twelve original signatories [6] to this Agreement are parties as of 1 January 1979 (or a successor undertaking which has been adopted by those original signatories), or if in practice a signatory applies the interest rates provisions of the relevant undertaking, an export credit practice which is in conformity with those provisions shall not be considered an export subsidy prohibited by this Agreement.

(*l*) Any other charge on the public account constituting an export subsidy in the sense of Article XVI of the General Agreement.

NOTES

[1] For the purpose of this Agreement:

The term " direct taxes " shall mean taxes on wages, profits, interest, rents, royalties, and all other forms of income, and taxes on the ownership of real property;

The term " import charges " shall mean tariffs, duties, and other fiscal charges not elsewhere enumerated in this note that are levied on imports;

The term " indirect taxes " shall mean sales, excise, turnover, value added, franchise, stamp, transfer, inventory and equipment taxes, border taxes and all taxes other than direct taxes and import charges;

" Prior stage " indirect taxes are those levied on goods or services used directly or indirectly in making the product;

" Cumulative " indirect taxes are multi-staged taxes levied where there is no mechanism for subsequent crediting of the tax if the goods or services subject to tax at one stage of production are used in a succeeding stage of production;

" Remission " of taxes includes the refund or rebate of taxes.

[2] The signatories recognize that deferral need not amount to an export subsidy where, for example, appropriate interest charges are collected. The signatories further recognize that nothing in this text prejudges the disposition by the CONTRACTING PARTIES of the specific issues raised in GATT document L/4422.

The signatories reaffirm the principle that prices for goods in transactions between exporting enterprises and foreign buyers under their or under the same control should for tax purposes be the prices which would be charged between independent enterprises acting at arm's length. Any signatory may draw the attention of another signatory to administrative or other practices which may contravene this principle and which result in a significant saving of direct taxes in export transactions. In such circumstances the signatories shall normally attempt to resolve their differences using the facilities of existing bilateral tax treaties or other specific international mechanisms, without prejudice to the rights and obligations of signatories under the General Agreement, including the right of consultation created in the preceding sentence.

Paragraph (*e*) is not intended to limit a signatory from taking measures to avoid the double taxation of foreign source income earned by its enterprises or the enterprises of another signatory.

Where measures incompatible with the provisions of paragraph (*e*) exist, and where major practical difficulties stand in the way of the signatory concerned bringing such measures promptly into conformity with the Agreement, the signatory concerned shall, without prejudice to the rights of other signatories under the General Agreement or this Agreement, examine methods of bringing these measures into conformity within a reasonable period of time.

In this connexion the European Economic Community has declared that Ireland intends to withdraw by 1 January 1981 its system of preferential tax measures related to exports, provided for under the Corporation Tax Act of 1976, whilst continuing nevertheless to honour legally binding commitments entered into during the lifetime of this system.

[3] Paragraph (*h*) does not apply to value-added tax systems and border-tax adjustment in lieu thereof; the problem of the excessive remission of value-added taxes is exclusively covered by paragraph (*g*).

[4] The signatories agree that nothing in this paragraph shall prejudge or influence the deliberations of the panel established by the GATT Council on 6 June 1978 (C/M/126).

[5] In evaluating the long-term adequacy of premium rates, costs and losses of insurance programmes, in principle only such contracts shall be taken into account that were concluded after the date of entry into force of this Agreement.

[6] An original signatory to this Agreement shall mean any signatory which adheres *ad referendum* to the Agreement on or before 30 June 1979.

AGREEMENT ON GOVERNMENT PROCUREMENT

PREAMBLE

Parties to this Agreement (hereinafter referred to as " Parties "),

Considering that Ministers agreed in the Tokyo Declaration of 14 September 1973 that comprehensive Multilateral Trade Negotiations in the framework of the General Agreement on Tariffs and Trade (hereinafter referred to as " General Agreement " or " GATT ") should aim, *inter alia*, to reduce or eliminate non-tariff measures or, where this is not appropriate, their trade restricting or distorting effects, and to bring such measures under more effective international discipline;

Considering that Ministers also agreed that negotiations should aim to secure additional benefits for the international trade of developing countries, and recognized the importance of the application of differential measures in ways which will provide special and more favourable treatment for them where this is feasible and appropriate;

Recognizing that in order to achieve their economic and social objectives to implement programmes and policies of economic development aimed at raising the standard of living of their people, taking into account their balance-of-payments position, developing countries may need to adopt agreed differential measures;

Considering that Ministers in the Tokyo Declaration recognized that the particular situation and problems of the least developed among the developing countries shall be given special attention and stressed the need to ensure that these countries receive special treatment in the context of any general or specific measures taken in favour of the developing countries during the negotiations;

Recognizing the need to establish an agreed international framework of rights and obligations with respect to laws, regulations, procedures and practices regarding government procurement with a view to achieving greater liberalization and expansion of world trade and improving the international framework for the conduct of world trade;

Recognizing that laws, regulations, procedures and practices regarding government procurement should not be prepared, adopted or applied to foreign or domestic products and to foreign or domestic suppliers so as to afford protection to domestic products or suppliers and should not discriminate among foreign products or suppliers;

Recognizing that it is desirable to provide transparency of laws, regulations, procedures and practices regarding government procurement;

Recognizing the need to establish international procedures on notification, consultation, surveillance and dispute settlement with a view to ensuring a fair, prompt and effective enforcement of the international provisions on government procurement and to maintain the balance of rights and obligations at the highest possible level;

Hereby agree as follows:

Article I

Scope and Coverage

1. This Agreement applies to:

    (*a*) any law, regulation, procedure and practice regarding the procurement of products by the entities [1] subject to this Agreement. This includes services incidental to the supply of products if the value of these incidental services does not exceed that of the products themselves, but not service contracts *per se*;

    (*b*) any procurement contract of a value of SDR 150,000 or more. [2] No procurement requirement shall be divided with the intent of reducing the value of the resulting contracts below SDR 150,000. If an individual requirement for the procurement of a product or products of the same type results in the award of more than one contract or in contracts being awarded in separate parts, the value of these recurring contracts in the twelve months subsequent to the initial contract shall be the basis for the application of this Agreement;

    (*c*) procurement by the entities under the direct or substantial control of Parties and other designated entities, with respect to their procurement procedures and practices. Until the review and further negotiations referred to in the Final Provisions, the coverage of this Agreement is specified by the lists of entities, and to the extent that rectifications, modifications or amendments may have been made, their successor entities, in Annex I.

---

[1] Throughout this Agreement, the word entities is understood to include agencies.

[2] For contracts below the threshold, the Parties shall consider, in accordance with paragraph 6 of Article IX, the application in whole or in part of this Agreement. In particular, they shall review the procurement practices and procedures utilized and the application of non-discrimination and transparency for such contracts in connexion with the possible inclusion of contracts below the threshold in this Agreement.

2. The Parties shall inform their entities not covered by this Agreement and the regional and local governments and authorities within their territories of the objectives, principles and rules of this Agreement, in particular the rules on national treatment and non-discrimination, and draw their attention to the overall benefits of liberalization of government procurement.

Article II

National Treatment and Non-Discrimination

1. With respect to all laws, regulations, procedures and practices regarding government procurement covered by this Agreement, the Parties shall provide immediately and unconditionally to the products and suppliers of other Parties offering products originating within the customs territories (including free zones) of the Parties, treatment no less favourable than:

   (a) that accorded to domestic products and suppliers; and

   (b) that accorded to products and suppliers of any other Party.

2. The provisions of paragraph 1 shall not apply to customs duties and charges of any kind imposed on or in connexion with importation, the method of levying such duties and charges, and other import regulations and formalities.

3. The Parties shall not apply rules of origin to products imported for purposes of government procurement covered by this Agreement from other Parties, which are different from the rules of origin applied in the normal course of trade and at the time of importation to imports of the same products from the same Parties.

Article III

Special and Differential Treatment for Developing Countries

Objectives

1. The Parties shall, in the implementation and administration of this Agreement, through the provisions set out in this Article, duly take into account the development, financial and trade needs of developing countries, in particular the least-developed countries, in their need to:

   (a) safeguard their balance-of-payments position and ensure a level of reserves adequate for the implementation of programmes of economic development;

   (b) promote the establishment or development of domestic industries including the development of small-scale and cottage industries in rural or backward areas; and economic development of other sectors of the economy;

(c) support industrial units so long as they are wholly or substantially dependent on government procurement;

(d) encourage their economic development through regional or global arrangements among developing countries presented to the CONTRACTING PARTIES to the GATT and not disapproved by them.

2. Consistently with the provisions of this Agreement, the Parties shall, in the preparation and application of laws, regulations and procedures affecting government procurement, facilitate increased imports from developing countries, bearing in mind the special problems of the least-developed countries and of those countries at low stages of economic development.

Coverage

3. With a view to ensuring that developing countries are able to adhere to this Agreement on terms consistent with their development, financial and trade needs, the objectives listed in paragraph 1 above shall be duly taken into account in the course of the negotiations with respect to the lists of entities of developing countries to be covered by the provisions of this Agreement. Developed countries, in the preparation of their lists of entities to be covered by the provisions of this Agreement shall endeavour to include entities purchasing products of export interest to developing countries.

Agreed exclusions

4. Developing countries may negotiate with other participants in the negotiation of this Agreement mutually acceptable exclusions from the rules on national treatment with respect to certain entities or products that are included in their lists of entities having regard to the particular circumstances of each case. In such negotiations, the considerations mentioned in paragraph 1(a)-(c) above shall be duly taken into account. Developing countries participating in regional or global arrangements among developing countries referred to in paragraph 1(d) above, may also negotiate exclusions to their lists, having regard to the particular circumstances of each case, taking into account, *inter alia*, the provisions on government procurement provided for in the regional or global arrangements concerned and taking into account, in particular, products which may be subject to common industrial development programmes.

5. After entry into force of this Agreement, the developing country Parties may modify their lists of entities in accordance with the provisions for modification of such lists contained in paragraph 5 of Article IX of this Agreement, having regard to their development, financial and trade needs,

or may request the Committee to grant exclusions from the rules on national treatment for certain entities or products that are included in their lists of entities, having regard to the particular circumstances of each case and taking duly into account the provisions of paragraph 1(*a*)-(*c*) above. The developing country Parties may also request, after entry into force of this Agreement, the Committee to grant exclusions for certain entities or products that are included in their lists in the light of their participation in regional or global arrangements among developing countries, having regard to the particular circumstances of each case and taking duly into account the provisions of paragraph 1(*d*) above. Each request to the Committee by a developing country Party relating to modification of a list shall be accompanied by documentation relevant to the request or by such information as may be necessary for consideration of the matter.

6. Paragraphs 4 and 5 above shall apply *mutatis mutandis* to developing countries acceding to this Agreement after its entry into force.

7. Such agreed exclusions as mentioned in paragraphs 4, 5 and 6 above shall be subject to review in accordance with the provisions of paragraph 13 of this Article.

Technical assistance for developing country Parties

8. Developed country Parties shall, upon request, provide all technical assistance which they may deem appropriate to developing country Parties in resolving their problems in the field of government procurement.

9. This assistance which shall be provided on the basis of non-discrimination among the developing country Parties shall relate, *inter alia*, to:

— the solution of particular technical problems relating to the award of a specific contract;

— any other problem which the Party making the request and another Party agree to deal with in the context of this assistance.

Information centres

10. The developed country Parties shall establish, individually or jointly, information centres to respond to reasonable requests from developing country Parties for information relating to, *inter alia*, laws, regulations, procedures and practices regarding government procurement, notices about proposed purchases which have been published, addresses of the entities covered by this Agreement, and the nature and volume of products purchased or to be purchased, including available information about future tenders. The Committee may also set up an information centre.

Special treatment for least-developed countries

11. Having regard to paragraph 6 of the Tokyo Declaration, special treatment shall be granted to the least-developed country Parties and to the suppliers in those countries with respect to products originating in those countries, in the context of any general or specific measures in favour of the developing country Parties. The Parties may also grant the benefits of this Agreement to suppliers in the least-developed countries which are not Parties, with respect to products originating in those countries.

12. Developed country Parties shall, upon request, provide assistance which they may deem appropriate to potential tenderers in the least-developed countries in submitting their tenders and selecting the products which are likely to be of interest to entities of developed countries as well as to suppliers in the least-developed countries and likewise assist them to comply with technical regulations and standards relating to products which are the subject of the proposed purchase.

Review

13. The Committee shall review annually the operation and effectiveness of this Article and after each three years of its operation on the basis of reports to be submitted by the Parties shall carry out a major review in order to evaluate its effects. As part of the three-yearly reviews and with a view to achieving the maximum implementation of the provisions of this Agreement, including in particular Article II, and having regard to the development, financial and trade situation of the developing countries concerned, the Committee shall examine whether exclusions provided for in accordance with the provisions of paragraphs 4 to 6 of this Article shall be modified or extended.

14. In the course of further rounds of negotiations in accordance with the provisions of Article IX, paragraph 6, the developing country Parties shall give consideration to the possibility of enlarging their lists of entities having regard to their economic, financial and trade situation.

Article IV

Technical Specifications

1. Technical specifications laying down the characteristics of the products to be purchased such as quality, performance, safety and dimensions, testing and test methods, symbols, terminology, packaging, marking and labelling, and conformity certification requirements prescribed by procurement entities, shall not be prepared, adopted or applied with a view to creating

obstacles to international trade nor have the effect of creating unnecessary obstacles to international trade.

2. Any technical specification prescribed by procurement entities shall, where appropriate:

    (*a*) be in terms of performance rather than design; and

    (*b*) be based on international standards, national technical regulations, or recognized national standards.

3. There shall be no requirement or reference to a particular trade mark or name, patent, design or type, specific origin or producer unless there is no sufficiently precise or intelligible way of describing the procurement requirements and provided that words such as " or equivalent " are included in the tenders.

Article V

Tendering Procedures

1. The Parties shall ensure that the tendering procedures of their entities are consistent with the provisions below. Open tendering procedures, for the purposes of this Agreement, are those procedures under which all interested suppliers may submit a tender. Selective tendering procedures, for the purposes of this Agreement, are those procedures under which, consistent with paragraph 7 and other relevant provisions of this Article, those suppliers invited to do so by the entity may submit a tender. Single tendering procedures, for the purposes of this Agreement, are those procedures where the entity contacts suppliers individually, only under the conditions specified in paragraph 15 below.

Qualification of suppliers

2. Entities, in the process of qualifying suppliers, shall not discriminate among foreign suppliers or between domestic and foreign suppliers. Qualification procedures shall be consistent with the following:

    (*a*) any conditions for participation in tendering procedures shall be published in adequate time to enable interested suppliers to initiate and, to the extent that it is compatible with efficient operation of the procurement process, complete the qualification procedures;

    (*b*) any conditions for participation required from suppliers, including financial guarantees, technical qualifications and information necessary for establishing the financial, commercial and technical capacity of suppliers, as well as the verification of qualifications, shall be no less favourable to foreign suppliers than to domestic suppliers and shall not discriminate among foreign suppliers;

(c) the process of, and the time required for, qualifying suppliers shall not be used in order to keep foreign suppliers off a suppliers' list or from being considered for a particular proposed purchase. Entities shall recognize as qualified suppliers such domestic or foreign suppliers who meet the conditions for participation in a particular proposed purchase. Suppliers requesting to participate in a particular proposed purchase who may not yet be qualified shall also be considered, provided there is sufficient time to complete the qualification procedure;

(d) entities maintaining permanent lists of qualified suppliers shall ensure that all qualified suppliers so requesting are included in the lists within a reasonably short time;

(e) any supplier having requested to become a qualified supplier shall be advised by the entities concerned of the decision in this regard. Qualified suppliers included on permanent lists by entities shall also be notified of the termination of any such lists or of their removal from them;

(f) nothing in sub-paragraphs (a) to (e) above shall preclude the exclusion of any supplier on grounds such as bankruptcy or false declarations, provided that such an action is consistent with the national treatment and non-discrimination provisions of this Agreement.

Notice of proposed purchase and tender documentation

3. Entities shall publish a notice of each proposed purchase in the appropriate publication listed in Annex II. Such notice shall constitute an invitation to participate in either open or selective tendering procedures.

4. Each notice of proposed purchase shall contain the following information:

(a) the nature and quantity of the products to be supplied, or envisaged to be purchased in the case of contracts of a recurring nature;

(b) whether the procedure is open or selective;

(c) any delivery date;

(d) the address and final date for submitting an application to be invited to tender or for qualifying for the suppliers' lists, or for receiving tenders, as well as the language or languages in which they must be submitted;

(e) the address of the entity awarding the contract and providing any information necessary for obtaining specifications and other documents;

(f) any economic and technical requirements, financial guarantees and information required from suppliers;

(*g*) the amount and terms of payment of any sum payable for the tender documentation.

The entity shall publish in one of the official languages of the GATT a summary of the notice of proposed purchase containing at least the following:

(i) subject matter of the contract;

(ii) time-limits set for the submission of tenders or an application to be invited to tender; and

(iii) addresses from which documents relating to the contracts may be requested.

5. To ensure optimum effective international competition under selective tendering procedures, entities shall, for each proposed purchase, invite tenders from the maximum number of domestic and foreign suppliers, consistent with the efficient operation of the procurement system. They shall select the suppliers to participate in the procedure in a fair and non-discriminatory manner.

6. (*a*) In the case of selective tendering procedures, entities maintaining permanent lists of qualified suppliers shall publish annually in one of the publications listed in Annex III, a notice of the following:

(i) the enumeration of the lists maintained, including their headings, in relation to the products or categories of products to be purchased through the lists;

(ii) the conditions to be filled by potential suppliers in view of their inscription on those lists and the methods according to which each of those conditions be verified by the entity concerned;

(iii) the period of validity of the lists, and the formalities for their renewal.

(*b*) Entities maintaining permanent lists of qualified suppliers may select suppliers to be invited to tender from among those listed. Any selection shall allow for equitable opportunities for suppliers on the lists.

(*c*) If, after publication of the notice under paragraph 3 above, a supplier not yet qualified requests to participate in a particular tender, the entity shall promptly start the procedure of qualification.

7. Suppliers requesting to participate in a particular proposed purchase shall be permitted to submit a tender and be considered provided, in the case of those not yet qualified, there is sufficient time to complete the qualification procedure under paragraphs 2-6 of this Article. The number of additional suppliers permitted to participate shall be limited only by the efficient operation of the procurement system.

8. If after publication of a notice of a proposed purchase but before the time set for opening or receipt of tenders as specified in the notices or the tender documentation, it becomes necessary to amend or re-issue the notice, the amendment or the re-issued notice shall be given the same circulation as the original documents upon which the amendment is based. Any significant information given to one supplier with respect to a particular proposed purchase shall be given simultaneously to all other suppliers concerned in adequate time to permit the suppliers to consider such information and to respond to it.

9. (a) Any prescribed time-limit shall be adequate to allow foreign as well as domestic suppliers to prepare and submit tenders before the closing of the tendering procedures. In determining any such time-limit, entities shall, consistent with their own reasonable needs, take into account such factors as the complexity of the proposed purchase, the extent of sub-contracting anticipated, and the normal time for transmitting tenders by mail from foreign as well as domestic points.

   (b) Consistent with the entity's own reasonable needs, any delivery date shall take into account the normal time required for the transport of goods from the different points of supply.

10. (a) In open procedures, the period for the receipt of tenders shall in no case be less than thirty days from the date of publication referred to in paragraph 3 of this Article.

   (b) In selective procedures not involving the use of a permanent list of qualified suppliers, the period for submitting an application to be invited to tender shall in no case be less than thirty days from the date of publication referred to in paragraph 3; the period for receipt of tenders shall in no case be less than thirty days from the date of issuance of the invitation to tender.

   (c) In selective procedures involving the use of a permanent list of qualified suppliers, the period for receipt of tenders shall in no case be less than thirty days from the date of the initial issuance of invitations to tender. If the date of initial issuance of invitations to tender does not coincide with the date of the publication referred to in paragraph 3, there shall in no case be less than thirty days between those two dates.

   (d) The periods referred to in (a), (b) and (c) above may be reduced either where a state of urgency duly substantiated by the entity renders impracticable the periods in question or in the case of the second or subsequent publications dealing with contracts of a recurring nature within the meaning of paragraph 4 of this Article.

11. If, in tendering procedures, an entity allows tenders to be submitted in several languages, one of those languages shall be one of the official languages of the GATT.

12. Tender documentation provided to suppliers shall contain all information necessary to permit them to submit responsive tenders, including the following:

   (*a*) the address of the entity to which tenders should be sent;

   (*b*) the address where requests for supplementary information should be sent;

   (*c*) the language or languages in which tenders and tendering documents must be submitted;

   (*d*) the closing date and time for receipt of tenders and the length of time during which any tender should be open for acceptance;

   (*e*) the persons authorized to be present at the opening of tenders and the date, time and place of this opening;

   (*f*) any economic and technical requirement, financial guarantees and information or documents required from suppliers;

   (*g*) a complete description of the products required or of any requirements including technical specifications, conformity certification to be fulfilled by the products, necessary plans, drawings and instructional materials;

   (*h*) the criteria for awarding the contract, including any factors other than price that are to be considered in the evaluation of tenders and the cost elements to be included in evaluating tender prices, such as transport, insurance and inspection costs, and in the case of foreign products, customs duties and other import charges, taxes and currency of payment;

   (*i*) the terms of payment;

   (*j*) any other terms or conditions.

13. (*a*) In open procedures, entities shall forward the tender documentation at the request of any supplier participating in the procedure, and shall reply promptly to any reasonable request for explanations relating thereto.

   (*b*) In selective procedures, entities shall forward the tender documentation at the request of any supplier requesting to participate and shall reply promptly to any reasonable request for explanations relating thereto.

   (*c*) Entities shall reply promptly to any reasonable request for relevant information submitted by a supplier participating in the tendering procedure, on condition that such information does not give that supplier an advantage over its competitors in the procedure for the award of the contract.

Submission, receipt and opening of tenders and awarding of contracts

14. The submission, receipt and opening of tenders and awarding of contracts shall be consistent with the following:

(*a*) tenders shall normally be submitted in writing directly or by mail. If tenders by telex, telegram or telecopy are permitted, the tender made thereby must include all the information necessary for the evaluation of the tender, in particular the definitive price proposed by the tenderer and a statement that the tenderer agrees to all the terms, conditions and provisions of the invitation to tender. The tender must be confirmed promptly by letter or by the despatch of a signed copy of the telex, telegram or telecopy. Tenders presented by telephone shall not be permitted. The content of the telex, telegram or telecopy shall prevail where there is a difference or conflict between that content and any documentation received after the time-limit; requests to participate in selective tendering procedures may be submitted by telex, telegram or telecopy;

(*b*) the opportunities that may be given to tenderers to correct unintentional errors between the opening of tenders and the awarding of the contract shall not be permitted to give rise to any discriminatory practice;

(*c*) a supplier shall not be penalized if a tender is received in the office designated in the tender documentation after the time specified because of delay due solely to mishandling on the part of the entity. Tenders may also be considered in other exceptional circumstances if the procedures of the entity concerned so provide;

(*d*) all tenders solicited under open and selective procedures by entities shall be received and opened under procedures and conditions guaranteeing the regularity of the openings as well as the availability of information from the openings. The receipt and opening of tenders shall also be consistent with the national treatment and non-discrimination provisions of this Agreement. To this effect, and in connexion with open procedures, entities shall establish provisions for the opening of tenders in the presence of either tenderers or their representatives, or an appropriate and impartial witness not connected with the procurement process. A report on the opening of tenders shall be drawn up in writing. This report shall remain with the entities concerned at the disposal of the government authorities responsible for the entity in order that it may be used if required under the procedures of Articles VI and VII of this Agreement;

(*e*) to be considered for award, a tender must, at the time of opening, conform to the essential requirements of the notices or tender documentation and be from suppliers which comply with the conditions for participation. If an entity has received a tender abnormally lower than other tenders submitted, it may enquire with the tenderer to ensure that it can comply with the conditions of participation and be capable of fulfilling the terms of the contract;

(*f*) unless in the public interest an entity decides not to issue the contract, the entity shall make the award to the tenderer who has been determined to be fully capable of undertaking the contract and whose tender, whether for domestic or foreign products, is either the lowest tender or the tender which in terms of the specific evaluation criteria set forth in the notices or tender documentation is determined to be the most advantageous;

(*g*) if it appears from evaluation that no one tender is obviously the most advantageous in terms of the specific evaluation criteria set forth in the notices or tender documentation, the entity shall, in any subsequent negotiations, give equal consideration and treatment to all tenders within the competitive range;

(*h*) entities should normally refrain from awarding contracts on the condition that the supplier provide offset procurement opportunities or similar conditions. In the limited number of cases where such requisites are part of a contract, Parties concerned shall limit the offset to a reasonable proportion within the contract value and shall not favour suppliers from one Party over suppliers from any other Party. Licensing of technology should not normally be used as a condition of award but instances where it is required should be as infrequent as possible and suppliers from one Party shall not be favoured over suppliers from any other Party.

Use of single tendering

15. The provisions of paragraphs 1-14 above governing open and selective tendering procedures need not apply in the following conditions, provided that single tendering is not used with a view to avoiding maximum possible competition or in a manner which would constitute a means of discrimination among foreign suppliers or protection to domestic producers:

(*a*) in the absence of tenders in response to an open or selective tender, or when the tenders submitted have been either collusive or do not conform to the essential requirements in the tender, or from suppliers who do not comply with the conditions for participation provided for in accordance with this Agreement, on condition, however, that the requirements of the initial tender are not substantially modified in the contract as awarded;

(b) when, for works of art or for reasons connected with protection of exclusive rights, such as patents or copyrights, the products can be supplied only by a particular supplier and no reasonable alternative or substitute exists;

(c) insofar as is strictly necessary when, for reasons of extreme urgency brought about by events unforeseeable by the entity, the products could not be obtained in time by means of open or selective tendering procedures;

(d) for additional deliveries by the original supplier which are intended either as parts replacement for existing supplies or installations, or as the extension of existing supplies or installations where a change of supplier would compel the entity to purchase equipment not meeting requirements of interchangeability with already existing equipment;

(e) when an entity purchases prototypes or a first product which are developed at its request in the course of, and for, a particular contract for research, experiment, study or original development. When such contracts have been fulfilled, subsequent purchases of products shall be subject to paragraphs 1-14 of this Article.[1]

16. Entities shall prepare a report in writing on each contract awarded under the provisions of paragraph 15 of this Article. Each report shall contain the name of the purchasing entity, value and kind of goods purchased, country of origin, and a statement of the conditions in paragraph 15 of this Article which prevailed. This report shall remain with the entities concerned at the disposal of the government authorities responsible for the entity in order that it may be used if required under the procedures of Articles VI and VII of this Agreement.

Article VI

Information and Review

1. Any law, regulation, judicial decision, administrative ruling of general application, and any procedure (including standard contract clauses) regarding government procurement covered by this Agreement, shall be published

---

[1] Original development of a first product may include limited production in order to incorporate the results of field testing and to demonstrate that the product is suitable for production in quantity to acceptable quality standards. It does not extend to quantity production to establish commercial viability or to recover research and development costs.

promptly by the Parties in the appropriate publications listed in Annex IV and in such a manner as to enable other Parties and suppliers to become acquainted with them. The Parties shall be prepared, upon request, to explain to any other Party their government procurement procedures. Entities shall be prepared, upon request, to explain to any supplier from a country which is a Party to this Agreement their procurement practices and procedures.

2.   Entities shall, upon request by any supplier, promptly provide pertinent information concerning the reasons why that supplier's application to qualify for the suppliers' list was rejected, or why that supplier was not invited or admitted to tender.

3.   Entities shall promptly, and in no case later than seven working days from the date of the award of a contract, inform the unsuccessful tenderers by written communication or publication that a contract has been awarded.

4.   Upon request by an unsuccessful tenderer, the purchasing entity shall promptly provide that tenderer with pertinent information concerning the reasons why the tender was not selected, including information on the characteristics and the relative advantages of the tender selected, as well as the name of the winning tenderer.

5.   Entities shall establish a contact point to provide additional information to any unsuccessful tenderer dissatisfied with the explanation for rejection of his tender or who may have further questions about the award of the contract. There shall also be procedures for the hearing and reviewing of complaints arising in connexion with any phase of the procurement process, so as to ensure that, to the greatest extent possible, disputes under this Agreement will be equitably and expeditiously resolved between the suppliers and the entities concerned.

6.   The government of the unsuccessful tenderer, which is a Party to this Agreement, may seek, without prejudice to the provisions under Article VII, such additional information on the contract award as may be necessary to ensure that the purchase was made fairly and impartially. To this end, the purchasing government shall provide information on both the characteristics and relative advantages of the winning tender and the contract price. Normally this latter information may be disclosed by the government of the unsuccessful tenderer provided it exercises this right with discretion. In cases where release of this information would prejudice competition in future tenders this information shall not be disclosed except after consultation with and agreement of the Party which gave the information to the government of the unsuccessful tenderer.

7.   Available information concerning individual contract awards shall be provided, upon a request, to any other Party.

8. Confidential information provided to any Party which would impede law enforcement or otherwise be contrary to the public interest or would prejudice the legitimate commercial interest of particular enterprises, public or private, or might prejudice fair competition between suppliers, shall not be revealed without formal authorization from the party providing the information.

9. The Parties shall collect and provide to the Committee on an annual basis statistics on their purchases. Such reports shall contain the following information with respect to contracts awarded by all procurement entities covered under this Agreement:

   (a) global statistics on estimated value of contracts awarded, both above and below the threshold value;

   (b) statistics on number and total value of contracts awarded above the threshold value, broken down by entities, categories of products and either nationality of the winning tenderer or country of origin of the product, according to a recognized trade or other appropriate classification system;

   (c) statistics on the total number and value of contracts awarded under each of the cases of Article V, paragraph 15.

Article VII

Enforcement of Obligations

Institutions

1. There shall be established under this Agreement a Committee on Government Procurement (referred to in this Agreement as " the Committee ") composed of representatives from each of the Parties. This Committee shall elect its own Chairman and shall meet as necessary but not less than once a year for the purpose of affording Parties the opportunity to consult on any matters relating to the operation of this Agreement or the furtherance of its objectives, and to carry out such other responsibilities as may be assigned to it by the Parties.

2. The Committee may establish *ad hoc* panels in the manner and for the purposes set out in paragraph 8 of this Article and working parties or other subsidiary bodies which shall carry out such functions as may be given to them by the Committee.

Consultations

3. Each Party shall afford sympathetic consideration to, and shall afford adequate opportunity for consultations regarding, representations made by

another Party with respect to any matter affecting the operation of this Agreement.

4. If any Party considers that any benefit accruing to it, directly or indirectly, under this Agreement is being nullified or impaired, or that the achievement of any objective of this Agreement is being impeded, by another Party or Parties, it may, with a view to reaching a mutually satisfactory resolution of the matter, request in writing consultations with the Party or Parties in question. Each Party shall afford sympathetic consideration to any request from another Party for consultations. The Parties concerned shall initiate requested consultations promptly.

5. The Parties engaged in consultations on a particular matter affecting the operation of this Agreement shall provide information concerning the matter subject to the provisions of Article VI, paragraph 8, and attempt to conclude such consultations within a reasonably short period of time.

Dispute settlement

6. If no mutually satisfactory solution has been reached as a result of consultations under paragraph 4 between the Parties concerned, the Committee shall meet at the request of any party to the dispute within thirty days of receipt of such a request to investigate the matter, with a view to facilitating a mutually satisfactory solution.

7. If no mutually satisfactory solution has been reached after detailed examination by the Committee under paragraph 6 within three months, the Committee shall, at the request of any party to the dispute establish a panel to:

    (*a*) examine the matter;

    (*b*) consult regularly with the parties to the dispute and give full opportunity for them to develop a mutually satisfactory solution;

    (*c*) make a statement concerning the facts of the matter as they relate to application of this Agreement and make such findings as will assist the Committee in making recommendations or giving rulings on the matter.

8. In order to facilitate the constitution of panels, the Chairman of the Committee shall maintain an informal indicative list of governmental officials experienced in the field of trade relations. This list may also include persons other than governmental officials. In this connexion, each Party shall be invited to indicate at the beginning of every year to the Chairman of the Committee the name(s) of the one or two persons whom the Parties would be willing to make available for such work. When a panel is established under paragraph 7, the Chairman, within seven days, shall propose to the parties to the dispute the composition of the panel consisting of three

or five members and preferably government officials. The parties directly concerned shall react within seven working days to nominations of panel members by the Chairman and shall not oppose nominations except for compelling reasons.

Citizens of countries whose governments are parties to a dispute shall not be eligible for membership of the panel concerned with that dispute. Panel members shall serve in their individual capacities and not as governmental representatives nor as representatives of any organization. Governments or organizations shall therefore not give them instructions with regard to matters before a panel.

9.   Each panel shall develop its own procedures. All Parties, having a substantial interest in the matter and having notified this to the Committee, shall have an opportunity to be heard. Each panel may consult with and seek information from any source it deems appropriate. Before a panel seeks such information from a source within the jurisdiction of a Party it shall inform the government of that Party. Any Party shall respond promptly and fully to any request by a panel for such information as the panel considers necessary and appropriate. Confidential information provided to the panel shall not be revealed without formal authorization from the government or person providing the information. Where such information is requested from the panel but release of such information by the panel is not authorized, a non-confidential summary of the information, authorized by the government or person providing the information, will be provided.

Where a mutually satisfactory solution to a dispute cannot be found or where the dispute relates to an interpretation of this Agreement, the panel should first submit the descriptive part of its report to the Parties concerned, and should subsequently submit to the parties to the dispute its conclusions, or an outline thereof, a reasonable period of time before they are circulated to the Committee. Where an interpretation of this Agreement is not involved and where a bilateral settlement of the matter has been found, the report of the panel may be confined to a brief description of the case and to reporting that a solution had been reached.

10.   The time required by panels will vary with the particular case. Panels should aim to deliver their findings, and where appropriate, recommendations, to the Committee without undue delay, taking into account the obligation of the Committee to ensure prompt settlement in cases of urgency, normally within a period of four months from the date the panel was established.

Enforcement

11.   After the examination is complete or after the report of a panel, working party or other subsidiary body is presented to the Committee, the Com-

mittee shall give the matter prompt consideration. With respect to these reports, the Committee shall take appropriate action normally within thirty days of receipt of the report unless extended by the Committee, including:

(*a*)   a statement concerning the facts of the matter;

(*b*)   recommendations to one or more Parties; and/or

(*c*)   any other ruling which it deems appropriate.

Any recommendations by the Committee shall aim at the positive resolution of the matter on the basis of the operative provisions of this Agreement and its objectives set out in the Preamble.

12.   If a Party to which recommendations are addressed considers itself unable to implement them, it should promptly furnish reasons in writing to the Committee. In that event, the Committee shall consider what further action may be appropriate.

13.   The Committee shall keep under surveillance any matter on which it has made recommendations or given rulings.

Balance of rights and obligations

14.   If the Committee's recommendations are not accepted by a party, or parties, to the dispute, and if the Committee considers that the circumstances are serious enough to justify such action, it may authorize a Party or Parties to suspend in whole or in part, and for such time as may be necessary, the application of this Agreement to any other Party or Parties, as is determined to be appropriate in the circumstances.

Article VIII

Exceptions to the Agreement

1.   Nothing in this Agreement shall be construed to prevent any Party from taking any action or not disclosing any information which it considers necessary for the protection of its essential security interests relating to the procurement of arms, ammunition or war materials, or to procurement indispensable for national security or for national defence purposes.

2.   Subject to the requirement that such measures are not applied in a manner which would constitute a means of arbitrary or unjustifiable discrimination between countries where the same conditions prevail or a disguised restriction on international trade, nothing in this Agreement shall be construed to prevent any Party from imposing or enforcing measures necessary to protect public morals, order or safety, human, animal or plant life or health, intellectual property, or relating to the products of handicapped persons, of philanthropic institutions or of prison labour.

Article IX

Final Provisions

1. *Acceptance and accession*

   (*a*) This Agreement shall be open for acceptance by signature or otherwise, by governments contracting parties to the GATT and by the European Economic Community whose agreed lists of entities are contained in Annex I.

   (*b*) Any government contracting party to the GATT not a Party to this Agreement may accede to it on terms to be agreed between that government and the Parties. Accession shall take place by the deposit with the Director-General to the CONTRACTING PARTIES to the GATT of an instrument of accession which states the terms so agreed.

   (*c*) This Agreement shall be open for acceptance by signature or otherwise by governments having provisionally acceded to the GATT, on terms related to the effective application of rights and obligations under this Agreement, which take into account rights and obligations in the instruments providing for their provisional accession, and whose agreed lists of entities are contained in Annex I.

   (*d*) This Agreement shall be open to accession by any other government on terms, related to the effective application of rights and obligations under this Agreement, to be agreed between that government and the Parties, by the deposit with the Director-General to the CONTRACTING PARTIES to the GATT of an instrument of accession which states the terms so agreed.

   (*e*) In regard to acceptance, the provisions of Article XXVI: 5(*a*) and (*b*) of the General Agreement would be applicable.

2. *Reservations*

   Reservations may not be entered in respect of any of the provisions of this Agreement.

3. *Entry into force*

   This Agreement shall enter into force on 1 January 1981 for the governments [1] which have accepted or acceded to it by that date. For each other

---

[1] For the purpose of this Agreement, the term " government " is deemed to include the competent authorities of the European Economic Community.

government, it shall enter into force on the thirtieth day following the date of its acceptance or accession to this Agreement.

4. *National legislation*

   (a) Each government accepting or acceding to this Agreement shall ensure, not later than the date of entry into force of this Agreement for it, the conformity of its laws, regulations and administrative procedures, and the rules, procedures and practices applied by the entities contained in its list annexed hereto, with the provisions of this Agreement.

   (b) Each Party shall inform the Committee of any changes in its laws and regulations relevant to this Agreement and in the administration of such laws and regulations.

5. *Rectifications or modifications*

   (a) Rectifications of a purely formal nature and minor amendments relating to Annexes I-IV to this Agreement shall be notified to the Committee and shall become effective provided there is no objection within thirty days to such rectifications or amendments.

   (b) Any modifications to lists of entities other than those referred to in sub-paragraph (a) may be made only in exceptional circumstances. In such cases, a Party proposing to modify its list of entities shall notify the Chairman of the Committee who shall promptly convene a meeting of the Committee. The Parties shall consider the proposed modification and consequent compensatory adjustments, with a view to maintaining a comparable level of mutually agreed coverage provided in this Agreement prior to such modification. In the event of agreement not being reached on any modification taken or proposed, the matter may be pursued in accordance with the provisions contained in Article VII of this Agreement, taking into account the need to maintain the balance of rights and obligations at the highest possible level.

6. *Reviews and negotiations*

   (a) The Committee shall review annually the implementation and operation of this Agreement taking into account the objectives thereof. The Committee shall annually inform the CONTRACTING PARTIES to the GATT of developments during the periods covered by such reviews.

   (b) Not later than the end of the third year from the entry into force of this Agreement and periodically thereafter, the Parties thereto shall undertake further negotiations, with a view to broadening and improving this Agreement on the basis of mutual reciprocity, having regard to the provisions of Article III relating to developing countries. In this connexion, the Committee shall, at an early stage, explore the possibilities of expanding the coverage of this Agreement to include service contracts.

7. *Amendments*

The Parties may amend this Agreement having regard, *inter alia*, to the experience gained in its implementation. Such an amendment, once the Parties have concurred in accordance with the procedures established by the Committee, shall not come into force for any Party until it has been accepted by such Party.

8. *Withdrawal*

Any Party may withdraw from this Agreement. The withdrawal shall take effect upon the expiration of sixty days from the day on which written notice of withdrawal is received by the Director-General to the CONTRACTING PARTIES to the GATT. Any Party may upon such notification request an immediate meeting of the Committee.

9. *Non-application of this Agreement between particular Parties*

This Agreement shall not apply as between any two Parties if either of the Parties, at the time either accepts or accedes to this Agreement, does not consent to such application.

10. *Notes and Annexes*

The notes and annexes to this Agreement constitute an integral part thereof.

11. *Secretariat*

This Agreement shall be serviced by the GATT secretariat.

12. *Deposit*

This Agreement shall be deposited with the Director-General to the CONTRACTING PARTIES to the GATT, who shall promptly furnish to each Party and each contracting party to the GATT a certified copy thereof, of each rectification or modification thereto pursuant to paragraph 5 and of each amendment thereto pursuant to paragraph 7, and a notification of each acceptance thereof or accession thereto pursuant to paragraph 1 and of each withdrawal therefrom pursuant to paragraph 8, of this Article.

13. *Registration*

This Agreement shall be registered in accordance with the provisions of Article 102 of the Charter of the United Nations.

Done at Geneva this twelfth day of April nineteen hundred and seventy-nine in a single copy, in the English, French and Spanish languages, each text being authentic, except as otherwise specified with respect to the lists of entities annexed hereto.

NOTES

Article I, paragraph 1

Having regard to general policy considerations relating to tied aid, including the objective of developing countries with respect to the untying of such aid, this Agreement does not apply to procurement made in furtherance of tied aid to developing countries so long as it is practised by Parties.

Article V, paragraph 14(h)

Having regard to the general policy considerations of developing countries in relation to government procurement, it is noted that under the provisions of paragraph 14(h) of Article V, developing countries may require incorporation of domestic content, offset procurement, or transfer of technology as criteria for award of contracts. It is noted that suppliers from one Party shall not be favoured over suppliers from any other Party.

Presidential Documents

Executive Order 12260 of December 31, 1980

Agreement on Government Procurement

By the authority vested in me as President by the Constitution and statutes of the United States of America, including Title III of the Trade Agreements Act of 1979 (19 U.S.C. 2511–2518), and Section 301 of Title 3 of the United States Code, and in order to implement the Agreement on Government Procurement, as defined in 19 U.S.C. 2518(1), it is hereby ordered as follows:

1–1 *Responsibilities.*

1–101. The obligations of the Agreement on Government Procurement (Agreement on Government Procurement, General Agreement on Tariffs and Trade, 12 April 1979, Geneva (GATT 1979)) apply to any procurement of eligible products by the Executive agencies listed in the Annex to this Order (eligible products are defined in Section 308 of the Trade Agreements Act of 1979; 19 U.S.C. 2518(4)). Such procurement shall be in accord with the policies and procedures of the Office of Federal Procurement Policy (41 U.S.C. 401 *et seq.*).

1–102. The United States Trade Representative, hereinafter referred to as the Trade Representative, shall be responsible for interpretation of the Agreement. The Trade Representative shall seek the advice of the interagency organization established under Section 242(a) of the Trade Expansion Act of 1962 (19 U.S.C. 1872(a)) and consult with affected Executive agencies, including the Office of Federal Procurement Policy.

1–103. The interpretation of Article VIII:1 of the Agreement shall be subject to the concurrence of the Secretary of Defense.

1–104. The Trade Representative shall determine, from time to time, the dollar equivalent of 150,000 Special Drawing Right units and shall publish that determination in the Federal Register. Procurement of less than 150,000 Special Drawing Right units is not subject to the Agreement or this Order (Article I:1(b) of the Agreement).

1–105. In order to ensure coordination of international trade policy with regard to the implementation of the Agreement, agencies shall consult in advance with the Trade Representative about negotiations with foreign governments or instrumentalities which concern government procurement.

1–2. *Delegations and Authorization.*

1–201. The functions vested in the President by Sections 301, 302, 304, 305(c) and 306 of the Trade Agreements Act of 1979 (19 U.S.C. 2511, 2512, 2514, 2515(c) and 2516) are delegated to the Trade Representative.

1–202. Notwithstanding the delegation in Section 1–201, the Secretary of Defense is authorized, in accord with Section 302(b)(3) of the Trade Agreements Act of 1979 (19 U.S.C. 2512(b)(3)), to waive the prohibitions specified therein.

Jimmy Carter

THE WHITE HOUSE,
December 31, 1980.

Billing code 3195-01-M

ANNEX

1. ACTION

2. Administrative Conference of the United States

3. American Battle Monuments Commission

4. Board for International Broadcasting

5. Civil Aeronautics Board

6. Commission on Civil Rights

7. Commodity Futures Trading Commission

8. Community Services Administration

9. Consumer Product Safety Commission

1C. Department of Agriculture (The Agreement on Government Procurement does not apply to procurement of agricultural products made in furtherance of agricultural support programs or human feeding programs)

11. Department of Commerce

12. Department of Defense (Excludes Corps of Engineers)

13. Department of Education

14. Department of Health and Human Services

15. Department of Housing and Urban Development

16. Department of the Interior (Excludes the Bureau of Reclamation)

17. Department of Justice

18. Department of Labor

19. Department of State

20. Department of the Treasury

21. Environmental Protection Agency

22. Equal Employment Opportunity Commission

23. Executive Office of the President

24. Export-Import Bank of the United States

25. Farm Credit Administration

26. Federal Communications Commission

27. Federal Deposit Insurance Corporation

28. Federal Home Loan Bank Board

29. Federal Maritime Commission

30. Federal Mediation and Conciliation Service

31. Federal Trade Commission

32. General Services Administration (Purchases by the National Tool Center, and the Region 9 Office in San Francisco, California are not included)

33. Interstate Commerce Commission

34. Merit Systems Protection Board

35. National Aeronautics and Space Administration

36. National Credit Union Administration

37. National Labor Relations Board

38. National Mediation Board

39. National Science Foundation

40. National Transportation Safety Board

41. Nuclear Regulatory Commission

42. Office of Personnel Management

43. Overseas Private Investment Corporation

44. Panama Canal Commission

45. Railroad Retirement Board

46. Securities and Exchange Commission

47. Selective Service System

48. Smithsonian Institution

49. United States Arms Control and Disarmament Agency

50. United States International Communication Agency

51. United States International Development Cooperation Agency

52. United States International Trade Commission

53. Veterans Administration

[FR Doc. 81-476
Filed 1-2-81: 3.10 pm]
Billing code 3195-01-C

262

OFFICE OF THE UNITED STATES TRADE REPRESENTATIVE

Determination Regarding Application of Agreement on Government Procurement and Waiver of Discriminatory Purchasing Requirements

Section 1–103 of Executive Order 12188 delegates the functions of the President under Section 2(b) of the Trade Agreements Act of 1979 ("the Act") (19 U.S.C. 2503) to the United States Trade Representative ("Trade Representative"), who shall exercise such authority with the advice of the Trade Policy Committee. Section 1–201 of Executive Order 12260 delegates the functions of the President under Sections 301 and 302 of the Act (19 U.S.C. 2511, 2512) to the Trade Representative. Executive Order 12260 also provides in section 1–104 that the Trade Representative shall determine, from time to time, the dollar equivalent of 150,000 Special Drawing Right units.

Now, therefore, I, Robert D. Hormats, Acting United States Trade Representative, in conformity with the provisions of Section 2 of the Act, Sections 301 and 302 of the Act, and Executive Orders 12188 and 12260, do hereby determine, effective on the date of signature of this notice, that, with respect to the Agreement on Government Procurement ("the Agreement"):

1. The countries or instrumentalities listed in Annex 1 have become parties to the Agreement, and will provide appropriate reciprocal competitive government procurement opportunities to United States products and suppliers of such products. In accordance with Section 301(b)(1) of the Act, each of these countries is designated for purposes of Section 301(a) of the Act.

2. The countries listed in Annex 2 are least developed countries, as defined in Section 308 of the Act (19 U.S.C. 2518). In accordance with Section 301(b)(4) of the Act, each of these countries is designated for purposes of Section 301(a) of the Act.

3. With respect to eligible products (as defined in Section 308(4) of the Act) of the countries or instrumentalities designated above for purposes of Section 301(a) of the Act, and suppliers of such products, the application of any law, regulation, procedure, or practice regarding Government procurement that would, if applied to such products and suppliers, result in treatment less favorable than that accorded—

(A) to United States products and suppliers of such products; or

(B) to eligible products of another foreign country or instrumentality which

is a party to the Agreement and suppliers of such products, shall be waived.

This waiver shall be applied by all Executive agencies listed in Annex A of Executive Order 12260 in consultation with, and when deemed necessary at the direction of, the Trade Representative.

4. The designations in paragraphs 1 and 2 above and the waiver in paragraph 3 above are subject to modification or withdrawal by the Trade Representative.

5. (a) Pursuant to Section 302 of the Act, Executive agencies are prohibited after January 1, 1981, from procuring any products (A) which are products of a foreign country or instrumentality which is not designated under Section 301(b) of the Act, and (B) which would otherwise be eligible products. This prohibition will last until such foreign country or instrumentality is designated under Section 301(b) of the Act.

(b) The above prohibition shall be deferred for a two-year period beginning January 1, 1981, except for products of major industrial countries. Major industrial countries include the member countries of the European Communities, Canada, and Japan.

(c) The above two-year delay may be terminated at any time (causing the prohibition to come into effect) for any or all countries.

6. The dollar equivalent of 150,000 Special Drawing Right units is $196,000. This determination may be modified from time to time as appropriate.

Dated: January 1, 1981.

Robert D. Hormats,
Acting United States Trade Representative.

Annex 1

Austria	Italy
Belgium	Japan
Canada	Luxembourg
Denmark	Netherlands
Federal Republic of	Norway
Germany	Singapore
Finland	Sweden
France	Switzerland
Hong Kong	United Kingdom
Ireland	

Annex 2

Bangladesh	Malawi
Benin	Maldives
Bhutan	Mali
Burundi	Nepal
Cape Verde	Niger
Central African Republic	Rwanda
Chad	Somalia
Comoros	Western Samoa
Gambia	Sudan
Guinea	Tanzania U.R.
Haiti	Uganda
Lesotho	Upper Volta
	Yemen AR

[FR Doc. 81–477 Filed 1–2–81, 3.32 pm]

BILLING CODE 3190-01-M

Statement Concerning Executive Order 12260 on Agreement on Government Procurement

On December 31, 1980, the President signed Executive Order 12260 ("the Order") implementing the Agreement on Government Procurement (the "Agreement") and Title III of the Trade Agreements Act of 1979 (the "Act") (19 U.S.C. 2511–2518), effective January 1, 1981.

The Agreement is one of the trade agreements concluded during the Tokyo Round of Multilateral Trade Negotiations. The Agreement was approved by the Congress by Section 2 of the Act (19 U.S.C. 2503). The United States Trade Representative ("Trade Representative"), acting under Section 2(b) of the Act and Section 1–103(b) of Executive Order 12188, accepted the Agreement on behalf of the United States without reservation on December 30, 1980. The Agreement enters into force with respect to the United States on January 1, 1981.

The purpose of the Order is to delineate agency responsibilities for implementing the Agreement and to delegate certain authority for implementing the Agreement. Specifically,

Section 1–101 of the Order requires all agencies listed in the Annex thereto to observe the obligations of the Agreement in their purchases of "eligible products". The definition of "eligible products" is that contained in section 308(4) of the Act (19 U.S.C. 2518(4)). To qualify as an eligible product, a product must satisfy three criteria. The product must be:

1. From a country or instrumentality that is a party to the Agreement;

2. Procured for an Executive agency which is specified in the Order as being subject to the Agreement;

3. Procured in large enough quantities that the contract price exceeds 150,000 Special Drawing Right units.

Section 1–102 gives the Trade Representative the responsibility to interpret the Agreement. This responsibility follows the Trade Representative's broader authority granted in section 1(b)(3) of Reorganization Plan No. 3 of 1979 (44 FR 69173, 93 Stat. 1381), to "issue policy guidance to departments and agencies on basic issues of policy and interpretation * * *" relating to, *inter alia*, the implementation of international trade agreements.

Section 1–103 provides that interpretation of Article VIII:1 of the

Agreement, relating to national defense, shall be subject to the concurrence of the Secretary of Defense.

Section 1–104 gives the Trade Representative the responsibility to make a determination of the dollar equivalent of the 150,000 Special Drawing Right units threshold for coverage of procurement contracts. The Special Drawing Right is the unit of account of the international monetary fund, and is a weighted average of the values of a group of currencies including the U.S. dollar. This determination will be published annually in the Federal Register, or more often if appropriate.

Section 1–105 provides that agencies shall consult in advance with the Trade Representative about negotiations with foreign governments or instrumentalities which concern government procurement. The provision was included to ensure the coordination of international trade policy as it relates to the implementation, including negotiations relating to additional coverage, of the Agreement.

Section 1–201 delegates the functions of the President under Title III of the Act to the Trade Representative with the exception of the functions of the President under Section 303 of the Act (19 U.S.C. 2513), which were previously delegated to the Trade Representative in Section 1–103(b) of Executive Order 12188. These functions include:

—Waiver of discriminatory purchasing requirements under Section 301(a) of the Act (19 U.S.C. 2511(a));
—Designation of eligible countries and instrumentalities under Section 301(b) of the Act (19 U.S.C. 2511(b));
—Prohibiting procurement from non-designated countries or instrumentalities under Section 302 of the Act (19 U.S.C. 2512), as well as implementing the two-year delay and case-by-case waiver of purchases under the same Section;
—Reporting and consultation requirements under Sections 302(c), 302(d), 304, 305 and 306 of the Act (19 U.S.C. 2512(c), 2512(d), 2514–2516); and
—Other functions of the President enumerated in Title III of the Act.

Section 1–202 implements the provisions of Section 302(b)(3) of the Act (19 U.S.C. 2512(b)(3)), authorizing the Secretary of Defense to waive the purchasing prohibition of Section 302(a)(1) in the context of reciprocal procurement agreements.

For agencies not included in the Annex to the Order, no change in present procurement practices will be required. Furthermore, to the extent procurement by agencies listed in the Annex is outside the Agreement, the Order will not apply. Procurement not covered by the Agreement includes:

—Contracts of a value not over 150,000 SDR's;
—Procurement by agencies not in the Order, even if done through agencies listed in the Order.
—Contracts where the value of services exceeds 50% of the contract price.

Also, service contracts *per se*, including construction contracts, research and development and transportation or cargo preference schemes, will not be affected by the Agreement.

Under the terms of the Agreement, procurements involving eligible products may be set aside for small business concerns; however, procurements involving eligible products may not be set aside for labor surplus area concerns unless the set-aside is also for small business concerns. The priority of Sections 15(e) and (f) of the Small Business Act, as amended by section 117 of Pub. L. 96–302 (94 Stat. 839), shall prevail.

The provisions of the Act and this Order do not relieve agencies of their obligations to implement the requirements of Pub. L. 95–507 (92 Stat. 1757, 15 U.S.C. 683).

Robert C. Cassidy,
General Counsel.

[FR Doc. 81–478 Filed 1–2–81; 3:32 pm]
BILLING CODE 3190-01-M

AGREEMENT ON IMPLEMENTATION
OF ARTICLE VII
OF THE GENERAL AGREEMENT
ON TARIFFS AND TRADE

GENERAL INTRODUCTORY COMMENTARY

1. The primary basis for customs value under this Agreement is " transaction value " as defined in Article 1. Article 1 is to be read together with Article 8 which provides, *inter alia,* for adjustments to the price actually paid or payable in cases where certain specific elements which are considered to form a part of the value for customs purposes are incurred by the buyer but are not included in the price actually paid or payable for the imported goods. Article 8 also provides for the inclusion in the transaction value of certain considerations which may pass from the buyer to the seller in the form of specified goods or services rather than in the form of money. Articles 2 to 7, inclusive, provide methods of determining the customs value whenever it cannot be determined under the provisions of Article 1.

2. Where the customs value cannot be determined under the provisions of Article 1 there should normally be a process of consultation between the customs administration and importer with a view to arriving at a basis of value under the provisions of Articles 2 or 3. It may occur, for example, that the importer has information about the customs value of identical or similar imported goods which is not immediately available to the customs administration in the port of importation. On the other hand, the customs administration may have information about the customs value of identical or similar imported goods which is not readily available to the importer. A process of consultation between the two parties will enable information to be exchanged, subject to the requirements of commercial confidentiality, with a view to determining a proper basis of value for customs purposes.

3. Articles 5 and 6 provide two bases for determining the customs value where it cannot be determined on the basis of the transaction value of the imported goods or of identical or similar imported goods. Under Article 5.1 the customs value is determined on the basis of the price at which the goods are sold in the condition as imported to an unrelated buyer in the country of importation. The importer also has the right to have goods which are further processed after importation valued under the provisions of Article 5 if he so requests. Under Article 6 the customs value is determined on the

basis of the computed value. Both these methods present certain difficulties and because of this the importer is given the right, under the provisions of Article 4, to choose the order of application of the two methods.

4.   Article 7 sets out how to determine the customs value in cases where it cannot be determined under the provisions of any of the preceding Articles.

PREAMBLE

Having regard to the Multilateral Trade Negotiations, the Parties to this Agreement (hereinafter referred to as " Parties "),

Desiring to further the objectives of the General Agreement on Tariffs and Trade (hereinafter referred to as " General Agreement " or " GATT ") and to secure additional benefits for the international trade of developing countries;

Recognizing the importance of the provisions of Article VII of the General Agreement and desiring to elaborate rules for their application in order to provide greater uniformity and certainty in their implementation;

Recognizing the need for a fair, uniform and neutral system for the valuation of goods for customs purposes that precludes the use of arbitrary or fictitious customs values;

Recognizing that the basis for valuation of goods for customs purposes should, to the greatest extent possible, be the transaction value of the goods being valued;

Recognizing that customs value should be based on simple and equitable criteria consistent with commercial practices and that valuation procedures should be of general application without distinction between sources of supply;

Recognizing that valuation procedures should not be used to combat dumping;

Hereby agree as follows:

PART I

RULES ON CUSTOMS VALUATION

Article 1

1.   The customs value of imported goods shall be the transaction value, that is the price actually paid or payable for the goods when sold for export to the country of importation adjusted in accordance with the provisions of Article 8, provided:

(*a*) that there are no restrictions as to the disposition or use of the goods by the buyer other than restrictions which:

   (i) are imposed or required by law or by the public authorities in the country of importation;

   (ii) limit the geographical area in which the goods may be resold; or

   (iii) do not substantially affect the value of the goods;

(*b*) that the sale or price is not subject to some condition or consideration for which a value cannot be determined with respect to the goods being valued;

(*c*) that no part of the proceeds of any subsequent resale, disposal or use of the goods by the buyer will accrue directly or indirectly to the seller, unless an appropriate adjustment can be made in accordance with the provisions of Article 8; and

(*d*) that the buyer and seller are not related, or where the buyer and seller are related, that the transaction value is acceptable for customs purposes under the provisions of paragraph 2 of this Article.

2. (*a*) In determining whether the transaction value is acceptable for the purposes of paragraph 1, the fact that the buyer and the seller are related within the meaning of Article 15 shall not in itself be grounds for regarding the transaction value as unacceptable. In such case the circumstances surrounding the sale shall be examined and the transaction value shall be accepted provided that the relationship did not influence the price. If, in the light of information provided by the importer or otherwise, the customs administration has grounds for considering that the relationship influenced the price, it shall communicate its grounds to the importer and he shall be given a reasonable opportunity to respond. If the importer so requests, the communication of the grounds shall be in writing.

   (*b*) In a sale between related persons, the transaction value shall be accepted and the goods valued in accordance with the provisions of paragraph 1 whenever the importer demonstrates that such value closely approximates to one of the following occurring at or about the same time:

   (i) the transaction value in sales to unrelated buyers of identical or similar goods for export to the same country of importation;

   (ii) the customs value of identical or similar goods as determined under the provisions of Article 5;

   (iii) the customs value of identical or similar goods as determined under the provisions of Article 6;

(iv) the transaction value in sales to unrelated buyers for export to the same country of importation of goods which would be identical to the imported goods except for having a different country of production provided that the sellers in any two transactions being compared are not related.

In applying the foregoing tests, due account shall be taken of demonstrated differences in commercial levels, quantity levels, the elements enumerated in Article 8 and costs incurred by the seller in sales in which he and the buyer are not related that are not incurred by the seller in sales in which he and the buyer are related.

(c) The tests set forth in paragraph 2(b) are to be used at the initiative of the importer and only for comparison purposes. Substitute values may not be established under the provisions of paragraph 2(b).

Article 2

1. (a) If the customs value of the imported goods cannot be determined under the provisions of Article 1, the customs value shall be the transaction value of identical goods sold for export to the same country of importation and exported at or about the same time as the goods being valued.

(b) In applying this Article, the transaction value of identical goods in a sale at the same commercial level and in substantially the same quantity as the goods being valued shall be used to determine the customs value. Where no such sale is found, the transaction value of identical goods sold at a different commercial level and/or in different quantities, adjusted to take account of differences attributable to commercial level and/or to quantity, shall be used, provided that such adjustments can be made on the basis of demonstrated evidence which clearly establishes the reasonableness and accuracy of the adjustment, whether the adjustment leads to an increase or a decrease in the value.

2. Where the costs and charges referred to in Article 8.2 are included in the transaction value, an adjustment shall be made to take account of significant differences in such costs and charges between the imported goods and the identical goods in question arising from differences in distances and modes of transport.

3. If, in applying this Article, more than one transaction value of identical goods is found, the lowest such value shall be used to determine the customs value of the imported goods.

Article 3

1. (a) If the customs value of the imported goods cannot be determined under the provisions of Articles 1 and 2, the customs value shall be the transaction value of similar goods sold for export to the same country of importation and exported at or about the same time as the goods being valued.

   (b) In applying this Article, the transaction value of similar goods in a sale at the same commercial level and in substantially the same quantity as the goods being valued shall be used to determine the customs value. Where no such sale is found, the transaction value of similar goods sold at a different commercial level and/or in different quantities, adjusted to take account of differences attributable to commercial level and/or to quantity, shall be used, provided that such adjustments can be made on the basis of demonstrated evidence which clearly establishes the reasonableness and accuracy of the adjustment, whether the adjustment leads to an increase or a decrease in the value.

2. Where the costs and charges referred to in Article 8.2 are included in the transaction value, an adjustment shall be made to take account of significant differences in such costs and charges between the imported goods and the similar goods in question arising from differences in distances and modes of transport.

3. If, in applying this Article, more than one transaction value of similar goods is found, the lowest such value shall be used to determine the customs value of the imported goods.

Article 4

If the customs value of the imported goods cannot be determined under the provisions of Articles 1, 2 and 3 the customs value shall be determined under the provisions of Article 5 or, when the customs value cannot be determined under that Article, under the provisions of Article 6 except that, at the request of the importer, the order of application of Articles 5 and 6 shall be reversed.

Article 5

1. (a) If the imported goods or identical or similar imported goods are sold in the country of importation in the condition as imported, the customs value of the imported goods under the provisions of

this Article shall be based on the unit price at which the imported goods or identical or similar imported goods are so sold in the greatest aggregate quantity, at or about the time of the importation of the goods being valued, to persons who are not related to the persons from whom they buy such goods, subject to deductions for the following:

(i) either the commissions usually paid or agreed to be paid or the additions usually made for profit and general expenses in connexion with sales in such country of imported goods of the same class or kind;

(ii) the usual costs of transport and insurance and associated costs incurred within the country of importation;

(iii) where appropriate, the costs and charges referred to in Article 8.2; and

(iv) the customs duties and other national taxes payable in the country of importation by reason of the importation or sale of the goods.

(b) If neither the imported goods nor identical nor similar imported goods are sold at or about the time of importation of the goods being valued, the customs value shall, subject otherwise to the provisions of paragraph 1 (a) of this Article, be based on the unit price at which the imported goods or identical or similar imported goods are sold in the country of importation in the condition as imported at the earliest date after the importation of the goods being valued but before the expiration of ninety days after such importation.

2.   If neither the imported goods nor identical nor similar imported goods are sold in the country of importation in the condition as imported, then, if the importer so requests, the customs value shall be based on the unit price at which the imported goods, after further processing, are sold in the greatest aggregate quantity to persons in the country of importation who are not related to the persons from whom they buy such goods, due allowance being made for the value added by such processing and the deductions provided for in paragraph 1(a) of this Article.

Article 6

1.   The customs value of imported goods under the provisions of this Article shall be based on a computed value. Computed value shall consist of the sum of:

(*a*) the cost or value of materials and fabrication or other processing employed in producing the imported goods;

(*b*) an amount for profit and general expenses equal to that usually reflected in sales of goods of the same class or kind as the goods being valued which are made by producers in the country of exportation for export to the country of importation;

(*c*) the cost or value of all other expenses necessary to reflect the valuation option chosen by the Party under Article 8.2.

2. No Party may require or compel any person not resident in its own territory to produce for examination, or to allow access to, any account or other record for the purposes of determining a computed value. However, information supplied by the producer of the goods for the purposes of determining the customs value under the provisions of this Article may be verified in another country by the authorities of the country of importation with the agreement of the producer and provided they give sufficient advance notice to the government of the country in question and the latter does not object to the investigation.

Article 7

1. If the customs value of the imported goods cannot be determined under the provisions of Articles 1 to 6, inclusive, the customs value shall be determined using reasonable means consistent with the principles and general provisions of this Agreement and of Article VII of the General Agreement and on the basis of data available in the country of importation.

2. No customs value shall be determined under the provisions of this Article on the basis of:

(*a*) the selling price in the country of importation of goods produced in such country;

(*b*) a system which provides for the acceptance for customs purposes of the higher of two alternative values;

(*c*) the price of goods on the domestic market of the country of exportation;

(*d*) the cost of production other than computed values which have been determined for identical or similar goods in accordance with the provisions of Article 6;

(*e*) the price of the goods for export to a country other than the country of importation;

(*f*) minimum customs values; or

(*g*) arbitrary or fictitious values.

3. If he so requests, the importer shall be informed in writing of the customs value determined under the provisions of this Article and the method used to determine such value.

Article 8

1. In determining the customs value under the provisions of Article 1, there shall be added to the price actually paid or payable for the imported goods:

- (*a*) the following, to the extent that they are incurred by the buyer but are not included in the price actually paid or payable for the goods:
    - (i) commissions and brokerage, except buying commissions;
    - (ii) the cost of containers which are treated as being one for customs purposes with the goods in question;
    - (iii) the cost of packing whether for labour or materials;
- (*b*) the value, apportioned as appropriate, of the following goods and services where supplied directly or indirectly by the buyer free of charge or at reduced cost for use in connexion with the production and sale for export of the imported goods, to the extent that such value has not been included in the price actually paid or payable:
    - (i) materials, components, parts and similar items incorporated in the imported goods;
    - (ii) tools, dies, moulds and similar items used in the production of the imported goods;
    - (iii) materials consumed in the production of the imported goods;
    - (iv) engineering, development, artwork, design work, and plans and sketches undertaken elsewhere than in the country of importation and necessary for the production of the imported goods;
- (*c*) royalties and licence fees related to the goods being valued that the buyer must pay, either directly or indirectly, as a condition of sale of the goods being valued, to the extent that such royalties and fees are not included in the price actually paid or payable;
- (*d*) the value of any part of the proceeds of any subsequent resale, disposal or use of the imported goods that accrues directly or indirectly to the seller.

2. In framing its legislation, each Party shall provide for the inclusion in or the exclusion from the customs value, in whole or in part, of the following:

(a) the cost of transport of the imported goods to the port or place of importation;

(b) loading, unloading and handling charges associated with the transport of the imported goods to the port or place of importation; and

(c) the cost of insurance.

3. Additions to the price actually paid or payable shall be made under this Article only on the basis of objective and quantifiable data.

4. No additions shall be made to the price actually paid or payable in determining the customs value except as provided in this Article.

Article 9

1. Where the conversion of currency is necessary for the determination of the customs value, the rate of exchange to be used shall be that duly published by the competent authorities of the country of importation concerned and shall reflect as effectively as possible, in respect of the period covered by each such document of publication, the current value of such currency in commercial transactions in terms of the currency of the country of importation.

2. The conversion rate to be used shall be that in effect at the time of exportation or the time of importation, as provided by each Party.

Article 10

All information which is by nature confidential or which is provided on a confidential basis for the purposes of customs valuation shall be treated as strictly confidential by the authorities concerned who shall not disclose it without the specific permission of the person or government providing such information, except to the extent that it may be required to be disclosed in the context of judicial proceedings.

Article 11

1. The legislation of each Party shall provide in regard to a determination of customs value for the right of appeal, without penalty, by the importer or any other person liable for the payment of the duty.

2. An initial right of appeal without penalty may be to an authority within the customs administration or to an independent body, but the legislation of each Party shall provide for the right of appeal without penalty to a judicial authority.

3. Notice of the decision on appeal shall be given to the appellant and the reasons for such decision shall be provided in writing. He shall also be informed of his rights of any further appeal.

Article 12

Laws, regulations, judicial decisions and administrative rulings of general application giving effect to this Agreement shall be published in conformity with Article X of the General Agreement by the country of importation concerned.

Article 13

If, in the course of determining the customs value of imported goods, it becomes necessary to delay the final determination of such customs value, the importer shall nevertheless be able to withdraw his goods from customs if, where so required, he provides sufficient guarantee in the form of a surety, a deposit or some other appropriate instrument, covering the ultimate payment of customs duties for which the goods may be liable. The legislation of each Party shall make provisions for such circumstances.

Article 14

The notes at Annex I to this Agreement form an integral part of this Agreement and the Articles of this Agreement are to be read and applied in conjunction with their respective notes. Annexes II and III also form an integral part of this Agreement.

Article 15

1. In this Agreement:

   (a) " customs value of imported goods " means the value of goods for the purposes of levying ad valorem duties of customs on imported goods;

   (b) " country of importation " means country or customs territory of importation; and

   (c) " produced " includes grown, manufactured and mined.

2. (*a*) In this Agreement " identical goods " means goods which are the same in all respects, including physical characteristics, quality and reputation. Minor differences in appearance would not preclude goods otherwise conforming to the definition from being regarded as identical.

(*b*) In this Agreement " similar goods " means goods which, although not alike in all respects, have like characteristics and like component materials which enable them to perform the same functions and to be commercially interchangeable. The quality of the goods, their reputation and the existence of a trademark are among the factors to be considered in determining whether goods are similar.

(*c*) The terms " identical goods " and " similar goods " do not include, as the case may be, goods which incorporate or reflect engineering, development, artwork, design work, and plans and sketches for which no adjustment has been made under Article 8.1(*b*)(iv) because such elements were undertaken in the country of importation.

(*d*) Goods shall not be regarded as " identical goods " or " similar goods " unless they were produced in the same country as the goods being valued.

(*e*) Goods produced by a different person shall be taken into account only when there are no identical goods or similar goods, as the case may be, produced by the same person as the goods being valued.

3. In this Agreement " goods of the same class or kind " means goods which fall within a group or range of goods produced by a particular industry or industry sector, and includes identical or similar goods.

4. For the purposes of this Agreement, persons shall be deemed to be related only if:

(*a*) they are officers or directors of one another's businesses;

(*b*) they are legally recognized partners in business;

(*c*) they are employer and employee;

(*d*) any person directly or indirectly owns, controls or holds 5 per cent or more of the outstanding voting stock or shares of both of them;

(*e*) one of them directly or indirectly controls the other;

(*f*) both of them are directly or indirectly controlled by a third person;

(*g*) together they directly or indirectly control a third person; or

(*h*) they are members of the same family.

5. Persons who are associated in business with one another in that one is the sole agent, sole distributor or sole concessionaire, however described, of the other shall be deemed to be related for the purposes of this Agreement if they fall within the criteria of paragraph 4 of this Article.

Article 16

Upon written request, the importer shall have the right to an explanation in writing from the customs administration of the country of importation as to how the customs value of his imported goods was determined.

Article 17

Nothing in this Agreement shall be construed as restricting or calling into question the rights of customs administrations to satisfy themselves as to the truth or accuracy of any statement, document or declaration presented for customs valuation purposes.

PART II

ADMINISTRATION, CONSULTATION AND DISPUTE SETTLEMENT

Institutions

Article 18

There shall be established under this Agreement:

1. A Committee on Customs Valuation (hereinafter referred to as the Committee) composed of representatives from each of the Parties. The Committee shall elect its own Chairman and shall normally meet once a year, or as is .otherwise envisaged by the relevant provisions of this Agreement, for the purpose of affording Parties the opportunity to consult on matters relating to the administration of the customs valuation system by any Party as it might affect the operation of this Agreement or the furtherance of its objectives and carrying out such other responsibilities as may be assigned to it by the Parties. The GATT secretariat shall act as the secretariat to the Committee.

2. A Technical Committee on Customs Valuation (hereinafter referred to as the Technical Committee) under the auspices of the Customs Cooperation Council, which shall carry out the responsibilities described in Annex II to this Agreement and shall operate in accordance with the rules of procedure contained therein.

Consultation

Article 19

1. If any Party considers that any benefit accruing to it, directly or indirectly, under this Agreement is being nullified or impaired, or that the achievement of any objective of this Agreement is being impeded, as a result of the actions of another Party or of other Parties, it may, with a view to reaching a mutually satisfactory solution of the matter, request consultations with the Party or Parties in question. Each Party shall afford sympathetic consideration to any request from another Party for consultations.

2. The Parties concerned shall initiate requested consultations promptly.

3. Parties engaged in consultations on a particular matter affecting the operation of this Agreement shall attempt to conclude such consultations within a reasonably short period of time. The Technical Committee shall provide, upon request, advice and assistance to Parties engaged in consultations.

Dispute settlement

Article 20

1. If no mutually satisfactory solution has been reached between the Parties concerned in consultations under Article 19 above, the Committee shall meet at the request of any party to the dispute, within thirty days of receipt of such a request, to investigate the matter, with a view to facilitating a mutually satisfactory solution.

2. In investigating the matter and in selecting its procedures, the Committee shall take into account whether the issues in dispute relate to commercial policy considerations or to questions requiring detailed technical consideration. The Committee may request on its own initiative that the Technical Committee carry out an examination, as provided in paragraph 4 below, of any question requiring technical consideration. Upon the request of any party to the dispute that considers the issues to relate to questions

of a technical nature, the Committee shall request the Technical Committee to carry out such an examination.

3.   During any phase of a dispute settlement procedure, competent bodies and experts in matters under consideration may be consulted; appropriate information and assistance may be requested from such bodies and experts. The Committee shall take into consideration the results of any work of the Technical Committee that pertain to the matter in dispute.

Technical issues

4.   When the Technical Committee is requested under the provisions of paragraph 2 above, it shall examine the matter and report to the Committee no later than three months from the date the technical issue was referred to it, unless the period is extended by mutual agreement between the parties to the dispute.

Panel proceedings

5.   In cases where the matter is not referred to the Technical Committee, the Committee shall establish a panel upon the request of any party to the dispute if no mutually satisfactory solution has been reached within three months from the date of the request to the Committee to investigate the matter. Where the matter is referred to the Technical Committee, the Committee shall establish a panel upon the request of any party to the dispute if no mutually satisfactory solution has been reached within one month from the date when the Technical Committee presents its report to the Committee.

6.   (a) When a panel is established, it shall be governed by the procedures as set forth in Annex III.

(b) If the Technical Committee has made a report on the technical aspects of the matter in dispute, the panel shall use this report as the basis for its consideration of the technical aspects of the matter in dispute.

Enforcement

7.   After the investigation is completed or after the report of the Technical Committee or panel is presented to the Committee, the Committee shall give the matter prompt consideration. With respect to panel reports, the Committee shall take appropriate action normally within thirty days of receipt of the report. Such action shall include:

(i) a statement concerning the facts of the matter; and

(ii) recommendations to one or more Parties or any other ruling which it deems appropriate.

8.   If a Party to which recommendations are addressed considers itself unable to implement them, it should promptly furnish reasons in writing to the Committee. In that event, the Committee shall consider what further action may be appropriate.

9.   If the Committee considers that the circumstances are serious enough to justify such action, it may authorize one or more Parties to suspend the application to any other Party or Parties of such obligations under this Agreement as it determines to be appropriate in the circumstances.

10.   The Committee shall keep under surveillance any matter on which it has made recommendations or given rulings.

11.   If a dispute arises between Parties relating to rights and obligations under this Agreement, Parties should complete the dispute settlement procedures under this Agreement before availing themselves of any rights which they have under the GATT, including invoking Article XXIII thereof.

PART III

SPECIAL AND DIFFERENTIAL TREATMENT

Article 21

1.   Developing country Parties may delay application of its provisions for a period not exceeding five years from the date of entry into force of this Agreement for such countries. Developing country Parties who choose to delay application of this Agreement shall notify the Director-General to the CONTRACTING PARTIES to the GATT accordingly.

2.   In addition to paragraph 1 above, developing country Parties may delay application of Article 1.2(*b*)(iii) and Article 6 for a period not exceeding three years following their application of all other provisions of this Agreement. Developing country Parties that choose to delay application of the provisions specified in this paragraph shall notify the Director-General to the CONTRACTING PARTIES to the GATT accordingly.

3.   Developed country Parties shall furnish, on mutually agreed terms, technical assistance to developing country Parties that so request. On this basis developed country Parties shall draw up programmes of technical assistance which may include, *inter alia*, training of personnel, assistance

in preparing implementation measures, access to sources of information regarding customs valuation methodology, and advice on the application of the provisions of this Agreement.

PART IV

FINAL PROVISIONS

Acceptance and accession

Article 22

1. This Agreement shall be open for acceptance by signature or otherwise by governments contracting parties to the GATT and by the European Economic Community.

2. This Agreement shall be open for acceptance by signature or otherwise by governments having provisionally acceded to the GATT, on terms related to the effective application of rights and obligations under this Agreement, which take into account rights and obligations in the instruments providing for their provisional accession.

3. This Agreement shall be open to accession by any other government on terms, related to the effective application of rights and obligations under this Agreement, to be agreed between that government and the Parties, by the deposit with the Director-General to the CONTRACTING PARTIES to the GATT of an instrument of accession which states the terms so agreed.

4. In regard to acceptance, the provisions of Article XXVI:5(*a*) and (*b*) of the General Agreement would be applicable.

Reservations

Article 23

Reservations may not be entered in respect of any of the provisions of this Agreement without the consent of the other Parties.

Entry into force

Article 24

This Agreement shall enter into force on 1 January 1981 for the governments [1] which have accepted or acceded to it by that date. For each other government it shall enter into force on the thirtieth day following the date of its acceptance or accession to this Agreement.

National legislation

Article 25

1. Each government accepting or acceding to this Agreement shall ensure, not later than the date of entry into force of this Agreement for it, the conformity of its laws, regulations and administrative procedures with the provisions of this Agreement.

2. Each Party shall inform the Committee of any changes in its laws and regulations relevant to this Agreement and in the administration of such laws and regulations.

Review

Article 26

The Committee shall review annually the implementation and operation of this Agreement taking into account the objectives thereof. The Committee shall annually inform the CONTRACTING PARTIES to the GATT of developments during the period covered by such reviews.

Amendments

Article 27

The Parties may amend this Agreement, having regard, *inter alia*, to the experience gained in its implementation. Such an amendment, once the Parties have concurred in accordance with procedures established by the

---

[1] The term " governments " is deemed to include the competent authorities of the European Economic Community.

Committee, shall not come into force for any Party until it has been accepted by such Party.

Withdrawal

Article 28

Any Party may withdraw from this Agreement. The withdrawal shall take effect upon the expiration of sixty days from the date on which written notice of withdrawal is received by the Director-General to the CONTRACTING PARTIES to the GATT. Any Party may, upon the receipt of such notice, request an immediate meeting of the Committee.

Secretariat

Article 29

This Agreement shall be serviced by the GATT secretariat except in regard to those responsibilities specifically assigned to the Technical Committee, which will be serviced by the secretariat of the Customs Co-operation Council.

Deposit

Article 30

This Agreement shall be deposited with the Director-General to the CONTRACTING PARTIES to the GATT, who shall promptly furnish to each Party and each contracting party to the GATT a certified copy thereof and of each amendment thereto pursuant to Article 27, and a notification of each acceptance thereof or accession thereto pursuant to Article 22 and of each withdrawal therefrom pursuant to Article 28.

Registration

Article 31

This Agreement shall be registered in accordance with the provisions of Article 102 of the Charter of the United Nations.

Done at Geneva this twelfth day of April nineteen hundred and seventy-nine in a single copy, in the English, French and Spanish languages, each text being authentic.

ANNEX I

INTERPRETATIVE NOTES

General Note

Sequential application of valuation methods

1. Articles 1 to 7, inclusive, define how the customs value of imported goods is to be determined under the provisions of this Agreement. The methods of valuation are set out in a sequential order of application. The primary method for customs valuation is defined in Article 1 and imported goods are to be valued in accordance with the provisions of this Article whenever the conditions prescribed therein are fulfilled.

2. Where the customs value cannot be determined under the provisions of Article 1, it is to be determined by proceeding sequentially through the succeeding Articles to the first such Article under which the customs value can be determined. Except as provided in Article 4, it is only when the customs value cannot be determined under the provisions of a particular Article that the provisions of the next Article in the sequence can be used.

3. If the importer does not request that the order of Articles 5 and 6 be reversed, the normal order of the sequence is to be followed. If the importer does so request but it then proves impossible to determine the customs value under the provisions of Article 6, the customs value is to be determined under the provisions of Article 5, if it can be so determined.

4. Where the customs value cannot be determined under the provisions of Articles 1 to 6, inclusive, it is to be determined under the provisions of Article 7.

Use of generally accepted accounting principles

1. " Generally accepted accounting principles " refers to the recognized consensus or substantial authoritative support within a country at a particular time as to which economic resources and obligations should be recorded as assets and liabilities, which changes in assets and liabilities should be recorded, how the assets and liabilities and changes in them should be measured, what information should be disclosed and how it should be disclosed, and which financial statements should be prepared. These standards may be broad guidelines of general application as well as detailed practices and procedures.

2. For the purposes of this Agreement, the customs administration of each party shall utilize information prepared in a manner consistent with generally accepted accounting principles in the country which is appropriate for the Article in question. For example, the determination of usual profit and general expenses under the provisions of Article 5 would be carried out utilizing information prepared in a manner consistent with generally accepted accounting principles of

the country of importation. On the other hand, the determination of usual profit and general expenses under the provisions of Article 6 would be carried out utilizing information prepared in a manner consistent with generally accepted accounting principles of the country of production. As a further example, the determination of an element provided for in Article 8.1 (*b*) (ii) undertaken in the country of importation would be carried out utilizing information in a manner consistent with the generally accepted accounting principles of that country.

Note to Article 1

Price actually paid or payable

The price actually paid or payable is the total payment made or to be made by the buyer to or for the benefit of the seller for the imported goods. The payment need not necessarily take the form of a transfer of money. Payment may be made by way of letters of credit or negotiable instruments. Payment may be made directly or indirectly. An example of an indirect payment would be the settlement by the buyer, whether in whole or in part, of a debt owed by the seller.

Activities undertaken by the buyer on his own account, other than those for which an adjustment is provided in Article 8, are not considered to be an indirect payment to the seller, even though they might be regarded as of benefit to the seller. The costs of such activities shall not, therefore, be added to the price actually paid or payable in determining the customs value.

The customs value shall not include the following charges or costs, provided that they are distinguished from the price actually paid or payable for the imported goods:

(*a*) charges for construction, erection, assembly, maintenance or technical assistance, undertaken after importation on imported goods such as industrial plant, machinery or equipment;

(*b*) the cost of transport after importation;

(*c*) duties and taxes of the country of importation.

The price actually paid or payable refers to the price for the imported goods. Thus the flow of dividends or other payments from the buyer to the seller that do not relate to the imported goods are not part of the customs value.

Paragraph 1 (a) (iii)

Among restrictions which would not render a price actually paid or payable unacceptable are restrictions which do not substantially affect the value of the goods. An example of such restrictions would be the case where a seller requires a buyer of automobiles not to sell or exhibit them prior to a fixed date which represents the beginning of a model year.

Paragraph 1 (b)

If the sale or price is subject to some condition or consideration for which a value cannot be determined with respect to the goods being valued, the transaction value shall not be acceptable for customs purposes. Some examples of this include:

(a) the seller establishes the price of the imported goods on condition that the buyer will also buy other goods in specified quantities;

(b) the price of the imported goods is dependent upon the price or prices at which the buyer of the imported goods sells other goods to the seller of the imported goods;

(c) the price is established on the basis of a form of payment extraneous to the imported goods, such as where the imported goods are semi-finished goods which have been provided by the seller on condition that he will receive a specified quantity of the finished goods.

However, conditions or considerations relating to the production or marketing of the imported goods shall not result in rejection of the transaction value. For example, the fact that the buyer furnishes the seller with engineering and plans undertaken in the country of importation shall not result in rejection of the transaction value for the purposes of Article 1. Likewise, if the buyer undertakes on his own account, even though by agreement with the seller, activities relating to the marketing of the imported goods, the value of these activities is not part of the customs value nor shall such activities result in rejection of the transaction value.

Paragraph 2

1. Paragraphs 2 (a) and 2 (b) provide different means of establishing the acceptability of a transaction value.

2. Paragraph 2 (a) provides that where the buyer and the seller are related, the circumstances surrounding the sale shall be examined and the transaction value shall be accepted as the customs value provided that the relationship did not influence the price. It is not intended that there should be an examination of the circumstances in all cases where the buyer and the seller are related. Such examination will only be required where there are doubts about the acceptability of the price. Where the customs administration have no doubts about the acceptability of the price, it should be accepted without requesting further information from the importer. For example, the customs administration may have previously examined the relationship, or it may already have detailed information concerning the buyer and the seller, and may already be satisfied from such examination or information that the relationship did not influence the price.

3. Where the customs administration is unable to accept the transaction value without further inquiry, it should give the importer an opportunity to supply such further detailed information as may be necessary to enable it to examine the circumstances surrounding the sale. In this context, the customs administration should be prepared to examine relevant aspects of the transaction, including the way in which the buyer and seller organize their commercial relations and the way in which the price in question was arrived at, in order to determine whether the relationship influenced the price. Where it can be shown that the buyer and seller, although related under the provisions of Article 15, buy from and sell to each other as if they were not related, this would demonstrate that the price had not been influenced by the relationship. As an example of this, if the price had been settled in a manner consistent with the normal pricing practices of the

industry in question or with the way the seller settles prices for sales to buyers who are not related to him, this would demonstrate that the price had not been influenced by the relationship. As a further example, where it is shown that the price is adequate to ensure recovery of all costs plus a profit which is representative of the firm's overall profit realized over a representative period of time (e.g. on an annual basis) in sales of goods of the same class or kind, this would demonstrate that the price had not been influenced.

4. Paragraph 2 (*b*) provides an opportunity for the importer to demonstrate that the transaction value closely approximates to a " test " value previously accepted by the customs administration and is therefore acceptable under the provisions of Article 1. Where a test under paragraph 2 (*b*) is met, it is not necessary to examine the question of influence under paragraph 2 (*a*). If the customs administration has already sufficient information to be satisfied, without further detailed inquiries, that one of the tests provided in paragraph 2 (*b*) has been met, there is no reason for it to require the importer to demonstrate that the test can be met. In paragraph 2 (*b*) the term " unrelated buyers " means buyers who are not related to the seller in any particular case.

Paragraph 2 (b)

A number of factors must be taken into consideration in determining whether one value " closely approximates " to another value. These factors include the nature of the imported goods, the nature of the industry itself, the season in which the goods are imported, and, whether the difference in values is commercially significant. Since these factors may vary from case to case, it would be impossible to apply a uniform standard such as a fixed percentage, in each case. For example, a small difference in value in a case involving one type of goods could be unacceptable while a large difference in a case involving another type of goods might be acceptable in determining whether the transaction value closely approximates to the " test " values set forth in Article 1.2 (*b*).

Note to Article 2

1. In applying Article 2, the customs administration shall, wherever possible, use a sale of identical goods at the same commercial level and in substantially the same quantities as the goods being valued. Where no such sale is found, a sale of identical goods that takes place under any one of the following three conditions may be used:

    (*a*) a sale at the same commercial level but in different quantities;

    (*b*) a sale at a different commercial level but in substantially the same quantities; or

    (*c*) a sale at a different commercial level and in different quantities.

2. Having found a sale under any one of these three conditions adjustments will then be made, as the case may be, for:

    (*a*) quantity factors only;

    (*b*) commercial level factors only; or

(*c*) both commercial level and quantity factors.

3. The expression " and/or " allows the flexibility to use the sales and make the necessary adjustments in any one of the three conditions described above.

4. For the purposes of Article 2, the transaction value of identical imported goods means a customs value, adjusted as provided for in paragraphs 1 (*b*) and 2 of this Article, which has already been accepted under Article 1.

5. A condition for adjustment because of different commercial levels or different quantities is that such adjustment, whether it leads to an increase or a decrease in the value, be made only on the basis of demonstrated evidence that clearly establishes the reasonableness and accuracy of the adjustments, e.g. valid price lists containing prices referring to different levels or different quantities. As an example of this, if the imported goods being valued consist of a shipment of 10 units and the only identical imported goods for which a transaction value exists involved a sale of 500 units, and it is recognized that the seller grants quantity discounts, the required adjustment may be accomplished by resorting to the seller's price list and using that price applicable to a sale of 10 units. This does not require that a sale had to have been made in quantities of 10 as long as the price list has been established as being *bona fide* through sales at other quantities. In the absence of such an objective measure, however, the determination of a customs value under the provisions of Article 2 is not appropriate.

Note to Article 3

1. In applying Article 3, the customs administration shall, wherever possible, use a sale of similar goods at the same commercial level and in substantially the same quantities as the goods being valued. Where no such sale is found, a sale of similar goods that takes place under any one of the following three conditions may be used:

(*a*) a sale at the same commercial level but in different quantities;

(*b*) a sale at a different commercial level but in substantially the same quantities; or

(*c*) a sale at a different commercial level and in different quantities.

2. Having found a sale under any one of these three conditions adjustments will then be made, as the case may be, for:

(*a*) quantity factors only;

(*b*) commercial level factors only; or

(*c*) both commercial level and quantity factors.

3. The expression " and/or " allows the flexibility to use the sales and make the necessary adjustments in any one of the three conditions described above.

4. For the purpose of Article 3, the transaction value of similar imported goods means a customs value, adjusted as provided for in paragraphs 1 (*b*) and 2 of this Article, which has already been accepted under Article 1.

5.   A condition for adjustment because of different commercial levels or different quantities is that such adjustment, whether it leads to an increase or a decrease in the value, be made only on the basis of demonstrated evidence that clearly establishes the reasonableness and accuracy of the adjustment, e.g. valid price lists containing prices referring to different levels or different quantities. As an example of this, if the imported goods being valued consist of a shipment of 10 units and the only similar imported goods for which a transaction value exists involved a sale of 500 units, and it is recognized that the seller grants quantity discounts, the required adjustment may be accomplished by resorting to the sellers' price list and using that price applicable to a sale of 10 units. This does not require that a sale had to have been made in quantities of 10 as long as the price list has been established as being *bona fide* through sales at other quantities. In the absence of such an objective measure, however, the determination of a customs value under the provisions of Article 3 is not appropriate.

Note to Article 5

1.   The term " unit price at which ... goods are sold in the greatest aggregate quantity " means the price at which the greatest number of units is sold in sales to persons who are not related to the persons from whom they buy such goods at the first commercial level after importation at which such sales take place.

2.   As an example of this, goods are sold from a price list which grants favourable unit prices for purchases made in larger quantities.

Sale quantity	Unit price	Number of sales	Total quantity sold at each price
1-10 units	100	10 sales of 5 units 5 sales of 3 units	65
11-25 units	95	5 sales of 11 units	55
over 25 units	90	1 sale of 30 units 1 sale of 50 units	80

The greatest number of units sold at a price is 80; therefore, the unit price in the greatest aggregate quantity is 90.

3.   As another example of this, two sales occur. In the first sale 500 units are sold at a price of 95 currency units each. In the second sale 400 units are sold at a price of 90 currency units each. In this example, the greatest number of units sold at a particular price is 500; therefore, the unit price in the greatest aggregate quantity is 95.

4.   A third example would be the following situation where various quantities are sold at various prices.

(a) *Sales*

Sale quantity	Unit price
40 units	100
30 units	90
15 units	100
50 units	95
25 units	105
35 units	90
5 units	100

(b) *Totals*

Total quantity sold	Unit price
65	90
50	95
60	100
25	105

In this example, the greatest number of units sold at a particular price is 65; therefore, the unit price in the greatest aggregate quantity is 90.

5. Any sale in the importing country, as described in paragraph 1 above, to a person who supplies directly or indirectly free of charge or at reduced cost for use in connection with the production and sale for export of the imported goods any of the elements specified in Article 8.1 (b), should not be taken into account in establishing the unit price for the purposes of Article 5.

6. It should be noted that " profit and general expenses " referred to in Article 5.1 should be taken as a whole. The figure for the purposes of this deduction should be determined on the basis of information supplied by or on behalf of the importer unless his figures are inconsistent with those obtaining in sales in the country of importation of imported goods of the same class or kind. Where the importer's figures are inconsistent with such figures, the amount for profit and general expenses may be based upon relevant information other than that supplied by or on behalf of the importer.

7. The " general expenses " include the direct and indirect costs of marketing the goods in question.

8. Local taxes payable by reason of the sale of the goods for which a deduction is not made under the provisions of Article 5.1 (a) (iv) shall be deducted under the provisions of Article 5.1 (a) (i).

9. In determining either the commissions or the usual profits and general expenses under the provisions of Article 5.1, the question whether certain goods are " of the same class or kind " as other goods must be determined on a case-by-case basis by reference to the circumstances involved. Sales in the country of importation of the narrowest group or range of imported goods of the same class or kind, which includes the goods being valued, for which the necessary information can be provided, should be examined. For the purposes of Article 5, " goods of the same class or kind " includes goods imported from the same country as the goods being valued as well as goods imported from other countries.

10. For the purposes of Article 5.1 (*b*), the " earliest date " shall be the date by which sales of the imported goods or of identical or similar imported goods are made in sufficient quantity to establish the unit price.

11. Where the method in Article 5.2 is used, deductions made for the value added by further processing shall be based on objective and quantifiable data relating to the cost of such work. Accepted industry formulas, recipes, methods of construction, and other industry practices would form the basis of the calculations.

12. It is. recognized that the method of valuation provided for in Article 5.2 would normally not be applicable when, as a result of the further processing, the imported goods lose their identity. However, there can be instances where, although the identity of the imported goods is lost, the value added by the processing can be determined accurately without unreasonable difficulty. On the other hand, there can also be instances where the imported goods maintain their identity but form such a minor element in the goods sold in the country of importation that the use of this valuation method would be unjustified. In view of the above, each situation of this type must be considered on a case-by-case basis.

Note to Article 6

1. As a general rule, customs value is determined under this Agreement on the basis of information readily available in the country of importation. In order to determine a computed value, however, it may be necessary to examine the costs of producing the goods being valued and other information which has to be obtained from outside the country of importation. Furthermore, in most cases the producer of the goods will be outside the jurisdiction of the authorities of the country of importation. The use of the computed value method will generally be limited to those cases where the buyer and seller are related, and the producer is prepared to supply to the authorities of the country of importation the necessary costings and to provide facilities for any subsequent verification which may be necessary.

2. The " cost or value " referred to in Article 6.1 (*a*) is to be determined on the basis of information relating to the production of the goods being valued supplied by or on behalf of the producer. It is to be based upon the commercial accounts of the producer, provided that such accounts are consistent with the generally accepted accounting principles applied in the country where the goods are produced.

3. The "cost or value" shall include the cost of elements specified in Article 8.1 (*a*) (ii) and (iii). It shall also include the value, apportioned as appropriate under the provisions of the relevant note to Article 8, of any element specified in Article 8.1 (*b*) which has been supplied directly or indirectly by the buyer for use in connexion with the production of the imported goods. The value of the elements specified in Article 8.1 (*b*) (iv) which are undertaken in the country of importation shall be included only to the extent that such elements are charged to the producer. It is to be understood that no cost or value of the elements referred to in this paragraph shall be counted twice in determining the computed value.

4.   The " amount for profit and general expenses " referred to in Article 6.1 (*b*) is to be determined on the basis of information supplied by or on behalf of the producer unless his figures are inconsistent with those usually reflected in sales of goods of the same class or kind as the goods being valued which are made by producers in the country of exportation for export to the country of importation.

5.   It should be noted in this context that the " amount for profit and general expenses " has to be taken as a whole. It follows that if, in any particular case, the producer's profit figure is low and his general expenses are high, his profit and general expenses taken together may nevertheless be consistent with that usually reflected in sales of goods of the same class or kind. Such a situation might occur, for example, if a product were being launched in the country of importation and the producer accepted a nil or low profit to offset high general expenses associated with the launch. Where the producer can demonstrate that he is taking a low profit on his sales of the imported goods because of particular commercial circumstances, his actual profit figures should be taken into account provided that he has valid commercial reasons to justify them and his pricing policy reflects usual pricing policies in the branch of industry concerned. Such a situation might occur, for example, where producers have been forced to lower prices temporarily because of an unforeseeable drop in demand, or where they sell goods to complement a range of goods being produced in the country of importation and accept a low profit to maintain competitivity. Where the producer's own figures for profit and general expenses are not consistent with those usually reflected in sales of goods of the same class or kind as the goods being valued which are made by producers in the country of exportation for export to the country of importation, the amount for profit and general expenses may be based upon relevant information other than that supplied by or on behalf of the producer of the goods.

6.   Where information other than that supplied by or on behalf of the producer is used for the purposes of determining a computed value, the authorities of the importing country shall inform the importer, if the latter so requests, of the source of such information, the data used and the calculations based upon such data, subject to the provisions of Article 10.

7.   The " general expenses " referred to in Article 6.1 (*b*) covers the direct and indirect costs of producing and selling the goods for export which are not included under Article 6.1 (*a*).

8.   Whether certain goods are " of the same class or kind " as other goods must be determined on a case-by-case basis with reference to the circumstances involved. In determining the usual profits and general expenses under the provisions of Article 6, sales for export to the country of importation of the narrowest group or range of goods, which includes the goods being valued, for which the necessary information can be provided, should be examined. For the purposes of Article 6, " goods of the same class or kind " must be from the same country as the goods being valued.

Note to Article 7

1.   Customs values determined under the provisions of Article 7 should, to the greatest extent possible, be based on previously determined customs values.

2. The methods of valuation to be employed under Article 7 should be those laid down in Articles 1 to 6, inclusive, but a reasonable flexibility in the application of such methods would be in conformity with the aims and provisions of Article 7.

3. Some examples of reasonable flexibility are as follows:

    (a) *Identical goods*—the requirement that the identical goods should be exported at or about the same time as the goods being valued could be flexibly interpreted; identical imported goods produced in a country other than the country of exportation of the goods being valued could be the basis for customs valuation; customs values of identical imported goods already determined under the provisions of Articles 5 and 6 could be used.

    (b) *Similar goods*—the requirement that the similar goods should be exported at or about the same time as the goods being valued could be flexibly interpreted; similar imported goods produced in a country other than the country of exportation of the goods being valued could be the basis for customs valuation; customs values of similar imported goods already determined under the provisions of Articles 5 and 6 could be used.

    (c) *Deductive method*—the requirement that the goods shall have been sold in the " condition as imported " in Article 5.1 (a) could be flexibly interpreted; the " ninety days " requirement could be administered flexibly.

Note to Article 8

Paragraph 1 (a) (i)

The term " buying commissions " means fees paid by an importer to his agent for the service of representing him abroad in the purchase of the goods being valued.

Paragraph 1 (b) (ii)

1. There are two factors involved in the apportionment of the elements specified in Article 8.1 (b) (ii) to the imported goods—the value of the element itself and the way in which that value is to be apportioned to the imported goods. The apportionment of these elements should be made in a reasonable manner appro priate to the circumstances and in accordance with generally accepted accounting principles.

2. Concerning the value of the element, if the importer acquires the element from a seller not related to him at a given cost, the value of the element is that cost. If the element was produced by the importer or by a person related to him, its value would be the cost of producing it. If the element had been previously used by the importer, regardless of whether it had been acquired or produced by such importer, the original cost of acquisition or production would have to be adjusted downward to reflect its use in order to arrive at the value of the element.

3. Once a value has been determined for the element, it is necessary to apportion that value to the imported goods. Various possibilities exist. For example, the value might be apportioned to the first shipment if the importer wishes to pay duty on the entire value at one time. As another example, the importer may request that the value be apportioned over the number of units produced up to the time of the first shipment. As a further example, he may request that the value be apportioned over the entire anticipated production where contracts or firm commitments exist for that production. The method of apportionment used will depend upon the documentation provided by the importer.

4. As an illustration of the above, an importer provides the producer with a mould to be used in the production of the imported goods and contracts with him to buy 10,000 units. By the time of arrival of the first shipment of 1,000 units, the producer has already produced 4,000 units. The importer may request the customs administration to apportion the value of the mould over 1,000 units, 4,000 units or 10,000 units.

Paragraph 1 (b) (iv)

1. Additions for the elements specified in Article 8.1 (*b*) (iv) should be based on objective and quantifiable data. In order to minimize the burden for both the importer and customs administration in determining the values to be added, data readily available in the buyer's commercial record system should be used in so far as possible.

2. For those elements supplied by the buyer which were purchased or leased by the buyer, the addition would be the cost of the purchase or the lease. No addition shall be made for those elements available in the public domain, other than the cost of obtaining copies of them.

3. The ease with which it may be possible to calculate the values to be added will depend on a particular firm's structure and management practice, as well as its accounting methods.

4. For example, it is possible that a firm which imports a variety of products from several countries maintains the records of its design centre outside the country of importation in such a way as to show accurately the costs attributable to a given product. In such cases, a direct adjustment may appropriately be made under the provisions of Article 8.

5. In another case, a firm may carry the cost of the design centre outside the country of importation as a general overhead expense without allocation to specific products. In this instance, an appropriate adjustment could be made under the provisions of Article 8 with respect to the imported goods by apportioning total design centre costs over total production benefiting from the design centre and adding such apportioned cost on a unit basis to imports.

6. Variations in the above circumstances will, of course, require different factors to be considered in determining the proper method of allocation.

7. In cases where the production of the element in question involves a number of countries and over a period of time, the adjustment should be limited to the value actually added to that element outside the country of importation.

Paragraph 1 (c)

1. The royalties and licence fees referred to in Article 8.1 (c) may include, among other things, payments in respect to patents, trademarks and copyrights. However, the charges for the right to reproduce the imported goods in the country of importation shall not be added to the price actually paid or payable for the imported goods in determining the customs value.

2. Payments made by the buyer for the right to distribute or resell the imported goods shall not be added to the price actually paid or payable for the imported goods if such payments are not a condition of the sale for export to the country of importation of the imported goods.

Paragraph 3

Where objective and quantifiable data do not exist with regard to the additions required to be made under the provisions of Article 8, the transaction value cannot be determined under the provisions of Article 1. As an illustration of this, a royalty is paid on the basis of the price in a sale in the importing country of a litre of a particular product that was imported by the kilogram and made up into a solution after importation. If the royalty is based partially on the imported goods and partially on other factors which have nothing to do with the imported goods (such as when the imported goods are mixed with domestic ingredients and are no longer separately identifiable, or when the royalty cannot be distinguished from special financial arrangements between the buyer and the seller), it would be inappropriate to attempt to make an addition for the royalty. However, if the amount of this royalty is based only on the imported goods and can be readily quantified, an addition to the price actually paid or payable can be made.

Note to Article 9

For the purposes of Article 9, " time of importation " may include the time of entry for customs purposes.

Note to Article 11

1. Article 11 provides the importer with the right to appeal against a valuation determination made by the customs administration for the goods being valued. Appeal may first be to a higher level in the customs administration, but the importer shall have the right in the final instance to appeal to the judiciary.

2. " Without penalty " means that the importer shall not be subject to a fine or threat of fine merely because he chose to exercise his right of appeal. Payment of normal court costs and lawyers' fees shall not be considered to be a fine.

3. However, nothing in Article 11 shall prevent a Party from requiring full payment of assessed customs duties prior to an appeal.

Note to Article 15

Paragraph 4

For the purposes of this Article, the term " persons " includes legal persons, where appropriate.

Paragraph 4 (e)

For the purposes of this Agreement, one person shall be deemed to control another when the former is legally or operationally in a position to exercise restraint or direction over the latter.

ANNEX II

TECHNICAL COMMITTEE ON CUSTOMS VALUATION

1. In accordance with Article 18 of this Agreement, the Technical Committee shall be established under the auspices of the Customs Co-operation Council with a view, at the technical level, towards uniformity in interpretation and application of this Agreement.

2. The responsibilities of the Technical Committee shall include the following:

(*a*) to examine specific technical problems arising in the day-to-day administration of the customs valuation system of Parties and to give advisory opinions on appropriate solutions based upon the facts presented;

(*b*) to study, as requested, valuation laws, procedures and practices as they relate to this Agreement and to prepare reports on the results of such studies;

(*c*) to prepare and circulate annual reports on the technical aspects of the operation and status of this Agreement;

(*d*) to furnish such information and advice on any matters concerning the valuation of imported goods for customs purposes as may be requested by any Party or the Committee. Such information and advice may take the form of advisory opinions, commentaries or explanatory notes;

(*e*) to facilitate, as requested, technical assistance to Parties with a view to furthering the international acceptance of this Agreement; and

(*f*) to exercise such other responsibilities as the Committee may assign to it.

General

3. The Technical Committee shall attempt to conclude its work on specific matters, especially those referred to it by Parties or the Committee, in a reasonably short period of time.

4.   The Technical Committee shall be assisted as appropriate in its activities by the Secretariat of the Customs Co-operation Council.

Representation

5.   Each Party shall have the right to be represented on the Technical Committee. Each Party may nominate one delegate and one or more alternates to be its representatives on the Technical Committee. Such a Party so represented on the Technical Committee is hereinafter referred to as a member of the Technical Committee. Representatives of members of the Technical Committee may be assisted by advisers. The GATT secretariat may also attend such meetings with observer status.

6.   Members of the Customs Co-operation Council who are not Parties may be represented at meetings of the Technical Committee by one delegate and one or more alternates. Such representatives shall attend meetings of the Technical Committee as observers.

7.   Subject to the approval of the Chairman of the Technical Committee, the Secretary-General of the Customs Co-operation Council (hereinafter referred to as " the Secretary-General ") may invite representatives of governments which are neither Parties nor members of the Customs Co-operation Council and representatives of international governmental and trade organizations to attend meetings of the Technical Committee as observers.

8.   Nominations of delegates, alternates and advisers to meetings of the Technical Committee shall be made to the Secretary-General.

Technical Committee meetings

9.   The Technical Committee shall meet as necessary but at least two times a year. The date of each meeting shall be fixed by the Technical Committee at its preceding session. The date of the meeting may be varied either at the request of any member of the Technical Committee concurred in by a simple majority of the members of the Technical Committee or, in cases requiring urgent attention, at the request of the Chairman.

10.   The meetings of the Technical Committee shall be held at the headquarters of the Customs Co-operation Council unless otherwise decided.

11.   The Secretary-General shall inform all members of the Technical Committee and those included under paragraphs 6 and 7 at least thirty days in advance, except in urgent cases, of the opening date of each session of the Technical Committee.

Agenda

12.   A provisional agenda for each session shall be drawn up by the Secretary-General and circulated to the members of the Technical Committee and to those included under paragraphs 6 and 7 at least thirty days in advance of the session, except in urgent cases. This agenda shall comprise all items whose inclusion has been approved by the Technical Committee during its preceding session, all items included by the Chairman on his own initiative, and all items whose inclusion

has been requested by the Secretary-General, by the Committee or by any member of the Technical Committee.

13. The Technical Committee shall determine its agenda at the opening of each session. During the session the agenda may be altered at any time by the Technical Committee.

Officers and conduct of business

14. The Technical Committee shall elect from among the delegates of its members a Chairman and one or more Vice-Chairmen. The Chairman and Vice-Chairmen shall each hold office for a period of one year. The retiring Chairman and Vice-Chairmen are eligible for re-election. A Chairman or Vice-Chairman who ceases to represent a member of the Technical Committee shall automatically lose his mandate.

15. If the Chairman is absent from any meeting or part thereof, a Vice-Chairman shall preside. In that event, the latter shall have the same powers and duties as the Chairman.

16. The Chairman of the meeting shall participate in the proceedings of the Technical Committee as such and not as the representative of a member of the Technical Committee.

17. In addition to exercising the powers conferred upon him elsewhere by these rules, the Chairman shall declare the opening and closing of each meeting, direct the discussion, accord the right to speak, and, pursuant to these rules, have control of the proceedings. The Chairman may also call a speaker to order if his remarks are not relevant.

18. During discussion of any matter a delegation may raise a point of order. In this event, the Chairman shall immediately state his ruling. If this ruling is challenged, the Chairman shall submit it to the meeting for decisions and it shall stand unless overruled.

19. The Secretary-General, or officers of the Secretariat designated by him, shall perform the secretarial work of meetings of the Technical Committee.

Quorum and voting

20. Representatives of a simple majority of the members of the Technical Committee shall constitute a quorum.

21. Each member of the Technical Committee shall have one vote. A decision of the Technical Committee shall be taken by a majority comprising at least two thirds of the members present. Regardless of the outcome of the vote on a particular matter, the Technical Committee shall be free to make a full report to the Committee and to the Customs Co-operation Council on that matter indicating the different views expressed in the relevant discussions.

Languages and records

22. The official languages of the Technical Committee shall be English, French and Spanish. Speeches or statements made in any of these three languages shall

be immediately translated into the other official languages unless all delegations agree to dispense with translation. Speeches or statements made in any other language shall be translated into English, French and Spanish, subject to the same conditions, but in that event the delegation concerned shall provide the translation into English, French or Spanish. Only English, French and Spanish shall be used for the official documents of the Technical Committee. Memoranda and correspondence for the consideration of the Technical Committee must be presented in one of the official languages.

23. The Technical Committee shall draw up a report of all its sessions and, if the Chairman considers it necessary, minutes or summary records of its meetings. The Chairman or his designee shall report on the work of the Technical Committee at each meeting of the Committee and at each meeting of the Customs Co-operation Council.

Annex III

AD HOC PANELS

1. *Ad hoc* panels established by the Committee under this Agreement shall have the following responsibilities:

   (*a*) to examine the matter referred to it by the Committee;

   (*b*) to consult with the parties to the dispute and give full opportunity for them to develop a mutually satisfactory solution; and

   (*c*) to make a statement concerning the facts of the matter as they relate to the application of the provisions of this Agreement and, make such findings as will assist the Committee in making recommendations or giving rulings on the matter.

2. In order to facilitate the constitution of panels, the Chairman of the Committee shall maintain an informal indicative list of government officials knowledgeable in the area of customs valuation and experienced in the field of trade relations and economic development. This list may also include persons other than government officials. In this connexion, each Party shall be invited to indicate at the beginning of every year to the Chairman of the Committee the name(s) of the one or two governmental experts whom the Parties would be willing to make available for such work. When a panel is established, the Chairman, after consultation with the Parties concerned, shall, within seven days of such establishment propose the composition of the panel consisting of three or five members and preferably government officials. The Parties directly concerned shall react within seven working days to nominations of panel members by the Chairman and shall not oppose nominations except for compelling reasons.

Citizens of countries whose governments are parties to a dispute shall not be eligible for membership of the panel concerned with that dispute. Panel members shall serve in their individual capacities and not as government representatives, nor as representatives of any organization. Governments or organizations shall therefore not give them instructions with regard to matters before a panel.

3.   Each panel shall develop its own working procedures. All Parties having a substantial interest in the matter and having notified this to the Committee shall have an opportunity to be heard. Each panel may consult and seek information and technical advice from any source it deems appropriate. Before a panel seeks such information or technical advice from a source within the jurisdiction of a Party, it shall inform the government of that Party. Any Party shall respond promptly and fully to any request by a panel for such information as the panel considers necessary and appropriate. Confidential information provided to the panel shall not be disclosed without the specific permission of the person or government providing such information. Where such information is requested from the panel but release of such information by the panel is not authorized, a non-confidential summary of the information, authorized by the person or government providing the information, will be provided.

4.   Where the parties to the dispute have failed to reach a satisfactory solution the panel shall submit its findings in writing. The report of a panel should normally set out the rationale behind its findings. Where a settlement of the matter is reached between the parties, the report of the panel may be confined to a brief description of the dispute and to a statement that a solution has been reached.

5.   Panels shall use such report of the Technical Committee as may have been issued under Article 20.4 of this Agreement as the basis for their consideration of issues that involve questions of a technical nature.

6.   The time required by panels will vary with the particular case. They should aim to deliver their findings, and where appropriate, recommendations, to the Committee without undue delay, normally within a period of three months from the date that the panel was established.

7.   To encourage development of mutually satisfactory solutions between the parties to a dispute and with a view to obtaining their comments, each panel should first submit the descriptive part of its report to the Parties concerned, and should subsequently submit to the parties to the dispute its conclusions, or an outline thereof, a reasonable period of time before they are circulated to the Parties.

PROTOCOL TO THE AGREEMENT
ON IMPLEMENTATION OF ARTICLE VII
OF THE GENERAL AGREEMENT
ON TARIFFS AND TRADE

The Parties to the Agreement on Implementation of Article VII of the General Agreement on Tariffs and Trade (hereinafter referred to as " the Agreement ").

Having regard to the Multilateral Trade Negotiations and to the desire expressed by the Trade Negotiations Committee at its meeting of 11 and 12 April 1979 to arrive at a single text of an Agreement on Implementation of Article VII of the General Agreement on Tariffs and Trade;

Recognizing that developing countries may have particular problems in applying the Agreement;

Considering that the provisions of Article 27 of the Agreement relating to amendments have not yet entered into force;

Hereby :

I

1.   *Agree* to the deletion of the provision of Article 1.2(*b*)(iv) of the Agreement;

2.   *Recognize* that the five-year delay in the application of the provisions of the Agreement by developing countries provided for in Article 21.1 may, in practice, be insufficient for certain developing countries. In such cases a developing country Party to the Agreement may request before the end of the period referred to in Article 21.1 an extension of such period, it being understood that the Parties to the Agreement will give sympathetic consideration to such a request in cases where the developing country in question can show good cause;

3.   *Recognize* that developing countries which currently value goods on the basis of officially established minimum values may wish to make a reservation to enable them to retain such values on a limited and transitional basis under such terms and conditions as may be agreed to by the Parties to the Agreement;

4. *Recognize* that developing countries which consider that the reversal of the sequential order at the request of the importer provided for in Article 4 of the Agreement may give rise to real difficulties for them may wish to make a reservation to Article 4 in the following terms:

" The Government of .... reserves the right to provide that the relevant provision of Article 4 of the Agreement shall apply only when the customs authorities agree to the request to reverse the order of Articles 5 and 6. "

If developing countries make such a reservation, the Parties to the Agreement shall consent to it under Article 23 of the Agreement;

5. *Recognize* that developing countries may wish to make a reservation with respect to Article 5.2 of the Agreement in the following terms:

" The Government of .... reserves the right to provide that Article 5.2 of the Agreement shall be applied in accordance with the provisions of the relevant note thereto whether or not the importer so requests. "

If developing countries make such a reservation, the Parties to the Agreement shall consent to it under Article 23 of the Agreement;

6. *Recognize* that certain developing countries have expressed concern that there may be problems in the implementation of Article 1 of the Agreement insofar as it relates to importations into their countries by sole agents, sole distributors and sole concessionaires. The Parties to the Agreement agree that, if such problems arise in practice in developing countries applying the Agreement, a study of this question shall be made, at the request of such countries, with a view to finding appropriate solutions;

7. *Agree* that Article 17 recognizes that in applying the Agreement, customs administrations may need to make enquiries concerning the truth or accuracy of any statement, document or declaration presented to them for customs valuation purposes. They further agree that the Article thus acknowledges that enquiries may be made which are, for example, aimed at verifying that the elements of value declared or presented to customs in connection with a determination of customs value are complete and correct. They recognize that Parties to the Agreement, subject to their national laws and procedures, have the right to expect the full co-operation of importers in these enquiries;

8. *Agree* that the price actually paid or payable includes all payments actually made or to be made as a condition of sale of the imported goods, by the buyer to the seller, or by the buyer to a third party to satisfy an obligation of the seller.

II

1. Upon the entry into force of the Agreement the provisions of this Protocol shall be deemed to be part of the Agreement.

2. This Protocol shall be deposited with the Director-General to the CONTRACTING PARTIES to the GATT. It is open for acceptance, by signature or otherwise, by signatories of the Agreement on Implementation of Article VII of the General Agreement on Tariffs and Trade and by other governments accepting or acceding to the Agreement pursuant to the provisions of Article 22 thereof.

Done at Geneva this first day of November 1979 in a single copy in the English, French and Spanish languages, each text being authentic.

AGREEMENT ON TECHNICAL
BARRIERS TO TRADE

PREAMBLE

Having regard to the Multilateral Trade Negotiations, the Parties to the Agreement on Technical Barriers to Trade (hereinafter referred to as " Parties " and " this Agreement ");

Desiring to further the objectives of the General Agreement on Tariffs and Trade (hereinafter referred to as " General Agreement " or " GATT ");

Recognizing the important contribution that international standards and certification systems can make in this regard by improving efficiency of production and facilitating the conduct of international trade;

Desiring therefore to encourage the development of such international standards and certification systems;

Desiring however to ensure that technical regulations and standards, including packaging, marking and labelling requirements, and methods for certifying conformity with technical regulations and standards do not create unnecessary obstacles to international trade;

Recognizing that no country should be prevented from taking measures necessary to ensure the quality of its exports, or for the protection of human, animal or plant life or health, of the environment, or for the prevention of deceptive practices, subject to the requirement that they are not applied in a manner which would constitute a means of arbitrary or unjustifiable discrimination between countries where the same conditions prevail or a disguised restriction on international trade;

Recognizing that no country should be prevented from taking measures necessary for the protection of its essential security interest;

Recognizing the contribution which international standardization can make to the transfer of technology from developed to developing countries;

Recognizing that developing countries may encounter special difficulties in the formulation and application of technical regulations and standards and methods for certifying conformity with technical regulations and standards, and desiring to assist them in their endeavours in this regard;

Hereby agree as follows:

Article 1

General provisions

1.1 General terms for standardization and certification shall normally have the meaning given to them by definitions adopted within the United Nations system and by international standardizing bodies taking into account their context and in the light of the object and purpose of this Agreement.

1.2 However, for the purposes of this Agreement the meaning of the terms given in Annex 1 applies. [1]

1.3 All products, including industrial and agricultural products, shall be subject to the provisions of this Agreement.

1.4 Purchasing specifications prepared by governmental bodies for production or consumption requirements of governmental bodies are not subject to the provisions of this Agreement but are addressed in the Agreement on Government Procurement, according to its coverage.

1.5 All references in this Agreement to technical regulations, standards, methods for assuring conformity with technical regulations or standards and certification systems shall be construed to include any amendments thereto and any additions to the rules or the product coverage thereof, except amendments and additions of an insignificant nature.

TECHNICAL REGULATIONS AND STANDARDS

Article 2

Preparation, adoption and application of technical regulations and standards by central government bodies

With respect to their central government bodies:

2.1 Parties shall ensure that technical regulations and standards are not prepared, adopted or applied with a view to creating obstacles to international trade. Furthermore, products imported from the territory of any Party shall be accorded treatment no less favourable than that accorded to like products of national origin and to like products originating in any other country in relation to such technical regulations or standards. They

---

[1] See page 29.

shall likewise ensure that neither technical regulations nor standards themselves nor their application have the effect of creating unnecessary obstacles to international trade.

2.2   Where technical regulations or standards are required and relevant international standards exist or their completion is imminent, Parties shall use them, or the relevant parts of them, as a basis for the technical regulations or standards except where, as duly explained upon request, such international standards or relevant parts are inappropriate for the Parties concerned, for *inter alia* such reasons as national security requirements; the prevention of deceptive practices; protection for human health or safety, animal or plant life or health, or the environment; fundamental climatic or other geographical factors; fundamental technological problems.

2.3   With a view to harmonizing technical regulations or standards on as wide a basis as possible, Parties shall play a full part within the limits of their resources in the preparation by appropriate international standardizing bodies of international standards for products for which they either have adopted, or expect to adopt, technical regulations or standards.

2.4   Wherever appropriate, Parties shall specify technical regulations and standards in terms of performance rather than design or descriptive characteristics.

2.5   Whenever a relevant international standard does not exist or the technical content of a proposed technical regulation or standard is not substantially the same as the technical content of relevant international standards, and if the technical regulation or standard may have a significant effect on trade of other Parties, Parties shall:

2.5.1   publish a notice in a publication at an early appropriate stage, in such a manner as to enable interested parties to become acquainted with it, that they propose to introduce a particular technical regulation or standard;

2.5.2   notify other Parties through the GATT secretariat of the products to be covered by technical regulations together with a brief indication of the objective and rationale of proposed technical regulations;

2.5.3   upon request, provide without discrimination, to other Parties in regard to technical regulations and to interested parties in other Parties in regard to standards, particulars or copies of the proposed technical regulation or standard and, whenever possible, identify the parts which in substance deviate from relevant international standards;

2.5.4   in regard to technical regulations allow, without discrimination, reasonable time for other Parties to make comments in writing, discuss these comments upon request, and take these written comments and the results of these discussions into account;

2.5.5 in regard to standards, allow reasonable time for interested parties in other Parties to make comments in writing, discuss these comments upon request with other Parties and take these written comments and the results of these discussions into account.

2.6 Subject to the provisions in the heading of Article 2, paragraph 5, where urgent problems of safety, health, environmental protection or national security arise or threaten to arise for a Party, that Party may omit such of the steps enumerated in Article 2, paragraph 5 as it finds necessary provided that the Party, upon adoption of a technical regulation or standard, shall:

2.6.1 notify immediately other Parties through the GATT secretariat of the particular technical regulation, the products covered, with a brief indication of the objective and the rationale of the technical regulation, including the nature of the urgent problems;

2.6.2 upon request provide, without discrimination other Parties with copies of the technical regulation and interested parties in other Parties with copies of the standard;

2.6.3 allow, without discrimination, other Parties with respect to technical regulations and interested parties in other Parties with respect to standards, to present their comments in writing upon request discuss these comments with other Parties and take the written comments and the results of any such discussion into account;

2.6.4 take also into account any action by the Committee as a result of consultations carried out in accordance with the procedures established in Article 14.

2.7 Parties shall ensure that all technical regulations and standards which have been adopted are published promptly in such a manner as to enable interested parties to become acquainted with them.

2.8 Except in those urgent circumstances referred to in Article 2, paragraph 6, Parties shall allow a reasonable interval between the publication of a technical regulation and its entry into force in order to allow time for producers in exporting countries, and particularly in developing countries, to adapt their products or methods of production to the requirements of the importing country.

2.9 Parties shall take such reasonable measures as may be available to them to ensure that regional standardizing bodies of which they are members comply with the provisions of Article 2, paragraphs 1 to 8. In addition

Parties shall not take measures which have the effect of, directly or indirectly, requiring or encouraging such bodies to act in a manner inconsistent with those provisions.

2.10 Parties which are members of regional standardizing bodies shall, when adopting a regional standard as a technical regulation or standard fulfil the obligations of Article 2, paragraphs 1 to 8 except to the extent that the regional standardizing bodies have fulfilled these obligations.

Article 3

Preparation, adoption and application of technical regulations and standards by local government bodies

3.1 Parties shall take such reasonable measures as may be available to them to ensure that local government bodies within their territories comply with the provisions of Article 2 with the exception of Article 2, paragraph 3, paragraph 5, sub-paragraph 2, paragraph 9 and paragraph 10, noting that provision of information regarding technical regulations referred to in Article 2, paragraph 5, sub-paragraph 3 and paragraph 6, sub-paragraph 2 and comment and discussion referred to in Article 2, paragraph 5, sub-paragraph 4 and paragraph 6, sub-paragraph 3 shall be through Parties. In addition, Parties shall not take measures which have the effect of, directly or indirectly, requiring or encouraging such local government bodies to act in a manner inconsistent with any of the provisions of Article 2.

Article 4

Preparation, adoption and application of technical regulations and standards by non-governmental bodies

4.1 Parties shall take such reasonable measures as may be available to them to ensure that non-governmental bodies within their territories comply with the provisions of Article 2, with the exception of Article 2, paragraph 5, sub-paragraph 2 and provided that comment and discussion referred to in Article 2, paragraph 5, sub-paragraph 4 and paragraph 6, sub-paragraph 3 may also be with interested parties in other Parties. In addition, Parties shall not take measures which have the effect of, directly or indirectly, requiring or encouraging such non-governmental bodies to act in a manner inconsistent with any of the provisions of Article 2.

ONFORMITY WITH TECHNICAL REGULATIONS AND STANDARDS

Article 5

*Determination of conformity with technical regulations or standards
by central government bodies*

5.1 Parties shall ensure that, in cases where a positive assurance is required that products conform with technical regulations or standards, central government bodies apply the following provisions to products originating in the territories of other Parties:

5.1.1 imported products shall be accepted for testing under conditions no less favourable than those accorded to like domestic or imported products in a comparable situation;

5.1.2 the test methods and administrative procedures for imported products shall be no more complex and no less expeditious than the corresponding methods and procedures, in a comparable situation for like products of national origin or originating in any other country;

5.1.3 any fees imposed for testing imported products shall be equitable in relation to any fees chargeable for testing like products of national origin or originating in any other country;

5.1.4 the results of tests shall be made available to the exporter or importer or their agents, if requested, so that corrective action may be taken if necessary;

5.1.5 the siting of testing facilities and the selection of samples for testing shall not be such as to cause unnecessary inconvenience for importers, exporters or their agents;

5.1.6 the confidentiality of information about imported products arising from or supplied in connection with such tests shall be respected in the same way as for domestic products.

5.2 However, in order to facilitate the determination of conformity with technical regulations and standards where such positive assurance is required, Parties shall ensure, whenever possible, that their central government bodies:

accept test results, certificates or marks of conformity issued by relevant bodies in the territories of other Parties; or rely upon self-certification by producers in the territories of other Parties;

even when the test methods differ from their own, provided they are satisfied that the methods employed in the territory of the exporting Party provide a sufficient means of determining conformity with the relevant technical regulations or standards. It is recognized that prior consultations may be necessary in order to arrive at a mutually satisfactory understanding regarding self-certification, test methods and results, and certificates or marks of conformity employed in the territory of the exporting Party, in particular in the case of perishable products or of other products which are liable to deteriorate in transit.

5.3   Parties ensure that test methods and administrative procedures used by central government bodies are such as to permit, so far as practicable, the implementation of the provisions in Article 5, paragraph 2.

5.4   Nothing in this Article shall prevent Parties from carrying out reasonable spot checks within their territories.

Article 6

Determination by local government bodies and non-governmental bodies of conformity with technical regulations or standards

6.1   Parties shall take such reasonable measures as may be available to them to ensure that local government bodies and non-governmental bodies within their territories comply with the provisions of Article 5. In addition, Parties shall not take measures which have the effect of, directly or indirectly, requiring or encouraging such bodies to act in a manner inconsistent with any of the provisions of Article 5.

CERTIFICATION SYSTEMS

Article 7

Certification systems operated by central government bodies

With respect to their central government bodies:

7.1   Parties shall ensure that certification systems are not formulated or applied with a view to creating obstacles to international trade. They shall likewise ensure that neither such certification systems themselves nor their application have the effect of creating unnecessary obstacles to international trade.

7.2   Parties shall ensure that certification systems are formulated and applied so as to grant access for suppliers of like products originating in the territories of other Parties under conditions no less favourable than those accorded to suppliers of like products of national origin or originating in any other country, including the determination that such suppliers are able and willing to fulfil the requirements of the system. Access for suppliers is obtaining certification from an importing Party under the rules of the system. Access for suppliers also includes receiving the mark of the system, if any, under conditions no less favourable than those accorded to suppliers of like products of national origin or originating in any other country.

7.3 Parties shall:

    7.3.1 publish a notice in a publication at an early appropriate stage, in such a manner as to enable interested parties to become acquainted with it, that they propose to introduce a certification system;

    7.3.2 notify the GATT secretariat of the products to be covered by the proposed system together with a brief description of the objective of the proposed system;

    7.3.3 upon request provide, without discrimination, to other Parties particulars or copies of the proposed rules of the system;

    7.3.4 allow, without discrimination, reasonable time for other Parties to make comments in writing on the formulation and operation of the system, discuss the comments upon request and take them into account.

7.4 However, where urgent problems of safety, health, environmental protection or national security arise or threaten to arise for a Party, that Party may omit such of the steps enumerated in Article 7, paragraph 3 as it finds necessary provided that the Party, upon adoption of the certification system, shall:

    7.4.1 notify immediately the other Parties through the GATT secretariat of the particular certification system and the products covered, with a brief indication of the objective and the rationale of the certification system including the nature of the urgent problems;

    7.4.2 upon request provide, without discrimination, other Parties with copies of the rules of the system;

    7.4.3 allow, without discrimination, other Parties to present their comments in writing, discuss these comments upon request and take the written comments and results of any such discussion into account.

7.5 Parties shall ensure that all adopted rules of certification systems are published.

Article 8

Certification systems operated
by local government and non-governmental bodies

8.1 Parties shall take such reasonable measures as may be available to them to ensure that local government bodies and non-governmental bodies within their territories when operating certification systems comply with the provisions of Article 7, except paragraph 3, sub-paragraph 2, noting that the provision of information referred to in Article 7, paragraph 3, sub-paragraph 3 and paragraph 4, sub-paragraph 2, the notification referred to in Article 7, paragraph 4, sub-paragraph 1, and the comment and discussion referred to in Article 7, paragraph 4, sub-paragraph 3, shall be through Parties. In addition, Parties shall not take measures which have the effect of, directly or indirectly, requiring or encouraging such bodies to act in a manner inconsistent with any of the provisions of Article 7.

8.2 Parties shall ensure that their central government bodies rely on certification systems operated by local government and non-governmental bodies only to the extent that these bodies and systems comply with the relevant provisions of Article 7.

Article 9

International and regional certification systems

9.1 Where a positive assurance, other than by the supplier, of conformity with a technical regulation or standard is required, Parties shall, wherever practicable, formulate international certification systems and become members thereof or participate therein.

9.2 Parties shall take such reasonable measures as may be available to them to ensure that international and regional certification systems in which relevant bodies within their territories are members or participants comply with the provisions of Article 7, with the exception of paragraph 2 having regard to the provisions of Article 9, paragraph 3. In addition, Parties shall not take any measures which have the effect of, directly or indirectly, requiring or encouraging such systems to act in a manner inconsistent with any of the provisions of Article 7.

9.3 Parties shall take such reasonable measures as may be available to them to ensure that international and regional certification systems, in which relevant bodies within their territories are members or participants, are formulated and applied so as to grant access for suppliers of like products originating in the territories of other Parties, under conditions no less favourable than those accorded to suppliers of like products originating in a member country, a participant country or in any other country, including the determination that such suppliers are able and willing to fulfil the requirements of the system. Access for suppliers is obtaining certification from an importing Party which is a member of or participant in the system, or from a body authorized by the system to grant certification, under the rules of the system. Access for suppliers also includes receiving the mark of the system, if any, under conditions no less favourable than those accorded to suppliers of like products originating in a member country or a participant country.

9.4   Parties shall ensure that their central government bodies rely on international or regional certification systems only to the extent that the systems comply with the provisions of Article 7 and Article 9, paragraph 3.

INFORMATION AND ASSISTANCE

Article 10

Information about technical regulations, standards and certification systems

10.1   Each Party shall ensure that an enquiry point exists which is able to answer all reasonable enquiries from interested parties in other Parties regarding:

10.1.1   any technical regulations adopted or proposed within its territory by central or local government bodies, by non-governmental bodies which have legal power to enforce a technical regulation, or by regional standardizing bodies of which such bodies are members or participants;

10.1.2   any standards adopted or proposed within its territory by central or local government bodies, or by regional standardizing bodies of which such bodies are members or participants;

10.1.3   any certification systems, or proposed certification systems, which are operated within its territory by central or local government bodies, or by non-governmental bodies which have legal power to enforce a technical regulation, or by regional certification bodies of which such bodies are members or participants;

10.1.4   the location of notices published pursuant to this Agreement, or the provision of information as to where such information can be obtained; and

10.1.5   the location of the enquiry points mentioned in Article 10, paragraph 2.

10.2 Each Party shall take such reasonable measures as may be available to it to ensure that one or more enquiry points exist which are able to answer all reasonable enquiries from interested parties in other Parties regarding:

10.2.1 any standards adopted or proposed within its territory by non-governmental standardizing bodies, or by regional standardizing bodies of which such bodies are members or participants; and

10.2.2 any certification systems, or proposed certification systems, which are operated within its territory by non-governmental certification bodies, or by regional certification bodies of which such bodies are members or participants.

10.3 Parties shall take such reasonable measures as may be available to them to ensure that where copies of documents are requested by other Parties, or by interested parties in other Parties in accordance with the provisions of this Agreement, they are supplied at the same price (if any) as to the nationals of the Party concerned.

10.4 The GATT secretariat will, when it receives notifications in accordance with the provisions of this Agreement, circulate copies of the notifications to all Parties and interested international standardizing and certification bodies and draw the attention of developing country Parties to any notifications relating to products of particular interest to them.

10.5 Nothing in this Agreement shall be construed as requiring:

10.5.1 the publication of texts other than in the language of the Party;

10.5.2 the provision of particulars or copies of drafts other than in the language of the Party; or

10.5.3 Parties to furnish any information, the disclosure of which they consider contrary to their essential security interests.

10.6 Notifications to the GATT secretariat shall be in English, French or Spanish.

10.7 Parties recognize the desirability of developing centralized information systems with respect to the preparation, adoption and application of all technical regulations, standards and certification systems within their territories.

Article 11

Technical assistance to other Parties

11.1 Parties shall, if requested, advise other Parties, especially the developing countries, on the preparation of technical regulations.

11.2 Parties shall, if requested, advise other Parties, especially the developing countries, and shall grant them technical assistance on mutually agreed terms and conditions regarding the establishment of national standardizing bodies and participation in the international standardizing bodies and shall encourage their national standardizing bodies to do likewise.

11.3 Parties shall, if requested, take such reasonable measures as may be available to them to arrange for the regulatory bodies within their territories to advise other Parties, especially the developing countries, and shall grant them technical assistance on mutually agreed terms and conditions regarding:

11.3.1 the establishment of regulatory bodies, or certification bodies for providing a certificate or mark of conformity with technical regulations; and

11.3.2 the methods by which their technical regulations can best be met.

11.4 Parties shall, if requested, take such reasonable measures as may be available to them to arrange for advice to be given to other Parties, especially the developing countries, and shall grant them technical assistance on mutually agreed terms and conditions regarding the establishment of certification bodies for proving a certificate or mark of conformity with standards adopted within the territory of the requesting Party.

11.5 Parties shall, if requested, advise other Parties, especially the developing countries, and shall grant them technical assistance on mutually agreed terms and conditions regarding the steps that should be taken by their producers, if they wish to take part in certification systems operated by governmental or non-governmental bodies within the territory of the Party receiving the request.

11.6 Parties which are members or participants of international or regional certification systems shall, if requested, advise other Parties, especially the developing countries, and shall grant them technical assistance on mutually agreed terms and conditions regarding the establishment of the institutions and legal framework which would enable them to fulfil the obligations of membership or participation in such systems.

11.7 Parties shall, if so requested, encourage certification bodies within their territories, if such bodies are members or participants of international or regional certification systems to advise other Parties, especially the developing countries, and should consider requests for technical assistance from them regarding the establishment of the institutions which would enable the relevant bodies within their territories to fulfil the obligations of membership or participation.

11.8 In providing advice and technical assistance to other Parties in terms of Article 11, paragraphs 1 to 7, Parties shall give priority to the needs of the least-developed countries.

Article 12

Special and differential treatment of developing countries

12.1   Parties shall provide differential and more favourable treatment to developing country Parties to this Agreement, through the following provisions as well as through the relevant provisions of their Articles of this Agreement.

12.2   Parties shall give particular attention to the provisions of this Agreement concerning developing countries' rights and obligations and shall take into account the special development, financial and trade needs of developing countries in the implementation of this Agreement both nationally and in the operation of this Agreement's institutional arrangements.

12.3   Parties shall, in the preparation and application of technical regulations, standards, test methods and certification systems, take account of the special development, financial and trade needs of developing countries, with a view to ensuring that such technical regulations, standards, test methods and certification systems and the determination of conformity with technical regulations and standards do not create unnecessary obstacles to exports from developing countries.

12.4   Parties recognize that, although international standards may exist, in their particular technological and socio-economic conditions, developing countries adopt certain technical regulations or standards, including test methods, aimed at preserving indigenous technology and production methods and processes compatible with their development needs. Parties therefore recognize that developing countries should not be expected to use international standards as a basis for their technical regulations or standards, including test methods, which are not appropriate to their development, financial and trade needs.

12.5   Parties shall take such reasonable measures as may be available to them to ensure that international standardizing bodies and international certification systems are organized and operated in a way which facilitates active and representative participation of relevant bodies in all Parties taking into account the special problems of developing countries.

12.6   Parties shall take such reasonable measures as may be available to them to ensure that international standardizing bodies, upon request of developing countries, examine the possibility of, and if practicable, prepare international standards concerning products of special interest to developing countries.

12.7   Parties shall, in accordance with the provisions of Article 11, provide technical assistance to developing countries to ensure that the preparation and application of technical regulations, standards, test methods and certification systems do not create unnecessary obstacles to the expansion and diversification of exports from developing countries.   In determining the terms and conditions of the technical assistance, account shall be taken of the stage of development of the requesting country and in particular of the least-developed countries.

12.8   It is recognized that developing countries may face special problems, including institutional and infrastructural problems, in the field of preparation and application of technical regulations, standards, test methods and certification systems.   It is further recognized that the special development and trade needs of developing countries, as well as their stage of technological development, may hinder their ability to discharge fully their obligations under this Agreement.   Parties, therefore, shall take this fact fully into account.   Accordingly, with a view to ensuring that developing countries are able to comply with this Agreement, the Committee is enabled to grant upon request specified, time-limited exceptions in whole or in part from obligations under this Agreement.   When considering such requests the Committee shall take into account the special problems, in the field of preparation and application of technical regulations, standards, test methods and certification systems and the special development and trade needs of the developing country, as well as its stage of technological development, which may hinder its ability to discharge fully its obligations under this Agreement.   The Committee shall in particular, take into account the special problems of the least-developed countries.

12.9   During consultations, developed countries shall bear in mind the special difficulties experienced by developing countries in formulating and implementing standards and technical regulations and methods of ensuring conformity with those standards and technical regulations, and in their desire to assist developing countries with their efforts in this direction, developed countries shall take account of the special needs of the former in regard to financing, trade and development.

12.10   The Committee shall examine periodically the special and differential treatment as laid down in this Agreement, granted to developing countries, on national and international levels.

INSTITUTIONS, CONSULTATION AND DISPUTE SETTLEMENT

Article 13

The Committee on Technical Barriers to Trade

There shall be established under this Agreement:

13.1   A Committee on Technical Barriers to Trade composed of representatives from each of the Parties (hereinafter referred to as "the Committee"). The Committe shall elect its own Chairman and shall meet as necessary but no less than once a year for the purpose of affording Parties the opportunity of consulting on any matters relating to the operation of this Agreement or the furtherance of its objectives and shall carry out such responsibilities as assigned to it under this Agreement or by the Parties;

13.2   Working parties, technical expert groups, panels or other bodies as may be appropriate, which shall carry out such responsibilities as may be assigned to them by the Committee in accordance with the relevant provisions of this Agreement.

13.3   It is understood that unnecessary duplication should be avoided between the work under this Agreement and that of governments in other technical bodies, e.g. the Joint FAO/WHO Codex Alimentarius Commission.   The Committee shall examine this problem with a view to minimizing such duplication.

Article 14

Consultation and dispute settlement

Consultation

14.1   Each Party shall afford sympathetic consideration to and adequate opportunity for prompt consultation regarding representations made by other Parties with respect to any matter affecting the operation of this Agreement.

14.2   If any Party considers that any benefit accruing to it, directly or indirectly, under this Agreement is being nullified or impaired, or that the attainment of any objective of this Agreement is being impeded, by another Party or Parties, and that its trade interests are significantly affected, the Party may make written representations or proposals to the other Party or Parties which it considers to be concerned.   Any Party shall give sympathetic consideration to the representations or proposals made to it, with a view to reaching a satisfactory resolution of the matter.

Dispute settlement

14.3 It is the firm intention of Parties that all disputes under this Agreement shall be promptly and expeditiously settled, particularly in the case of perishable products.

14.4 If no solution has been reached after consultations under Article 14, paragraphs 1 and 2, the Committee shall meet at the request of any Party to the dispute within thirty days of receipt of such a request, to investigate the matter with a view to facilitating a mutually satisfactory solution.

14.5 In investigating the matter and in selecting, subject, *inter alia*, to the provisions of Article 14, paragraphs 9 and 14, the appropriate procedures the Committee shall take into account whether the issues in dispute relate to commercial policy considerations and/or to questions of a technical nature requiring detailed consideration by experts.

14.6 In the case of perishable products the Committee shall, in keeping with Article 14, paragraph 3, consider the matter in the most expeditious manner possible with a view to facilitating a mutually satisfactory solution within three months of the request for the Committee investigation.

14.7 It is understood that where disputes arise affecting products with a definite crop cycle of twelve months, every effort whould be made by the Committee to deal with these disputes within a period of twelve months.

14.8 During any phase of a dispute settlement procedure including the earliest phase, competent bodies and experts in matters under consideration may be consulted and invited to attend the meetings of the Committee; appropriate information and assistance may be requested from such bodies and experts.

Technical issues

14.9 If no mutually satisfactory solution has been reached under the procedures of Article 14, paragraph 4 within three months of the request for the Committee investigation, upon the request of any Party to the dispute who considers the issues to relate to questions of a technical nature the Committee shall establish a technical expert group and direct it to:

examine the matter;

consult with the Parties to the dispute and give full opportunity for them to develop a mutually satisfactory solution;

make a statement concerning the facts of the matter; and

make such findings as will assist the Committee in making recommendations or giving rulings on the mater, including *inter alia*, and if appropriate, findings concerning the detailed scientific judgments involved, whether the measure was necessary for the protection of human, animal or plant life or health, and whether a legitimate scientific judgment is involved.

14.10 Technical expert groups shall be governed by the procedures of Annex 2. [1]

14.11 The time required by the technical expert group considering questions of a technical nature will vary with the particular case. The technical expert group should aim to deliver its findings to the Committee within six months from the date the technical issue was referred to it, unless extended by mutual agreement between the Parties to the dispute.

14.12 Reports should set out the rationale behind any findings that they make.

14.13 If no mutually satisfactory solution has been reached after completion of the procedures in this Article, and any Party to the dispute requests a panel, the Committee shall establish a panel which shall operate under the provisions of Article 14, paragraphs 15 to 18.

Panel proceedings

14.14 If no mutually satisfactory solution has been reached under the procedures of Article 14, paragraph 4 within three months of the request for the Committee investigation and the procedures of Article 14, paragraphs 9 to 13 have not been invoked, the Committee shall, upon request of any Party to the dispute, establish a panel.

14.15 When a panel is established, the Committee shall direct it to:

examine the matter;

consult with Parties to the dispute and give full opportunity for them to develop a mutually satisfactory solution;

make a statement concerning the facts of the matter as they relate to the application of provisions of this Agreement and make such findings as will assist the Committee in making recommendations or giving rulings on the matter.

14.16 Panels shall be governed by the procedures in Annex 3. [2]

14.17 Panels shall use the report of any technical expert group established under Article 14, paragraph 9 as the basis for its consideration of issues that involve questions of a technical nature.

---

[1] See page 31.
[2] See page 31.

14.18   The time required by panels will vary with the particular case. They should aim to deliver their findings, and where appropriate, recommendations to the Committee without undue delay, normally within a period of four months from the date that the panel was established.

Enforcement

14.19   After the investigation is complete or after the report of a technical expert group, working group, panel or other body is presented to the Committee, the Committee shall give the matter prompt consideration. With respect to panel reports, the Committee shall take appropriate action normally within thirty days of receipt of the report, unless extended by the Committee, including:

a statement concerning the facts of the matter; or

recommendations to one or more Parties; or

any other ruling which it deems appropriate.

14.20   If a Party to which recommendations are addressed considers itself unable to implement them, it should promptly furnish reasons in writing to the Committee.   In that event the Committee shall consider what further action may be appropriate.

14.21   If the Committee considers that the circumstances are serious enough to justify such action, it may authorize one or more Parties to suspend, in respect of any other Party, the application of such obligations under this Agreement as it determines to be appropriate in the circumstances. In this respect, the Committee may, *inter alia*, authorize the suspension of the application of obligations, including those in Articles 5 to 9, in order to restore mutual economic advantage and balance of rights and obligations.

14.22   The Committee shall keep under surveillance any matter on which it has made recommendations or given rulings.

Other provisions relating to dispute settlement

Procedures

14.23   If disputes arise between Parties relating to rights and obligations of this Agreement, Parties should complete the dispute settlement procedures under this Agreement before availing themselves of any rights which they have under the GATT.   Parties recognize that, in any case so referred to the CONTRACTING PARTIES, any finding, recommendation or ruling pursuant to Article 14, paragraphs 9 to 18 may be taken into account by the CONTRACTING PARTIES, to the extent they relate to matters involving equivalent rights and obligations under the General Agreement.   When Parties resort to GATT Article XXIII, a determination under that Article shall be based on GATT provisions only.

Levels of obligation

14.24   The dispute settlement provisions set out above can be invoked in cases where a Party considers that another Party has not achieved satisfactory results under Articles 3, 4, 6, 8 and 9 and its trade interests are significantly affected.   In this respect, such results shall be equivalent to those envisaged in Articles 2, 5 and 7 as if the body in question were a Party.

Processes and production methods

14.25   The dispute settlement procedures set out above can be invoked in cases where a Party considers that obligations under this Agreement are being circumvented by the drafting of requirements in terms of processes and production methods rather than in terms of characteristics of products.

Retroactivity

14.26   To the extent that a Party considers that technical regulations, standards, methods for assuring conformity with technical regulations or standards, or certification systems which exist at the time of entry into force of this Agreement are not consistent with the provisions of this Agreement, such regulations, standards, methods and systems shall be subject to the provisions in Articles 13 and 14 of this Agreement, in so far as they are applicable.

FINAL PROVISIONS

Article 15

Final provisions

Acceptance and accession

15.1   This Agreement shall be open for acceptance by signature or otherwise, by governments contracting parties to the GATT, and by the European Economic Community.

15.2   This Agreement shall be open for acceptance by signature or otherwise by governments having provisionally acceded to the GATT, on terms related to the effective application of rights and obligations under this Agreement, which take into account rights and obligations in the instruments providing for their provisional accession.

15.3 This Agreement shall be open to accession by any other government on terms, related to the effective application of rights and obligations under this Agreement, to be agreed between that government and the Parties, by the deposit with the Director-General to the CONTRACTING PARTIES to the GATT of an instrument of accession which states the terms so agreed.

15.4 In regard to acceptance, the provisions of Article XXVI: 5(*a*) and (*b*) of the General Agreement would be applicable.

Reservations

15.5 Reservations may not be entered in respect of any of the provisions of this Agreement without the consent of the other Parties.

Entry into force

15.6 This Agreement shall enter into force on 1 January 1980 for the governments [1] which have accepted or acceded to it by that date. For each other government it shall enter into force on the thirtieth day following the date of its acceptance or accession to this Agreement.

Review

15.7 Each Party shall, promptly after the date on which this Agreement enters into force for the Party concerned, inform the Committee of measures in existence or taken to ensure the implementation and administration of this Agreement. Any changes of such measures thereafter shall also be notified to the Committee.

15.8 The Committee shall review annually the implementation and operation of this Agreement taking into account the objectives thereof. The Committee shall annually inform the CONTRACTING PARTIES to the GATT of developments during the period covered by such reviews.

15.9 Not later than the end of the third year from the entry into force of this Agreement and at the end of each three-year period thereafter, the Committee shall review the operation and implementation of this Agreement, including the provisions relating to transparency, with a view to adjusting the rights and obligations of this Agreement where necessary to ensure mutual economic advantage and balance of rights and obligations, without prejudice to the provisions of Article 12, and where appropriate proposing amendments to the text of this Agreement having regard, *inter alia*, to the experience gained in its implementation.

---

[1] The term " government " is deemed to include the competent authorities of the European Economic Community.

Amendments

15.10   The Parties may amend this Agreement having regard, *inter alia*, to the experience gained in its implementation.   Such an amendment, once the Parties have concurred in accordance with procedures established by the Committee, shall not come into force for any Party until it has been accepted by such Party.

Withdrawal

15.11   Any Party may withdraw from this Agreement.   The withdrawal shall take effect upon the expiration of sixty days from the day on which written notice of withdrawal is received by the Director-General to the CONTRACTING PARTIES to the GATT.   Any Party may upon such notification request an immediate meeting of the Committee.

Non-application of this Agreement between particular Parties

15.12   This Agreement shall not apply as between any two Parties if either of the Parties, at the time either accepts or accedes to this Agreement, does not consent to such application.

Annexes

15.13   The annexes to this Agreement constitute an integral part thereof.

Secretariat

15.14   This Agreement shall be serviced by the GATT secretariat.

Deposit

15.15   This Agreement shall be deposited with the Director-General to the CONTRACTING PARTIES to the GATT, who shall promptly furnish to each Party and each contracting party to the GATT a certified copy thereof and of each amendment thereto pursuant to Article 15, paragraph 10 and a notification of each acceptance thereof or accession thereto pursuant to Article 15, paragraphs 1 to 3 and of each withdrawal therefrom pursuant to Article 15, paragraph 11.

Registration

15.16   This Agreement shall be registered in accordance with the provisions of Article 102 of the Charter of the United Nations.

Done at Geneva this twelfth day of April nineteen hundred and seventy-nine in a single copy, in the English, French and Spanish languages, each text being authentic.

ANNEX 1

TERMS AND THEIR DEFINITIONS FOR THE
SPECIFIC PURPOSES OF THIS AGREEMENT

Note: References to the definitions of international standardizing bodies in the explanatory notes are made as they stood in March 1979.

1. *Technical specification*

A specification contained in a document which lays down characteristics of a product such as levels of quality, performance, safety or dimensions. It may include, or deal exclusively with terminology, symbols, testing and test methods, packaging, marking or labelling requirements as they apply to a product.

Explanatory note:
This Agreement deals only with technical specifications relating to products. Thus the wording of the corresponding Economic Commission for Europe/International Organization for Standardization definition is amended in order to exclude services and codes of practice.

2. *Technical regulation*

A technical specification, including the applicable administrative provisions, with which compliance is mandatory.

Explanatory note:
The wording differs from the corresponding Economic Commission for Europe International Organization for Standardization definition because the latter is based on the definition of regulation which is not defined in this Agreement. Furthermore the Economic Commission for Europe/International Organization for Standardization definition contains a normative element which is included in the operative provisions of this Agreement. For the purposes of this Agreement, this definition covers also a standard of which the application has been made mandatory not by separate regulation but by virtue of a general law.

3. *Standard*

A technical specification approved by a recognized standardizing body for repeated or continuous application, with which compliance is not mandatory.

Explanatory note:
The corresponding Economic Commission for Europe/International Organization for Standardization definition contains several normative elements which are not included in the above definition. Accordingly, technical specifications which are not based on consensus are covered by this Agreement. This definition does not

cover technical specifications prepared by an individual company for its own production or consumption requirements. The word " body " covers also a national standardizing system.

4. *International body or system*

A body or system whose membership is open to the relevant bodies of at least all Parties to this Agreement.

5. *Regional body or system*

A body or system whose membership is open to the relevant bodies of only some of the Parties.

6. *Central government body*

Central government, its ministries and departments or any body subject to the control of the central government in respect of the activity in question.

Explanatory note :

In the case of the European Economic Community the provisions governing central government bodies apply. However, regional bodies or certification systems may be established within the European Economic Community, and in such cases would be subject to the provisions of this Agreement on regional bodies or certification systems.

7. *Local government body*

A government other than a central government (e.g. states, provinces, Länder, cantons, municipalities, etc.), its ministries or departments or. any body subject to the control of such a government in respect of the activity in question.

8. *Non-governmental body*

A body other than a central government body or a local government body, including a non-governmental body which has legal power to enforce a technical regulation.

9. *Standardizing body*

A governmental or non-governmental body, one of whose recognized activities is in the field of standardization.

10. *International standard*

A standard adopted by an international standardizing body.

Explanatory note :

The wording differs from the corresponding Economic Commission for Europe/ International Organization for Standardization definition in order to make it consistent with other definitions of this Agreement.

TECHNICAL EXPERT GROUPS

The following procedures shall apply to technical expert groups established in accordance with the provisions of Article 14.

1. Participation in technical expert groups shall be restricted to persons, preferably government officials, of professional standing and experience in the field in question.

2. Citizens of countries whose central governments are Parties to a dispute shall not be eligible for membership of the technical expert group concerned with that dispute. Members of technical expert groups shall serve in their individual capacities and not as government representatives, nor as representatives of any organization. Governments or organizations shall therefore not give them instructions with regard to matters before a technical expert group.

3. The Parties to a dispute shall have access to all relevant information provided to a technical expert group, unless it is of a confidential nature. Confidential information provided to the technical expert group shall not be revealed without formal authorization from the government or person providing the information. Where such information is requested from the technical expert group but release of such information by the technical expert group is not authorized, a non-confidential summary of the information will be provided by the government or person supplying the information.

4. To encourage development of mutually satisfactory solutions between the Parties and with a view to obtaining their comments, each technical expert group should first submit the descriptive part of its report to the Parties concerned, and should subsequently submit to the Parties to the dispute its conclusions, or an outline thereof, a reasonable period of time before they are circulated to the Parties.

Annex 3

PANELS

The following procedures shall apply to panels established in accordance with the provisions of Article 14.

1. In order to facilitate the constitution of panels, the Chairman of the Committee shall maintain an informal indicative list of government officials knowledgeable in the area of technical barriers to trade and experienced in the field of trade

relations and economic development. This list may also include persons other than government officials. In this connexion, each Party shall be invited to indicate at the beginning of every year to the Chairman of the Committee the name(s) of the one or two governmental experts whom the Parties would be willing to make available for such work. When a panel is established under Article 14, paragraph 13 or Article 14, paragraph 14, the Chairman, within seven days shall propose the composition of the panel consisting of three or five members, preferably government officials. The Parties directly concerned shall react within seven working days to nominations of panel members by the Chairman and shall not oppose nominations except for compelling reasons. Citizens of countries whose central governments are Parties to a dispute shall not be eligible for membership of the panel concerned with that dispute. Panel members shall serve in their individual capacities and not as government representatives, nor as representatives of any organization. Governments or organizations shall therefore not give them instructions with regard to matters before a panel.

2. Each panel shall develop its own working procedures. All Parties having a substantial interest in the matter and having notified this to the Committee, shall have an opportunity to be heard. Each panel may consult and seek information and technical advice from any source it deems appropriate. Before a panel seeks such information or technical advice from a source within the jurisdiction of a Party, it shall inform the government of that Party. In case such consultation with competent bodies and experts is necessary it should be at the earliest possible stage of the dispute settlement procedure. Any Party shall respond promptly and fully to any request by a panel for such information as the panel considers necessary and appropriate. Confidential information provided to the panel shall not be revealed without formal authorization from the government or person providing the information. Where such information is requested from the panel but release of such information by the panel is not authorized, a non-confidential summary of the information will be provided by the government or person supplying the information.

3. Where the Parties to a dispute have failed to come to a satisfactory solution, the panel shall submit its findings in a written form. Panel reports should normally set out the rationale behind any findings and recommendations that it makes. Where a bilateral settlement of the matter has been found, the report of the panel may be confined to a brief description of the case and to reporting that a solution has been reached.

4. To encourage development of mutually satisfactory solutions between the Parties and with a view to obtaining their comments, each panel should first submit the descriptive part of its report to the Parties concerned, and should subsequently submit to the Parties to the dispute its conclusions, or an outline thereof, a reasonable period of time before they are circulated to the Parties.

AGREEMENT ON IMPORT LICENSING PROCEDURES

PREAMBLE

Having regard to the Multilateral Trade Negotiations, the Parties to this Agreement on Import Licensing Procedures (hereinafter referred to as " Parties " and " this Agreement ");

Desiring to further the objectives of the General Agreement on Tariffs and Trade (hereinafter referred to as " General Agreement " or " GATT ");

Taking into account the particular trade, development and financial needs of developing countries;

Recognizing the usefulness of automatic import licensing for certain purposes and that such licensing should not be used to restrict trade;

Recognizing that import licensing may be employed to administer measures such as those adopted pursuant to the relevant provisions of the GATT;

Recognizing also that the inappropriate use of import licensing procedures may impede the flow of international trade;

Desiring to simplify, and bring transparency to, the administrative procedures and practices used in international trade, and to ensure the fair and equitable application and administration of such procedures and practices;

Desiring to provide for a consultative mechanism and the speedy, effective and equitable resolution of disputes arising under this Agreement;

Hereby agree as follows:

Article 1

General provisions

1.   For the purpose of this Agreement, import licensing is defined as administrative procedures [1] used for the operation of import licensing regimes

---

[1] Those procedures referred to as " licensing " as well as other similar administrative procedures.

requiring the submission of an application or other documentation (other than that required for customs purposes) to the relevant administrative body as a prior condition for importation into the customs territory of the importing country.

2.   The Parties shall ensure that the administrative procedures used to implement import licensing regimes are in conformity with the relevant provisions of the GATT including its annexes and protocols, as interpreted by this Agreement, with a view to preventing trade distortions that may arise from an inappropriate operation of those procedures, taking into account the economic development purposes and financial and trade needs of developing countries.

3.   The rules for import licensing procedures shall be neutral in application and administered in a fair and equitable manner.

4.   The rules and all information concerning procedures for the submission of applications, including the eligibility of persons, firms and institutions to make such applications, and the lists of products subject to the licensing requirement shall be published promptly in such a manner as to enable governments and traders to become acquainted with them.   Any changes in either the rules concerning licensing procedures or the list of products subject to import licensing shall also be promptly published in the same manner. Copies of these publications shall also be made available to the GATT Secretariat.

5.   Application forms and, where applicable, renewal forms shall be as simple as possible.   Such documents and information as are considered strictly necessary for the proper functioning of the licensing regime may be required on application.

6.   Application procedures and, where applicable, renewal procedures shall be as simple as possible. Applicants shall have to approach only one administrative body previously specified in the rules referred to in paragraph 4 above in connexion with an application and shall be allowed a reasonable period therefor. In cases where it is strictly indispensable that more than one administrative body is to be approached in connexion with an application, these shall be kept to the minimum number possible.

7.   No application shall be refused for minor documentation errors which do not alter basic data contained therein. No penalty greater than necessary to serve merely as a warning shall be imposed in respect of any omission or mistake in documentation or procedures which is obviously made without fraudulent intent or gross negligence.

8.   Licensed imports shall not be refused for minor variations in value, quantity or weight from the amount designated on the licence due to

differences occurring during shipment, differences incidental to bulk loading and other minor differences consistent with normal commercial practice.

9.   The foreign exchange necessary to pay for licensed imports shall be made available to licence holders on the same basis as to importers of goods not requiring import licences.

10.   With regard to security exceptions, the provisions of Article XXI of the GATT apply.

11.   The provisions of this Agreement shall not require any Party to disclose confidential information which would impede law enforcement or otherwise be contrary to the public interest or would prejudice the legitimate commercial interests of particular enterprises, public or private.

Article 2

Automatic import licensing [1]

1.   Automatic import licensing is defined as import licensing where approval of the application is freely granted.

2.   The following provisions [2], in addition to those in paragraphs 1 to 11 of Article 1 and paragraph 1 of Article 2 above, shall apply to automatic import licensing procedures:

   (a)   Automatic licensing procedures shall not be administered in a manner so as to have restricting effects on imports subject to automatic licensing;

   (b)   Parties recognize that automatic import licensing may be necessary whenever other appropriate procedures are not available. Automatic import licensing may be maintained as long as the circumstances which gave rise to its introduction prevail or as long as its underlying administrative purposes cannot be achieved in a more appropriate way;

   (c)   Any person, firm or institution which fulfils the legal requirements of the importing country for engaging in import operations involving products subject to automatic licensing shall be equally eligible to apply for and to obtain import licences;

---

[1] Those import licensing procedures requiring a security which have no restrictive effects on imports, are to be considered as falling within the scope of paragraphs 1 and 2 of Article 2 below.

[2] A developing country Party, which has specific difficulties with the requirements of sub-paragraphs (d) and (e) below may, upon notification to the Committee referred to in paragraph 1 of Article 4, delay the application of these sub-paragraphs by not more than two years the date of entry into force of this Agreement for such Party.

(*d*) Applications for licences may be submitted on any working day prior to the customs clearance of the goods;

(*e*) Applications for licences when submitted in appropriate and complete form shall be approved immediately on receipt, to the extent administratively feasible, but within a maximum of ten working days.

Article 3

Non-automatic import licensing

The following provisions, in addition to those in paragraphs 1 to 11 of Article 1 above, shall apply to non-automatic import licensing procedures, that is, import licensing procedures not falling under paragraphs 1 and 2 of Article 2 above:

(*a*) Licensing procedures adopted, and practices applied, in connexion with the issuance of licences for the administration of quotas and other import restrictions, shall not have trade restrictive effects on imports additional to those caused by the imposition of the restriction;

(*b*) Parties shall provide, upon the request of any Party having an interest in the trade in the product concerned, all relevant information concerning:

  (i) the administration of the restrictions;

  (ii) the import licences granted over a recent period;

  (iii) the distribution of such licences among supplying countries;

  (iv) where practicable, import statistics (i.e. value and/or volume) with respect to the products subject to import licensing. The developing countries would not be expected to take additional administrative or financial burdens on this account;

(*c*) Parties administering quotas by means of licensing shall publish the overall amount of quotas to be applied by quantity and/or value, the opening and closing dates of quotas, and any change thereof;

(*d*) In the case of quotas allocated among supplying countries, the Party applying the restrictions shall promptly inform all other Parties having an interest in supplying the product concerned of the shares in the quota currently allocated, by quantity or value, to the various supplying countries and shall give public notice thereof;

(*e*) Where there is a specific opening date for the submission of licensing applications, the rules and product lists referred to in paragraph 4 of Article 1 shall be published as far in advance as possible of such date, or immediately after the announcement of the quota or other measure involving an import licensing requirement;

(f) Any person, firm or institution which fulfils the legal requirements of the importing country shall be equally eligible to apply and to be considered for a licence. If the licence application is not approved, the applicant shall, on request, be given the reasons therefor and shall have a right of appeal or review in accordance with the domestic legislation or procedures of the importing country;

(g) The period for processing of applications shall be as short as possible;

(h) The period of licence validity shall be of reasonable duration and not be so short as to preclude imports. The period of licence validity shall not preclude imports from distant sources, except in special cases where imports are necessary to meet unforeseen short-term requirements;

(i) When administering quotas, Parties shall not prevent importation from being effected in accordance with the issued licences, and shall not discourage the full utilization of the quotas;

(j) When issuing licences, Parties shall take into account the desirability of issuing licences for products in economic quantities;

(k) In allocating licences, Parties should consider the import performance of the applicant, including whether licences issued to the applicant have been fully utilized, during a recent representative period;

(l) Consideration shall be given to ensuring a reasonable distribution of licences to new importers, taking into account the desirability of issuing licences for products in economic quantities. In this regard, special consideration should be given to those importers importing products originating in developing countries and, in particular, the least-developed countries;

(m) In the case of quotas administered through licences which are not allocated among supplying countries, licence holders [1] shall be free to choose the sources of imports. In the case of quotas allocated among supplying countries, the licence shall clearly stipulate the country or countries;

(n) In applying paragraph 8 of Article 1 above, compensating adjustments may be made in future licence allocations where imports exceeded a previous licence level.

---

[1] Sometimes referred to as " quota holders ".

Article 4

Institutions, consultation and dispute settlement

1.   There shall be established under this Agreement a Committee on Import Licensing composed of representatives from each of the Parties (referred to in this Agreement as " the Committee "). The Committee shall elect its own Chairman and shall meet as necessary for the purpose of affording Parties the opportunity of consulting on any matters relating to the operation of this Agreement or the furtherance of its objectives.

2.   Consultations and the settlement of disputes with respect to any matter affecting the operation of this Agreement, shall be subject to the procedures of Articles XXII and XXIII of the GATT.

Article 5

Final provisions

1. *Acceptance and accession*

   (*a*)   This Agreement shall be open for acceptance by signature or otherwise, by governments contracting parties to the GATT and by the European Economic Community.

   (*b*)   This Agreement shall be open for acceptance by signature or otherwise by governments having provisionally acceded to the GATT, on terms related to the effective application of rights and obligations under this Agreement, which take into account rights and obligations in the instruments providing for their provisional accession.

   (*c*)   This Agreement shall be open to accession by any other government on terms, related to the effective application of rights and obligations under this Agreement, to be agreed between that government and the Parties, by the deposit with the Director-General to the CONTRACTING PARTIES to the GATT of an instrument of accession which states the terms so agreed.

   (*d*)   In regard to acceptance, the provisions of Article XXVI:5(*a*) and (*b*) of the General Agreement would be applicable.

2. *Reservations*

   Reservations may not be entered in respect of any of the provisions of this Agreement without the consent of the other Parties.

3. *Entry into force*

This Agreement shall enter into force on 1 January 1980 for the governments [1] which have accepted or acceded to it by that date. For each other government it shall enter into force on the thirtieth day following the date of its acceptance or accession to this Agreement.

4. *National legislation*

(*a*) Each government accepting or acceding to this Agreement shall ensure, not later than the date of entry into force of this Agreement for it, the conformity of its laws, regulations and administrative procedures with the provisions of this Agreement.

(*b*) Each Party shall inform the Committee of any changes in its laws and regulations relevant to this Agreement and in the administration of such laws and regulations.

5. *Review*

The Committee shall review as necessary, but at least once every two years, the implementation and operation of this Agreement taking into account the objectives thereof and shall inform the CONTRACTING PARTIES to the GATT of developments during the period covered by such reviews.

6. *Amendments*

The Parties may amend this Agreement, having regard, *inter alia*, to the experience gained in its implementation. Such an amendment, once the Parties have concurred in accordance with procedures established by the Committee, shall not come into force for any Party until it has been accepted by such Party.

7. *Withdrawal*

Any Party may withdraw from this Agreement. The withdrawal shall take effect upon the expiration of sixty days from the day on which written notice of withdrawal is received by the Director-General to the CONTRACTING PARTIES to the GATT. Any Party may upon such notification request an immediate meeting of the Committee.

---

[1] For the purpose of this Agreement, the term " governments " is deemed to include the competent authorities of the European Economic Community.

8. *Non-application of this Agreement between particular Parties*

This Agreement shall not apply as between any two Parties if either of the Parties, at the time either accepts or accedes to this Agreement, does not consent to such application.

9. *Secretariat*

This Agreement shall be serviced by the GATT secretariat.

10. *Deposit*

This Agreement shall be deposited with the Director-General to the CONTRACTING PARTIES to the GATT, who shall promptly furnish to each Party and each contracting party to the GATT a certified copy thereof and of each amendment thereto pursuant to paragraph 6, and a notification of each acceptance thereof or accession thereto pursuant to paragraph 1 and of each withdrawal therefrom pursuant to paragraph 7 of this Article.

11. *Registration*

This Agreement shall be registered in accordance with the provisions of Article 102 of the Charter of the United Nations.

Done at Geneva this twelfth day of April, nineteen hundred and seventy-nine in a single copy, in the English, French and Spanish languages, each text being authentic.

AGREEMENT ON TRADE IN CIVIL AIRCRAFT

PREAMBLE

Signatories[1] to the Agreement on Trade in Civil Aircraft, hereinafter referred to as " this Agreement ";

Noting that Ministers on 12-14 September 1973 agreed the Tokyo Round of Multilateral Trade Negotiations should achieve the expansion and ever-greater liberalization of world trade through, *inter alia*, the progressive dismantling of obstacles to trade and the improvement of the international framework for the conduct of world trade;

Desiring to achieve maximum freedom of world trade in civil aircraft, parts and related equipment, including elimination of duties, and to the fullest extent possible, the reduction or elimination of trade restricting or distorting effects;

Desiring to encourage the continued technological development of the aeronautical industry on a world-wide basis;

Desiring to provide fair and equal competitive opportunities for their civil aircraft activities and for their producers to participate in the expansion of the world civil aircraft market;

Being mindful of the importance in the civil aircraft sector of their overall mutual economic and trade interests;

Recognizing that many Signatories view the aircraft sector as a particularly important component of economic and industrial policy;

Seeking to eliminate adverse effects on trade in civil aircraft resulting from governmental support in civil aircraft development, production, and marketing while recognizing that such governmental support, of itself, would not be deemed a distortion of trade;

Desiring that their civil aircraft activities operate on a commercially competitive basis, and recognizing that government-industry relationships differ widely among them;

Recognizing their obligations and rights under the General Agreement on Tariffs and Trade, hereinafter referred to as " the GATT ", and under other multilateral agreements negotiated under the auspices of the GATT;

---

[1] The term " Signatories " is hereinafter used to mean Parties to this Agreement.

Recognizing the need to provide for international notification, consultation, surveillance and dispute settlement procedures with a view to ensuring a fair, prompt and effective enforcement of the provisions of this Agreement and to maintain the balance of rights and obligations among them;

Desiring to establish an international framework governing conduct of trade in civil aircraft;

Hereby agree as follows:

Article 1

Product Coverage

1.1 This Agreement applies to the following products:

    (*a*) all civil aircraft,

    (*b*) all civil aircraft engines and their parts and components,

    (*c*) all other parts, components, and sub-assemblies of civil aircraft,

    (*d*) all ground flight simulators and their parts and components,

whether used as original or replacement equipment in the manufacture, repair, maintenance, rebuilding, modification or conversion of civil aircraft.

1.2 For the purposes of this Agreement " civil aircraft " means (*a*) all aircraft other than military aircraft and (*b*) all other products set out in Article 1.1 above.

Article 2

Customs Duties and Other Charges

2.1 Signatories agree:

    2.1.1   to eliminate by 1 January 1980, or by the date of entry into force of this Agreement, all customs duties and other charges [1] of any kind levied on, or in connexion with, the importation of products, classified for customs purposes under their respective tariff headings listed in the Annex, if such products are for use in a civil aircraft and incorporation therein, in the course of its manufacture, repair, maintenance, rebuilding, modification or conversion;

---

[1] " Other charges " shall have the same meaning as in Article II of the GATT.

2.1.2   to eliminate by 1 January 1980, or by the date of entry into force of this Agreement, all customs duties and other charges [1] of any kind levied on repairs on civil aircraft;

2.1.3   to incorporate in their respective GATT Schedules by 1 January 1980, or by the date of entry into force of this Agreement, duty-free or duty-exempt treatment for all products covered by Article 2.1.1 above and for all repairs covered by Article 2.1.2 above.

2.2   Each Signatory shall: (*a*) adopt or adapt an end-use system of customs administration to give effect to its obligations under Article 2.1 above; (*b*) ensure that its end-use system provides duty-free or duty-exempt treatment that is comparable to the treatment provided by other Signatories and is not an impediment to trade; and (*c*) inform other Signatories of its procedures for administering the end-use system.

Article 3

Technical Barriers to Trade

3.1   Signatories note that the provisions of the Agreement on Technical Barriers to Trade apply to trade in civil aircraft. In addition, Signatories agree that civil aircraft certification requirements and specifications on operating and maintenance procedures shall be governed, as between Signatories, by the provisions of the Agreement on Technical Barriers to Trade.

Article 4

Government-Directed Procurement, Mandatory Sub-Contracts and Inducements

4.1   Purchasers of civil aircraft should be free to select suppliers on the basis of commercial and technological factors.

4.2   Signatories shall not require airlines, aircraft manufacturers, or other entities engaged in the purchase of civil aircraft, nor exert unreasonable pressure on them, to procure civil aircraft from any particular source, which would create discrimination against suppliers from any Signatory.

---

[1] " Other charges " shall have the same meaning as in Article II of the GATT.

4.3 Signatories agree that the purchase of products covered by this Agreement should be made only on a competitive price, quality and delivery basis. In conjunction with the approval or awarding of procurement contracts for products covered by this Agreement a Signatory may, however, require that its qualified firms be provided with access to business opportunities on a competitive basis and on terms no less favourable than those available to the qualified firms of other Signatories. [1]

4.4 Signatories agree to avoid attaching inducements of any kind to the sale or purchase of civil aircraft from any particular source which would create discrimination against suppliers from any Signatory.

Article 5

Trade Restrictions

5.1 Signatories shall not apply quantitative restrictions (import quotas) or import licensing requirements to restrict imports of civil aircraft in a manner inconsistent with applicable provisions of the GATT. This does not preclude import monitoring or licensing systems consistent with the GATT.

5.2 Signatories shall not apply quantitative restrictions or export licensing or other similar requirements to restrict, for commercial or competitive reasons, exports of civil aircraft to other Signatories in a manner inconsistent with applicable provisions of the GATT.

Article 6

Government Support, Export Credits, and Aircraft Marketing

6.1 Signatories note that the provisions of the Agreement on Interpretation and Application of Articles VI, XVI and XXIII of the General Agreement on Tariffs and Trade (Agreement on Subsidies and Countervailing Measures) apply to trade in civil aircraft. They affirm that in their participation in, or support of, civil aircraft programmes they shall seek to avoid adverse

---

[1] Use of the phrase " access to business opportunities . . . on terms no less favourable . . . " does not mean that the amount of contracts awarded to the qualified firms of one Signatory entitles the qualified firms of other Signatories to contracts of a similar amount.

effects on trade in civil aircraft in the sense of Articles 8.3 and 8.4 of the Agreement on Subsidies and Countervailing Measures. They also shall take into account the special factors which apply in the aircraft sector, in particular the widespread governmental support in this area, their international economic interests, and the desire of producers of all Signatories to participate in the expansion of the world civil aircraft market.

6.2   Signatories agree that pricing of civil aircraft should be based on a reasonable expectation of recoupment of all costs, including non-recurring programme costs, identifiable and pro-rated costs of military research and development on aircraft, components, and systems that are subsequently applied to the production of such civil aircraft, average production costs, and financial costs.

Article 7

Regional and Local Governments

7.1   In addition to their other obligations under this Agreement, Signatories agree not to require or encourage, directly or indirectly, regional and local governments and authorities, non-governmental bodies, and other bodies to take action inconsistent with provisions of this Agreement.

Article 8

Surveillance, Review, Consultation, and Dispute Settlement

8.1   There shall be established a Committee on Trade in Civil Aircraft (hereinafter referred to as " the Committee ") composed of representatives of all Signatories. The Committee shall elect its own Chairman. It shall meet as necessary, but not less than once a year, for the purpose of affording Signatories the opportunity to consult on any matters relating to the operation of this Agreement, including developments in the civil aircraft industry, to determine whether amendments are required to ensure continuance of free and undistorted trade, to examine any matter for which it has not been possible to find a satisfactory solution through bilateral consultations, and to carry out such responsibilities as are assigned to it under this Agreement, or by the Signatories.

8.2   The Committee shall review annually the implementation and operation of this Agreement taking into account the objectives thereof. The Committee shall annually inform the CONTRACTING PARTIES to the GATT of developments during the period covered by such review.

8.3 Not later than the end of the third year from the entry into force of this Agreement and periodically thereafter, Signatories shall undertake further negotiations, with a view to broadening and improving this Agreement on the basis of mutual reciprocity.

8.4 The Committee may establish such subsidiary bodies as may be appropriate to keep under regular review the application of this Agreement to ensure a continuing balance of mutual advantages. In particular, it shall establish an appropriate subsidiary body in order to ensure a continuing balance of mutual advantages, reciprocity and equivalent results with regard to the implementation of the provisions of Article 2 above related to product coverage, the end-use systems, customs duties and other charges.

8.5 Each Signatory shall afford sympathetic consideration to and adequate opportunity for prompt consultation regarding representations made by another Signatory with respect to any matter affecting the operation of this Agreement.

8.6 Signatories recognize the desirability of consultations with other Signatories in the Committee in order to seek a mutually acceptable solution prior to the initiation of an investigation to determine the existence, degree and effect of any alleged subsidy. In those exceptional circumstances in which no consultations occur before such domestic procedures are initiated, Signatories shall notify the Committee immediately of initiation of such procedures and enter into simultaneous consultations to seek a mutually agreed solution that would obviate the need for countervailing measures.

8.7 Should a Signatory consider that its trade interests in civil aircraft manufacture, repair, maintenance, rebuilding, modification or conversion have been or are likely to be adversely affected by any action by another Signatory, it may request review of the matter by the Committee. Upon such a request, the Committee shall convene within thirty days and shall review the matter as quickly as possible with a view to resolving the issues involved as promptly as possible and in particular prior to final resolution of these issues elsewhere. In this connexion the Committee may issue such rulings or recommendations as may be appropriate. Such review shall be without prejudice to the rights of Signatories under the GATT or under instruments multilaterally negotiated under the auspices of the GATT, as they affect trade in civil aircraft. For the purposes of aiding consideration of the issues involved, under the GATT and such instruments, the Committee may provide such technical assistance as may be appropriate.

8.8 Signatories agree that, with respect to any dispute related to a matter covered by this Agreement, but not covered by other instruments multilaterally negotiated under the auspices of the GATT, the provisions of Articles XXII and XXIII of the General Agreement and the provisions of the Understanding related to Notification, Consultation, Dispute Settlement and Surveillance shall be applied, *mutatis mutandis*, by the Signatories and the Committee for the purposes of seeking settlement of such dispute. These procedures shall also be applied for the settlement of any dispute related to a matter covered by this Agreement and by another instrument multilaterally negotiated under the auspices of the GATT, should the parties to the dispute so agree.

Article 9

Final Provisions

9.1 *Acceptance and Accession*

9.1.1   This Agreement shall be open for acceptance by signature or otherwise by governments contracting parties to the GATT and by the European Economic Community.

9.1.2   This Agreement shall be open for acceptance by signature or otherwise by governments having provisionally acceded to the GATT, on terms related to the effective application of rights and obligations under this Agreement, which take into account rights and obligations in the instruments providing for their provisional accession.

9.1.3   This Agreement shall be open to accession by any other government on terms, related to the effective application of rights and obligations under this Agreement, to be agreed between that government and the Signatories, by the deposit with the Director-General to the CONTRACTING PARTIES to the GATT of an instrument of accession which states the terms so agreed.

9.1.4   In regard to acceptance, the provisions of Article XXVI: 5(*a*) and (*b*) of the General Agreement would be applicable.

9.2 *Reservations*

9.2.1   Reservations may not be entered in respect of any of the provisions of this Agreement without the consent of the other Signatories.

9.3 *Entry into Force*

9.3.1   This Agreement shall enter into force on 1 January 1980 for the governments [1] which have accepted or acceded to it by that date.

---

[1] For the purpose of this Agreement, the term " government " is deemed to include the competent authorities of the European Economic Community.

For each other government it shall enter into force on the thirtieth day following the date of its acceptance or accession to this Agreement.

9.4 *National Legislation*

9.4.1   Each government accepting or acceding to this Agreement shall ensure, not later than the date of entry into force of this Agreement for it, the conformity of its laws, regulations and Administrative procedures with the provisions of this Agreement.

9.4.2   Each Signatory shall inform the Committee of any changes in its laws and regulations relevant to this Agreement and in the administration of such laws and regulations.

9.5 *Amendments*

9.5.1   The Signatories may amend this Agreement, having regard, *inter alia*, to the experience gained in its implementation. Such an amendment, once the Signatories have concurred in accordance with the procedures established by the Committee, shall not come into force for any Signatory until it has been accepted by such Signatory.

9.6 *Withdrawal*

9.6.1   Any Signatory may withdraw from this Agreement. The withdrawal shall take effect upon the expiration of twelve months from the day on which written notice of withdrawal is received by the Director-General to the CONTRACTING PARTIES to the GATT. Any Signatory may upon such notification request an immediate meeting of the Committee.

9.7 *Non-Application of this Agreement Between Particular Signatories*

9.7.1   This Agreement shall not apply as between any two Signatories if either of the Signatories, at the time either accepts or accedes to this Agreement, does not consent to such application.

9.8 *Annex*

9.8.1   The Annex to this Agreement forms an integral part thereof.

9.9 *Secretariat*

9.9.1   This Agreement shall be serviced by the GATT secretariat.

9.10 *Deposit*

9.10.1   This Agreement shall be deposited with the Director-General to the CONTRACTING PARTIES to the GATT who shall promptly furnish to each Signatory and each contracting party to the GATT a certified copy thereof and of each amendment thereto pursuant to Article 9.5 and a notification of each acceptance thereof or accession thereto pursuant to Article 9.1, or each withdrawal therefrom pursuant to Article 9.6.

9.11 *Registration*

9.11.1   This Agreement shall be registered in accordance with the provisions of Article 102 of the Charter of the United Nations.

Done at Geneva this twelfth day of April nineteen hundred and seventy-nine in a single copy, in the English and French languages, each text being authentic, except as otherwise specified with respect to the various lists in the Annex. [1]

ANNEX

PRODUCT COVERAGE

Signatories agree that products classified for customs purposes under their respective tariff headings listed below [2] shall be accorded duty-free or duty-exempt treatment, if such products are for use in a civil aircraft and incorporation therein, in the course of its manufacture, repair, maintenance, rebuilding, modification or conversion.

These products shall not include:

— an incomplete or unfinished product, unless it has the essential characteristics of a complete or finished civil aircraft part, component, sub-assembly or item of equipment. [3]

— materials in any form (e.g., sheets, plates, profile shapes, strips, bars, pipes, tubes, or other shapes) unless they have been cut to size or shape or shaped for incorporation in civil aircraft. [3]

— raw materials and consumable goods.

---

[1] The lists are not reproduced.

[2] The product lists are not reproduced.

[3] E.g., an article which has a civil aircraft manufacturer's parts number.

INTERNATIONAL DAIRY ARRANGEMENT

PREAMBLE

Recognizing the importance of milk and dairy products to the economy of many countries [1] in terms of production, trade and consumption;

Recognizing the need, in the mutual interests of producers and consumers, and of exporters and importers, to avoid surpluses and shortages, and to maintain prices at an equitable level;

Noting the diversity and interdependence of dairy products;

Noting the situation in the dairy products market, which is characterized by very wide fluctuations and the proliferation of export and import measures;

Considering that improved co-operation in the dairy products sector contributes to the attainment of the objectives of expansion and liberalization of world trade, and the implementation of the principles and objectives concerning developing countries agreed upon in the Tokyo Declaration of Ministers dated 14 September 1973 concerning the Multilateral Trade Negotiations;

Determined to respect the principles and objectives of the General Agreement on Tariffs and Trade (hereinafter referred to as " General Agreement " or " GATT ") [2] and, in carrying out the aims of this Arrangement, effectively to implement the principles and objectives agreed upon in the said Tokyo Declaration;

The participants to the present Arrangement have, through their representatives, agreed as follows:

---

[1] In this Arrangement and in the Protocols annexed thereto, the term " country " is deemed to include the European Economic Community.

[2] This preambular provision applies only among participants that are contracting parties to the GATT.

PART ONE

GENERAL PROVISIONS

Article I

Objectives

The objectives of this Arrangement shall be, in accordance with the principles and objectives agreed upon in the Tokyo Declaration of Ministers dated 14 September 1973 concerning the Multilateral Trade Negotiations,

— to achieve the expansion and ever greater liberalization of world trade in dairy products under market conditions as stable as possible, on the basis of mutual benefit to exporting and importing countries;

— to further the economic and social development of developing countries.

Article II

Product Coverage

1. This Arrangement applies to the dairy products sector. For the purpose of this Arrangement, the term " dairy products " is deemed to include the following products, as defined in the Customs Co-operation Council Nomenclature:

	CCCN
(a) Milk and cream, fresh, not concentrated or sweetened	04.01
(b) Milk and cream, preserved, concentrated or sweetened	04.02
(c) Butter	04.03
(d) Cheese and curd	04.04
(e) Casein	ex 35.01

2. The International Dairy Products Council established in terms of Article VII: 1(a) of this Arrangement (hereinafter referred to as the Council) may decide that the Arrangement is to apply to other products in which dairy products referred to in paragraph 1 of this Article have been incorporated if it deems their inclusion necessary for the implementation of the objectives and provisions of this Arrangement.

Article III

Information

1.   The participants agree to provide regularly and promptly to the Council the information required to permit it to monitor and assess the overall situation of the world market for dairy products and the world market situation for each individual dairy product.

2.   Participating developing countries shall furnish the information available to them. In order that these participants may improve their data collection mechanisms, developed participants, and any developing participants able to do so, shall consider sympathetically any request to them for technical assistance.

3.   The information that the participants undertake to provide pursuant to paragraph 1 of this Article, according to the modalities that the Council shall establish, shall include data on past performance, current situation and outlook regarding production, consumption, prices, stocks and trade, including transactions other than normal commercial transactions, in respect of the products referred to in Article II of this Arrangement, and any other information deemed necessary by the Council. Participants shall also provide information on their domestic policies and trade measures, and on their bilateral, plurilateral or multilateral commitments, in the dairy sector and shall make known, as early as possible, any changes in such policies and measures that are likely to affect international trade in dairy products. The provisions of this paragraph shall not require any participant to disclose confidential information which would impede law enforcement or otherwise be contrary to the public interest or would prejudice the legitimate commercial interests of particular enterprises, public or private.

> *Note*: It is understood that under the provisions of this Article, the Council instructs the secretariat to draw up, and keep up to date, an inventory of all measures affecting trade in dairy products, including commitments resulting from bilateral, plurilateral and multilateral negotiations.

Article IV

Functions of the International Dairy Products Council and Co-operation between the Participants to this Arrangement

1.   The Council shall meet in order to:
   (*a*) make an evaluation of the situation in and outlook for the world market for dairy products, on the basis of a status report prepared

by the secretariat with the documentation furnished by participants in accordance with Article III of this Arrangement, information arising from the operation of the Protocols covered by Article VI of this Arrangement, and any other information available to it;

(*b*) review the functioning of this Arrangement.

2. If after an evaluation of the world market situation and outlook, referred to in paragraph 1(*a*) of this Article, the Council finds that a serious market disequilibrium, or threat of such a disequilibrium, which affects or may affect international trade, is developing for dairy products in general or for one or more products, the Council will proceed to identify, taking particular account of the situation of developing countries, possible solutions for consideration by governments.

3. Depending on whether the Council considers that the situation defined in paragraph 2 of this Article is temporary or more durable, the measures referred to in paragraph 2 of this Article could include short-, medium- or long-term measures to contribute to improve the overall situation of the world market.

4. When considering measures that could be taken pursuant to paragraphs 2 and 3 of this Article, due account shall be taken of the special and more favourable treatment, to be provided for developing countries, where this is feasible and appropriate.

5. Any participant may raise before the Council any matter [3] affecting this Arrangement, *inter alia*, for the same purposes provided for in paragraph 2 of this Article. Each participant shall promptly afford adequate opportunity for consultation regarding such matter [1] affecting this Arrangement.

6. If the matter affects the application of the specific provisions of the Protocols annexed to this Arrangement, any participant which considers that its trade interests are being seriously threatened and which is unable to reach a mutually satisfactory solution with the other participant or participants concerned, may request the Chairman of the Committee for the relevant Protocol established under Article VII: 2(*a*) of this Arrangement, to convene a special meeting of the Committee on an urgent basis so as to determine as rapidly as possible, and within four working days if requested, any measures which may be required to meet the situation. If a satisfactory

---

[1] It is confirmed that the term "matter" in this paragraph includes any matter which is covered by multilateral agreements negotiated within the framework of the Multilateral Trade Negotiations, in particular those bearing on export and import measures. It is further confirmed that the provisions of Article IV:5 and this footnote are without prejudice to the rights and obligations of the parties to such agreements.

solution cannot be reached, the Council shall, at the request of the Chairman of the Committee for the relevant Protocol, meet within a period of not more than fifteen days to consider the matter with a view to facilitating a satisfactory solution.

Article V

Food Aid and Transactions other than Normal Commercial Transactions

1. The participants agree:

    (*a*) In co-operation with FAO and other interested organizations, to foster recognition of the value of dairy products in improving nutritional levels and of ways and means through which they may be made available for the benefit of developing countries.

    (*b*) In accordance with the objectives of this Arrangement, to furnish, within the limits of their possibilities, dairy products to developing countries by way of food aid. Participants should notify the Council in advance each year, as far as practicable, of the scale, quantities and destinations of their proposed contributions of such food aid. Participants should also give, if possible, prior notification to the Council of any proposed amendments to the notified programme. It would be understood that contributions could be made bilaterally or through joint projects or through multilateral programmes, particularly the World Food Programme.

    (*c*) Recognizing the desirability of harmonizing their efforts in this field, as well as the need to avoid harmful interference with normal patterns of production, consumption and international trade, to exchange views in the Council on their arrangements for the supply and requirements of dairy products as food aid or on concessional terms.

2. Donated exports to developing countries, exports destined for relief purposes or welfare purposes in developing countries, and other transactions which are not normal commercial transactions shall be effected in accordance with the FAO "Principles of Surplus Disposal and Consultative Obligations". Consequently, the Council shall co-operate closely with the Consultative Sub-Committee on Surplus Disposal.

3. The Council shall, in accordance with conditions and modalities that it will establish, upon request, discuss, and consult on, all transactions other than normal commercial transactions and other than those covered by the Agreement on Interpretation and Application of Articles VI, XVI and XXIII of the General Agreement on Tariffs and Trade.

PART TWO

Article VI

Protocols

1.   Without prejudice to the provisions of Articles I to V of this Arrangement, the products listed below shall be subject to the provisions of the Protocols annexed to this Arrangement:

Annex I

— *Protocol Regarding Certain Milk Powders*
Milk powder and cream powder, excluding whey powder

Annex II

— *Protocol Regarding Milk Fat*
Milk fat

Annex III

— *Protocol Regarding Certain Cheeses*
Certain cheeses

PART THREE

Article VII

Administration of the Arrangement

1.   *International Dairy Products Council*

   (*a*) An International Dairy Products Council shall be established within the framework of the GATT. The Council shall comprise representatives of all participants to the Arrangement and shall carry out all the functions which are necessary to implement the provisions of the Arrangement. The Council shall be serviced by the GATT secretariat. The Council shall establish its own rules of procedure.

(b) *Regular and special meetings*

The Council shall normally meet at least twice each year. However, the Chairman may call a special meeting of the Council either on his own initiative, at the request of the Committees established under paragraph 2(*a*) of this Article, or at the request of a participant to this Arrangement.

(c) *Decisions*

The Council shall reach its decisions by consensus. The Council shall be deemed to have decided on a matter submitted for its consideration if no member of the Council formally objects to the acceptance of a proposal.

(d) *Co-operation with other organizations*

The Council shall make whatever arrangements are appropriate for consultation or co-operation with intergovernmental and non-governmental organizations.

(e) *Admission of observers*

(i) The Council may invite any non-participating country to be represented at any meeting as an observer.

(ii) The Council may also invite any of the organizations referred to in paragraph 1(*d*) of this Article to attend any meeting as an observer.

2. *Committees*

(a) The Council shall establish a Committee to carry out all the functions which are necessary to implement the provisions of the Protocol Regarding Certain Milk Powders, a Committee to carry out all the functions which are necessary to implement the provisions of the Protocol Regarding Milk Fat and a Committee to carry out all the functions which are necessary to implement the provisions of the Protocol Regarding Certain Cheeses. Each of these Committees shall comprise representatives of all participants to the relevant Protocol. The Committees shall be serviced by the GATT secretariat. They shall report to the Council on the exercise of their functions.

(b) *Examination of the market situation*

The Council shall make the necessary arrangements, determining the modalities for the information to be furnished under Article III of this Arrangement, so that

— the Committee of the Protocol Regarding Certain Milk Powders may keep under constant review the situation in and the evolution of the international market for the products covered by this Protocol, and the conditions under which the provisions of this Protocol are applied by participants, taking into account the evolution of prices in international trade in each of the other dairy products having implications for the trade in products covered by this Protocol;

— the Committee of the Protocol Regarding Milk Fat may keep under constant review the situation in and the evolution of the international market for the products covered by this Protocol, and the conditions under which the provisions of this Protocol are applied by participants, taking into account the evolution of prices in international trade in each of the other dairy products having implications for the trade in products covered by this Protocol;

— the Committee of the Protocol Regarding Certain Cheeses may keep under constant review the situation in and the evolution of the international market for the products covered by this Protocol, and the conditions under which the provisions of this Protocol are applied by participants, taking into account the evolution of prices in international trade in each of the other dairy products having implications for the trade in products covered by this Protocol.

(c) *Regular and special meetings*

Each Committee shall normally meet at least once each quarter. However, the Chairman of each Committee may call a special meeting of the Committee on his own initiative or at the request of any participant.

(d) *Decisions*

Each Committee shall reach its decisions by consensus. A committee shall be deemed to have decided on a matter submitted for its consideration if no member of the Committee formally objects to the acceptance of a proposal.

PART FOUR

Article VIII

Final Provisions

1. *Acceptance* [1]

(*a*) This Arrangement is open for acceptance, by signature or otherwise, by governments members of the United Nations, or of one of its specialized agencies and by the European Economic Community.

(*b*) Any government [2] accepting this Arrangement may at the time of acceptance make a reservation with regard to its acceptance of any of the Protocols annexed to the Arrangement. This reservation is subject to the approval of the participants.

(*c*) This Arrangement shall be deposited with the Director-General to the CONTRACTING PARTIES to the GATT who shall promptly furnish a certified copy thereof and a notification of each acceptance thereof to each participant. The texts of this Arrangement in the English, French and Spanish languages shall all be equally authentic.

(*d*) Acceptance of this Arrangement shall carry denunciation of the Arrangement Concerning Certain Dairy Products, done at Geneva on 12 January 1970 which entered into force on 14 May 1970, for participants having accepted that Arrangement and denunciation of the Protocol Relating to Milk Fat, done at Geneva on 2 April 1973 which entered into force on 14 May 1973, for participants having accepted that Protocol. Such denunciation shall take effect on the date of entry into force of this Arrangement.

2. *Provisional application*

Any government may deposit with the Director-General to the CONTRACTING PARTIES to the GATT a declaration of provisional application of this Arrangement. Any government depositing such a declaration shall provisionally apply this Arrangement and be provisionally regarded as participating in this Arrangement.

---

[1] The terms " acceptance " or " accepted " as used in this Article include the completion of any domestic procedures necessary to implement the provisions of this Arrangement.

[2] For the purpose of this Arrangement, the term " government " is deemed to include the competent authorities of the European Economic Community.

3. *Entry into force*

   (a) This Arrangement shall enter into force, for those participants having accepted it, on 1 January 1980. For participants accepting this Arrangement after that date, it shall be effective from the date of their acceptance.

   (b) The validity of contracts entered into before the date of entry into force of this Arrangement is not affected by this Arrangement.

4. *Validity*

This Arrangement shall remain in force for three years. The duration of this Arrangement shall be extended for further periods of three years at a time, unless the Council, at least eighty days prior to each date of expiry, decides otherwise.

5. *Amendment*

Except where provision for modification is made elsewhere in this Arrangement the Council may recommend an amendment to the provisions of this Arrangement. The proposed amendment shall enter into force upon acceptance by the governments of all participants.

6. *Relationship between the Arrangement and the Annexes*

The following shall be deemed to be an integral part of this Arrangement, subject to the provisions of paragraph 1(b) of this Article:

— the Protocols mentioned in Article VI of this Arrangement and contained in its Annexes I, II and III;

— the lists of reference points mentioned in Article 2 of the Protocol Regarding Certain Milk Powders, Article 2 of the Protocol Regarding Milk Fat, and Article 2 of the Protocol Regarding Certain Cheeses, contained in Annexes I(a), II(a) and III(a) respectively;

— the schedules of price differentials according to milk fat content mentioned in Article 3: 4, note 3 of the Protocol Regarding Certain Milk Powders and Article 3: 4, note 1 of the Protocol Regarding Milk Fat, contained in Annexes I(b) and II(b) respectively;

— the register of processes and control measures referred to in Article 3:5 of the Protocol Regarding Certain Milk Powders, contained in Annex Ic.

7. *Relationship between the Arrangement and the GATT*

Nothing in this Arrangement shall affect the rights and obligations of participants under the GATT.[1]

8. *Withdrawal*

    (*a*) Any participant may withdraw from this Arrangement. Such withdrawal shall take effect upon the expiration of sixty days from the day on which written notice of withdrawal is received by the Director-General to the CONTRACTING PARTIES to the GATT.

    (*b*) Subject to such conditions as may be agreed upon by the participants, any participant may withdraw from any of the Protocols annexed to this Arrangement. Such withdrawal shall take effect upon the expiration of sixty days from the day on which written notice of withdrawal is received by the Director-General to the CONTRACTING PARTIES to the GATT.

Done at Geneva this twelfth day of April nineteen hundred and seventy-nine.

ANNEX I

PROTOCOL REGARDING CERTAIN MILK POWDERS

PART ONE

Article 1

Product Coverage

1. This Protocol applies to milk powder and cream powder falling under CCCN heading No. 04.02, excluding whey powder.

---

[1] This provision applies only among participants that are contracting parties to the GATT.

PART TWO

Article 2

Pilot Products

1. For the purpose of this Protocol, minimum export prices shall be established for the pilot products of the following description:

(a) Designation: *Skimmed milk powder*
Milk fat content: less than or equal to 1.5 per cent by weight
Water content: less than or equal to 5 per cent by weight

(b) Designation: *Whole milk powder*
Milk fat content: 26 per cent by weight
Water content: less than or equal to 5 per cent by weight

(c) Designation: *Buttermilk po..der* [1]
Milk fat content: less than or equal to 11 per cent by weight
Water content: less than or equal to 5 per cent by weight

Packaging: in packages normally used in the trade, of a net content by weight of not less than 25 kgs., or 50 lbs., as appropriate

Terms of sale: f.o.b. ocean-going vessels from the exporting country or free-at-frontier exporting country.
By derogation from this provision, reference points are designated for the countries listed in Annex I(a). [2] The Committee established in pursuance of Article VII:2(a) of the Arrangement (hereinafter referred to as the Committee) may amend the contents of that Annex.
Prompt payment against documents.

Article 3

Minimum Prices

Level and observance of minimum prices

1. Participants undertake to take the steps necessary to ensure that the export prices of the products defined in Article 2 of this Protocol shall not be less than the minimum prices applicable under the present Protocol. If the products are exported in the form of goods in which they have been incorporated, participants shall take the steps necessary to avoid the circumvention of the price provisions of this Protocol.

2. (a) The minimum price levels set out in the present Article take account, in particular, of the current market situation, dairy prices in producing participants, the need to ensure an appropriate relationship between the

---

[1] Derived from the manufacture of butter and anhydrous milk fat.

[2] Annex I(a) is not reproduced.

minimum prices established in the Protocols to the present Arrangement, the need to ensure equitable prices to consumers, and the desirability of maintaining a minimum return to the most efficient producers in order to ensure stability of supply over the longer term.

(b) The minimum prices provided for in paragraph 1 of the present Article applicable at the date of entry into force of this Protocol are fixed at:

(i) US$425 per metric ton for the skimmed milk powder defined in Article 2 of this Protocol.

(ii) US$725 per metric ton for the whole milk powder defined in Article 2 of this Protocol.

(iii) US$425 per metric ton for the buttermilk powder defined in Article 2 of this Protocol.

3. (a) The levels of the minimum prices specified in the present Article can be modified by the Committee, taking into account, on the one hand, the results of the operation of the Protocol and, on the other hand, the evolution of the situation of the international market.

(b) The levels of the minimum prices specified in the present Article shall be subject to review at least once a year by the Committee. The Committee shall meet in September of each year for this purpose. In undertaking this review the Committee shall take account in particular, to the extent relevant and necessary, of costs faced by producers, other relevant economic factors of the world market, the need to maintain a long-term minimum return to the most economic producers, the need to maintain stability of supply and to ensure acceptable prices to consumers, and the current market situation and shall have regard to the desirability of improving the relationship between the levels of the minimum prices set out in paragraph 2(b) of the present Article and the dairy support levels in the major producing participants.

Adjustment of minimum prices

4. If the products actually exported differ from the pilot products in respect of the fat content, packaging or terms of sale, the minimum prices shall be adjusted so as to protect the minimum prices established in this Protocol for the products specified in Article 2 of this Protocol according to the following provisions:

Milk fat content:

If the milk fat content of the milk powders described in Article 1 of the present Protocol excluding buttermilk powder [1] differs from the milk fat content of the pilot products as defined in Article 2:1(a) and (b) of the present Protocol, then for each full percentage point of milk fat as from 2 per cent, there shall be an upward adjustment of the minimum price in proportion to the difference between the minimum prices established for the pilot products defined in Article 2:1(a) and (b) of the present Protocol. [2]

---

[1] As defined in Article 2:1(c) of this Protocol.

[2] See Annex I(b), "Schedule of price differentials according to milk fat content". (Annex I(b) is not reproduced).

Packaging:

> If the products are offered otherwise than in packages normally used in the trade, of a net content by weight of not less than 25 kgs. or 50 lbs., as appropriate, the minimum prices shall be adjusted so as to reflect the difference in the cost of packaging from the type of package specified above.

Terms of sale:

> If sold on terms other than f.o.b. from the exporting country or free-at-frontier exporting country [1], the minimum prices shall be calculated on the basis of the minimum f.o.b. prices specified in paragraph 2(*b*) of this Article, plus the real and justified costs of the services provided; if the terms of the sale include credit, this shall be charged for at the prevailing commercial rates in the country concerned.

Exports and imports of skimmed milk powder and buttermilk powder for purposes of animal feed

5.   By derogation from the provisions of paragraphs 1 to 4 of this Article participants may, under the conditions defined below, export or import, as the case may be, skimmed milk powder and buttermilk powder for purposes of animal feed at prices below the minimum prices provided for in this Protocol for these products. Participants may make use of this possibility only to the extent that they subject the products exported or imported to the processes and control measures which will be applied in the country of export or destination so as to ensure that the skimmed milk powder and buttermilk powder thus exported or imported are used exclusively for animal feed. These processes and control measures shall have been approved by the Committee and recorded in a register established by it. [2] Participants wishing to make use of the provisions of this paragraph shall give advance notification of their intention to do so to the Committee which shall meet, at the request of a participant, to examine the market situation. The participants shall furnish the necessary information concerning their transactions in respect of skimmed milk powder and buttermilk powder for purposes of animal feed, so that the Committee may follow developments in this sector and periodically make forecasts concerning the evolution of this trade.

Special conditions of sales

6.   Participants undertake within the limit of their institutional possibilities to ensure that practices such as those referred to in Article 4 of this Protocol do not have the effect of directly or indirectly bringing the export prices of the products subject to the minimum price provisions below the agreed minimum prices.

---

[1] See Article 2.

[2] See Annex I(*c*), " Register of Processes and Control Measures ". It is understood that exporters would be permitted to ship skimmed milk powder and buttermilk powder for animal feed purposes in an unaltered state to importers which have had their processes and control measures inserted in the Register. In this case, exporters would inform the Committee of their intention to ship unaltered skimmed milk powder and/or buttermilk powder for animal feed purposes to those importers which have their processes and control measures registered. (Annex I(*c*) is not reproduced).

Field of application

7.   For each participant, this Protocol is applicable to exports of the products specified in Article 1 of this Protocol manufactured or repacked inside its own customs territory.

Transactions other than normal commercial transactions

8.   The provisions of paragraphs 1 to 7 of this Article shall not be regarded as applying to donated exports to developing countries or to exports destined for relief purposes or food-related development purposes or welfare purposes in developing countries.

Article 4

Provision of Information

1.   In cases where prices in international trade of the products covered by Article 1 of this Protocol are approaching the minimum prices mentioned in Article 3:2(*b*) of this Protocol, and without prejudice to the provisions of Article III of the Arrangement, participants shall notify to the Committee all the relevant elements for evaluating their own market situation and, in particular, credit or loan practices, twinning with other products, barter or three-sided transactions, refunds or rebates, exclusivity contracts, packaging costs and details of the packaging, so that the Committee can make a verification.

Article 5

Obligations of Exporting Participants

1.   Exporting participants agree to use their best endeavours, in accordance with their institutional possibilities, to supply on a priority basis the normal commercial requirements of developing importing participants, especially those used for food-related development purposes and welfare purposes.

Article 6

Co-operation of Importing Participants

1.   Participants which import products covered by Article 1 of this Protocol undertake in particular:

   (*a*)   to co-operate in implementing the minimum prices objective of this Protocol and to ensure, as far as possible, that the products covered by Article 1 of this Protocol are not imported at less than the appropriate customs valuation equivalent to the prescribed minimum prices;

   (*b*)   without prejudice to the provisions of Article III of the Arrangement and Article 4 of this Protocol, to supply information concerning imports of products covered by Article 1 of this Protocol from non-participants;

(c) to consider sympathetically proposals for appropriate remedial action if imports at prices inconsistent with the minimum prices threaten the operation of this Protocol.

2. Paragraph 1 of this Article shall not apply to imports of skimmed milk powder and buttermilk powder for purposes of animal feed, provided that such imports are subject to the measures and procedures provided for in Article 3:5 of this Protocol.

PART THREE

Article 7

Derogations

1. Upon request by a participant, the Committee shall have the authority to grant derogations from the provisions of Article 3, paragraphs 1 to 5 of this Protocol in order to remedy difficulties which observance of minimum prices could cause certain participants. The Committee shall pronounce on such a request within three months from the date of the request.

Article 8

Emergency Action

1. Any participant, which considers that its interests are seriously endangered by a country not bound by this Protocol, can request the Chairman of the Committee to convene an emergency meeting of the Committee within two working days to determine and decide whether measures would be required to meet the situation. If such a meeting cannot be arranged within the two working days and the commercial interests of the participant concerned are likely to be materially prejudiced, that participant may take unilateral action to safeguard its position, on the condition that any other participants likely to be affected are immediately notified. The Chairman of the Committee shall also be formally advised immediately notified. The Chairman of the Committee shall also be formally advised immediately of the full circumstances of the case and shall be requested to call a special meeting of the Committee at the earliest possible moment.

ANNEX II

PROTOCOL REGARDING MILK FAT

PART ONE

Article 1

Product Coverage

1. This Protocol applies to milk fat falling under CCCN heading No. 04.03, having a milk fat content equal to or greater than 50 per cent by weight.

PART TWO

Article 2

Pilot Products

1. For the purpose of this Protocol, minimum export prices shall be established for the pilot products of the following descriptions:

(*a*) Designation: *Anhydrous milk fat*
Milk fat content: 99.5 per cent by weight

(*b*) Designation: *Butter*
Milk fat content: 80 per cent by weight

Packaging:
In packages normally used in the trade, of a net content by weight of not less than 25 kgs. or 50 lbs, as appropriate.

Terms of sale:
F.o.b. from the exporting country or free-at-frontier exporting country.
By derogation from this provision, reference points are designated for the countries listed in Annex II(*a*). [1] The Committee established in pursuance of Article VII:2(a) of the Arrangement (hereinafter referred to as the Committee) may amend the contents of that Annex.
Prompt payment against documents.

---

[1] Annex II(*a*) is not reproduced.

Article 3

Minimum Prices

Level and observance of minimum prices

1. Participants undertake to take the steps necessary to ensure that the export prices of the products defined in Article 2 of this Protocol shall not be less than the minimum prices applicable under the present Protocol. If the products are exported in the form of goods in which they have been incorporated, participants shall take the steps necessary to avoid the circumvention of the price provisions of this Protocol.

2. (a) The minimum price levels set out in the present Article take account, in particular, of the current market situation, dairy prices in producing participants, the need to ensure an appropriate relationship between the minimum prices established in the Protocols to the present Arrangement, the need to ensure equitable prices to consumers, and the desirability of maintaining a minimum return to the most efficient producers in order to ensure stability of supply over the longer term.

   (b) The minimum prices provided for in paragraph 1 of the present Article applicable at the date of entry into force of this Protocol are fixed at:

   (i) US$1,100 per metric ton for the anhydrous milk fat defined in Article 2 of this Protocol.

   (ii) US$925 per metric ton for the butter defined in Article 2 of this Protocol.

3. (a) The levels of the minimum prices specified in the present Article can be modified by the Committee, taking into account, on the one hand, the results of the operation of the Protocol and, on the other hand, the evolution of the situation of the international market.

   (b) The levels of the minimum prices specified in the present Article shall be subject to review at least once a year by the Committee. The Committee shall meet in September of each year for this purpose. In undertaking this review the Committee shall take account in particular, to the extent relevant and necessary, of costs faced by producers, other relevant economic factors of the world market, the need to maintain a long-term minimum return to the most economic producers, the need to maintain stability of supply and to ensure acceptable prices to consumers, and the current market situation and shall have regard to the desirability of improving the relationship between the levels of the minimum prices set out in paragraph 2(b) of the present Article and the dairy support levels in the major producing participants.

Adjustment of minimum prices

4. If the products actually exported differ from the pilot products in respect of the fat content, packaging or terms of sale, the minimum prices shall be adjusted

so as to protect the minimum prices established in this Protocol for the products specified in Article 2 of this Protocol according to the following provisions:

Milk fat content:

If the milk fat content of the product defined in Article 1 of the present Protocol differs from the milk fat content of the pilot products as defined in Article 2 of the present Protocol then, if the milk fat content is equal to or greater than 82 per cent or less than 80 per cent, the minimum price of this product shall be, for each full percentage point by which the milk fat content is more than or less than 80 per cent, increased or reduced in proportion to the difference between the minimum prices established for the pilot products defined in Article 2 of the present Protocol.

Packaging:

If the products are offered otherwise than in packages normally used in the trade, of a net content by weight of not less than 25 kgs. or 50 lbs., as appropriate, the minimum prices shall be adjusted so as to reflect the difference in the cost of packaging from the type of package specified above.

Terms of sale:

If sold on terms other than f.o.b. from the exporting country or free-at-frontier exporting country [1], the minimum prices shall be calculated on the basis of the minimum f.o.b. prices specified in paragraph 2(b) of this Article, plus the real and justified costs of the services provided; if the terms of the sale include credit, this shall be charged for at the prevailing commercial rates in the country concerned.

Special conditions of sales

5.   Participants undertake within the limit of their institutional possibilities to ensure that practices such as those referred to in Article 4 of this Protocol do not have the effect of directly or indirectly bringing the export prices of the products subject to the minimum price provisions below the agreed minimum prices.

Field of application

6.   For each participant, this Protocol is applicable to exports of the products specified in Article 1 of this Protocol manufactured or repacked inside its own customs territory.

Transactions other than normal commercial transactions

7.   The provisions of paragraphs 1 to 6 of this Article shall not be regarded as applying to donated exports to developing countries or to exports destined for relief purposes or food-related development purposes or welfare purposes in developing countries.

---

[1] See Article 2.

Article 4

Provision of Information

1. In cases where prices in international trade of the products covered by Article 1 of this Protocol are approaching the minimum prices mentioned in Article 3:2(*b*) of this Protocol, and without prejudice to the provisions of Article III of the Arrangement, participants shall notify to the Committee all the relevant elements for evaluating their own market-situation and, in particular, credit or loan practices, twinning with other products, barter or three-sided transactions, refunds or rebates, exclusivity contracts, packaging costs and details of the packaging, so that the Committee can make a verification.

Article 5

Obligations of Exporting Participants

1. Exporting participants agree to use their best endeavours, in accordance with their institutional possibilities, to supply on a priority basis the normal commercial requirements of developing importing participants, especially those used for food-related development purposes and welfare purposes.

Article 6

Co-operation of Importing Participants

1. Participants which import products covered by Article 1 of this Protocol undertake in particular:

(*a*) to co-operate in implementing the minimum prices objective of this Protocol and to ensure, as far as possible, that the products covered by Article 1 of this Protocol are not imported at less than the appropriate customs valuation equivalent to the prescribed minimum prices;

(*b*) without prejudice to the provisions of Article III of the Arrangement and Article 4 of this Protocol, to supply information concerning imports of products covered by Article 1 of this Protocol from non-participants;

(*c*) to consider sympathetically proposals for appropriate remedial action if imports at prices inconsistent with the minimum prices threaten the operation of this Protocol.

PART THREE

Article 7

Derogations

1. Upon request by a participant, the Committee shall have the authority to grant derogations from the provisions of Article 3, paragraphs 1 to 4 of this Protocol in order to remedy difficulties which observance of minimum prices could cause certain participants. The Committee shall pronounce on such a request within three months from the date of the request.

Article 8

Emergency Action

1. Any participant, which considers that its interests are seriously endangered by a country not bound by this Protocol, can request the Chairman of the Committee to convene an emergency meeting of the Committee within two working days to determine and decide whether measures would be required to meet the situation. If such a meeting cannot be arranged within the two working days and the commercial interests of the participant concerned are likely to be materially prejudiced, that participant may take unilateral action to safeguard its position, on the condition that any other participants likely to be affected are immediately notified. The Chairman of the Committee shall also be formally advised immediately of the full circumstances of the case and shall be requested to call a special meeting of the Committee at the earliest possible moment.

ANNEX III

PROTOCOL REGARDING CERTAIN CHEESES

PART ONE

Article 1

Product Coverage

1. This Protocol applies to cheeses falling under CCCN heading No. 04.04, having a fat content in dry matter, by weight, equal to or more than 45 per cent and a dry matter content, by weight, equal to or more than 50 per cent.

PART TWO

Article 2

Pilot Product

1. For the purpose of this Protocol, a minimum export price shall be established for the pilot product of the following description:

Designation: *Cheese*

Packaging:

> In packages normally used in the trade of a net content by weight of not less than 20 kgs. or 40 lbs., as appropriate.

Terms of sale:

> F.o.b. from the exporting country or free-at-frontier exporting country.

> By derogation from this provision, reference points are designated for the countries listed in Annex III(a). [1] The Committee established in pursuance of Article VII:2(a) of the Arrangement (hereinafter referred to as the Committee) may amend the contents of that Annex.

> Prompt payment against documents.

Article 3

Minimum Price

Level and observance of minimum price

1. Participants undertake to take the steps necessary to ensure that the export prices of the products defined in Articles 1 and 2 of this Protocol shall not be less than the minimum price applicable under the present Protocol. If the products are exported in the form of goods in which they have been incorporated, participants shall take the steps necessary to avoid the circumvention of the price provisions of this Protocol.

2. (a) The minimum price level set out in the present Article takes account, in particular, of the current market situation, dairy prices in producing participants, the need to ensure an appropriate relationship between the minimum prices established in the Protocols to the present Arrangement, the need to ensure equitable prices to consumers, and the desirability of maintaining a minimum return to the most efficient producers in order to ensure stability of supply over the longer term.

---

[1] Annex III(a) is not reproduced.

(*b*) The minimum price provided for in paragraph 1 of the present Article applicable at the date of entry into force of this Protocol is fixed at US$800 per metric ton.

3. (*a*) The level of the minimum price specified in the present Article can be modified by the Committee, taking into account, on the one hand, the results of the operation of the Protocol and, on the other hand, the evolution of the situation of the international market.

(*b*) The level of the minimum price specified in the present Article shall be subject to review at least once a year by the Committee. The Committee shall meet in September of each year for this purpose. In undertaking this review the Committee shall take account in particular, to the extent relevant and necessary, of costs faced by producers, other relevant economic factors of the world market, the need to maintain a long-term minimum return to the most economic producers, the need to maintain stability of supply and to ensure acceptable prices to consumers, and the current market situation and shall have regard to the desirability of improving the relationship between the level of the minimum price set out in paragraph 2(*b*) of the present Article and the dairy support levels in the major producing participants.

Adjustment of minimum price

4. If the products actually exported differ from the pilot product in respect of the packaging or terms of sale, the minimum price shall be adjusted so as to protect the minimum price established in this Protocol, according to the following provisions:

Packaging:

If the products are offered otherwise than in packages as specified in Article 2, the minimum price shall be adjusted so as to reflect the difference in the cost of packaging from the type of package specified above.

Terms of sale:

If sold on terms other than f.o.b. from the exporting country or free-at-frontier exporting country [1], the minimum price shall be calculated on the basis of the minimum f.o.b. price specified in paragraph 2(*b*) of this Article, plus the real and justified costs of the services provided; if the terms of the sale include credit, this shall be charged for at the prevailing commercial rates in the country concerned.

Special conditions of sale

5. Participants undertake within the limit of their institutional possibilities to ensure that practices such as those referred to in Article 4 of this Protocol do not have the effect of directly or indirectly bringing the export prices of the products subject to the minimum price provisions below the agreed minimum price.

---

[1] See Article 2.

Field of application

6. For each participant, this Protocol is applicable to exports of the products specified in Article 1 of this Protocol manufactured or repacked inside its own customs territory.

Transactions other than normal commercial transactions

7. The provisions of paragraphs 1 to 6 of this Article shall not be regarded as applying to donated exports to developing countries or to exports destined for relief purposes or food-related development purposes or welfare purposes in developing countries.

Article 4

Provision of Information

1. In cases where prices in international trade of the products covered by Article 1 of this Protocol are approaching the minimum price mentioned in Article 3:2(*b*) of this Protocol and without prejudice to the provisions of Article III of the Arrangement participants shall notify to the Committee all the relevant elements for evaluating their own market situation and, in particular, credit or loan practices twinning with other products, barter or three-sided transactions, refunds or rebates, exclusivity contracts, packaging costs and details of the packaging, so that the Committee can make a verification.

Article 5

Obligations of Exporting Participants

1. Exporting participants agree to use their best endeavours, in accordance with their institutional possibilities, to supply on a priority basis the normal commercial requirements of developing importing participants, especially those used for food-related development purposes and welfare purposes.

Article 6

Co-operation of Importing Participants

1. Participants which import products covered by Article 1 of this Protocol undertake in particular:

(*a*) to co-operate in implementing the minimum price objective of this Protocol and to ensure, as far as possible, that the products covered by Article 1 of this Protocol are not imported at less than the appropriate customs valuation equivalent to the prescribed minimum price;

(*b*) without prejudice to the provisions of Article III of the Arrangement and Article 4 of this Protocol, to supply information concerning imports of products covered by Article 1 of this Protocol from non-participants;

(*c*) to consider sympathetically proposals for appropriate remedial action if imports at prices inconsistent with the minimum price threaten the operation of this Protocol

PART THREE

Article 7

Derogations

1.   Upon request by a participant, the Committee shall have the authority to grant derogations from the provisions of Article 3, paragraphs 1 to 4 of this Protocol in order to remedy difficulties which observance of minimum prices could cause certain participants. The Committee shall pronounce on such a request within thirty days from the date of the request.

2.   The provisions of Article 3:1 to 4 shall not apply to exports, in exceptional circumstances, of small quantities of natural unprocessed cheese which would be below normal export quality as a result of deterioration or production faults. Participants exporting such cheese shall notify the GATT secretariat in advance of their intention to do so. Participants shall also notify the Committee quarterly of all sales of cheese effected under the provisions of this paragraph, specifying in respect of each transaction, the quantities, prices and destinations involved.

Article 8

Emergency Action

1.   Any participant, which considers that its interests are seriously endangered by a country not bound by this Protocol, can request the Chairman of the Committee to convene an emergency meeting of the Committee within two working days to determine and decide whether measures would be required to meet the situation. If such a meeting cannot be arranged within the two working days and the commercial interests of the participant concerned are likely to be materially prejudiced, that participant may take unilateral action to safeguard its position, on the condition that any other participants likely to be affected are immediately notified. The Chairman of the Committee shall also be formally advised immediately of the full circumstances of the case and shall be requested to call a special meeting of the Committee at the earliest possible moment.

ARRANGEMENT REGARDING BOVINE MEAT

PREAMBLE

Convinced that increased international co-operation should be carried out in such a way as to contribute to the achievement of greater liberalization, stability and expansion in international trade in meat and live animals;

Taking into account the need to avoid serious disturbances in international trade in bovine meat and live animals;

Recognizing the importance of production and trade in bovine meat and live animals for the economies of many countries, especially for certain developed and developing countries;

Mindful of their obligations to the principles and objectives of the General Agreement on Tariffs and Trade (hereinafter referred to as " General Agreement " or " GATT "); [1]

Determined, in carrying out the aims of this Arrangement to implement the principles and objectives agreed upon in the Tokyo Declaration of Ministers, dated 14 September 1973 concerning the Multilateral Trade Negotiations, in particular as concerns special and more favourable treatment for developing countries;

The participants in the present Arrangement have, through their representatives, agreed as follows:

PART ONE

GENERAL PROVISIONS

Article I

Objectives

The objectives of this Arrangement shall be:

(1) to promote the expansion, ever greater liberalization and stability of the international meat and livestock market by facilitating the progressive dismantling of obstacles and restrictions to world trade in bovine meat

---

[1] This provision applies only among GATT contracting parties.

and live animals, including those which compartmentalize this trade, and by improving the international framework of world trade to the benefit of both consumer and producer, importer and exporter;

(2) to encourage greater international co-operation in all aspects affecting the trade in bovine meat and live animals with a view in particular to greater rationalization and more efficient distribution of resources in the international meat economy;

(3) to secure additional benefits for the international trade of developing countries in bovine meat and live animals through an improvement in the possibilities for these countries to participate in the expansion of world trade in these products by means of *inter alia*:

(*a*) promoting long-term stability of prices in the context of an expanding world market for bovine meat and live animals; and

(*b*) promoting the maintenance and improvement of the earnings of developing countries that are exporters of bovine meat and live animals;

the above with a view thus to deriving additional earnings, by means of securing long-term stability of markets for bovine meat and live animals;

(4) to further expand trade on a competitive basis taking into account the traditional position of efficient producers.

Article II

Product Coverage

This Arrangement applies to bovine meat. For the purpose of this Arrangement, the term " bovine meat " is considered to include:

	CCCN
(*a*) Live bovine animals	01.02
(*b*) Meat and edible offals of bovine animals, fresh, chilled or frozen	ex 02.01
(*c*) Meat and edible offals of bovine animals, salted, in brine, dried or smoked	ex 02.06
(*d*) Other prepared or preserved meat or offal of bovine animals	ex 16.02

and any other product that may be added by the International Meat Council, as established under the terms of Article V of this Arrangement, in order to accomplish the objectives and provisions of this Arrangement.

Article III

Information and Market Monitoring

1. All participants agree to provide regularly and promptly to the Council, the information which will permit the Council to monitor and assess the overall situation of the world market for meat and the situation of the world market for each specific meat.

2. Participating developing countries shall furnish the information available to them. In order that these countries may improve their data collection mechanism, developed participants, and any developing participants able to do so, shall consider sympathetically any request to them for technical assistance.

3. The information that the participants undertake to provide pursuant to paragraph 1 of this Article, according to the modalities that the Council shall establish, shall include data on past performance and current situation and an assessment of the outlook regarding production (including the evolution of the composition of herds), consumption, prices, stocks of and trade in the products referred to in Article II, and any other information deemed necessary by the Council, in particular on competing products. Participants shall also provide information on their domestic policies and trade measures including bilateral and plurilateral commitments in the bovine sector, and shall notify as early as possible any changes in such policies and measures that are likely to affect international trade in live bovine animals and meat. The provisions of this paragraph shall not require any participant to disclose confidential information which would impede law enforcement or otherwise be contrary to the public interest or would prejudice the legitimate commercial interests of particular enterprises, public or private.

4. The secretariat of the Arrangement shall monitor variations in market data, in particular herd sizes, stocks, slaughterings and domestic and international prices, so as to permit early detection of the symptoms of any serious imbalance in the supply and demand situation. The secretariat shall keep the Council apprized of significant developments on world markets, as well as prospects for production, consumption, exports and imports.

> *Note:* It is understood that under the provisions of this Article, the Council instructs the secretariat to draw up, and keep up to date, an inventory of all measures affecting trade in bovine meat and live animals, including commitments resulting from bilateral, plurilateral and multilateral negotiations.

Article IV

*Functions of the International Meat Council
and Co-operation between the Participants to this Arrangement*

1. The Council shall meet in order to:

   (*a*) evaluate the world supply and demand situation and outlook on the basis of an interpretative analysis of the present situation and of probable developments drawn up by the secretariat of the Arrangement, on the basis of documentation provided in conformity with Article III of the present Arrangement, including that relating to the operation of domestic and trade policies and of any other information available to the secretariat;

   (*b*) proceed to a comprehensive examination of the functioning of the present Arrangement;

   (*c*) provide an opportunity for regular consultation on all matters affecting international trade in bovine meat.

2. If after evaluation of the world supply and demand situation referred to in paragraph 1 (*a*) of this Article, or after examination of all relevant information pursuant to paragraph 3 of Article III, the Council finds evidence of a serious imbalance or a threat thereof in the international meat market, the Council will proceed by consensus, taking into particular account the situation in developing countries, to identify, for consideration by governments, possible solutions to remedy the situation consistent with the principles and rules of GATT.

3. Depending on whether the Council considers that the situation defined in paragraph 2 of this Article is temporary or more durable, the measures referred to in paragraph 2 of this Article could include short-, medium-, or long-term measures taken by importers as well as exporters to contribute to improve the overall situation of the world market consistent with the objectives and aims of the Arrangement, in particular the expansion, ever greater liberalization, and stability of the international meat and livestock markets.

4. When considering the suggested measures pursuant to paragraphs 2 and 3 of this Article, due consideration shall be given to special and more favourable treatment to developing countries, where this is feasible and appropriate.

5. The participants undertake to contribute to the fullest possible extent to the implementation of the objectives of this Arrangement set forth in Article I. To this end, and consistent with the principles and rules of the

General Agreement, participants shall, on a regular basis, enter into the discussions provided in Article IV:1 (*c*) with a view to exploring the possibilities of achieving the objectives of the present Arrangement, in particular the further dismantling of obstacles to world trade in bovine meat and live animals. Such discussions should prepare the way for subsequent consideration of possible solutions of trade problems consistent with the rules and principles of the GATT, which could be jointly accepted by all the parties concerned, in a balanced context of mutual advantages.

6. Any participant may raise before the Council any matter [1] affecting this Arrangement, *inter alia*, for the same purposes provided for in paragraph 2 of this Article. The Council shall, at the request of a participant, meet within a period of not more than fifteen days to consider any matter [1] affecting the present Arrangement.

PART TWO

Article V

Administration of the Arrangement

1. *International Meat Council*

An International Meat Council shall be established within the framework of the GATT. The Council shall comprise representatives of all participants to the Arrangement and shall carry out all the functions which are necessary to implement the provisions of the Arrangement. The Council shall be serviced by the GATT secretariat. The Council shall establish its own rules of procedure, in particular the modalities for consultations provided for in Article IV.

2. *Regular and special meetings*

The Council shall normally meet at least twice each year. However the Chairman may call a special meeting of the Council either on his own, initiative, or at the request of a participant to this Arrangement.

---

[1] *Note:* It is confirmed that the term " matter " in this paragraph includes any matter which is covered by multilateral agreements negotiated within the framework of the Multilateral Trade Negotiations, in particular those bearing on export and import measures. It is further confirmed that the provisions of Article IV, paragraph 6, and this footnote are without prejudice to the rights and obligations of the Parties to such agreements.

3. Decisions

The Council shall reach its decisions by consensus. The Council shall be deemed to have decided on a matter submitted for its consideration if no member of the Council formally objects to the acceptance of a proposal.

4. Co-operation with other organizations

The Council shall make whatever arrangements are appropriate for consultation or co-operation with intergovernmental and non-governmental organizations.

5. Admission of observers

(a) The Council may invite any non-participating country to be represented at any of its meetings as an observer.

(b) The Council may also invite any of the organizations referred to in paragraph 4 of this Article to attend any of its meetings as an observer.

PART THREE

Article VI

Final Provisions

1. Acceptance [1]

(a) This Arrangement is open for acceptance, by signature or otherwise, by governments members of the United Nations, or of one of its specialized agencies and by the European Economic Community.

(b) Any government [2] accepting this Arrangement may at the time of acceptance make a reservation with regard to its acceptance of any of the provisions in the present Arrangement. This reservation is subject to the approval of the participants.

(c) This Arrangement shall be deposited with the Director-General to the CONTRACTING PARTIES to the GATT who shall promptly furnish a certified copy thereof and a notification of each acceptance thereof to each participant. The texts of this Arrangement in the English, French and Spanish languages shall all be equally authentic.

---

[1] The terms " acceptance " or " accepted " as used in this Article include the completion of any domestic procedures necessary to implement the provisions of this Arrangement.

[2] For the purpose of this Arrangement, the term " government " is deemed to include the competent authorities of the European Economic Community.

(*d*) The entry into force of this Arrangement shall entail the abolition of the International Meat Consultative Group.

2. *Provisional application*

Any government may deposit with the Director-General to the CONTRACTING PARTIES to the GATT a declaration of provisional application of this Arrangement. Any government depositing such a declaration shall provisionally apply this Arrangement and be provisionally regarded as participating in this Arrangement.

3. *Entry into force*

This Arrangement shall enter into force, for those participants having accepted it, on 1 January 1980. For participants accepting this Arrangement after that date, it shall be effective from the date of their acceptance.

4. *Validity*

This Arrangement shall remain in force for three years. The duration of this Arrangement shall be extended for further periods of three years at a time, unless the Council, at least eighty days prior to each date of expiry, decides otherwise.

5. *Amendment*

Except where provision for modification is made elsewhere in this Arrangement the Council may recommend an amendment to the provisions of this Arrangement. The proposed amendment shall enter into force upon acceptance by the governments of all participants.

6. *Relationship between the Arrangement and the GATT*

Nothing in this Arrangement shall affect the rights and obligations of participants under the GATT.[1]

7. *Withdrawal*

Any participant may withdraw from this Arrangement. Such withdrawal shall take effect upon the expiration of sixty days from the date on which written notice of withdrawal is received by the Director-General to the CONTRACTING PARTIES to the GATT.

---

[1] This provision applies only among GATT contracting parties.

DIFFERENTIAL AND MORE FAVOURABLE TREATMENT RECIPROCITY AND FULLER PARTICIPATION OF DEVELOPING COUNTRIES

Decision of 28 November 1979

Following negotiations within the framework of the Multilateral Trade Negotiations, the CONTRACTING PARTIES *decide* as follows:

1. Notwithstanding the provisions of Article I of the General Agreement, contracting parties may accord differential and more favourable treatment to developing countries [1], without according such treatment to other contracting parties.

2. The provisions of paragraph 1 apply to the following [2]:

(*a*) preferential tariff treatment accorded by developed contracting parties to products originating in developing countries in accordance with the Generalized System of Preferences [3];

(*b*) differential and more favourable treatment with respect to the provisions of the General Agreement concerning non-tariff measures governed by the provisions of instruments multilaterally negotiated under the auspices of the GATT;

(*c*) regional or global arrangements entered into amongst less-developed contracting parties for the mutual reduction or elimination of tariffs and, in accordance with criteria or conditions which may be prescribed by the CONTRACTING PARTIES, for the mutual reduction or elimination of non-tariff measures, on products imported from one another;

(*d*) special treatment on the least developed among the developing countries in the context of any general or specific measures in favour of developing countries.

---

[1] The words " developing countries " as used in this text are to be understood to refer also to developing territories.

[2] It would remain open for the CONTRACTING PARTIES to consider on an *ad hoc* basis under the GATT provisions for joint action any proposals for differential and more favourable treatment not falling within the scope of this paragraph.

[3] As described in the Decision of the CONTRACTING PARTIES of 25 June 1971, relating to the establishment of " generalized, non-reciprocal and non-discriminatory preferences beneficial to the developing countries ".

3. Any differential and more favourable treatment provided under this clause:

(a) shall be designed to facilitate and promote the trade of developing countries and not to raise barriers to or create undue difficulties for the trade of any other contracting parties;

(b) shall not constitute an impediment to the reduction or elimination of tariffs and other restrictions to trade on a most-favoured-nation basis;

(c) shall in the case of such treatment accorded by developed contracting parties to developing countries be designed and, if necessary, modified, to respond positively to the development, financial and trade needs of developing countries.

4. Any contracting party taking action [1] to introduce an arrangement pursuant to paragraphs 1, 2 and 3 above or subsequently taking action to introduce modification or withdrawal of the differential and more favourable treatment so provided shall:

(a) notify the CONTRACTING PARTIES and furnish them with all the information they may deem appropriate relating to such action;

(b) afford adequate opportunity for prompt consultations at the request of any interested contracting party with respect to any difficulty or matter that may arise. The CONTRACTING PARTIES shall, if requested to do so by such contracting party, consult with all contracting parties concerned with respect to the matter with a view to reaching solutions satisfactory to all such contracting parties.

5. The developed countries do not expect reciprocity for commitments made by them in trade negotiations to reduce or remove tariffs and other barriers to the trade of developing countries, i.e., the developed countries do not expect the developing countries, in the course of trade negotiations, to make contributions which are inconsistent with their individual development, financial and trade needs. Developed contracting parties shall therefore not seek, neither shall less-developed contracting parties be required to make, concessions that are inconsistent with the latter's development, financial and trade needs.

6. Having regard to the special economic difficulties and the particular development, financial and trade needs of the least-developed countries, the developed countries shall exercise the utmost restraint in seeking any concessions or contributions for commitments made by them to reduce or

---

[1] Nothing in these provisions shall affect the rights of contracting parties under the General Agreement.

remove tariffs and other barriers to the trade of such countries, and the least-developed countries shall not be expected to make concessions or contributions that are inconsistent with the recognition of their particular situation and problems.

7.   The concessions and contributions made and the obligations assumed by developed and less-developed contracting parties under the provisions of the General Agreement should promote the basic objectives of the Agreement, including those embodied in the Preamble and in Article XXXVI. Less-developed contracting parties expect that their capacity to make contributions or negotiated concessions or take other mutually agreed action under the provisions and procedures of the General Agreement would improve with the progressive development of their economies and improvement in their trade situation and they would accordingly expect to participate more fully in the framework of rights and obligations under the General Agreement.

8.   Particular account shall be taken of the serious difficulty of the least-developed countries in making concessions and contributions in view of their special economic situation and their development, financial and trade needs.

9.   The contracting parties will collaborate in arrangements for review of the operation of these provisions, bearing in mind the need for individual and joint efforts by contracting parties to meet the development needs of developing countries and the objectives of the General Agreement.

DECLARATION ON TRADE MEASURES TAKEN
FOR BALANCE-OF-PAYMENTS PURPOSES

Adopted on 28 November 1979

The *CONTRACTING PARTIES*,

Having regard to the provisions of Articles XII and XVIII:B of the General Agreement;

Recalling the procedures for consultations on balance-of-payments restrictions approved by the Council on 28 April 1970 (BISD, Eighteenth Supplement, pages 48-53) and the procedures for regular consultations on balance-of-payments restrictions with developing countries approved by the Council on 19 December 1972 (BISD, Twentieth Supplement, pages 47-49);

Convinced that restrictive trade measures are in general an inefficient means to maintain or restore balance-of-payments equilibrium;

Noting that restrictive import measures other than quantitative restrictions have been used for balance-of-payments purposes;

Reaffirming that restrictive import measures taken for balance-of-payments purposes should not be taken for the purpose of protecting a particular industry or sector;

Convinced that the contracting parties should endeavour to avoid that restrictive import measures taken for balance-of-payments purposes stimulate new investments that would not be economically viable in the absence of the measures;

Recognizing that the less-developed contracting parties must take into account their individual development, financial and trade situation when implementing restrictive import measures taken for balance-of-payments purposes;

Recognizing that the impact of trade measures taken by developed countries on the economies of developing countries can be serious;

Recognizing that developed contracting parties should avoid the imposition of restrictive trade measures for balance-of-payments purposes to the maximum extent possible,

Agree as follows:

1. The procedures for examination stipulated in Articles XII and XVIII shall apply to all restrictive import measures taken for balance-of-payments

purposes. The application of restrictive import measures taken for balance-of-payments purposes shall be subject to the following conditions in addition to those provided for in Articles XII, XIII, XV and XVIII without prejudice to other provisions of the General Agreement:

(a) in applying restrictive import measures contracting parties shall abide by the disciplines provided for in the GATT and give preference to the measure which has the least disruptive effect on trade [1];

(b) the simultaneous application of more than one type of trade measure for this purpose should be avoided;

(c) whenever practicable, contracting parties shall publicly announce a time schedule for the removal of the measures.

The provisions of this paragraph are not intended to modify the substantive provisions of the General Agreement.

2. If, notwithstanding the principles of this Declaration, a developed contracting party is compelled to apply restrictive import measures for balance-of-payments purposes, it shall, in determining the incidence of its measures, take into account the export interests of the less-developed contracting parties and may exempt from its measures products of export interest to those contracting parties.

3. Contracting parties shall promptly notify to the GATT the introduction or intensification of all restrictive import measures taken for balance-of-payments purposes. Contracting parties which have reason to believe that a restrictive import measure applied by another contracting party was taken for balance-of-payments purposes may notify the measure to the GATT or may request the GATT secretariat to seek information on the measure and make it available to all contracting parties if appropriate.

4. All restrictive import measures taken for balance-or-payments purposes shall be subject to consultation in the GATT Committee on Balance-of-Payments Restrictions (hereafter referred to as " Committee ").

5. The membership of the Committee is open to all contracting parties indicating their wish to serve on it. Efforts shall be made to ensure that the composition of the Committee reflects as far as possible the characteristics of the contracting parties in general in terms of their geographical location, external financial position and stage of economic development.

6. The Committee shall follow the procedures for consultations on balance-of-payments restrictions approved by the Council on 28 April 1970 and set

---

[1] It is understood that the less-developed contracting parties must take into account their individual development, financial and trade situation when selecting the particular measure to be applied.

out in BISD, Eighteenth Supplement, pages 48-53, (hereinafter referred to as " full consultation procedures ") or the procedures for regular consultations on balance-of-payments restrictions with developing countries approved by the Council on 19 December 1972 and set out in BISD, Twentieth Supplement, pages 47-49, (hereinafter referred to as " simplified consultation procedures ") subject to the provisions set out below.

7. The GATT secretariat, drawing on all appropriate sources of information, including the consulting contracting party, shall with a view to facilitating the consultations in the Committee prepare a factual background paper describing the trade aspects of the measures taken, including aspects of particular interest to less-developed contracting parties. The paper shall also cover such other matters as the Committee may determine. The GATT secretariat shall give the consulting contracting party the opportunity to comment on the paper before it is submitted to the Committee.

8. In the case of consultations under Article XVIII:12 (b) the Committee shall base its decision on the type of procedure on such factors as the following:

   (a) the time elapsed since the last full consultations;
   (b) the steps the consulting contracting party has taken in the light of conclusions reached on the occasion of previous consultations;
   (c) the changes in the overall level or nature of the trade measures taken for balance-of-payments purposes;
   (d) the changes in the balance-of-payments situation or prospects;
   (e) whether the balance-of-payments problems are structural or temporary in nature.

9. A less-developed contracting party may at any time request full consultations.

10. The technical assistance services of the GATT secretariat shall, at the request of a less-developed consulting contracting party, assist it in preparing the documentation for the consultations.

11. The Committee shall report on its consultations to the Council. The reports on full consultations shall indicate:

   (a) the Committee's conclusions as well as the facts and reasons on which they are based;
   (b) the steps the consulting contracting party has taken in the light of conclusions reached on the occasion of previous consultations;
   (c) in the case of less-developed contracting parties, the facts and reasons on which the Committee based its decision on the procedure followed; and

(*d*) in the case of developed contracting parties, whether alternative economic policy measures are available.

If the Committee finds that the consulting contracting party's measures

(*a*) are in important respects related to restrictive trade measures maintained by another contracting party [1] or

(*b*) have a significant adverse impact on the export interests of a less-developed contracting party,

it shall so report to the Council which shall take such further action as it may consider appropriate.

12.   In the course of full consultations with a less-developed contracting party the Committee shall, if the consulting contracting party so desires, give particular attention to the possibilities for alleviating and correcting the balance-of-payments problem through measures that contracting parties might take to facilitate an expansion of the export earnings of the consulting contracting party, as provided for in paragraph 3 of the full consultation procedures.

13.   It the Committee finds that a restrictive import measure taken by the consulting contracting party for balance-of-payments purposes is inconsistent with the provisions of Articles XII, XVIII:B or this Declaration, it shall, in its report to the Council, make such findings as will assist the Council in making appropriate recommendations designed to promote the implementation of Articles XII and XVIII:B and this Declaration. The Council shall keep under surveillance any matter on which it has made recommendations.

---

[1] It is noted that such a finding is more likely to be made in the case of recent measures than of measures in effect for some considerable time.

SAFEGUARD ACTION FOR DEVELOPMENT PURPOSES

Decision of 28 November 1979

1. THE CONTRACTING PARTIES recognize that the implementation by less-developed contracting parties of programmes and policies of economic development aimed at raising the standard of living of the people may involve in addition to the establishment of particular industries [1] the development of new or the modification or extension of existing production structures with a view to achieving fuller and more efficient use of resources in accordance with the priorities of their economic development. Accordingly, they agree that a less-developed contracting party may, to achieve these objectives, modify or withdraw concessions included in the appropriate schedules annexed to the General Agreement as provided for in Section A of Article XVIII or, where no measure consistent with the other provisions of the General Agreement is practicable to achieve these objectives, have recourse to Section C of Article XVIII, with the additional flexibility provided for below. In taking such action the less-developed contracting party concerned shall give due regard to the objectives of the General Agreement and to the need to avoid unnecessary damage to the trade of other contracting parties.

2. The CONTRACTING PARTIES recognize further that there may be unusual circumstances where delay in the application of measures which a less-developed contracting party wishes to introduce under Section A or Section C of Article XVIII may give rise to difficulties in the application of its programmes and policies of economic development for the aforesaid purposes. They agree, therefore, that in such circumstances, the less-developed contracting party concerned may deviate from the provisions of Section A and paragraphs 14, 15, 17 and 18 of Section C to the extent necessary for introducing the measures contemplated on a provisional basis immediately after notification.

3. It is understood that all other requirements of the preambular part of Article XVIII and of Sections A and C of that Article, as well as the Notes and Supplementary Provisions set out in Annex I under these Sections will continue to apply to the measures to which this Decision relates.

4. The CONTRACTING PARTIES shall review this Decision in the light of experience with its operation, with a view to determining whether it should be extended, modified or discontinued.

---

[1] As referred to in paragraphs 2, 3, 7, 13 and 22 of Article XVIII and in the Note to these paragraphs.

UNDERSTANDING REGARDING NOTIFICATION, CONSULTATION, DISPUTE SETTLEMENT AND SURVEILLANCE

Adopted on 28 November 1979

1. The CONTRACTING PARTIES reaffirm their adherence to the basic GATT mechanism for the management of disputes based on Articles XXII and XXIII. [1] With a view to improving and refining the GATT mechanism, the CONTRACTING PARTIES agree as follows:

Notification

2. Contracting parties reaffirm their commitment to existing obligations under the General Agreement regarding publication and notification. [2]

3. Contracting parties moreover undertake, to the maximum extent possible, to notify the CONTRACTING PARTIES of their adoption of trade measures affecting the operation of the General Agreement, it being understood that such notification would of itself be without prejudice to views on the consistency of measures with or their relevance to rights and obligations under the General Agreement. Contracting parties should endeavour to notify such measures in advance of implementation. In other cases, where prior notification has not been possible, such measures should be notified promptly *ex post facto*. Contracting parties which have reason to believe that such trade measures have been adopted by another contracting party may seek information on such measures bilaterally, from the contracting party concerned.

Consultations

4. Contracting parties reaffirm their resolve to strengthen and improve the effectiveness of consultative procedures employed by contracting parties. In that connexion, they undertake to respond to requests for consultations promptly and to attempt to conclude consultations expeditiously, with a view to reaching mutually satisfactory conclusions. Any requests for consultations should include the reasons therefor.

---

[1] It is noted that Article XXV may, as recognized by the CONTRACTING PARTIES, *inter alia*, when they adopted the report of the Working Party on particular difficulties connected with trade in primary products (L/930), also afford an appropriate avenue for consultation and dispute settlement in certain circumstances.

[2] See secretariat note, Notifications required from contracting parties (MTN/FR/W/17, dated 1 August 1978).

5. During consultations, contracting parties should give special attention to the particular problems and interests of less-developed contracting parties.

6. Contracting parties should attempt to obtain satisfactory adjustment of the matter in accordance with the provisions of Article XXIII:1 before resorting to Article XXIII:2.

Dispute settlement

7. The CONTRACTING PARTIES agree that the customary practice of the GATT in the field of dispute settlement, described in the Annex, should be continued in the future, with the improvements set out below. They recognize that the efficient functioning of the system depends on their will to abide by the present understanding. The CONTRACTING PARTIES reaffirm that the customary practice includes the procedures for the settlement of disputes between developed and less-developed countries adopted by the CONTRACTING PARTIES in 1966 (BISD, fourteenth supplement, page 18) and that these remain available to less-developed contracting parties wishing to use them.

8. If a dispute is not resolved through consultations the contracting parties concerned may request an appropriate body or individual to use their good offices with a view to the conciliation of the outstanding differences between the parties. If the unresolved dispute is one in which a less-developed contracting party has brought a complaint against a developed contracting party, the less-developed contracting party may request the good offices of the Director-General who, in carrying out his tasks, may consult with the Chairman of the CONTRACTING PARTIES and the Chairman of the Council.

9. It is understood that requests for conciliation and the use of the dispute settlement procedures of Article XXIII:2 should not be intended or considered as contentious acts and that, if disputes arise, all contracting parties will engage in these procedures in good faith in an effort to resolve the disputes. It is also understood that complaints and counter-complaints in regard to distinct matters should not be linked.

10. It is agreed that if a contracting party invoking Article XXIII: 2 requests the establishment of a panel to assist the CONTRACTING PARTIES to deal with the matter, the CONTRACTING PARTIES would decide on its establishment in accordance with standing practice. It is also agreed that the CONTRACTING PARTIES would similarly decide to establish a working party if this were requested by a contracting party invoking the Article. It is further agreed that such requests would be granted only after the contracting party concerned had had an opportunity to study the complaint and respond to it before the CONTRACTING PARTIES.

11. When a panel is set up, the Director-General, after securing the agreement of the contracting parties concerned, should propose the composition of the panel, of three or five members depending on the case, to the CONTRACTING PARTIES for approval. The members of a panel would preferably be governmental. It is understood that citizens of countries whose governments [1] are parties to the dispute would not be members of the panel concerned with that dispute. The panel should be constituted as promptly as possible and normally not later than thirty days from the decision by the CONTRACTING PARTIES.

12. The parties to the dispute would respond within a short period of time, i.e., seven working days, to nominations of panel members by the Director-General and would not oppose nominations except for compelling reasons.

13. In order to facilitate the constitution of panels, the Director-General should maintain an informal indicative list of governmental and non-governmental persons qualified in the fields of trade relations, economic development, and other matters covered by the General Agreement, and who could be available for serving on panels. For this purpose, each contracting party would be invited to indicate at the beginning of every year to the Director-General the name of one or two persons who would be available for such work. [2]

14. Panel members would serve in their individual capacities and not as government representatives, nor as representatives of any organization. Governments would therefore not give them instructions nor seek to influence them as individuals with regard to matters before a panel. Panel members should be selected with a view to ensuring the independence of the members, a sufficiently diverse background and a wide spectrum of experience. [3]

15. Any contracting party having a substantial interest in the matter before a panel, and having notified this to the Council, should have an opportunity to be heard by the panel. Each panel should have the right to seek information and technical advice from any individual or body which it deems appropriate. However, before a panel seeks such information or advice from any individual or body within the jurisdiction of a State it shall inform the

---

[1] In the case customs unions or common markets are parties to a dispute, this provision applies to citizens of all member countries of the customs unions or common markets.

[2] The coverage of travel expenses should be considered within the limits of budgetary possibilities.

[3] A statement is included in the Annex describing the current practice with respect to inclusion on panels of persons from developing countries.

government of that State. Any contracting party should respond promptly and fully to any request by a panel for such information as the panel considers necessary and appropriate. Confidential information which is provided should not be revealed without formal authorization from the contracting party providing the information.

16. The function of panels is to assist the CONTRACTING PARTIES in discharging their responsibilities under Article XXIII:2. Accordingly, a panel should make an objective assessment of the matter before it, including an objective assessment of the facts of the case and the applicability of and conformity with the General Agreement and, if so requested by the CONTRACTING PARTIES, make such other findings as will assist the CONTRACTING PARTIES in making the recommendations or in giving the rulings provided for in Article XXIII:2. In this connexion, panels should consult regularly with the parties to the dispute and give them adequate opportunity to develop a mutually satisfactory solution.

17. Where the parties have failed to develop a mutually satisfactory solution, the panel should submit its findings in a written form. The report of a panel should normally set out the rationale behind any findings and recommendations that it makes. Where a bilateral settlement of the matter has been found, the report of the panel may be confined to a brief description of the case and to reporting that a solution has been reached.

18. To encourage development of mutually satisfactory solutions between the parties and with a view to obtaining their comments, each panel should first submit the descriptive part of its report to the parties concerned, and should subsequently submit to the parties to the dispute its conclusions, or an outline thereof, a reasonable period of time before they are circulated to the CONTRACTING PARTIES.

19. If a mutually satisfactory solution is developed by the parties to a dispute before a panel, any contracting party with an interest in the matter has a right to enquire about and be given appropriate information about that solution in so far as it relates to trade matters.

20. The time required by panels will vary with the particular case. [1] However, panels should aim to deliver their findings without undue delay, taking into account the obligation of the CONTRACTING PARTIES to ensure prompt settlement. In cases of urgency the panel would be called upon to deliver its findings within a period normally of three months from the time the panel was established.

---

[1] An explanation is included in the Annex that " in most cases the proceedings of the panels have been completed within a reasonable period of time, extending from three to nine months ".

21.   Reports of panels and working parties should be given prompt consideration by the CONTRACTING PARTIES. The CONTRACTING PARTIES should take appropriate action on reports of panels and working parties within a reasonable period of time. If the case is one brought by a less-developed contracting party, such action should be taken in a specially convened meeting, if necessary. In such cases, in considering what appropriate action might be taken the CONTRACTING PARTIES shall take into account not only the trade coverage of measures complained of, but also their impact on the economy of less-developed contracting parties concerned.

22.   The CONTRACTING PARTIES shall keep under surveillance any matter on which they have made recommendations or given rulings. If the CONTRACTING PARTIES' recommendations are not implemented within a reasonable period of time, the contracting party bringing the case may ask the CONTRACTING PARTIES to make suitable efforts with a view to finding an appropriate solution.

23.   If the matter is one which has been raised by a less-developed contracting party, the CONTRACTING PARTIES shall consider what further action they might take which would be appropriate to the circumstances.

Surveillance

24.   The CONTRACTING PARTIES agree to conduct a regular and systematic review of developments in the trading system. Particular attention would be paid to developments which affect rights and obligations under the GATT, to matters affecting the interests of less-developed contracting parties, to trade measures notified in accordance with this understanding and to measures which have been subject to consultation, conciliation or dispute settlement procedures laid down in this understanding.

Technical assistance

25.   The technical assistance services of the GATT secretariat shall, at the request of a less-developed contracting party, assist it in connexion with matters dealt with in this understanding.

AGREEMENT ON IMPLEMENTATION OF ARTICLE VI
OF THE GENERAL AGREEMENT ON TARIFFS AND TRADE

The Parties to this Agreement (hereinafter referred to as "Parties"),

Recognizing that anti-dumping practices should not constitute an un-justifiable impediment to international trade and that anti-dumping duties may be applied against dumping only if such dumping causes or threatens material injury to an established industry or materially retards the estab-lishment of an industry;

Considering that it is desirable to provide for equitable and open pro-cedures as the basis for a full examination of dumping cases;

Taking into account the particular trade, development and financial needs of developing countries;

Desiring to interpret the provisions of Article VI of the General Agree-ment on Tariffs and Trade (hereinafter referred to as "General Agreement" or "GATT") and to elaborate rules for their application in order to provide greater uniformity and certainty in their implementation; and

Desiring to provide for the speedy, effective and equitable settlement of disputes arising under this Agreement;

Hereby agree as follows:

PART I

ANTI-DUMPING CODE

Article 1

Principles

The imposition of an anti-dumping duty is a measure to be taken only under the circumstances provided for in Article VI of the General Agree-ment and pursuant to investigations initiated [1] and conducted in accordance

---

[1] The term "initiated" as used hereinafter means the procedural action by which a Party formally commences an investigation as provided in paragraph 6 of Article 6.

with the provisions of this Code. The following provisions govern the application of Article VI of the General Agreement in so far as action is taken under anti-dumping legislation or regulations.

Article 2

Determination of Dumping

1. For the purpose of this Code a product is to be considered as being dumped, i.e. introduced into the commerce of another country at less than its normal value, if the export price of the product exported from one country to another is less than the comparable price, in the ordinary course of trade, for the like product when destined for consumption in the exporting country.

2. Throughout this Code the term "like product" ("produit similaire") shall be interpreted to mean a product which is identical, i.e. alike in all respects to the product under consideration, or in the absence of such a product, another product which, although not alike in all respects, has characteristics closely resembling those of the product under consideration.

3. In the case where products are not imported directly from the country of origin but are exported to the country of importation from an intermediate country, the price at which the products are sold from the country of export to the country of importation shall normally be compared with the comparable price in the country of export. However, comparison may be made with the price in the country of origin, if, for example, the products are merely trans-shipped through the country of export, or such products are not produced in the country of export, or there is no comparable price for them in the country of export.

4. When there are no sales of the like product in the ordinary course of trade in the domestic market of the exporting country or when, because of the particular market situation, such sales do not permit a proper comparison, the margin of dumping shall be determined by comparison with a comparable price of the like product when exported to any third country which may be the highest such export price but should be a representative price, or with the cost of production in the country of origin plus a reasonable amount for administrative, selling and any other costs and for profits. As a general rule, the addition for profit shall not exceed the profit normally realized on sales of products of the same general category in the domestic market of the country of origin.

5. In cases where there is no export price or where it appears to the authorities [1] concerned that the export price is unreliable because of association or a compensatory arrangement between the exporter and the importer or a third party, the export price may be constructed on the basis of the price at which the imported products are first resold to an independent buyer, or if the products are not resold to an independent buyer, or not resold in the condition as imported, on such reasonable basis as the authorities may determine.

6. In order to effect a fair comparison between the export price and the domestic price in the exporting country (or the country of origin) or, if applicable, the price established pursuant to the provisions of Article VI:1 *(b)* of the General Agreement, the two prices shall be compared at the same level of trade, normally at the ex-factory level, and in respect of sales made at as nearly as possible the same time. Due allowance shall be made in each case, on its merits, for the differences in conditions and terms of sale, for the differences in taxation, and for the other differences affecting price comparability. In the cases referred to in paragraph 5 of Article 2 allowance for costs, including duties and taxes, incurred between importation and resale, and for profits accruing, should also be made.

7. This Article is without prejudice to the second Supplementary Provision to paragraph 1 of Article VI in Annex I to the General Agreement.

Article 3

Determination of Injury [2]

1. A determination of injury for purposes of Article VI of the General Agreement shall be based on positive evidence and involve an objective examination of both (*a*) the volume of the dumped imports and their effect on prices in the domestic market for like products, and (*b*) the consequent impact of these imports on domestic producers of such products.

2. With regard to volume of the dumped imports the investigating authorities shall consider whether there has been a significant increase in dumped imports, either in absolute terms or relative to production or consumption

---

[1] When in this Code the term "authorities" is used, it shall be interpreted as meaning authorities at an appropriate, senior level.

[2] Under this Code the term "injury" shall, unless otherwise specified, be taken to mean material injury to a domestic industry, threat of material injury to a domestic industry or material retardation of the establishment of such an industry and shall be interpreted in accordance with the provisions of this Article.

in the importing country. With regard to the effect of the dumped imports on prices, the investigating authorities shall consider whether there has been a significant price undercutting by the dumped imports as compared with the price of a like product of the importing country, or whether the effect of such imports is otherwise to depress prices to a significant degree or prevent price increases, which otherwise would have occurred, to a significant degree. No one or several of these factors can necessarily give decisive guidance.

3. The examination of the impact on the industry concerned shall include an evaluation of all relevant economic factors and indices having a bearing on the state of the industry such as actual and potential decline in output, sales, market share, profits, productivity, return on investments, or utilization of capacity; factors affecting domestic prices; actual and potential negative effects on cash flow, inventories, employment, wages, growth, ability to raise capital or investments. This list is not exhaustive, nor can one or several of these factors necessarily give decisive guidance.

4. It must be demonstrated that the dumped imports are, through the effects [1] of dumping, causing injury within the meaning of this Code. There may be other factors [2] which at the same time are injuring the industry, and the injuries caused by other factors must not be attributed to the dumped imports.

5. The effect of the dumped imports shall be assessed in relation to the domestic production of the like product when available data permit the separate identification of production in terms of such criteria as: the production process, the producers' realizations, profits. When the domestic production of the like product has no separate identity in these terms the effects of the dumped imports shall be assessed by the examination of the production of the narrowest group or range of products, which includes the like product, for which the necessary information can be provided.

6. A determination of threat of injury shall be based on facts and not merely on allegation, conjecture or remote possibility. The change in circumstances which would create a situation in which the dumping would cause injury must be clearly foreseen and imminent. [3]

---

[1] As set forth in paragraphs 2 and 3 of this Article.

[2] Such factors include, *inter alia*, the volume and prices of imports not sold at dumping prices, contraction in demand or changes in the patterns of consumption, trade restrictive practices of and competition between the foreign and domestic producers, developments in technology and the export performance and productivity of the domestic industry.

[3] One example, though not an exclusive one, is that there is convincing reason to believe that there will be, in the immediate future, substantially increased importations of the product at dumped prices.

7. With respect to cases where injury is threatened by dumped imports, the application of anti-dumping measures shall be studied and decided with special care.

Article 4

Definition of Industry

1. In determining injury the term "domestic industry" shall be interpreted as referring to the domestic producers as a whole of the like products or to those of them whose collective output of the products constitutes a major proportion of the total domestic production of those products, except that

(i) when producers are related [1] to the exporters or importers or are themselves importers of the allegedly dumped product, the industry may be interpreted as referring to the rest of the producers;

(ii) in exceptional circumstances the territory of a Party may, for the production in question, be divided into two or more competitive markets and the producers within each market may be regarded as a separate industry if (a) the producers within such market sell all or almost all of their production of the product in question in that market, and (b) the demand in that market is not to any substantial degree supplied by producers of the product in question located elsewhere in the territory. In such circumstances, injury may be found to exist even where a major portion of the total domestic industry is not injured provided there is a concentration of dumped imports into such an isolated market and provided further that the dumped imports are causing injury to the producers of all or almost all of the production within such market.

2. When the industry has been interpreted as referring to the producers in a certain area, i.e. a market as defined in paragraph 1(ii), anti-dumping duties shall be levied [2] only on the products in question consigned for final consumption to that area. When the constitutional law of the importing country does not permit the levying of anti-dumping duties on such a basis, the importing Party may levy the anti-dumping duties without limitation only if (1) the exporters shall have been given an opportunity to cease exporting at dumped prices to the area concerned or otherwise give assurances pursuant to Article 7 of this Code, and adequate assurances in this

---

[1] An understanding among Parties should be developed defining the word "related" as used in this Code.

[2] As used in this Code "levy" shall mean the definitive or final legal assessment or collection of a duty or tax.

regard have not been promptly given, and (2) such duties cannot be levied on specific producers which supply the area in question.

3.   Where two or more countries have reached under the provisions of Article XXIV:8(*a*) of the General Agreement such a level of integration that they have the characteristics of a single, unified market, the industry in the entire area of integration shall be taken to be the industry referred to in paragraph 1 above.

4.   The provisions of paragraph 5 of Article 3 shall be applicable to this Article.

Article 5

Initiation and Subsequent Investigation

1.   An investigation to determine the existence, degree and effect of any alleged dumping shall normally be initiated upon a written request by or on behalf of the industry [1] affected. The request shall include sufficient evidence of (*a*) dumping; (*b*) injury within the meaning of Article VI of the General Agreement as interpreted by this Code and (*c*) a causal link between the dumped imports and the alleged injury. If in special circumstances the authorities concerned decide to initiate an investigation without having received such a request, they shall proceed only if they have sufficient evidence on all points under (*a*) to (*c*) above.

2.   Upon initiation of an investigation and thereafter, the evidence of both dumping and injury caused thereby should be considered simultaneously. In any event the evidence of both dumping and injury shall be considered simultaneously (*a*) in the decision whether or not to initiate an investigation, and (*b*) thereafter, during the course of the investigation, starting on a date not later than the earliest date on which in accordance with the provisions of this Code provisional measures may be applied, except in the cases provided for in paragraph 3 of Article 10 in which the authorities accept the request of the exporters.

3.   An application shall be rejected and an investigation shall be terminated promptly as soon as the authorities concerned are satisfied that there is not sufficient evidence of either dumping or of injury to justify proceeding with the case. There should be immediate termination in cases where the margin of dumping or the volume of dumped imports, actual or potential, or the injury is negligible.

---

[1] As defined in Article 4.

4. An anti-dumping proceeding shall not hinder the procedures of customs clearance.

5. Investigations shall, except in special circumstances, be concluded within one year after their initiation.

Article 6

Evidence

1. The foreign suppliers and all other interested parties shall be given ample opportunity to present in writing all evidence that they consider useful in respect of the anti-dumping investigation in question. They shall also have the right, on justification, to present evidence orally.

2. The authorities concerned shall provide opportunities for the complainant and the importers and exporters known to be concerned and the governments of the exporting countries, to see all information that is relevant to the presentation of their cases, that is not confidential as defined in paragraph 3 below, and that is used by the authorities in an anti-dumping investigation, and to prepare presentations on the basis of this information.

3. Any information which is by nature confidential (for example, because its disclosure would be of significant competitive advantage to a competitor or because its disclosure would have a significantly adverse effect upon a person supplying the information or upon a person from whom he acquired the information) or which is provided on a confidential basis by parties to an anti-dumping investigation shall, upon cause shown, be treated as such by the investigating authorities. Such information shall not be disclosed without specific permission of the party submitting it.[1] Parties providing confidential information may be requested to furnish non-confidential summaries thereof. In the event that such parties indicate that such information is not susceptible of summary, a statement of the reasons why summarization is not possible must be provided.

4. However, if the authorities concerned find that a request for confidentiality is not warranted and if the supplier is either unwilling to make the information public or to authorize its disclosure in generalized or summary form, the authorities would be free to disregard such information unless it can be demonstrated to their satisfaction from appropriate sources that the information is correct.[2]

---

[1] Parties are aware that in the territory of certain Parties disclosure pursuant to a narrowly drawn protective order may be required.

[2] Parties agree that requests for confidentiality should not be arbitrarily rejected.

5. In order to verify information provided or to obtain further details the authorities may carry out investigations in other countries as required, provided they obtain the agreement of the firms concerned and provided they notify the representatives of the government of the country in question and unless the latter object to the investigation.

6. When the competent authorities are satisfied that there is sufficient evidence to justify initiating an anti-dumping investigation pursuant to Article 5, the Party or Parties the products of which are subject to such investigation and the exporters and importers known to the investigating authorities to have an interest therein and the complainants shall be notified and a public notice shall be given.

7. Throughout the anti-dumping investigation all parties shall have a full opportunity for the defence of their interests. To this end, the authorities concerned shall, on request, provide opportunities for all directly interested parties to meet those parties with adverse interests, so that opposing views may be presented and rebuttal arguments offered. Provision of such opportunities must take account of the need to preserve confidentiality and of the convenience to the parties. There shall be no obligation on any party to attend a meeting and failure to do so shall not be prejudicial to that party's case.

8. In cases in which any interested party refuses access to, or otherwise does not provide, necessary information within a reasonable period or significantly impedes the investigation, preliminary and final findings [1], affirmative or negative, may be made on the basis of the facts available.

9. The provisions of this Article are not intended to prevent the authorities of a Party from proceeding expeditiously with regard to initiating an investigation, reaching preliminary or final findings, whether affirmative or negative, or from applying provisional or final measures, in accordance with the relevant provisions of this Code.

Article 7

Price Undertakings

1. Proceedings may [2] be suspended or terminated without the imposition of provisional measures or anti-dumping duties upon receipt of satisfactory voluntary undertakings from any exporter to revise its prices or to cease

---

[1] Because of different terms used under different systems in various countries the term "finding" is hereinafter used to mean a formal decision or determination.

[2] The word "may" shall not be interpreted to allow the simultaneous continuation of proceedings with the implementation of price undertakings except as provided in paragraph 3.

exports to the area in question at dumped prices so that the authorities are satisfied that the injurious effect of the dumping is eliminated. Price increases under such undertakings shall not be higher than necessary to eliminate the margin of dumping.

2. Price undertakings shall not be sought or accepted from exporters unless the authorities of the importing country have initiated an investigation in accordance with the provisions of Article 5 of this Code. Undertakings offered need not be accepted if the authorities consider their acceptance impractical, for example, if the number of actual or potential exporters is too great, or for other reasons.

3. If the undertakings are accepted, the investigation of injury shall nevertheless be completed if the exporter so desires or the authorities so decide. In such a case, if a determination of no injury or threat thereof is made, the undertaking shall automatically lapse except in cases where a determination of no threat of injury is due in large part to the existence of a price undertaking. In such cases the authorities concerned may require that an undertaking be maintained for a reasonable period consistent with the provisions of this Code.

4. Price undertakings may be suggested by the authorities of the importing country, but no exporter shall be forced to enter into such an undertaking. The fact that exporters do not offer such undertakings, or do not accept an invitation to do so, shall in no way prejudice the consideration of the case. However, the authorities are free to determine that a threat of injury is more likely to be realized if the dumped imports continue.

5. Authorities of an importing country may require any exporter from whom undertakings have been accepted to provide periodically information relevant to the fulfilment of such undertakings, and to permit verification of pertinent data. In case of violation of undertakings, the authorities of the importing country may take, under this Code in conformity with its provisions, expeditious actions which may constitute immediate application of provisional measures using the best information available. In such cases definitive duties may be levied in accordance with this Code on goods entered for consumption not more than ninety days before the application of such provisional measures, except that any such retroactive assessment shall not apply to imports entered before the violation of the undertaking.

6. Undertakings shall not remain in force any longer than anti-dumping duties could remain in force under this Code. The authorities of an importing country shall review the need for the continuation of any price undertaking, where warranted, on their own initiative or if interested exporters or importers of the product in question so request and submit positive information substantiating the need for such review.

7. Whenever an anti-dumping investigation is suspended or terminated pursuant to the provisions of paragraph 1 above and whenever an undertaking is terminated, this fact shall be officially notified and must be published. Such notices shall set forth at least the basic conclusions and a summary of the reasons therefor.

Article 8

Imposition and Collection of Anti-dumping Duties

1. The decision whether or not to impose an anti-dumping duty in cases where all requirements for the imposition have been fulfilled and the decision whether the amount of the anti-dumping duty to be imposed shall be the full margin of dumping or less, are decisions to be made by the authorities of the importing country or customs territory. It is desirable that the imposition be permissive in all countries or customs territories Parties to this Agreement, and that the duty be less than the margin, if such lesser duty would be adequate to remove the injury to the domestic industry.

2. When an anti-dumping duty is imposed in respect of any product, such anti-dumping duty shall be collected in the appropriate amounts in each case, on a non-discriminatory basis on imports of such product from all sources found to be dumped and causing injury, except as to imports from those sources, from which price undertakings under the terms of this Code have been accepted. The authorities shall name the supplier or suppliers of the product concerned. If, however, several suppliers from the same country are involved, and it is impracticable to name all these suppliers, the authorities may name the supplying country concerned. If several suppliers from more than one country are involved, the authorities may name either all the suppliers involved, or, if this is impracticable, all the supplying countries involved.

3. The amount of the anti-dumping duty must not exceed the margin of dumping as established under Article 2. Therefore, if subsequent to the application of the anti-dumping duty it is found that the duty so collected exceeds the actual dumping margin, the amount in excess of the margin shall be reimbursed as quickly as possible.

4. Within a basic price system the following rules shall apply, provided that their application is consistent with the other provisions of this Code:
   If several suppliers from one or more countries are involved, anti-dumping duties may be imposed on imports of the product in question found to have been dumped and to be causing injury from the country

or countries concerned, the duty being equivalent to the amount by which the export price is less than the basic price established for this purpose, not exceeding the lowest normal price in the supplying country or countries where normal conditions of competition are prevailing. It is understood that, for products which are sold below this already established basic price, a new anti-dumping investigation shall be carried out in each particular case, when so demanded by the interested parties and the demand is supported by relevant evidence. In cases where no dumping is found, anti-dumping duties collected shall be reimbursed as quickly as possible. Furthermore, if it can be found that the duty so collected exceeds the actual dumping margin, the amount in excess of the margin shall be reimbursed as quickly as possible.

5.   Public notice shall be given of any preliminary or final finding whether affirmative or negative and of the revocation of a finding. In the case of affirmative finding each such notice shall set forth the findings and conclusions reached on all issues of fact and law considered material by the investigating authorities, and the reasons and basis therefor. In the case of a negative finding, each notice shall set forth at least the basic conclusions and a summary of the reasons therefor. All notices of findings shall be forwarded to the Party or Parties the products of which are subject to such finding and to the exporters known to have an interest therein.

Article 9

Duration of Anti-Dumping Duties

1.   An anti-dumping duty shall remain in force only as long as, and to the extent necessary to counteract dumping which is causing injury.

2.   The investigating authorities shall review the need for the continued imposition of the duty, where warranted, on their own initiative or if any interested party so requests and submits positive information substantiating the need for review.

Article 10

Provisional Measures

1.   Provisional measures may be taken only after a preliminary affirmative finding has been made that there is dumping and that there is sufficient evidence of injury, as provided for in (a) to (c) of paragraph 1 of Article 5.

Provisional measures shall not be applied unless the authorities concerned judge that they are necessary to prevent injury being caused during the period of investigation.

2. Provisional measures may take the form of a provisional duty or, preferably, a security — by cash deposit or bond — equal to the amount of the anti-dumping duty provisionally estimated, being not greater than the provisionally estimated margin of dumping. Withholding of appraisement is an appropriate provisional measure, provided that the normal duty and the estimated amount of the anti-dumping duty be indicated and as long as the withholding of appraisement is subject to the same conditions as other provisional measures.

3. The imposition of provisional measures shall be limited to as short a period as possible, not exceeding four months or, on decision of the authorities concerned, upon request by exporters representing a significant percentage of the trade involved to a period not exceeding six months.

4. The relevant provisions of Article 8 shall be followed in the application of provisional measures.

Article 11

Retroactivity

1. Anti-dumping duties and provisional measures shall only be applied to products which enter for consumption after the time when the decision taken under paragraph 1 of Article 8 and paragraph 1 of Article 10, respectively, enters into force, except that in cases:

(i) Where a final finding of injury (but not of a threat thereof or of a material retardation of the establishment of an industry) is made or, in the case of a final finding of threat of injury, where the effect of the dumped imports would, in the absence of the provisional measures, have led to a finding of injury, anti-dumping duties may be levied retroactively for the period for which provisional measures, if any, have been applied.

If the anti-dumping duty fixed in the final decision is higher than the provisionally paid duty, the difference shall not be collected. If the duty fixed in the final decision is lower than the provisionally paid duty or the amount estimated for the purpose of the security, the difference shall be reimbursed or the duty recalculated, as the case may be.

(ii) Where for the dumped product in question the authorities determine

(a) either that there is a history of dumping which caused injury or that the importer was, or should have been, aware that the exporter practises dumping and that such dumping would cause injury, and

(b) that the injury is caused by sporadic dumping (massive dumped imports of a product in a relatively short period) to such an extent that, in order to preclude it recurring, it appears necessary to levy an anti-dumping duty retroactively on those imports,

the duty may be levied on products which were entered for consumption not more than 90 days prior to the date of application of provisional measures.

2. Except as provided in paragraph 1 above where a finding of threat of injury or material retardation is made (but no injury has yet occurred) a definitive anti-dumping duty may be imposed only from the date of the finding of threat of injury or material retardation and any cash deposit made during the period of the application of provisional measures shall be refunded and any bonds released in an expeditious manner.

3. Where a final finding is negative any cash deposit made during the period of the application of provisional measures shall be refunded and any bonds released in an expeditious manner.

Article 12

Anti-Dumping Action on behalf of a Third Country

1. An application for anti-dumping action on behalf of a third country shall be made by the authorities of the third country requesting action.

2. Such an application shall be supported by price information to show that the imports are being dumped and by detailed information to show that the alleged dumping is causing injury to the domestic industry concerned in the third country. The government of the third country shall afford all assistance to the authorities of the importing country to obtain any further information which the latter may require.

3. The authorities of the importing country in considering such an application shall consider the effects of the alleged dumping on the industry concerned as a whole in the third country; that is to say the injury shall not be assessed in relation only to the effect of the alleged dumping on the industry's exports to the importing country or even on the industry's total exports.

4. The decision whether or not to proceed with a case shall rest with the importing country. If the importing country decides that it is prepared to take action, the initiation of the approach to the CONTRACTING PARTIES seeking their approval for such action shall rest with the importing country.

Article 13

Developing Countries

It is recognized that special regard must be given by developed countries to the special situation of developing countries when considering the application of anti-dumping measures under this Code. Possibilities of constructive remedies provided for by this Code shall be explored before applying anti-dumping duties where they would affect the essential interests of developing countries.

PART II

Article 14

Committee on Anti-Dumping Practices

1.   There shall be established under this Agreement a Committee on Anti-Dumping Practices (hereinafter referred to as the "Committee") composed of representatives from each of the Parties. The Committee shall elect its own Chairman and shall meet not less than twice a year and otherwise as envisaged by relevant provisions of this Agreement at the request of any Party. The Committee shall carry out responsibilities as assigned to it under this Agreement or by the Parties and it shall afford Parties the opportunity of consulting on any matters relating to the operation of the Agreement or the furtherance of its objectives. The GATT secretariat shall act as the secretariat to the Committee.

2.   The Committee may set up subsidiary bodies as appropriate.

3.   In carrying out their functions, the Committee and any subsidiary bodies may consult with and seek information from any source they deem appropriate. However, before the Committee or a subsidiary body seeks such information from a source within the jurisdiction of a Party, it shall inform the Party involved. It shall obtain the consent of the Party and any firm to be consulted.

4.   Parties shall report without delay to the Committee all preliminary or final anti-dumping actions taken. Such reports will be available in the GATT secretariat for inspection by government representatives. The Parties shall also submit, on a semi-annual basis, reports of any anti-dumping actions taken within the preceding six months.

Article 15

Consultation, Conciliation and Dispute Settlement [1]

1. Each Party shall afford sympathetic consideration to, and shall afford adequate opportunity for consultation regarding, representations made by another Party with respect to any matter affecting the operation of this Agreement.

2. If any Party considers that any benefit accruing to it, directly or indirectly, under this Agreement is being nullified or impaired, or that the achievement of any objective of the Agreement is being impeded, by another Party or Parties, it may, with a view to reaching a mutually satisfactory resolution of the matter, request in writing consultations with the Party or Parties in question. Each Party shall afford sympathetic consideration to any request from another Party for consultation. The Parties concerned shall initiate consultation promptly.

3. If any Party considers that the consultation pursuant to paragraph 2 has failed to achieve a mutually agreed solution and final action has been taken by the administering authorities of the importing country to levy definitive anti-dumping duties or to accept price undertakings, it may refer the matter to the Committee for conciliation. When a provisional measure has a significant impact and the Party considers the measure was taken contrary to the provisions of paragraph 1 of Article 10 of this Agreement, a Party may also refer such matter to the Committee for conciliation. In cases where matters are referred to the Committee for conciliation, the Committee shall meet within thirty days to review the matter, and, through its good offices, shall encourage the Parties involved to develop a mutually acceptable solution. [2]

4. Parties shall make their best efforts to reach a mutually satisfactory solution throughout the period of conciliation.

5. If no mutually agreed solution has been reached after detailed examination by the Committee under paragraph 3 within three months, the Committee shall, at the request of any party to the dispute, establish a panel to examine the matter, based upon:

(a) a written statement of the Party making the request indicating how a benefit accruing to it, directly or indirectly, under this

---

[1] If disputes arise between Parties relating to rights and obligations under this Agreement, Parties should complete the dispute settlement procedures under this Agreement before availing themselves of any rights which they have under the GATT.

[2] In this connexion the Committee may draw Parties' attention to those cases in which, in its view, there are no reasonable bases supporting the allegations made.

Agreement has been nullified or impaired, or that the achieving of the objectives of the Agreement is being impeded, and

(b) the facts made available in conformity with appropriate domestic procedures to the authorities of the importing country.

6. Confidential information provided to the panel shall not be revealed without formal authorization from the person or authority providing the information. Where such information is requested from the panel but release of such information by the panel is not authorized, a non-confidential summary of the information, authorized by the authority or person providing the information, will be provided.

7. Further to paragraphs 1-6 the settlement of disputes shall *mutatis mutandis* be governed by the provisions of the Understanding regarding Notification, Consultation, Dispute Settlement and Surveillance. Panel members shall have relevant experience and be selected from Parties not parties to the dispute.

PART III

Article 16

Final Provisions

1. No specific action against dumping of exports from another Party can be taken except in accordance with the provisions of the General Agreement, as interpreted by this Agreement. [1]

Acceptance and accession

2. (a) This Agreement shall be open for acceptance by signature or otherwise by governments contracting parties to the GATT and by the European Economic Community.

(b) This Agreement shall be open for acceptance by signature or otherwise by governments having provisionally acceded to the GATT, on terms related to the effective application of rights and obligations under this Agreement, which take into account rights and obligations in the instruments providing for their provisional accession.

---

[1] This is not intended to preclude action under other relevant provisions of the General Agreement, as appropriate.

(c) This Agreement shall be open to accession by any other government on terms, related to the effective application of rights and obligations under this Agreement, to be agreed between that government and the Parties, by the deposit with the Director-General to the CONTRACTING PARTIES to the GATT of an instrument of accession which states the terms so agreed.

(d) In regard to acceptance, the provisions of Article XXVI:5(a) and (b) of the General Agreement would be applicable.

Reservations

3. Reservations may not be entered in respect of any of the provisions of this Agreement without the consent of the other Parties.

Entry into force

4. This Agreement shall enter into force on 1 January 1980 for the governments [1] which have accepted or acceded to it by that date. For each other government it shall enter into force on the thirtieth day following the date of its acceptance or accession to this Agreement.

Denunciation of the 1967 Agreement

5. Acceptance of this Agreement shall carry denunciation of the Agreement on Implementation of Article VI of the General Agreement on Tariffs and Trade, done at Geneva on 30 June 1967, which entered into force on 1 July 1968, for Parties to the 1967 Agreement. Such denunciation shall take effect for each Party to this Agreement on the date of entry into force of this Agreement for each such Party.

National legislation

6. (a) Each government accepting or acceding to this Agreement shall take all necessary steps, of a general or particular character, to ensure, not later than the date of entry into force of this Agreement for it, the conformity of its laws, regulations and administrative procedures with the provisions of this Agreement as they may apply for the Party in question.

(b) Each Party shall inform the Committee of any changes in its laws and regulations relevant to this Agreement and in the administration of such laws and regulations.

---

[1] The term "government" is deemed to include the competent authorities of the European Economic Community.

Review

7. The Committee shall review annually the implementation and operation of this Agreement taking into account the objectives thereof. The Committee shall annually inform the CONTRACTING PARTIES to the GATT of developments during the period covered by such reviews.

Amendments

8. The Parties may amend this Agreement having regard, *inter alia*, to the experience gained in its implementation. Such an amendment, once the Parties have concurred in accordance with procedures established by the Committee, shall not come into force for any Party until it has been accepted by such Party.

Withdrawal

9. Any Party may withdraw from this Agreement. The withdrawal shall take effect upon the expiration of sixty days from the day on which written notice of withdrawal is received by the Director-General to the CONTRACTING PARTIES to the GATT. Any Party may upon such notification request an immediate meeting of the Committee.

Non-application of this Agreement between particular Parties

10. This Agreement shall not apply as between any two Parties if either of the Parties, at the time either accepts or accedes to this Agreement, does not consent to such application.

Secretariat

11. This Agreement shall be serviced by the GATT secretariat.

Deposit

12. This Agreement shall be deposited with the Director-General to the CONTRACTING PARTIES to the GATT, who shall promptly furnish to each Party and each contracting party to the GATT a certified copy thereof and of each amendment thereto pursuant to paragraph 8, and a notification of each acceptance thereof or accession thereto pursuant to paragraph 2, and of each withdrawal therefrom pursuant to paragraph 9 of this Article.

Registration

13. This Agreement shall be registered in accordance with the provisions of Article 102 of the Charter of the United Nations.

Done at Geneva this twelfth day of April nineteen hundred and seventy-nine in a single copy, in the English, French and Spanish languages, each text being authentic.

PROCES-VERBAL

Opened for signature following the meeting of the Trade Negotiations
Committee on 11-12 April 1979

---

1. Having participated in the Multilateral Trade Negotiations, the representatives of the Governments and the EEC Commission agree that the texts listed below in respect of which they have signed the present Procès-Verbal embody the results of their negotiations. They acknowledge that the texts may be subject to rectifications of a purely formal character that do not affect the substance or meaning of the texts in any way except as otherwise indicated in the text on tariff negotiations.

2. These representatives agree that by signing the present Procès-Verbal they indicate their intention to submit the relevant texts or legal instruments to be formulated on the basis of the said texts for the consideration of their respective authorities with a view to seeking approval of, or other decisions on, the relevant texts or instruments in accordance with appropriate procedures in their respective countries. Representatives may indicate that their signature evidences their intention to seek approval or decision.

3. Representatives may indicate that their signature to the present Procès-Verbal relates only to certain of the texts listed below which they will specify.

4. It is appreciated that some delegations participating in the Multilateral Trade Negotiations may not be in a position to sign the present Procès-Verbal immediately in relation to all or certain of the texts listed below. They are invited to do so at their earliest convenience.

5. It is recognized that representatives of least-developed countries participating in the Multilateral Trade Negotiations may need time to examine the results of the negotiations in the light of paragraph 6 of the Tokyo Declaration before they can sign the Procès-Verbal.

6. The representatives signing the present Procès-Verbal agree that the work on safeguards referred to in paragraph 3(d) of the Tokyo Declaration should be continued within the framework and in terms of that Declaration as a matter of urgency, taking into account the work already done, with the objective of reaching agreement before 15 July 1979.

7. Texts (k) and (l) are the result of negotiations only amongst the representatives of certain governments identified in the documents.

8. The representatives have taken note of the statements made in relation to various texts at the TNC meeting of 11-12 April 1979 as contained in MTN/P/5.

<u>Texts</u>

(a) Agreement on Technical Barriers to Trade MTN/NTM/W/192/Rev.5

(b) Agreement on Government Procurement MTN/NTM/W/211/Rev.2 and Add.1

(c) Agreement on Interpretation and Application of Articles VI, XVI and XXIII of the General Agreement on Tariffs and Trade MTN/NTM/W/236 and Corr.1

(d) Arrangement on Bovine Meat Annex to MTN/ME/8

(e) International Dairy Arrangement
    (i) MTN/DP/8, Annexes A and B

    or

    (ii) MTN/DP/8, Annex C

(f) Agreement on Implementation of Article VII of the General Agreement on Tariffs and Trade
    (i) MTN/NTM/W/229/Rev.1

    or

    (ii) MTN/NTM/W/229/Rev.1 as amended by MTN/NTM/W/222/Rev.1

(g) Agreement on Import Licensing Procedures MTN/NTM/W/231/Rev.2

(h) Multilateral Agricultural Framework MTN/27

(i) Texts prepared by Group "Framework" MTN/FR/W/20/Rev.2

(j) Tariff Negotiations MTN/26/Rev.2

(k) Agreement on Trade in Civil Aircraft prepared by a number of delegations MTN/W/38, Corr.1 and Add.1

(l) Agreement on Implementation of Article VI of the General Agreement on Tariffs and Trade prepared by a number of delegations
    (i) MTN/NTM/W/232, Add.1/Rev.1 Add.2 and Corr.1

    or

    (ii) MTN/NTM/W/232, Add.1/Rev.1 Add.2 and Corr.1 as amended by MTN/NTM/W/241/Rev.1

GATT MINISTERIAL DECLARATION

1.   The Contracting Parties to the General Agreement on Tariffs and
Trade have met at Ministerial level on 24-29 November 1982. They recognize
that the multilateral trading system, of which the General Agreement is the
legal foundation, is seriously endangered. In the current crisis of the world
economy, to which the lack of convergence in national economic policies has
contributed, protectionist pressures on governments have multiplied, disregard
of GATT disciplines has increased and certain shortcomings in the functioning
of the GATT system have been accentuated. Conscious of the role of the GATT
system in furthering economic well-being and an unprecedented expansion of
world trade, and convinced of the lasting validity of the basic principles and
objectives of the General Agreement in a world of increasing economic
interdependence, the Contracting Parties are resolved to overcome these
threats to the system.

2.   The deep and prolonged crisis of the world economy has severely
depressed levels of production and trade. In many countries growth rates are
low or negative; there is growing unemployment and a climate of uncertainty,
exacerbated by persistent inflation, high rates of interest and volatile
exchange rates, which seriously inhibit investment and structural adjustment
and intensify protectionist pressures. Many countries, and particularly
developing countries, now face critical difficulties created by the
combination of uncertain and limited access to export markets, declining
external demand, a sharp fall in commodity prices and the high cost of
borrowing. The import capacity of developing countries, which is essential to
their economic growth and development, is being impaired and is no longer
serving as a dynamic factor sustaining the exports of the developed world.
Acute problems of debt servicing threaten the stability of the financial
system.

3.   In the field of trade, the responses of governments to the
challenges of the crisis have too often been inadequate and inward-looking.
Import restrictions have increased and a growing proportion of them have for
various reasons been applied outside GATT disciplines, thus undermining the
multilateral trading system. Trade patterns have also been adversely affected
by certain forms of economic assistance for production and exports and by some
restrictive trade measures applied for non-economic purposes. In the
depressed economic circumstances these measures, together with continuing
pressures for further protective action, have contributed to further delays in
necessary structural adjustment, increased economic uncertainty and
discouraged productive investment.

4.   The results of the Tokyo Round, including in particular the
implementation on schedule of the tariff reductions, have provided some
impetus to the functioning of the trading system. However, despite the
strength and resilience which it has shown, the stresses on the system, which
are reflected in the growing number and intensity of disputes between
contracting parties, many of which remain unresolved, have made more
pronounced certain shortcomings in its functioning. Existing strains have
been aggravated by differences of perception regarding the balance of rights
and obligations under the GATT, the way in which these rights and obligations
have been implemented and the extent to which the interests of different
contracting parties have been met by the GATT. There are also concerns over

the manner in which rights are being pursued as well as the manner in which obligations are being fulfilled. Disagreements persist over the interpretation of some important provisions and over their application. Disciplines governing the restriction of trade through safeguard measures are inadequate; there is widespread dissatisfaction with the application of GATT rules and the degree of liberalization in relation to agricultural trade, even though such trade has continued to expand; trade in textiles and clothing continues to be treated under an Arrangement which is a major derogation from the General Agreement - a matter of critical importance to developing countries in particular. Such differences and imbalances are particularly detrimental to the stability of the international trading system when they concern access to the markets of major trading countries or when, through the use of export subsidies, competition among major suppliers is distorted.

5.   The Contracting Parties recognize that the interdependence of national economies means that no country can solve its trade problems in isolation and also that solutions would be greatly facilitated by parallel efforts in the financial and monetary fields. In this light, they commit themselves to reduce trade frictions, overcome protectionist pressures, avoid using export subsidies inconsistent with Article XVI of the GATT and promote the liberalization and expansion of trade. They are therefore determined to create, through concerted action, a renewed consensus in support of the GATT system, so as to restore and reinforce confidence in its capacity to provide a stable predictable trading environment and respond to new challenges.

6.   The Contracting Parties have accordingly decided:

-      to reaffirm their commitment to abide by their GATT obligations and to support and improve the GATT trading system, so that it may contribute vigorously to the further liberalization and expansion of trade based on mutual commitment, mutual advantage and overall reciprocity, and the most-favored-nation clause;

-      to preserve, in the operation and functioning of GATT instruments, the unity and consistency of the GATT system; and

-      to ensure the GATT provides a continuing forum for negotiation and consultation, in which an appropriate balance of rights and obligations can be assured for all contracting parties and the rules and procedures of the system are effectively and fairly applied, on the basis of agreed interpretations, for the economic development and benefit of all.

7.   In drawing up the work programme and priorities for the 1980's, the contracting parties undertake, individually and jointly;

(i)   to make determined efforts to ensure that trade policies and measures are consistent with GATT principles and rules and to resist protectionist pressures in the formulation and implementation of national trade policy and in proposing legislation; and also to refrain from taking or maintaining any measures inconsistent with GATT and to make determined efforts to avoid measures which would limit or distort international trade;

(ii) to give fullest consideration, in the application of measures falling within the GATT framework, and in the general exercise of their GATT rights, to the trading interests of other contracting parties and the shared objective of trade liberalization and expansion;

(iii) to abstain from taking restrictive trade measures, for reasons of a non-economic character, not consistent with the General Agreement;

(iv) (a) to ensure the effective implementation of GATT rules and provisions and specifically those concerning the developing countries, thereby furthering the dynamic role of developing countries in international trade;

(b) to ensure special treatment for the least-developed countries, in the context of differential and more favourable treatment for developing countries, in order to ameliorate the grave economic situation of these countries;

(v) to bring agriculture more fully into the multilateral trading system by improving the effectiveness of GATT rules, provisions and disciplines and through their common interpretation; to seek to improve terms of access to markets; and to bring export competition under greater discipline. To this end a major two-year work programme shall be undertaken.

(vi) to bring into effect expeditiously a comprehensive understanding on safeguards to be based on the principles of the General Agreement;

(vii) to ensure increased transparency of trade measures and the effective resolution of disputes through improvements in the operation of the pertinent procedures, supported by a determination to comply with rulings and respect recommendations;

(viii) to examine ways and means of, and to pursue measures aimed at, liberalizing trade in textiles and clothing, including the eventual application of the General Agreement, after the expiry of the 1981 Protocol extending the Arrangement Regarding International Trade in Textiles, it being understood that in the interim the parties to the Arrangement shall adhere strictly to its rules;

(ix) to give continuing consideration to changes in the trading environment so as to ensure that the GATT is responsive to these changes.

SAFEGUARDS

The Contracting Parties decide:

1. That, having regard to the objectives and disciplines of the General Agreement, there is need for an improved and more efficient safeguard system which provides for greater predictability and clarity and also greater security and equity for both importing and exporting countries, so as to preserve the results of trade liberalization and avoid the proliferation of restrictive measures; and

2.   That to this end, effect should be given to a comprehensive understanding to be based on the principles of the General Agreement which would contain, _inter alia_, following elements:

(i)   Transparency;

(ii)   Coverage;

(iii)   Objective criteria for action including the concept of serious injury or threat thereof;

(iv)   Temporary nature, degressivity and structural adjustments;

(v)   Compensation and retaliation; and

(vi)   Notification, consultation, multilateral surveillance and dispute settlement with particular reference to the role and functions of the Safeguards Committee.

3.   That such an understanding should be drawn up by the Council for adoption by the Contracting Parties not later than their 1983 Session.

GATT RULES AND ACTIVITIES RELATING TO DEVELOPING COUNTRIES

The Contracting Parties:

1.   Instruct the Committee on Trade and Development bearing in mind particularly the special responsibility of the developed contracting parties in this regard, to consult on a regular basis with contracting parties individually or collectively, as appropriate to examine how individual contracting parties have responded to the requirements of Part IV.

2.   Urge contracting parties to implement more effectively Part IV and the Decision of 28 November 1979 regarding "differential and more favourable treatment, reciprocity and fuller participation of developing countries":

3.   Urge contracting parties to work towards further improvement of GSP or MFN treatment for products of particular export interest to least-developed countries, and the elimination or reduction of non-tariff measures affecting such products;

4.   Agree to strengthen the technical cooperation programme of GATT;

5.   Instruct the Committee on Trade and Development to carry out an examination of the prospects for increasing trade between developed and developing countries and the possibilities in GATT for facilitating this objective;

To this effect, the Contracting Parties are also taking the decisions annexed and decide to review the action taken in these areas at their 1984 Session.

DISPUTE SETTLEMENT PROCEDURES

The Contracting Parties:

Agree that the Understanding on Notification, Consultation, Surveillance, and Dispute Settlement negotiated during the Tokyo Round (hereinafter referred to as the "Understanding") provides the essential framework or procedures for the settlement of disputes among contracting parties and that no major change is required in this framework, but that there is scope for more effective use of the existing mechanism and for specific improvements in procedures to this end;

And agree further that:

(i)   With reference to paragraph 8 of the Understanding, if a dispute is is not resolved through consultations, any party to a dispute may, with the agreement of the other party, seek the good offices of the Director-General or of an individual or group of persons nominated by the Director-General. This conciliatory process would be carried out expeditiously, and the Director-General would inform the Council of the outcome of the conciliatory process. Conciliation proceedings, and in particular positions taken by the parties to the dispute during conciliation, shall be confidential, without prejudice to the rights of either party in any further proceedings under Article XXIII:2. It remain open at any time during any conciliatory process for either party to the dispute to refer the matter to Contracting Parties.

(ii)   In order to ensure more effective compliance with the provisions of paragraphs 11 and 12 of the Understanding, the Director-General shall inform the Council of any case in which it has not been found possible to meet the time limits for the establishment of a panel.

(iii)   With reference to paragraph 13 of the Understanding, contracting parties will co-operate effectively with the Director-General in making suitably qualified experts available to serve on panels. Where experts are not drawn from Geneva, any expenses, including travel and subsistence allowance, shall be met from the GATT budget.

(iv)   The secretaries of GATT has the responsibility of assisting the panel, especially on the legal, historical and procedural aspects of the matters dealt with.

(v)   The terms of reference of a panel should be formulated so as to permit a clear finding with respect to any contravention of GATT provisions and/or on the question of nullification and impairment of benefits. In terms of paragraph 16 of the Understanding, and after reviewing the facts of the case, the applicability of GATT provisions and the arguments advanced, the panel should come to such a finding. Where a finding establishing a contravention of GATT provisions or nullification and impairment is made, the panel should make such suggestions as appropriate for dealing with the matter as would assist the Contracting Parties in making recommendations to the contracting parties which they consider to be concerned, or give a ruling on the matter, as appropriate.

(vi) Panels would aim to deliver their findings without undue delay, as provided in paragraph 20 of the Understanding. If a complete report cannot be made within the period foreseen in that paragraph, panels would be expected to so advise the Council and the report should be submitted as soon as possible thereafter.

(vii) Reports of panels should be given prompt consideration by the Contracting Parties. Where a decision on the findings contained in a report calls for a ruling or recommendation by the Council, the Council may allow the contracting party concerned a reasonable specified time to indicate what action it proposes to take with a view of to a satisfactory settlement of the matter, before making any recommendation or ruling on the basis of the report.

(viii) The recommendation or ruling made by the Contracting Parties shall be aimed at achieving a satisfactory settlement of the matter in accordance with GATT obligations. In furtherance of the provisions of paragraph 22 of the Understanding the Council shall periodically review the action taken pursuant to such recommendations. The contracting party to which such a recommendation has been addressed, shall report within a reasonable specified period on action taken or on its reasons for not implementing the recommendation or ruling by the Contracting Parties. The contracting party bringing the case may also ask the Contracting Parties to make suitable efforts with a view to finding an appropriate solution as provided in paragraph 22 of the Understanding.

(ix) The further action taken by the Contracting Parties in the above circumstances might include a recommendation for compensatory adjustment with respect to other products or authorization for the suspension of such concessions or other obligations as foreseen in Article XXIII:2, as the Contracting Parties may determine to be appropriate in the circumstances.

(x) The Parties to a dispute would fully participate in the consideration of the matter by the Contracting parties under paragraph (vii) above, including the consideration of any rulings or recommendations the Contracting Parties might make pursuant to Article XXIII:2 of the General Agreement, and their views would be fully recorded. They would likewise participate and have their views recorded in the considerations of the further actions provided for under paragraphs (viii) and (ix) above. The Contracting Parties reaffirmed that consensus will continue to be the traditional method of resolving disputes; however, they agreed that obstruction in the process of dispute settlement shall be avoided. 1/ It is understood that the decisions in this process cannot add to or diminish the rights and obligations provided in the General Agreement.

TRADE IN AGRICULTURE

With the purpose of accelerating the achievement of the objectives of the General Agreement, including Part IV, and recognizing that there is an

---

1/ This does not prejudice the provisions on decision making in the General

urgent need to find lasting solutions to the problems of trade in agricultural products, the Contracting Parties decide:

1.   That the following matters be examined, in the light of the objectives, principles and relevant provisions of the General Agreement and also taking into account the effects of national agricultural policies, with the purpose of making appropriate recommendations. The examination shall cover all measures affecting trade, market access and competition and supply in agricultural products, including subsidies and other forms of assistance.

    (i)   Trade measures affecting market access and supplies, with a view to achieving greater liberalization in the trade of agricultural products, with respect to tariffs and non-tariff measures, on a basis of overall reciprocity and mutual advantage under the General Agreement.

    (ii)   The operation of the General Agreement as regards subsidies affecting agriculture, especially export subsidies, with a view to examining its effectiveness. in the light of actual experience, in promoting the objectiveness of the General Agreement and avoiding subsidization seriously prejudicial to the trade or interests of contracting parties. Other forms of export assistance will be included in this examination.

    (iii)   Trade measures affecting agriculture maintained under exceptions or derogations without prejudice to the rights or contracting parties under the General Agreement.

2.   That in carrying out the tasks enumerated above, full account shall be taken of the need for a balance of rights and obligations under the GATT, and of the special needs of developing countries in the light of the GATT provisions providing for differential and more favourable treatment for such contracting parties. Full account shall also be taken of specific characteristics and problems in agriculture, of the scope for improving the operation of GATT rules, provisions and disciplines and agreed interpretations of its provisions.

3.   That for the purposes of carrying out this work, an improved and unified system of notifications shall be introduced so as to ensure full transparency.

4.   That a Committee on Trade in Agriculture shall be established, open to all contracting parties, for the purpose of carrying out the tasks enumerated above and of making recommendations with a view to achieving greater liberalization in the trade of agricultural products. The Committee will report periodically on the results achieved and make appropriate recommendations to the Council and the Contracting Parties for consideration not later than their 1984 Session.

TROPICAL PRODUCTS

The Contracting Parties decide to carry out, on the basis of the work programme pursued by the Committee on Trade and Development, consultations and appropriate negotiations aimed at further liberalization of trade in tropical products, including in their processed and semi-processed forms, and to review the progress achieved in eliminating or reducing existing obstacles to trade in tropical products at their 1984 Session.

QUANTITATIVE RESTRICTIONS AND OTHER NON-TARIFF MEASURES

The Contracting Parties decide:

1.   To review, in a group created for the purpose, existing quantitative restrictions and other non-tariff measures, the grounds on which these are maintained, and their conformity with the provisions of the General Agreement, so as to achieve the elimination of quantitative restrictions which are not in conformity with the General Agreement or their being brought into conformity with the General Agreement, and also to achieve progress in liberalizing other quantitative restrictions and non-tariff measures, adequate attention being given to the need for action on quantitative restrictions and other measures affecting products of particular export interest to developing countries; and

2.   That the group should make progress reports to the Council and that its complete report containing its findings and conclusions should be available for consideration by the Contracting Parties at their 1984 Session.

TARIFFS

The Contracting Parties decide:

1.   That prompt attention should be given to the problems of escalation of tariffs on products with increased processing with a view to effective action towards the elimination or reduction of such escalation where it inhibits international trade, taking into account the concerns relating to exports of developing countries; and agree

2.   That wide acceptance of a common system for classifying products for tariff and statistical purposes would facilitate world trade and therefore recommend prompt action towards the introduction of such a system. They take note of the ongoing work to this end in the Custom Co-operation Council. They further agree that, if such a system is introduced, the general level of benefits provided by GATT concessions must be maintained, that existing concessions should normally remain unchanged and that any negotiations that may prove necessary should be initiated promptly so as to avoid any undue delay in the implementation of a system. They also agree that technical support shall be provided by the GATT secretariat to developing contracting parties in order to fully assist their participation in such a process.

MTN AGREEMENTS AND ARRANGEMENTS

The Contracting Parties decide to review the operation of the MFN Agreements and Arrangements, taking into account reports from the Committees or Council concerned, with a view to determining what action if any is called for, in terms of their decision of November 1979. The Contracting Parties further agree that, for this purpose, the review should focus on the adequacy and effectiveness of these Agreements and Arrangements and the obstacles to the acceptance of these Agreements and Arrangements by interested parties.

STRUCTURAL ADJUSTMENT AND TRADE POLICY

The Contracting Parties decide to continue the work on structural adjustment and trade policy in order to focus on the interaction between structural adjustment and the fulfillment of the objectives of the General Agreement, and to review the results of this work at their 1983 Session.

TRADE IN COUNTERFEIT GOODS

The Contracting Parties instruct the Council to examine the question of counterfeit goods with a view to determining the appropriateness of joint action in the GATT framework on the trade aspects of commercial counterfeiting and, if such joint action is found to be appropriate, the modalities for such action, having full regard to the competence of other international organizations. For the purposes of such examination, Contracting Parties request the Director-General to hold consultations with the Director-General of WIPO in order to clarify the legal and institutional aspects involved.

EXPORT OF DOMESTICALLY PROHIBITED GOODS

The Contracting Parties decide that contracting parties shall, to the maximum extent feasible, notify GATT of any goods produced and exported by them by banned by their national authorities for sale on their domestic markets on grounds of human health and safety. At their 1984 Session, the Contracting Parties will consider in the light of experience gained with this notification procedure, the need for study of problems relevant to the GATT in relation to exports of domestically prohibited goods and of any action that may be appropriate to deal with such problems.

EXPORT CREDITS FOR CAPITAL GOODS

The Contracting Parties:

1.   Are aware that official export credit provisions on capital goods which apply to developing countries may pose problems for the expansion of imports into these countries consistent with their trade and development needs;

2.   Therefore recommend that contracting parties, members of those international arrangements concerning official export credit matters, when reviewing or revising their various international undertakings, give special

attention to relevant credit provisions, including specific terms and conditions, in order to facilitate the expansion of developing countries' imports of capital goods consistent with their trade and development needs; and

3.   Request the Director-General of the GATT to consult with the contracting parties concerned and report to the 39th Session.

TEXTILES AND CLOTHING

The Contracting Parties decide:

1.   To carry out on a priority basis a study of:

   (i)   the importance of textiles and clothing in world trade and particularly for the trade prospects of developing countries;

   (ii) the impact on economic activity and prospects of countries participating in textiles trade, of the existing systems of restraints and restrictions relating to textiles and clothing, principally the MFA:

   (iii) consequences for economic and trade prospects in these countries of phasing out on the basis of the provisions of the General Agreement, or of the continued maintenance, of the restraints and restrictions applied under the existing textile and clothing regimes, principally the MFA; and

2.   To examine expeditiously, taking into account the results of such a study, modalities of further trade liberalization in textiles and clothing including the possibilities for bringing about the full application of GATT provisions to this sector of trade.

3.   This work should be completed for consideration by the Contracting Parties at their 1984 Session.

PROBLEMS OF TRADE IN CERTAIN NATURAL RESOURCE PRODUCTS

The Contracting Parties decide:

1.   That problems relating to trade in the following natural resource products including in their semi-processed and processed forms, falling under the competence of the General Agreement relating to tariffs, non-tariff measures and other factors affecting trade, should be examined with a view to recommending possible solutions:

   (a) Non-ferrous metals and minerals

   (b) Forestry products

   (c) Fish and fisheries products

2.   That for this purpose the Council should decide, for each of these three items, the terms of reference, time frame and procedures.

EXCHANGE RATE FLUCTUATIONS AND THEIR EFFECT ON TRADE

The Contracting Parties decide

To request the Director-General to consult the Managing Director of the International Monetary Fund on the possibility of a study of the effects of erratic fluctuations in exchange rates on international trade, to report to the Council on the results of these consultations and to forward any such study to the Council so that it may consider any implications for the General Agreement.

DUAL PRICING AND RULES OF ORIGIN

The Contracting Parties decide:

To request the Council to make arrangements for studies of dual-pricing practices and rules of origin; and

To consider what further action may be necessary with regard to these matters when the results of these studies are available.

SERVICES

The Contracting Parties decide:

1.   To recommend to each contracting party with an interest in services of different types to undertake, as far as it is able, national examination of the issues in this sector.

2.   To invite contracting parties to exchange information on such matters among themselves, inter alia through international organizations such as GATT. The compilation and distribution of such information should be based on as uniform a format as possible.

3.   To review the results of these examinations, along with the information and comments provided by relevant international organizations, at their 1984 Session and to consider whether any multilateral action in these matters is appropriate and desirable.

ANNEX

GATT RULES AND ACTIVITIES RELATING TO DEVELOPING COUNTRIES

The Contracting Parties:

1.   Decide, in order to improve the review and surveillance procedures in regard to the implementation of Part IV, that:

(a)   the Committee on Trade and Development, bearing in mind particularly the special responsibility of the developed contracting parties in this regard, shall adopt a programme of consultations with contracting parties individually or collectively, as appropriate, to examine how individual contracting parties have responded to the requirements of Part IV;

(b)   each such consultation shall be based on information supplied by the contracting party or parties in question and additional factual material prepared by the secretariat;

(c)   the Committee on Trade and Development shall also examine other aspects of existing procedures for reviewing the implementation of Part IV and for dealing with problems relating to the application of its provisions, and prepare guidelines for their improvement.

2.   Invite the Committee on Trade and Development to review the operation of the Enabling Clause as provided for in its paragraph 9, with a view to its more effective implementation, _inter alia_, with respect to objectivity and transparency of modifications to GSP schemes and the operation of consultative provisions relating to differential and more favourable treatment for developing countries;

3.   Invite contracting parties to pursue action as follows towards facilitating trade of least-developed countries and reducing tariff and non-tariff obstacles to their exports:

(a)   further improve GSP or mfn treatment for products of particular export interest to least-developed countries, with the objective of providing fullest possible duty-free access to such products;

(b)   use, upon request and where feasible, of more flexible requirements for rules of origin for products of particular export interest to least-developed countries;

(c)   eliminate or reduce non-tariff measures affecting products of particular export interest to least-developed countries;

(d)   facilitate the participation of least-developed countries in MTN Agreements and Arrangements;

(e)   strengthen the technical assistance facilities of the GATT secretariat targeted to the special requirements of least-developed countries;

(f)   strengthen trade promotion activities, through the ITC and other initiatives, such as by encouraging the establishment of import promotion offices in importing countries;

(g)   give more emphasis to the discussion and examination of policy issues of interest to least-developed countries in the context of further efforts to liberalize trade.

4.   Decide to strengthen the Technical Co-operation programme of the GATT with a view to facilitating the more effective participation of developing countries in the GATT trading system:

(a)   by responding to increasing requests for seminars and other
      technical assistance activities;

(b)   by permitting increased participation in the GATT Commercial Policy
      Courses, and the inclusion in the training programme of a regular
      course in the Spanish language;

(c)   by encouraging, in the context of this programme, appropriate
      contributions from individual contracting parties.

5.   Invite contracting parties individually to grant new voluntary
contributions or provide other forms of assistance to the ITC.

ABOUT THE AUTHOR

Leslie Alan Glick is a graduate of Cornell University and Cornell Law School. He practices law in Washington, D.C. specializing in international trade and business law, intellectual property law, maritime and fisheries law. He has represented many U.S. and foreign companies in trade matters for the past 12 years. He is also the author of a book entitled Trading with Saudi Arabia: A Guide to the Shipping, Trade, Investments and Tax Laws of Saudi Arabia published by Allanheld Osmun in the United States and Croom Helm in London. He is also the author of Chapter 34, "Legal Aspects of Trade with Mexico", in a two volume treatise entitled DOING BUSINESS in MEXICO published by Matthew Bender & Co. In addition, he is the author of numerous law review articles on international law and trade in the Harvard International Law Journal, Cornell Law Review, Federal Bar News and Journal, and other publications. He currently serves as chairman of the International Trade and Customs Law Committee of the Federal Bar Association, where he has organized numerous programs on international trade.